JOHN SOANE

AN ACCIDENTAL ROMANTIC

GILLIAN DARLEY

YALE UNIVERSITY PRESS   NEW HAVEN & LONDON

© 1999 Gillian Darley

Designed by Kate Gallimore
Typeset in Baskerville and Castellar by SX Composing DTP
Printed in Hong Kong

Library of Congress Catalog Card Number: 99-62198

ISBN 0 300 08165 0

Illustration on page ii: John Soane by Christopher Hunneman, *c.* 1776 (see fig. 14).
Endpapers: Joseph Gandy *A Selection of Buildings Erected from the Design of J. Soane Esq RA between 1780 and 1815* (see fig. 168).

CONTENTS

PREFACE AND
ACKNOWLEDGEMENTS

I have heard the comment, more than once, that visiting Sir John Soane's Museum is like a journey inside someone's head. That 'most psychological' house, which has intrigued, puzzled and delighted me ever since my first visit long ago is the reason for this biography. Which other architect leaves you quite as haunted by his absence, by so many carefully unanswered clues? If the house at Lincoln's Inn Fields is laden with hints, it is even more heavily weighted down by riddles. This book is an attempt to elucidate at least some of the questions which lie behind Soane's uncomfortable architectural genius.

This is a biography, not an architectural monograph. I have concentrated on pulling the background to his buildings into focus, convinced that by so doing John Soane's life, as a whole, has the potential to illuminate his architecture and its development. Soane is a fascinating, perverse character and the path that he cut for himself through society, the arts and the professions is a telling one – a story of an age of possibilities and of an awkward, vulnerable and proud individual within it.

By ensuring that his museum and house would remain intact for future generations Soane intended to construct his own memorial. Despite his insistence that this was an academic exercise, the union of the arts and architecture, for the instruction of future generations of young architects (but, poignantly, not his own sons), the house is, above all, an autobiographical statement – with all the ambiguities that that suggests.

What kind of man was this near-contemporary of Turner and Blake, or for that matter of Goya, Goethe and Beethoven? Other eighteenth-century architects, William Chambers or Robert Adam for instance, do not provoke such interest when you enter one of their buildings. In Soane's case, the man, the sheer individualism of his work, the narrative and the sequence of the house and the objects within it, suggest that we need to find an answer and he arranged it that we should. In case the house and contents alone do not reveal enough he contributed a massive archive of printed and manuscript material to help in the quest. Someone who leaves quite as much evidence behind for a biographer ('strange work' it would be, said one writer after his death) is trailing their coat, to the extent that I have felt occasionally that I was under my subject's watchful eye. I have attempted to be neither too credulous nor too judgemental: despite the control that Soane exerted over the evidence of his life and work, there is much to be found beyond 13 Lincoln's Inn Fields.

The quantity of explanation that Soane offered about his professional and later personal life is itself a paradox. Soane thought that by his own obsessive processes of reiteration and self-justification he would stand higher in the judgement of his successors. Yet Soane's tortuous working and reworking of everything in his life, from the sources of his architecture, as illuminated in his Royal Academy lectures, to the terrible toils in which he entwined his family latterly does little to clarify matters. In the conduct of his life and work he was a man who needed others upon which to model himself; his guides and his heroes stand together: Sir William Chambers and Jean-Jacques Rousseau, Napoleon and George Dance, David Garrick and Sir Christopher Wren, Shakespeare and William Pitt the younger, William Beckford and John Philip Kemble.

To be born in the 1750s and to die in the 1830s was to embark on an extraordinary journey. The route took in the processes of industrialisation, European turmoil and revolution, social readjustments and domestic convulsions. Modernisation fell under every conceivable heading. Soane, always prepared to be guided in his choice of reading or sources of information, was remarkably open (at times even suggestible) to the observations of others, the thoughts of those he respected or the opinions of those he trusted. Himself a terse and parsimonious correspondent (and diarist) he still drew from his old friends, by no means a homogeneous group, either socially or geographically, a range of insight and intelligence on countless topics, all of which he devoured.

Soane had begun to realise, around 1810, that there was unlikely to be an architectural succession within his own family, on the model of the Brettinghams, Adams, Wyatts or Dances. Surveying the wreckage of his dynastic hopes, Soane transferred to his extraordinary house/museum the task of keeping the flame of remembrance alive. Every architectural move or purchase that Soane took thereafter was directed to the widest audience: young architects and after them, posterity. Soane's considerable (but never secure) sense of his own achievement was finally sealed by the concrete evidence of his professional life – 13 Lincoln's Inn Fields, as secured for the public by Act of Parliament in 1833.

Close acquaintance with Soane over the last few years has not been easy. There are episodes in the family papers which are shocking in their ruthless and persistent cruelty to innocent outsiders, daughters-in-law or grandchildren (and which perhaps explain why the former assistant curator of the museum did not allow access to them – well over a century after Soane's death). They cannot be ignored, but need not be dwelt on pruriently. Soane was, in the old cliché, his own worst enemy – his delightful, perceptive wife, Eliza, and his oldest and most steadfast friends (and he had many) knew this and rarely failed to remind him of the fact.

Sir John Summerson, curator of the museum from 1945 until 1984, considered that Soane exhibited evidence of a streak of instability, even paranoia; certainly, if so, heredity provides some explanation for the actions of George Soane, whose inconsistencies of behaviour and judgement easily surpassed his father's. Soane's behaviour seemed to follow a cyclical pattern; at moments (often exacerbated by bad physical health and, especially, the fear of blindness) he lost his reason, sense and self-control. At these moments the claims of kinship and friendship counted for little.

Soane had no capacity for self-knowledge, as his more courageous friends would remind him. He was naïve, impressionable, easily thrown off course. A self-made man, he was also resolutely willing to learn and practise social skills and must have done so fast and effectively. This left him exposed; a practised operator in high circles, yet with the thinnest of skins. He was far from unique in this position; the late eighteenth century was a period of great social mobility and in the arts there seems to have been little hindrance to those of humble birth, indeed, quite the reverse.

The journey between the labouring world and the liberal arts was well-travelled and, in architecture, far from clearly defined. In common with many of his contemporaries, Soane climbed nimbly from the manual trades to the professional classes and beyond. In Soane's case, the leap was sudden and momentous – in one short bound, from hod-carrier to archi-tectural apprentice. Farington spitefully harped upon Soane's social ori-gins because he had found an exposed nerve. The diarist's version of events is important because he recorded the day-to-day gossip in their closely connected circles.

Soane had no recourse to the comforts and sense of containment offered by organised religion; he could never fall back on faith. His dynas-tic enterprise was, in some senses, his own spiritual journey. He was, if not a convinced atheist as his son George wrote, then a very resolute non-believer. Freemasonry was, like the many literary and intellectual institu-tions which he also supported, a non-denominational society into which he fitted with ease.

When troubled, Soane depended on solutions to man's difficulties offered by other men, either in the light-hearted fictional offerings of *Gil Blas* or the soul-searching desperation of *King Lear*. He leant on Rousseau's *Confessions* in preference to the King James Bible. Words from the stage yielded him more introspection than those from the pulpit. Anti-clerical in every bone, Soane must have allowed himself a grim smile as he suggested to his son George that he might consider a church living as a way out of his financial troubles.

Soane's character impinges on his practice because he saw almost every professional difficulty in personal terms. In an important example, a thread running through many of the troubles in his middle years, his reac-tion to the young Robert Smirke and his work (and from that, his difficul-ties at the Royal Academy) can be seen, on closer examination, to be entirely based on his dislike of the individual – the result of accumulated small grievances and petty jealousies.

Soane's personal relationship to his patrons and clients was the key to the quality of his architecture. At the opposite extreme from James Wyatt, all too ready to take another commission, all too unready to exert himself in its execution, Soane was the most conscientious and thorough of architects in every situation. When circumstances promised well, he would do any-thing to ensure that a major commission led to the best result, on several occasions investing his own money in a building project. His house at Lincoln's Inn Fields epitomises his work for a perfect client – himself.

There is evidence in the long and often melancholy story of Soane's life that he was a man often beyond self-control. His actions and reactions were frequently ill-considered and irrational – as damaging to him, personally and professionally, as they could possibly be. It took immense understand-ing and forbearance to see the best in Soane or to forgive him as so many did. His defence is offered by the solid evidence of the loyalty that he inspired in clients, on the grounds of his abilities as an architect with a level of dedication, professionalism and inspiration rarely met in a single man. Proof came from the highest level; for over thirty years he was the personal architect of the two longest serving Prime Ministers of the period, William Pitt the younger and Lord Liverpool. At the other social extreme, but tending to the same conclusion, is the loyalty of the men with whom he worked; the joiners, bricklayers, plasterers, masons, model-makers and others who became his close colleagues, in some cases for their entire working lives.

Similarly, if his architectural language was one of classicism and his intellect tended towards an Enlightenment view of the world, then his personality was a maelstrom of conflict – at times as troubled as a demonic Fuseli painting. A romantic urge, often manifesting itself in the form of sentimentality, theatricality and his incubus, self-pity, lay beneath his ordered, suppressive personality. With romanticism came aspiration; he was inevitably an admirer of Napoleon. This tension insinuates itself into the most remarkable architectural passages in his work, whether these are the weightless domestic interiors such as his own exquisite breakfast room or the hugely complex arrangements at the Bank of England.

The recurring theme in criticism of his work was that of wilfulness and a search for originality at all cost, the 'Soane style'. There is an irony in this, for he was everlastingly in search of precedent. It is in the search for his own, individual voice – however steeped in the classical language of architecture – and in the break with precedents and peers that Soane's romanticism lies.

During Soane's busiest periods, the 1790s, early 1800s and the 1820s, his public offices and official work have been divided into separate chapters from his own house and other domestic commissions, resulting in the occasional deviation from the chronology in the book.

My first debts among many during the preparation of this book are to the staff at Sir John Soane's Museum. The Curator, Margaret Richardson and the Deputy Curator, Helen Dorey were encouraging from the start and shared their knowledge and expertise with me, making valuable comments and corrections to the manuscript, as did Daniel Abramson via e-mail in the USA. At Lincoln's Inn Fields Susan Palmer, the Archivist, was a model of kindly patience and helpfulness in making material available, reading and commenting on the text and, in particular, checking my references against the somewhat arcane system which the museum is obliged to retain as historical evidence. The Museum Study Group has offered a continual and companionable exchange of ideas and information and the organiser, the museum's Assistant Director (Education) Christopher Woodward also read my draft and offered his own stimulating comments.

I have had help from archivists and librarians in the following places: the Bank of England (Archives and Museum), the Central Archives of the British Museum, the Paul Mellon Centre for Studies in British Art, the Institution of Civil Engineers, the Guildhall Library, the Public Record Office, St Bartholomew's Hospital, the United Grand Lodge of England (Freemasons Hall), Walthamstow (Vestry House Museum), Chertsey Museum, local history collections in the London Borough of Ealing, Margate and Southampton, the Royal Academy, the Royal College of Surgeons, the Royal Opera House Covent Garden, the Society of Antiquaries, the Royal Institution, the Royal Society, the Royal Society of Arts, the Artists' General Benevolent Institution, the Garrick Club, the

Athenaeum Club, the Library of the Huguenot Society, Lambeth Palace Library, the House of Lords Record Office, the London Metropolitan Archive, the Theatre Museum, the Fitzwilliam Museum Cambridge, County Record Offices of Norfolk, Surrey and Berkshire and City Record Offices in Birmingham and the Corporation of London. Any author who has the serendipitous pleasures (and extended loans) of the London Library at their disposal is fortunate and to the staff of that fine library as well as to their counterparts in the new (and old) British Library, including the India Office Library and Manuscripts Collections, many thanks.

I have also been kindly received by many owners and administrators of Soane houses, despite sometimes giving them insufficient warning, and I offer them collective thanks. At Mulgrave Castle, where I examined papers relating to Soane's work there, the Estate Manager Mr Shepherd was helpful and welcoming. There is also a long list of people who have helped me; at their head must come Andrew Saint who uncomplainingly interrupted the season of peace and goodwill to read the manuscript and responded with both wit and wisdom; while in Paris Charlotte Ellis and Martin Mead were kind and meticulous in sorting out my howlers. Ptolemy Dean was generous in sharing his architectural insights and was an inspiriting guide to several Soane buildings. Others who shared my enthusiasm or offered ideas, snippets of material or patiently answered questions include: Stephen Astley, John Gage, the late Alain Gaucher, John and Eileen Harris, Rosemary Hill, Peter Inskip, Emmeline Leary, Jill Lever, Philippa Lewis, Adam Mars-Jones, Joe Mordaunt Crook, Evelyn Newby, Robert O'Farrell, Philip Orchard, Jon Piggott, Frank Salmon, Tom Stacey, John Taylor and the Walpole Residents Association. David Watkin falls last in this alphabetical list but must be the first person to whom anyone working on Soane is indebted.

In the later stages this book has been produced at astonishing speed, in order that it can be published to coincide with the Royal Academy exhibition. I was lucky enough to receive a last-minute Hawthornden Fellowship in November 1998 which gave me a fortnight of total immersion in a place of extraordinary beauty, Hawthornden Castle, and I owe a huge debt to Drue Heinz, the Admissions Committee and to the Administrator, Adam Czerniawski, for those invaluable uninterrupted days. Yale University Press, more used to such pressures than I, were superbly calm; to John Nicoll, Kate Gallimore and Sally Nicholls, my thanks for their unflappability and charm. Caroline Dawnay, my agent, has been a great support.

Research and the early stages of writing this book began gently but, because of the time-scale, it has recently became a dominating presence, a fact which my friends, colleagues and family may have noticed by my absence – if not physical, then mental. Our daughter has surely visited more Soane buildings than any other small girl and has even found holidays diverted to follow Soane's footsteps. Michael, a historian manqué with a lawyer's eye for the weak spot in an argument, read the text and offered shrewd observations. Between them, Susannah and Michael have cheerfully endured life in a domestic no man's land. My loving thanks are quite inadequate.

Gillian Darley   *London*

1

BEGINNINGS

John Soane's life, or at least the edited version, began at 5 a.m. on 18 March 1778, the moment at which he left London for Italy, King George III's proud travelling scholar chosen from among the handful of most promising students of the Royal Academy Schools. In his notebooks, sparse as they are, hardly a year passed without a mention of the anniversary of his momentous journey.[1]

Soane, aged twenty-four, had made a speedy and strenuous ascent from obscure beginnings; throughout his life he deliberately avoided all mention of his origins. In 1784, the year of his marriage and in which he took his first pupil, he added the 'e' to his name and amended every previous reference to John Soan, extinguishing the last vestige of his earlier self.

Soane's silence about his youth is inconsistent – he never underestimated his disadvantages. As part of the story of his remarkable professional ascent, a humble birth would have made a perfect starting point. But when, as Sir John Soane, he arranged the details of his life in the privately printed *Memoirs of the Professional Life of an Architect* of 1835, he told no more of his childhood than that he was 'led by a natural inclination to study architecture'.

The few known facts and his extreme reticence about his background suggest a sudden crisis in the family. Soane's absolute terror of debt and his own punctilious attitude towards financial matters, both in his own prompt settlement of accounts and in recalling outstanding debts, point to a sudden downturn which took a respectable artisan family into poverty.[2]

John Soan, senior, was a bricklayer or builder, baptised at the parish church of St Thomas of Canterbury at Goring-on-Thames in 1714, the son of William Soan and his wife Susanna. In 1738, Soan married Martha Marcy, from nearby Basildon.[3] Since all the Soan siblings were baptised in Goring and their father was buried there, they probably lived in the Oxfordshire village,[4] a bridging point to Streatley on the Berkshire side of the river. The only documented record of the family's whereabouts comes much later, in 1761 when Soan rented a house for £4 10s per year from Timothy Tyrrell of Reading. However there is no doubt that the setting of John Soane's earliest years was the Thames Valley, in the lush landscape between Pangbourne and Goring (fig. 1).[5]

That stretch of river still preserves much of its seductive beauty. Steeply wooded hillsides and extensive water meadows are the backdrop

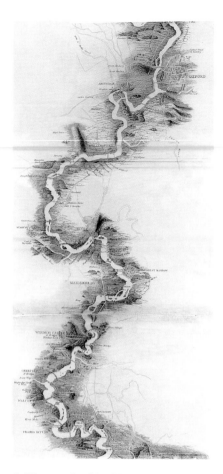

1. The stretch of the Thames that Soane knew best; born at Goring, schooled at Reading, his family then moved to Chertsey. Tombleson's Thames by W. G. Fearnside, London, 1834.

2. St Bartholomew's Basildon where Soane's father, the local bricklayer may have helped rebuild the tower in 1734.

to hamlets in which the surviving older cottages are built in brick, flint and framed timber, often all three combined. The materials are local, skilfully and inventively handled. The walls of the houses and barns are enlivened by patterned brickwork, chequered, banded or even dated, the soft, tomato tones given their definition by opalescent grey or blue vitrified headers. Often flintwork, roughly cut, has been dropped in, gritty panels slotted between the brick courses. Sometimes, instead, creamy chunks of chalk are used. The work of a bricklayer offered possibilities for quiet ingenuity. John Soan may have pointed out his own work to his son. Tradition has it that in 1734 he rebuilt the tower of Lower Basildon church (fig. 2),[6] still presiding over a huddle of farms and barns down on the water meadows.

Later, J.M.W. Turner caught both the calm of these meadows, where curious cattle came down to the water's edge to gaze as he moored his boat to sketch or fish from it (fig. 3), and the dominant, though distant, Reading skyline, punctured by the silhouettes of the abbey and the three major churches. These peaceful late summer scenes were only one face of a landscape receptive to the changes in seasons but always at the mercy of the Thames. The waters could rise with little warning, swelled by storm water which tore away everything in its path. But even on calm days, the river was hazardous.

In August 1757 the *Oxford Gazette and Reading Mercury* reported on the inquest and verdict of accidental death in the case of James Pattin, a hard-working Goring bricklayer who had been pulled out of the river near Caversham Mill, having been 'seen in liquor about eight o'clock the evening before'. The life of a casual labourer was uncertain, seasonal and hard. Soane's father may have been a respectable artisan, even a master craftsman, who fell on hard times or just a jobbing bricklayer dependent on piece-work, as his elder brother William became.

Around these riverside villages, Whitchurch and Pangbourne, Goring and Streatley, Lower Basildon, or above, the upland hamlets of Upper Basildon, Whitchurch Hill or Goring Heath, John Soan remains one of many anonymous figures behind the rich local building history. Only his son, John Soane, eager to chronicle his own life and achievements, could have left some record of his father's work on the farmhouses, mills, barns and cottages of the area and this he steadfastly refused to do.

In childhood, Soane must have known architectural highpoints of the district. These included the Alnutt almshouses at Goring Heath, built by a Lord Mayor of London in the 1720s, their chapel sporting a jaunty Dutch gable and crisply cut brick pilasters. Out in the fields of Upper Basildon was the mysterious 'Nobe's Tomb' a stone mausoleum commemorating the life of a Quaker, built in 1699. On the river there were two neighbouring Elizabethan mansions, Hardwick Court and Mapledurham House – homes of two Catholic families and fine representatives of an architecture for which there was little sympathy in the eighteenth century.

Everywhere flints, picked off the fields, were used as light-hearted ornament on gates and outbuildings; Soane's fondness for rustic architecture must have been grounded in these local touches just as much as in theories about the primitive origins of classical building forms. But brick was the material Soane understood and enjoyed best. He revelled in its potential –

in the rhythms, effects and structural opportunities of the material when expertly handled. He knew about clays, the firing process, the variants of bricks and tiles available. Soane's specifications were detailed and expert because he had been schooled in the craft.

Soane was instinctively drawn to the creative handling of materials. Later he measured the dimensions of southern Italian roofing tiles, sketched the honeycomb patterns of Roman reticulated stonework, counted ancient brick courses and noted the mixes and thickness of plaster.[7] He quickly extended his knowledge to cover stonemasonry, carpentry and all the complex range of detailing and construction that would be required of him. Whether building the Bank of England or a timber-framed barn, these observations stood him in good stead.

Periodically in adult life Soane would interrupt an expedition to the excellent trout-fishing waters around Pangbourne, usually with one or other of his old friends from Reading, and find time to to visit buildings in the area. He continually returned to the area of his birth.[8] Memory played so large a part in Soane's work that this stretch of country with its wealth of vernacular buildings is one of the most significant, if carefully unacknowledged, strands in his architectural thought.

Soane's mother is a less obscure figure. A portrait Soane commissioned from John Downman of 'the Old Lady' – as she was known in the family – a couple of years before her death shows a close resemblance to her son (fig. 4), sharing the long, thin face – compared to the back of a spoon by one of his pupils – terminated by a fiercely prominent chin and cold thin lips. Martha Soan may have come from a different social background from her husband.[9] In the early 1800s several Marcys visited Pitshanger Manor, Soane's elegant Ealing villa and show-piece, suggesting that they were presentable in a way that Soane's siblings (who did not) were not. Of these William (born 1741), Deborah (born 1744), Susanna (born 1746) and Martha (born 1749) were the surviving children, all baptised at

3. An unfinished oil sketch by J.M.W. Turner of the church and mill at Goring, painted in 1805, possibly begun in Soane's company.

4. Martha Soan, Soane's mother, 'the Old Lady' as she was known, aged eighty-four in a painting by John Downman of 1798.

Goring. Two children were buried in infancy, the first-born (also William, born in 1739 and buried six months later) and an earlier John, buried in 1751 with no record of his baptism. Deborah died, aged twenty-two, in 1766.[10]

There is no baptismal record at Goring, or apparently elsewhere, for John Soane himself who was born on 10 September 1753, which perhaps points to a move or family disruptions around the time of his birth. However, as only the second surviving son, twelve years younger than William, Martha Soan's ambitions for her children were heavily vested in John, her last-born.

Soane was dutiful towards his mother but never referred to his father, who died in April 1768 when he was fourteen. From then on, William became the head of his family, but not an elder brother to whom Soane wanted to draw much attention although Soane provided him with financial support in later years of bad health and failing eyesight.

The Soan family lived, whatever their own circumstances, in a very prosperous part of the country. Reading was surrounded by rich farmland and stood on heavy clay soils, ideal for brick and tile-making. Large brickfields lay to the west of the town and, in the later nineteenth century, whole streets were built in strident polychrome brick to advertise the local trade.

The town lay at the meeting point of two major rivers, the Kennet and the Thames (the latter navigable from London to Oxford and beyond), and on the coaching route to Bath. Eighteenth-century Reading had a flourishing economy, based on a wide range of specialist trades developed after the failure of the broadcloth industry, and on its position as an entrepôt, with numerous wharves and warehouses standing along the banks of the Kennet (increasingly canalised during Soane's lifetime). It was a purposeful town, its merchants adapting quickly to changing circumstances. Later waves of prosperity, which, from the mid-eighteenth century onwards included, in rapid succession, the introduction of canals, railways and, finally, major roads and motorways, have largely obliterated the signs of incremental growth that might have remained visible in a less prosperous town.

Based upon its abbey school, founded at the latest in the fifteenth century, Reading had a proud educational reputation. By the mid-eighteenth century there were dozens of small schools, serving both the children of the local population and those from further afield. Reflecting this high level of literacy the *Reading Mercury*, founded in 1723, was one of the first provincial newspapers in Britain.[11] Prosperous merchants, energetic businessmen and professionals, literate and cultured people, formed the upper levels of society in the county town of Berkshire; the kind of people with whom Soane remained most at ease throughout his life.

On the evidence of a number of books inscribed with their names, all four of Soane's elder siblings were literate, although William went into his father's trade as a bricklayer not long after John's birth, and lived in very reduced circumstances. Soane always had great respect and understanding for tradesmen in the building industry, some of whom he worked with during his entire professional life. These men represented the upper echelons of the world from which he came.

From the age of eight John Soane attended, according to established anecdote,[12] a private school in Reading run by William Baker. Such schools were rarely recorded; there was no official scrutiny of these establishments and they sprang up anywhere that a dozen or so children could be housed and offered the required basics: mathematics, Latin, perhaps a modern language and a smattering of literature.

By chance, we have a glimpse of Baker's school some twenty years later in the pages of the Reverend Dr Thomas Frognall Dibdin's *Reminiscences*. Dibdin, whose parents had died in Calcutta when he was a small child (and who became a minor figure in Soane's extensive demonology), was being put through school by a venomous great aunt who paid £20 per annum for his education, board and lodging at a small and congenial establishment run by a Mr John Man and his wife. Their house was in Hosier's Lane, which ran for a short way parallel to the major routes leading west out of town, Oxford Road and Bath Road, before petering out. It was, said Dibdin, an 'obscure part of town'.

John Man was 'a singular, naturally clever, and kind-hearted man: had a mechanical turn; and could construct electrifying apparatuses, and carve a picture frame'. His wife was as kind, if less eccentric, and the boarders were brought up with their four small children, in such a family atmosphere that the orphan Dibdin called them father and mother. Also living in the house was the former schoolmaster, Man's father-in-law William Baker, who after forty years had handed over the small establishment into the capable hands of his daughter and her husband.

In Dibdin's fond account, Baker's study door was always open to the schoolboys and wearing a large, fluffy wig and an exotic dark green oriental gown, he would show them interesting books, discuss literary subjects and offer encouragement in their work. His own son, also William, became a printer, having 'damaged his health in the pursuit of mathematics', described in the introduction to his book *Peregrinations of the Mind* as passing 'the hours of amusement and all other vacant time in the library of his father'. In his case, bookishness had apparently gone too far.

Man seemed to have a more balanced attitude to learning while sharing old Baker's passion for books. Dibdin describes how he bought them 'by the *sack-full*' and, himself to become an exceptionally unreliable bibliographer, traced his contagion with 'the electric spark of the BIBLIOMANIA' from here.[13]

If there was any remaining doubt as to whether Soane attended Baker's school, this description is persuasive. Soane's own passion for the printed page dates from those early years under Baker's roof. For the rest of his life, he could always find pleasure in books; when he travelled he made straight for the bookshops; when he felt unhappy, he rearranged his shelves or bought more volumes. He borrowed books and lent them to his friends. He encouraged his pupils and assistants to share his enthusiasm; he enjoyed quotations and classical literary references. He liked nothing better than to design a library for a favourite client. Even when his eyesight was failing, he ensured that someone was available to read to him.

The puzzle is how a bricklayer found the means to pay for his family's education. The pressure that Soane placed upon his own sons (and, after them, his grandsons) to achieve the best from their education, suggests that similar exhortations were made to him, the youngest in the family and promising student as he must have been. Perhaps Soane's father was prospering at this point or someone had spotted his obvious abilities and helped pay for his schooling or possibly Baker admitted him at a reduced rate. If he had received charity himself it might explain his reticence about his early years as well as his own generosity to the deserving and his implacability to those he judged undeserving – for whatever, often illogical, reason.

On John Soan's death the family joined the eldest son William who had moved to Chertsey in Surrey, remaining there for the rest of his life. Later the pleasant town became a second home to Soane's wife and children, who built up a circle of friends there while visiting William and his family and old Mrs Soan. For some time, one of her daughters also lived in Chertsey.[14] For Soane, a major attraction was the Chertsey Abbey fishpond: throughout his life fishing was the one relaxation guaranteed to distract him entirely from his professional cares. He passed many happy hours with his rod, a pleasure which he shared with several of his closest friends, the young Timothy Tyrrell (with whom he was possibly at school) included.

Chertsey was, like Reading, an ancient abbey town and dependent for its commercial life on its position at an important crossing point of the Thames; close enough to London to attract City men, politicians and nabobs to the pleasant hills and countryside around. The main roads, London, Guildford and Windsor Streets, indicated the likely destinations of those who passed through. The Crown Inn and the Swan Inn, the latter kept by the Daniell family since the 1750s, provided travellers with comfortable lodgings and a change of horses. Thomas Daniell and his nephew William became Royal Academicians and later – to Soane's considerable dismay – provided a regular conduit for information on his activities, reputation and family between London and Chertsey.

Chertsey provides the first, semi-apocryphal, word of Soane's career. He is glimpsed crouched at the foot of his brother's ladder – buried in a book rather than attending to his task as hod-carrier for William, who was at work at Ongar Hall. The description, in Brayley's *History of Surrey*, of the 'illiterate and ill-conditioned elder brother . . . who plodded through life as a petty bricklayer' is given plausibility by the fact that Soane's close friend John Britton assisted with the volume.[15] The scene hints at the family's descent in the world, the educated boy acting as a reluctant manual labourer, and offers it the light of hindsight, since readers in the 1840s well knew the heights to which the grumpy bricklayer's assistant had risen in the course of his career.

Fortunately, in 1768, William introduced his bright young brother to someone who was to become a key figure in his life and future career.[16] James Peacock was a surveyor, already employed as the right-hand man to the rising City architect George Dance the younger (fig. 5) – a partnership which lasted until Peacock's death in 1814. He appears to have had a Chertsey connection and the meeting must have taken place there.[17]

James Peacock, cheerful, efficient but not architecturally ambitious, was a few years older than Dance. He was something of a dreamer; a social reformer who published titles such as *Proposals for a Magnificent Establishment* and an inventor, developing a novel water filtration system which he pursued with great tenacity for decades. A sprightly wit marked his several publications, even on the title-page. Οικιδια, or *Nutshells*, was an architectural patternbook directed, tongue in cheek, at small builders. The

5. George Dance jun. in 1814 just before he retired from architectural practice, drawn by a fellow portraitist G. H. Harlow.

author Jose MacPacke was described as a 'bricklayer's labourer': the name was an anagram of James Peacock. His irony and facility with words suggest a tempting, but unproven, connection to another, younger, Peacock also with Chertsey connections, the satirical novelist Thomas Love Peacock.[18]

In introducing the fifteen-year-old John Soane to Dance, himself only twenty-seven, Peacock offered the boy a start in life beyond his wildest imagination, a huge first step beyond the uncertain, impoverished world of the casual labourer.[19] It led to some kind of paid employment for Soane in Dance's office as a messenger or errand-boy, certainly not as an articled pupil, nor as the 'foot-boy' as Joseph Farington, the painter and diarist, recorded while also noting, more truthfully, that Dance was eager to encourage 'an inclination he discovered in him for drawing'.[20]

Soane, like any fifteen-year-old from a small country town, must have found London both overwhelming and exciting, a fearful place as well as an inspiring one. From the Dances' house on the corner of Moorfields and Chiswell Street, near the northern boundaries of the City of London, which had been the family home for many years, the household which Soane now joined, he could explore the city end to end. Always a tireless walker, he discovered how the intricate street pattern of the medieval city suddenly exploded at intervals to reveal its treasures.

London was densely veined with its pre-Great Fire street patterns, foul lanes, courts and alleys jostling the ordered brick terraces of Queen Anne and Georgian development. The body of the city, its houses and inns, shops and workshops functioned around its architecturally dominant major organs, the structures of the state, religion, law, corporation, commerce and trade. The scale and variety of their fabric and history was overwhelming. Yet there was no overall framework; Wren's plans had been consigned to history and John Gwynn's recent efforts had met with no success.[21] Throughout Soane's working life London would be put together piecemeal; bridges, roads, major public buildings were added with little coherence.

Near Chiswell Street were the Mansion House, by Dance's father, George, senior, and the Bank of England, in the process of being transformed by Sir Robert Taylor. Dwarfing them and dominating everything was Wren's St Paul's Cathedral. A dense crop of towers and spires, the sixty-nine City churches, sprang up like seedlings at the foot of the dome. Beyond Temple Bar to the west were the remnants of the riverside palaces, such as old Northumberland House, as well as Inigo Jones's sophisticated Covent Garden piazza with its Doric church and, even further west, his Banqueting House in Whitehall (fig. 6). The vast gothic hull of Westminster Hall loomed beyond and Westminster Abbey, with Hawksmoor's recently remodelled west front, lay behind it in turn. On the riverside was a warren of wharves and quays, packed on to the banks of the Thames near the City. All invited exploration from one who was 'devoted to architecture from my childhood'.

At little more than Soane's age then, George Dance had been sent to Italy for six years by his father. He returned in December 1764, an honorary member of the Academies of Parma and S. Luca in Rome. In the company of his suave elder brother, the painter Nathaniel Dance,[22] who had been in Rome some time, George Dance made many social and pro-

6. Whitehall, painted *c.* 1775 by William Marlow, looking north towards Charing Cross, Inigo Jones's Banqueting House is in the right near foreground, while the spire of James Gibbs's St Martin in the Fields can be seen in the distance. The entrance to Kent and Vardy's Horse Guards building is to the left.

fessional contacts – among them, the actor David Garrick (in whose theatre company their much older brother James, who assumed the stage name of Love, had played), Cardinal Corsini and Thomas Pitt, nephew of William Pitt the elder, on whose 'extraordinarily fine character and fine sense' he reported to his father, hoping that the friendship would serve him well back in England.[23] More often the assorted *milordi inglesi* appeared in his cheerful caricatures as loungers and lay-abeds (fig. 7).

During the year in which Soane began to work for him, 1768, Dance inherited his father's post as Clerk to the City Works – in effect, architect to the City of London.[24] Dance and Peacock were at the very heart of the contemporary development of London, both in the City and those areas of London which became desirable once the new Blackfriars Bridge (opened in 1769) linked the City to the Surrey side of the Thames. Many of Dance's ambitious plans, especially those for the area around St George's Fields in Southwark, came to nothing (usually because of difficulties with private landowners) but as author of several official reports on subjects including London Bridge, housing standards and conditions in gaols and, above all, in his visionary schemes for the expansion of the Port of London and the docks during the Napoleonic wars,[25] he proved himself both an inspired architect and an enlightened city planner.

In 1768 both George and Nathaniel Dance became founder members of the Royal Academy. George Dance was one of only five architects among the thirty-six members.[26] A convivial man, the fifth son of a large family of actors, singers and painters, he was a good musician and an excellent draughtsman, portraying his friends and contemporaries for relaxation. He inscribed an album of his drawings: 'These gigs and odd roaring, ranting, smiling and frowning, capering, sluts, boobys, Kings etc . . . have been all drawn by George Dance Esquire RA.'[27] Life around Dance and Peacock must have been light-hearted, the office ringing with laughter as well as urgent business.

Living within Dance's household exposed Soane to an immeasurably different world from his own and offered him infinite possibilities. Access to Dance's library, and probably Peacock's too, familiarised Soane with the texts and folios, English, French and Italian, which provided the intellectual underpinning of mid-eighteenth century architecture. A recent addition, the second edition of William Chambers's *Treatise on Civil Architecture* in 1768, provided a trustworthy modern guide to the classical orders, rules, ornament and usage.

As a boy Soane owned manuals for calculation and measuring as well as volumes on geometry, 'optics' and a Greek grammar while his few works of classical literature, Virgil and Ovid, were a tribute to tastes nurtured by Baker. He also possessed at least two architectural books: Matthew Brettingham's *Plans and Elevations of . . . Holkham* (1761), presented by the author in 1769, and John Evelyn's translation of Fréart's *Parallel of the Five Orders* (1707).[28]

The elder George Dance had died in February 1768 and was buried at St Luke's, Old Street, a church which he, as a mason, had helped to build. The most important commission that immediately fell on young Dance's shoulders was for Newgate Prison, for a two-headed client – the City (who had provided the Old Bailey site) and the government (who paid for the building). By the spring of 1769 the designs were well under way.[29] Construction began the following year.

By a real stroke of luck Soane found himself in the household and office of a well-travelled architect with a choice and secure practice and an excellent library. Dance was a fine draughtsman with a superb grasp of spatial and structural possibilities. His first important job, the newest City church, All Hallows, London Wall had showed him to be an inventive,

Morning amusement previous to a jaunt to Tivoli

7. A pen and ink caricature by George Dance jun. showing two hung-over Grand Tourists being roused by a third for a jaunt to Tivoli. Dance was in Rome in the early 1760s although this may have been a later and indelible memory of the jaded and wealthy young men he had met.

open-minded designer whose years in Italy had given him the confidence to step beyond strict neoclassical norms. Newgate was a particularly expressive example of *architecture parlante* – its function graphically signalled by the massive rusticated carapace which cut off the institution from the city around it and sealed its inhabitants safely within (fig. 8). The long shadow of his sponsor at the Accademia di S. Luca, Piranesi, fell over the scheme. With little more than external ornament to display his abilities and inspiration, Dance modulated the extended stone curtilage walls – without windows – in such a fashion that, in Sir John Summerson's phrase, he achieved 'a sort of architectural poetry'.[30]

Nevertheless Dance's generous scheme, with big courtyards and plenty of ventilation to prevent the spread of contagious diseases which laid waste the populations of eighteenth-century prisons, was continually subject to financial cut-backs.[31] The result was a dense, airless set of buildings, a caricature of the original plan in which seperate blocks and adjacent courtyards made the best use of the wedge of City land. As built, it offered Soane a well-remembered lesson in functional and textural ingenuity on a tight urban site; it also taught him about the constraints of the public purse and the architectural price paid for unenlightened clients.

Among the signatories to early contract drawings for the prison was the successful builder and carpenter George Wyatt – Surveyor of Sewers, Lamps and Pavements in the City and a Common Councillor of the ward of Farringdon Without.[32] Working for Dance, Soane may well have met the man whose niece he would later marry. Wyatt, Dance and Peacock were all City liverymen; respectively in the Drapers', Merchant Taylors' and Joiners' Companies.[33] The ancient networks of the City were always effective conduits of influence and patronage; Soane was well-placed here to observe them.

If Soane was no more than an errand boy to begin with, by 1769 he was involved in Dance's first commission beyond the City, remodelling a house in Ealing, a small village to the west of London. Pitshanger Manor was a neat brick villa owned by Thomas Gurnell, a leading Quaker banker, City merchant and partner in Gurnell, Hoare and Harman.[34] Dance added a two-storey wing to the south of the house, providing a ground floor dining-room and first floor drawing-room. While working at Pitshanger, he came to know the family well and, though not a Quaker, in 1772 he married Mary, Gurnell's twenty-year-old daughter.

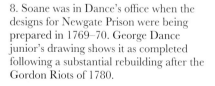

8. Soane was in Dance's office when the designs for Newgate Prison were being prepared in 1769–70. George Dance junior's drawing shows it as completed following a substantial rebuilding after the Gordon Riots of 1780.

Dance was eager to encourage his protégé. It was no doubt at his instigation (and probably with his good references) that Soane applied to become a student of the Royal Academy schools (fig. 9).[35] In October 1771 aged just eighteen, he joined the school which had recently moved from premises in Pall Mall to Old Somerset House by courtesy of George III. In its first year, 1769, of the seventy-seven students, only three had been architects. Still a small minority, the numbers were gradually rising.

The Royal Academy schools were free, and financed by the annual exhibitions (though for the first few uncertain years the king met any deficit). Their dependence was total; the Academy was a body 'whose government, elections, and all other matters are wholly [?in] the King's breast. This circumstance must entirely silence all envious cabals, all designing manoeuvres, and all intriguing solicitations.'[36]

Unlike the other students, architects, because of the system of pupillage in which most were serving, were exempt from academic drawing exercises and could present their hours in an office in lieu of those in the studios.[37] Their time at the Royal Academy was spent in the library and attending lectures. The Library, already stocked with many leading European and British treatises and architectural publications, was the creation of Sir William Chambers who, as treasurer, released the funds but also had determined views on what was admissible.[38] Soane hungrily spent hours copying extracts from the volumes on the shelves.[39]

The architecture lectures were delivered, on winter Monday evenings, by the Professor, Thomas Sandby.[40] Some professors gave their lectures intermittently, if at all, but Sandby was particularly punctilious in his duties. In him, Soane met quite another model of the successful architect – someone whose career had been entirely built on a chance connection to royalty.[41] Although steeped in a painterly appreciation of the picturesque and sublime possibilities of the landscape, he could not be considered a leading architect

Sandby's major building, the impressive, double height Freemasons' Hall on Great Queen Street, off Drury Lane, was built while Soane was at the Royal Academy. Sandby (probably through the good offices of his patron the Duke of Cumberland who later became Grand Master)[42] had been appointed Grand Architect of the Order of Freemasons in 1775 and his new headquarters building gave the freemasons – by now established for some fifty years – greater visibility and a permanent presence in London. Before, they had met in any available premises, taking their 'instruments' with them. With its links to the monarchy, English freemasonry remained comfortably inside established society, in contrast to freemasonic tendencies to either republicanism or occultism in France and elsewhere.[43] Soane was always exceptionally alert to the processes of patronage and Sandby's career offered him another variant to observe.

Sandby's lectures were pedestrian, but comprehensive. They owed more than he admitted to Chambers.[44] Soane conscientiously attended his course (unchanged year after year) from 1771 until 1775, copying out the lectures in full. Sandby's longueurs could be forgiven when, in his sixth and final lecture, he unscrolled his splendid illustrations for a Bridge of Magnificence, one of which extended more than half the width of the

9. Zoffany's 1771–2 group portrait of Royal Academicians, shown in the Life Class. The two women academicians are represented by their portraits out of delicacy. Unlike painters and sculptors, architectural students only attended the Royal Academy after their working day in an office, to benefit from lectures and use of the library.

room. Soane never forgot the moment; neither the subject nor the theatrical impact (fig. 10).[45]

The Royal Academy Schools aimed to add another dimension to a young architect's training. The library and the lectures provided food for his mind and, in addition, he had opportunities to refine his draughtsmanship and presentation – competing with his peers for the various prizes. The best work was displayed at the exhibition. The Royal Academy Schools suited Soane's needs perfectly, though perhaps not many others'. Few of Soane's peers continued in architecture and fewer still achieved distinction.

The realities of daily practice were gleaned in the long hours of pupillage in an architect's office. Their French student counterparts may have learned about perspective, drainage and fortification in the classroom, arguing with their professors and visiting important buildings, but the English learned their profession as they went, an apprenticeship or pupillage comparable to those in medicine and law.

After four years Dance felt that Soane might benefit from new experience. In 1772 Dance was about to start work on his major City commission, the Guildhall, and his marriage to Mary Gurnell was soon followed by a large family, altering his domestic arrangements.[46] Soane was 'with his approbation placed in the office of an eminent builder in extensive practice'.[47] He was Henry Holland.

Holland, eldest son of a master builder, had been in partnership with Lancelot (Capability) Brown since 1771 and two years later married Brown's daughter, a move which further cemented the partnership. As Soane joined the office, work included the early stages of a large speculative development of 89 acres to the west of London, leased from Lord Cadogan's estate and capitalised by Holland's father. Hans Town was named after Sir Hans Sloane, Cadogan's distinguished father-in-law, a physician and botanist whose collections formed the basis of the British Museum.

In Holland's office Soane was a clerk earning £60 per annum, involved in many varied commissions from the building of Sloane Street[48] to several country house commissions. Soane is known to have worked on at least three: Claremont in Surrey, for Lord Clive,[49] Benham Park, Berkshire, begun the following year for Lord Craven and Cadland, on the Hampshire coast near Fawley, for Robert Drummond, the banker. Soane was responsible for measuring up and final calculations in order to settle the tradesmens' bills.

10. Joseph Gandy after John Soane, Design for a Triumphal Bridge; one of a number of presentation drawings of 1799 based upon Soane's Royal Academy Gold Medal winning drawing of 1776.

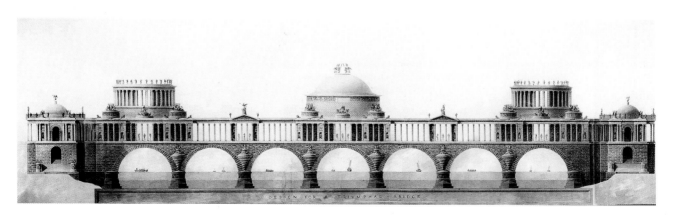

With Dance he had seen something of the fine art of architecture and begun to grasp the arcane processes of patronage but it was with Holland that he learned the real business of building. As a junior employee he had to measure, estimate, draw up contracts and bills, as well as produce record drawings. This was the office (if not the practice) on which he would model his own and long afterwards he used Holland's bill and price books to guide him.[50]

Soane must have become increasingly aware of how helpful family connections (and a solid financial inheritance) could be. In his own profession he could observe the dynastic networks of the Adam, Brettingham and Wyatt families, while at first hand, with Dance and Holland, he witnessed the advantages of birth, inherited contacts and sinecures, links forged by political allegiance or City connections, as well as those made through marriage.

George Dance's father had been the Clerk of Works to the City of London from 1735, and George became his father's assistant before inheriting his position. His maternal grandfather, James Gould, was the surveyor to the South Sea Company and his father-in-law, Thomas Gurnell, was a wealthy City merchant. Even without ability, young George Dance could hardly have failed in architecture. Henry Holland's father was a rich master builder, with extensive City contacts within the Tylers' and Bricklayers' Companies, while his business partner, soon his father-in-law, assured him many a useful professional *entrée*.

In Holland's office Soane saw the architect-builders' practice, in which distinctions between the professional architect, the specifier and contractor became impossibly blurred. It led to his deep distrust of any confusion in roles. Where speculative development was involved an enormous financial commitment was required, especially in volatile periods such as during the current War of American Independence, and even if the individual architect was as honest and efficient as Henry Holland there were innumerable potential conflicts which could be as detrimental to the architecture and to the client as to the construction.

When submitting work to the Royal Academy Soane gave his employer's address as his own, the usual practice. In 1772 both Soane and Richard Holland, his fellow student at the Royal Academy and Henry Holland's cousin, gave their address as the Holland family house, 31 Half Moon Street,[51] which runs between Piccadilly and Curzon Street. From the end of the street Green Park can be glimpsed. Just round the corner stands 94 Piccadilly, Matthew Brettingham's town house designed in the mid-1750s for Lord Egremont. Several other recently built mansions shared the view over the park.[52]

The next address Soane gave, in 1774, was 'at Mr Holland's Hertford Street', a recently developed road east of Park Lane and running into Curzon Street from the north. This part of Mayfair was built from the mid-1760s onwards and later the Hollands had an interest in at least ten houses.[53] The Hollands moved to No. 17 shortly after their marriage. If, as has been presumed, Soane was still living in Henry Holland's household, he now found himself on the edge of London, a city insatiably pushing west, with Hans Town (just beginning) part of the rapid transformation of the rural landscape into an urban one. He had moved well away from the City, to a fashionable quarter which was changing rapidly as the mansions of the aristocracy became sandwiched by the new terraced streets.[54]

One of these new Mayfair town houses belonged to, and is assumed to have been designed by, Thomas Pitt, nephew of the first Earl of Chatham. Camelford House was built in 1773-4 on land belonging to the Grosvenor Estate.[55] In 1775 Pitt took a further lease from the estate on a plot in adjoining Hereford Street and built two houses for sale. Before long Soane was employed there by John Crunden, an associate of Holland's, to check bills for completed work.[56]

Gradually Soane's life must have become less solitary, his attitude to London less fearful. With fellow students and contemporaries such as Richard Holland, later to leave architecture for the family building business, Soane was finding friends who shared his pleasures and interests.[57] The only hints to the young man Soane had become in his early twenties lie in the pages of his commonplace book of 1776[58] where he heightened his emotions by some appropriate reading. The extracts he chose suggest that he was harbouring an unrequited love; a suitably Rousseauesque pose since early in the *Confessions* Soane's hero refers to having 'spent my days in silent longing in the presence of those I most loved'. There is a quotation from *Much Ado about Nothing*, in which Benedick protests that he will live a bachelor but the 'fire that is closest kept, burns most of all'. Of all his notebooks, largely made up of dry observations, this is the most emotionally consistent and suggests that he had found some time for a sentimental life, beyond his unstinting efforts to fashion himself as an architect. Most probably, his student pleasures were not for the record.

Throughout his life Soane's reading matter never changed. The novels of these early years remained his favourites; *Gil Blas*, whether in Le Sage's original French, in Italian or in Smollett's translation, Sterne, Molière, Richardson, Rousseau's *Julie, ou La Nouvelle Héloïse* were his staples. Dictionaries, travel diaries and architectural treatises made up the remainder of his earliest library[59] and it was to many titles in this first selection that he held fast. His reading was the conventional literary diet that the new subscription libraries and the flourishing booksellers satisfied.[60]

Among Soane's known friends from these student years[61] Edward Foxhall who entered the Royal Academy schools in December 1775 became a carver, upholsterer and furniture-maker. He also acted as an agent at auctions. John Hobcraft, later to work with Soane as a joiner, was another student of architecture at the Royal Academy, entering six months before him. Richard Holland, as we have seen, became a successful builder. The only one to remain in architecture was Robert Furze Brettingham, who entered the schools in 1775, the fourth generation of a well-known Norfolk family of builders and architects – taking his mother's family name to reinforce his connection to the Brettingham dynasty.

If the subsequent careers of Soane's fellow students showed the breadth of options available, for Soane there could be no alternative to architecture. In his early months as a student at the Royal Academy, the talk of the town was James Wyatt's Pantheon on Oxford Street, the 'winter Ranelagh', which opened in 1772 (fig. 11). In the astonishing Byzantine hall – based upon the great rotunda of Hagia Sofia in Constantinople – with its green and purple lamps and its subtle hidden top-lighting, Soane experienced and would always remember the grandeur and unabashed theatricality of Wyatt's pleasure house.[62] Yet when Fanny Burney's heroine Evelina[63] went to the Pantheon she was struck by its beauty but also its solemnity: 'it has more the appearance of a chapel than of a place of diversion: and, though I was quite charmed with the magnificence of the room, I felt that I could not be as gay and thoughtless there as at Ranelagh, for there is something in it which rather inspires awe . . . than mirth and pleasure.' The Pantheon became a fashionable mecca for all visitors to London. To Horace Walpole it seemed like a lost city of antiquity; 'Baalbec in all its glory'.[64] For a twenty-year-old architectural student, it was a swift journey to an infinitely exotic country.

During these years Soane watched architectural reputations rise, such as James Wyatt's, and saw others fall. Listening to his fellow students at the Royal Academy, some of them pupils in leading architectural offices, he heard the latest gossip. The most spectacular establishment was the Adam brothers' at Lower Grosvenor Street with its continual passage of highly paid foreign artists and droves of lowly drawing office assistants labouring on their developments. As leading builders, a good season might see as many as 3,000 men working for them.[65] In 1772 the architectural world watched the failure of the brothers' speculative venture at the Adelphi and as, undaunted, they embarked the following year as partners in another scheme in Marylebone, on Portland Place.

At the other extreme was the politically astute Sir William Chambers (fig. 12), as well-connected at court as at Westminster and in the wider cultural life of the capital, his pupils guided into key positions, his professional life untainted by any potential conflict of financial or contractural interests. In 1776 construction began on the great riverside complex of Somerset House, an elegantly diplomatic tribute to both the English Palladians and the French academic neoclassicists. There was no more impressive public building to be seen. Chambers, the widely acknowledged leader of the profession, was the man upon whom to model an architectural career (and office) of the kind Soane envisaged.

Hardly had he enrolled at the Royal Academy, than Soane had set about producing his Silver Medal drawing, the set subject an elevation of Old Somerset House, but he missed the handing-in date. The Silver Medal, competed for by the architectural students, was won by Thomas Whetten, a rich pupil of Chambers's. In 1772, with time on his side, Soane was successful with an elevation of the Banqueting House, Whitehall. The Royal Academy Silver Medal was the first marker of a recently enrolled student's progress and, far beyond that, the biennial Gold Medal marked graduation for the most able. The covetable travelling studentship, the gift of the king, was the most desirable of all. Soane's tenacious pursuit of these prizes offers a first sighting of his steely ambition.

At the distribution of prizes, including Soane's Silver Medal, on 10 December 1772, the President of the Royal Academy, Sir Joshua Reynolds (fig. 12), delivered his fifth Discourse. His homily on the pursuit of excellence, even at the expense of small imperfections, could have been tailored for Soane's ear. He counselled younger students to 'choose some particular walk in which you may exercise all your powers; in order that each of you may become the first in his way'.[66] Soane read and annotated the published *Discourses*.

11. James Wyatt's Pantheon, Oxford Street seen in its heyday as a social meeting place ('the winter Ranelagh'), painting attributed to William Hodges and William Parr (1770–2).

Soane's ambition made him precipitate, as if he had less time to achieve what others could take by virtue of their social position. His attempt to win the Gold Medal in 1774 was unsuccessful, let down particularly by his *prova*, a test in which the student had five hours to draw a subject without preparation. Soane saw, with mortification and for the second time, Thomas Whetten succeeding where he had failed. But in 1776 Soane gained the Gold Medal comfortably, gaining thirteen out of sixteen votes. The set project had been a Triumphal Bridge[67] – the subject which had fired Soane when Sandby illustrated his version at the Royal Academy earlier that year. Soane had persuaded the Academy both to allow him to sit the *prova* on a different day and on a different subject, and even then his sketch was unfinished.[68] Soane's design process was essentially lengthy, he needed time to mull over options and disliked being pressed. The *prova* did not suit his working method at all but the set subject, with its long preparation period and academic subject matter, showed Soane's newly acquired skills at their best.

With the Gold Medal Soane was now eligible for the three-year travelling scholarship to Rome. He had persuaded Sir William Chambers to show his drawings to the king and in the version of events reported by Farington, George III had personally approved Soane's scholarship without further ado.[69] Despite the intervention of the monarch and the leading architect, the president considered this irregular and Sir Joshua asked that the academicians be asked, in due process, to elect the next travelling scholar. In December 1777 an election was held and Soane easily gained his scholarship, by twenty votes, from the only other candidate, none other than Thomas Whetten.

In the meantime, Soane had set up on his own – in reality no more than a separate address from Holland for whom he continued to work. He was also preparing his first publication, *Designs in Architecture*, at the behest of the Taylor brothers who had approached him in December 1776.[70] The initial proposal for an eighty-plate folio volume, including a British Senate House, bridges, churches, villas and mansions shrank into a small format volume with thirty-seven copper-plate engravings, selling for 6 shillings and published in 1778.

The designs were for garden seats, eyecatchers and picturesque structures in classical or gothick dress, gauche and confused, such as the Moresque dairy, with round-headed windows and a low saucer dome (fig. 13). Plans, where given, were simple in the extreme. There is no dedicatee. The Taylors, aware of the demand for such titles, the most prestigious of which was Chambers's *Designs for Chinese Buildings* (1757), had successfully cornered the market for such architectural snippets – Soane's book, published at their expense was reprinted three times, the last in 1797. Appearing as the author headed for Rome, it was, together with his works on the walls at the Royal Academy, Soane's *curriculum vitae*.

His student exhibits at the Royal Academy had been designs for a 'nobleman's town-house', a 'gentleman's villa', a garden building and, in 1775, another town house. Now in 1777 his exhibit was more adventurous, a mausoleum, in memory of James King, a fellow Royal Academy student tragically drowned on a boating expedition at Greenwich. Soane melodramatically claimed that he, a non-swimmer, had intended to join the party until the last moment, but had been saved by his decision to work on his Gold Medal submission ('my being employed on the drawings of the bridge preserved me from a watery grave'): fate – in an appropriately architectural guise – had saved him.[71]

Soane's laborious preparations for any presentation drawings indicated that he was not a natural draughtsman.[72] However many years he spent beside Dance, he could never emulate his master's innate brilliance with pencil or pen. He may have found comfort in a little book, the anonymous

12. Architecture, sculpture and painting epitomised by, respectively, Sir William Chambers, Joseph Wilton and Sir Joshua Reynolds, painted by J.F. Rigaud as the Royal Academy moved into their premises within Chamber's new Somerset House.

13. The Moresque dairy, plate XXXIII from Soane's youthful *Designs in Architecture* (1778), an unconvincing attempt to combine the oriental and the occidental.

Essay on the Qualifications and Duties of an Architect. 'How superficially they judge who imagine fine drawing a principal if not the only qualification requisite for a good architect . . . to draw fine is one thing, and to design well is another . . . often a good design is condemned because it is ill drawn and on the contrary a bad design approved because it is well drawn.' Published in 1773, and full of lively good sense, it was subtitled 'useful hints for the young architect or surveyor.' Everything points to it being written by James Peacock, Soane's fatherly mentor during his years in Dance's office.[73]

The little book might have been written for Soane. Emphasising the importance of a sound knowledge of the building trades for an architect – however finely educated and widely travelled he might be – the author has much to say about building up a practice. 'Use every opportunity to improve yourself' and once you have a family to support, 'seek employment with the greatest diligence though with an apparent indifference . . . making your court to great men but seldom, lest you appear troublesome'. Sometimes 'you will be obliged to make application to those very persons . . . who ought rather to have applied to you'. He offers advice in dealing with a tricky client: if after examining whether you have done your duty, acted honestly and uprightly and faithfully discharged your duty, and he still remains dissatisfied, it is best to resign.

The architect may profess to know everything, but never will, while the surveyor has the advantage of knowing who to ask, through his connections. 'Be careful to gain the good-will of the workmen under you . . . be always ready to assist them to the utmost of your power and plead their cause if at any time they or their families are in distress.' When you find an honest and industrious tradesman, recommend him. 'An experienced workman may sometimes give you a hint that may prove of no small utility in business.' Soane must have had the continual benefit of Peacock's wisdom in person throughout his early and formative years in London. He forgot not a word of it.

The young John Soane, preparing to set off for Rome, was tall and bonily thin, with an intense, uncertain gaze. His face, like his mother's in old age, was exceptionally elongated, with small, rather hooded eyes, a prominent brow and tight lips. The dominant feature was a heavy chin, to which the nose was no match. Without a wig, his hair was dark and wavy. An early portrait (fig. 14), by his fellow Royal Academy student, Hunneman, enlarges the eyes but captures the hesitancy in the awkward mouth. Another, by Nathaniel Dance (George's brother), shows him in a wig, looking very uncertain of himself (fig. 15). Soane's remained a face which reflected displeasure better than good cheer. All his portraits detect a certain ambiguity of expression; a half-smile, a sideways look.

An unusual feature was Soane's voice, randomly rising and falling between a masculine bass and a high treble, described in later life as a 'singular undulation.'[74] When angered, it rose to become shrill but very quiet; in real fury, Soane fell silent. (A practice which he extended to his arguments on paper; exasperating those with whom he was in dispute by refusing to reply or acknowledge any communication.) The voice mirrored his personality, in which there was little middle ground, no compromise. The length and angularity of the face was reflected in his physique generally and the etiolated impression became accentuated with age. Soane would

not soften into obesity; he ate and drank with enthusiasm but burned off his pleasures with both nervous and physical energy.

Despite the setbacks and delays, after five years in Holland's office and a short period of independence, Soane was ready for Rome. For a twenty-four-year old country builder's son, even one by then familiar with metropolitan fashions and attitudes, the journey was a thrilling, but alarming, prospect. Whatever his route south, he would cross several national borders, each state separated from the last with its own controls and currencies, languages and dialects. Travelling could be dangerous, the political situation was always prone to change, and cheap lodgings and transport were, at best, uncomfortable.

The excitement lay in the experience of finally seeing the great buildings of classical antiquity for himself; rather than drily or inaccurately recorded in the familiar engravings. He would see them in all weathers, all lights. He would be able to touch the worn ancient stones and brickwork, climb ladders to record the actual dimensions of their mouldings and columns, he could match the writings of antiquity to their setting and see the Latin words and names, lettered on to the tablets and monuments around him. Perched on half-excavated mounds of earth or stonework, he could immerse himself in ancient Rome – a city still visible.

Equally familiar on the page, but impossible to visualize without its

14. (above, left) Portrait of the confident young architect with dividers by his Royal Academy fellow student Christopher Hunneman, painted *c.* 1776. Soane valued the painting highly – it was still hanging in his attic bedroom at Lincoln's Inn Fields in the 1830s.

15. (above, right) A more hesitant, formal portait of the young Soane in a powdered wig aged twenty-one. Drawing by Nathaniel Dance RA, George's elder brother.

landscape, Paestum in southern Italy promised a first impression of Greece. Soane hoped that other journeys, perhaps even as far as to Greece itself, might be possible. Everywhere he would be able to hear, and before long speak, living and colloquial Italian and as he travelled, find the companionship of others with whom to compare his impressions and experiences. Among the Grand Tourists he might find, if he was as assiduous as Chambers, patrons enough for a lifetime's work. As he prepared to leave London, everything was before him, everything was possible.

2

TO ROME AND NAPLES

Soane had used the year before he left for Rome to good effect. Desperately impatient to get there, he distracted himself with work and preparations (fig. 16). Finally the moment arrived; at 5 a.m. on 18 March 1778 the adventure began.

Soane's travelling companion from London to Paris and then on to Rome was his fellow student from the Royal Academy schools, Robert Furze Brettingham, who may have had useful contacts in Italy through his uncle, Matthew Brettingham.[1] As fellow students, Brettingham and Soane had probably worked together in recent months in London. In whatever capacity, the two young men knew each other well enough to be confident of being congenial travelling companions.

George Dance, having himself spent six fruitful and highly enjoyable years abroad, arriving in Rome in May 1759, had advice, contacts and his own experience to offer Soane. It may have been Dance who provided an introduction to Piranesi and it was certainly his example that Soane followed in becoming a member of the Academy in Parma. But Soane's most valuable guidance lay in a letter which Sir William Chambers, the elder statesman of the architectural profession and Treasurer of the Royal Academy, had written some years earlier to another architect taking the same route. Edward Stevens, who had worked in his office, never returned, dying in Rome in 1775.[2] The letter, a copy of which Chambers gave to Soane, was a masterly summary of the education which lay ahead for an eager and receptive young architect.

No one offered a better example of the practical uses to which a period of study in Rome could be put than Chambers. From the dozen or so potential patrons, mostly aristocrats, whom he had met in Italy, nine had become clients.[3] It was, he wrote to Stevens, essential for students to 'make a better use of their time now than they formerly used to do, for unless they study hard and acquire superior talents, they will do little here; this country [is] swarming so with artists of all kinds, that unless a man does much better than his neighbours, he will have but an indifferent chance of making his way'.

Chambers went on to guide Stevens, and in his footsteps Soane, to works that had stood the test of time; 'Always see with your own eyes . . . [you] must discover their true beauties, and the secrets by which they are produced.' No architect should be a sole example but: 'Work in the same

16. Soane's first of many plans for a 'British Senate House' which he later titled 'sketch for a House of Parliament before I went abroad!'.

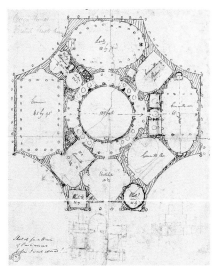

quarry with M. Angelo, Vignola, Peruzzi and Palladio, use their materials, search for more, and endeavour to unite the grand manner of the two first, with the elegance, simplicity, and purity of the last.' He added Bernini and Pietro da Cortona, while counselling Stevens to correct the 'luxuriant, bold, and perhaps licentious Style' with Palladian simplicity and chasteness – 'endeavour to avoid the faults and blend the perfections of all'. In Rome and around Naples Chambers advised Stevens to sketch antique fragments, but also to draw from life and study painting and sculpture, for 'you cannot be a master in your own art without great judgement in these' (Reynolds's advice almost to the letter).

Chambers gave Soane his architectural and artistic bearings in Italy. He may also have provided another introduction to Piranesi, of whom he had written 'he is full of matter: extravagant 'tis true, often absurd, but from his overflowings you may gather information'.[4] Soane claimed that Piranesi personally presented him with four prints but offered no other details. (Later he bought many of his volumes and prints.) Since Piranesi died that year, their meeting may have been brief. Soane seldom underplayed his encounters with great men.

Chambers may also have guided Soane towards key buildings and people in Paris. He had attended Blondel's influential Ecole des Arts during 1749–50 and remained in regular touch with his fellow students. For almost twenty-five years he had kept abreast of the major developments in French architecture, through correspondence, publications and, most immediate of all, reports of new work brought by his French visitors to London. Finally, he achieved his long-planned return to Paris in 1774 to see the fruits of the building boom that had followed the ending of the Seven Years' War in 1763. He was a close friend of several key men in the profession, M.-J. Peyre, Charles de Wailly, P.-L. Moreau-Desproux and J.-D. Leroy, as well as leading amateurs and artists and was shown the pick of contemporary Parisian buildings – all steeped in Roman influence – on his visit.

Chambers's pupil and biographer Thomas Hardwick – whom Soane knew from the Royal Academy Schools and soon encountered in Rome – had also spent some weeks in Paris in the autumn of 1776. He went armed with advice from his master who pointed him to Ledoux's *pavillon* for Mademoiselle Guimart (his own Parisian sketchbook included five *hôtels* by the architect), Gondoin's Ecole de Chirugie (fig. 17), the church of Sainte Roche (which by then included Boullée's Calvaire) and J.-D. Antoine's Hôtel des Monnaies (fig. 18), all of which Hardwick faithfully drew.[5] It is no coincidence that all these buildings were of particular interest to Soane, cited later in his lectures and writings.

Eighteen months later, when Soane and Brettingham arrived in Paris on their way to Rome, they found the city still in the grip of a building boom. Medieval Paris was a huddled core to a capital in an ambitiously expansive mood epitomised by the just completed Place Louis XV (later the Place de la Concorde), straddling the Champs-Elysées and the Tuileries. Numerous speculative developments were springing up along the great northern Boulevard and in the *faubourgs*, together with magnificent town houses such as Brongniart's Hôtel de Monaco and Boullée's Hôtel de Brunoy.[6]

We have sparse information about Soane and Brettingham's stay in Paris but know from Soane's incomplete notes that they called upon Jean-

Rodolphe Perronet, who as *Inspecteur des ponts et chaussées* was the most distinguished civil engineer in France, although his early experience had been in an architect's office. Born in 1708, Perronet was, despite his age, intensely and ever-increasingly active as a teacher and builder.[7] Chambers knew Perronet, sponsoring his nomination for membership of the Royal Society – official recognition came to him earlier in England than it did in France.[8] Both innovator and link to the past, and a contributor of many of the articles on engineering to Diderot's and d'Alembert's *Encyclopédie*, the bible of Enlightenment thought, Perronet was a pivotal figure.

An inventor of technological wizardry of all sorts, Perronet had a public gallery of ingenious devices which included an underwater saw for submerged piling and offered an explanation of how copper balls 5 foot in diameter were used to roll into place the massive rock supporting Peter the Great's statue in St. Petersburg, which so impressed Soane that he recalled it in a lecture almost forty years later.[9]

Soane was intrigued by Perronet's Pont de Neuilly (fig. 19) with its revolutionary construction, soon widely imitated, allowing the roadway to be flattened out over elliptical arches.[10] But, with the insouciance of youth, he judged Perronet 'an excellent engineer . . . but a very indifferent architect'.[11] Interestingly, Soane was enthusiastic about the wider implications of the new bridge, intended to form a link in a grand western approach to Paris, running 'in two straight lines and a great part of it on the level' from Saint-Germain-en-Laye through the Bois de Boulogne to the Place Louis XV and on to the Tuileries. The sheer scale of the scheme made a lasting impression on Soane and heightened his contempt for the way in which Wren and Gwynn's urban proposals had been blocked. He believed that London too deserved a grand route and late in life he energetically returned to the idea.

Years later Soane would buy the impressive folio volumes of Perronet's major works, in which his engineering achievements were celebrated in a series of superb and informative engravings. The distinguished engineer also provides a link to Claude-Nicolas Ledoux, since he was *Commissaire du Roi aux Salines de Lorraine et de Franche-Comté* from 1771 and built the dramatic saltworks at Arc-et-Senans, almost complete by 1778. Perronet became *Inspecteur général des Salines* in 1775.

Chambers's interest in Ledoux's Parisian town houses (quite unknown and unpublished in England in 1774) may well have been prompted by Perronet.[12] In early 1778 when Soane and Brettingham were in Paris, Ledoux was designing the Hôtel Théllusson, which was to be a radical version of the Parisian *hôtel* with its massive arch, framing a park in miniature and the exedra of the house – a building of great importance to Soane. His critical admiration for Ledoux, who had revolutionised the plan of the French town house by using diagonal axes and inserting circular and oval rooms, led to him being the first English architect known to have bought his published works.[13]

A rare survival of Soane's impressions were his thoughts on Moreau-Desproux's Opera House on the rue Saint-Honoré, the Théâtre de l'Opéra at the Palais-Royal, completed in 1770, only to burn to the ground in 1781. 'Simple but not inelegant', Soane noted (and stored it away for future use) its handsome vestibule, with Doric columns and flights of steps. He noticed that the balconies were designed largely so that

17. Interior of l'Ecole de Chirugie (Médecine), Jacques Gondoin's admired medical school of 1769–75, a major recent building Soane may have visited when he passed through Paris in March 1778, on the way to Rome.

18. William Chambers's drawing of the riverside façade of Jacques-Denis Antoine's Hôtel des Monnaies (the Mint) just completed in 1774 when Chambers revisited Paris. It influenced the Strand elevation of his Somerset House

19. Hubert Robert's painting shows the moment in 1772 when the timber centres were removed from the arches of the Pont de Neuilly. Perronet's novel almost flat bridge was much admired by Soane on engineering rather than architectural grounds.

the occupants could themselves be seen to best advantage (no nonsense about sight-lines to the stage).[14]

Unlike Rome, Paris offered no well-trodden path for a visitor to follow. Beyond the city Chambers may have also pointed Soane to some of the latest examples of French garden design, evocative exercises such as the *jardin d'illusion* just completed for the Duc de Chartres at Monceau and begun in 1773,[15] or the Désert de Retz at Chambourcy, begun in 1774. Their contrived ruins amidst planted groves and water, evoked a seductive classical civilisation, tempting allusions for eager English travellers to Italy. No landscape was more visited than Rousseau's tomb at Ermenonville, situated under a grove of poplars on an island in the lake. Although he could not have seen Rousseau's grave since he did not die until the summer of 1778, Soane knew of it and drew both the site and the inscription onto the flyleaf of his copy of the *Confessions*.[16]

On 29 March the travellers went to Versailles to have their passports endorsed, enabling them to travel on through French territory.[17] The English in France were understandably nervous, since the French had just formed an alliance with the Americans.

Frustratingly, there is no record of the route that Soane and Brettingham took on their month long journey south to Rome. Years later Soane referred to his disappointment in never visiting the Roman remains at Saint-Rémy in Provence, suggesting that the two men did not take the usual winter route, via the Mediterranean coast, Orange and Nîmes. Presumably they were eager to reach Rome as quickly as possible and, as spring was approaching and the snows retreating, they could have taken the Alpine route due south over the Mont Cenis pass. On his way home Soane had eagerly planned to travel via France, suggesting that he had left these treasures of Roman antiquity as a treat for the return journey.

On arriving in Rome on 2 May, travel-weary from their weeks spent racketing over rough roads in jolting carriages and nights spent in cheap, often filthy inns, Soane and Brettingham would have immediately visited the English Coffee House, at the Piazza di Spagna, to introduce themselves into the circle of expatriate artists in Rome. It was the point from which everyone arriving in the city took their bearings, as much socially as physically; a meeting place in the immensity of the unfamiliar city. Thomas Jones, the painter, had made it his first port of call on arrival with Thomas Hardwick on a gloomy late November morning in 1776 and found a great gathering of artist friends and new acquaintances in a gloomy dirty cellar.

Newcomers were wise to observe the social behaviour and grouping of the Grand Tourists. The Romans, observed Jones, had their own classification for the English, putting them into 'three classes or degrees – like the positive, comparative and superlative of the grammarians'. First came the artists, in Rome for study, improvement and professional advancement. The second group included 'Mezzi Cavalieri' (literally, half gentlemen), of private means and perhaps with a servant, occasionally seen at the English Coffee House (fig. 20). The third class were true 'Cavalieri or Milordi Inglesi' who moved in an entirely superior circle, surrounded by their satellites – 'travelling tutors, antiquarians, dealers in *virtu*, English grooms, French valets and Italian running footmen'.[18] It was this latter category of person that Soane, with Chambers's advice in mind, would search out but it was the lesser gentry and merchants who would become Soane's travelling companions and lifelong friends.

Otherwise Soane's attention was quickly absorbed by his intense excitement at finally standing in front of the remains of Roman classical antiquity (fig. 21). Structures familiar only from the pages of treatises and motifs copied in countless English country houses and public buildings were finally before him in the original; to be touched, measured and above all, learned from. Some surprised by their scale, others by their ruinous state. Engravers tended to clean up reality and alter dimensions. The Forum was only partially exposed, with earth banked up around the great monuments such as the Arch of Titus (fig. 22), stranded amidst the detritus of eighteenth-century city life. Until the mid-century, classical Rome had been a valuable source of building materials and portable antique fragments for anyone who cared to help themselves. Pillage and neglect had desecrated the great monuments of antiquity, yet their grandeur and authenticity were overwhelming.

Soane wasted no time. His first recorded letter home to London was to his erstwhile colleague, the carver Henry Wood, 'my attention is entirely taken up in the seeing and examining the numerous and inestimable

20. A drawing of a Roman coffee house in the 1770s by David Allan shows home comforts on foreign shores, with billiards and a Grandfather clock for the homesick Grand Tourist.

21. Watercolour by Smith of Warwick showing the Colosseum and the Arch of Constantine (left) in 1802, earth banked up over the monuments and life going on around these remnants of classical Rome.

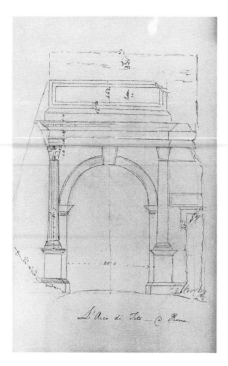

22. Soane's measured drawing of the Arch of Titus, Rome, undertaken on ladders in order to meticulously record every detail of the dimensions.

remains of Antiquity . . . you are no stranger to the zeal and attachment I have for them.' Wood, with whom he had worked on Holland's Hans Town development, knew how frantic he had been to start his journey to Rome, how impatient to see the evidence for himself.

Soane's first dated drawing, 21 May, was of S. Agnese fuori le Mura, followed by several other early churches – almost antique with their reused columns and classical capitals. He recorded their clear, elemental plans as well as sections and occasional details. Constantly in his hand in these early weeks were the two volumes of *Letters from Italy* by Anna Miller (*née* Riggs), published the previous year, but referring to a visit during 1770 and 1771. A respected guidebook for Grand Tourists, it offered a winning and enthusiastic combination of practicalities, factual and historic information, spiced up with a few dropped names.

Fortunately for Soane, none of the other young English architects in Rome at the time showed much sign of either his ambition or application. Charles Heathcote Tatham, writing to Henry Holland in 1795, had heard of Soane's envied reputation. As Tatham put it, 'Mr Soane's good fortune was singularly brilliant and auspicious, much depending upon his own instinctive industry and merit, but so much more upon the prosperity of the times'.[19] He compared that against the current politically volatile situation, offering scant professional opportunity, since the few wealthy travellers were 'continually on the wing'. By 1796, busy collecting and arranging transport for the antique fragments he had found for Holland (and which eventually became Soane's property), he commented 'As to connections, it is mere wild goose game.'

The handful of British architects in Rome had so little time and so much to see that collaborating and pooling the results of their studies seemed a practical expedient. Thomas Hardwick, returned to Rome from Naples in June 1778 and he and Soane produced a number of measured ground plans and other drawings, without much concern for who had done what. Sometimes one copied directly from the work of the other. The arrangement was, however, destined to lead to misunderstandings.

On the whole Soane did not fit in easily with his peers,[20] despite his friendship with the kindly and uncompetitive Robert Brettingham. Hardwick was an able draughtsman but as an architect searching for future patronage he was no match for Soane. The third architect in Rome at this time, John Henderson, a Scot who had been there for several years, was soon eclipsed by Soane's efforts. These three, with Jacob More the painter, went south in September to see Vesuvius, which was active once again. Soane was not of the party. He missed four pleasant days which included a visit to Pompeii, sailing across the Bay of Baia and a moonlight visit to Pozzuoli. The tour set More on a lifetime's production of pot-boilers, depicting Vesuvius erupting and the Bay of Naples by moonlight.[21]

The artists and architects were nervously aware of the growing political tension between England and France over the summer of 1778, which might render their journey home very difficult and hasty. However, the news proved not too alarming and Soane settled down, going out of Rome to Tivoli, to explore Hadrian's Villa, the most evocative of Roman sites with its massive brick standing structures, its subterranean passages and above all its redolent atmosphere. There he had a first sight of the Temple of Vesta, a tiny building which would possess him as few others did and to which George Dance had probably first drawn his attention.[22] While in Rome itself he concentrated on a careful investigation of the Colosseum.

By August Soane had to prepare his submission for the Royal Academy summer exhibition the following year. He chose to design a British Senate House (fig. 23), composed as he put it later, in flowery prose, 'in the gay morning of youthful fancy, amid all the wild imagination of a youthful mind animated by the contemplation of the majestic ruins of the sublime works of Imperial Rome.' In its final form, lettered in *sans serif*,[23] the dominant central form was the flattened dome of the Pantheon, from which long colonnades stretch out, embracing courtyards front and rear. It was a grandiose vision, comparable in its ambitions to the earlier Triumphal Bridge design, its pedigree intermittently French, intermittently classical Roman, admixed with Bernini. Later Robert Brettingham helpfully passed back his uncle Matthew's remarks on the composition which he thought 'shewed considerable inventive facility and originality but was deficient in practical acquaintance with the accommodation necessary in such a great national structure'.[24]

Soane's fellow artists in Rome could display their work in studios or on the walls of other dilettanti, to tempt any potential patrons. It was in their studios in the artists' quarter around the Piazza de Spagna, and in their company, that an ambitious architect would make contact with the important *cognoscenti* among the Grand Tourists. For an architect there was, apart from seeking out classical fragments for sale and offering measured drawings of the major buildings, no easy or immediate way of securing patronage. The prospects were long-term and inevitably uncertain. Soane's flair was to identify and cultivate those whom he sensed might be persuaded to give him a chance in the future.

Soane first met Frederick Hervey, the Bishop of Derry, that autumn (fig. 24): there was no odder Grand Tourist. His Italian tour of 1777–9 was his third and although on this occasion he had brought his wife and youngest daughter Louisa with him, they preferred to settle down in one

23. Design for a British Senate House redrawn by Joseph Gandy in *c.* 1810–11 after the drawing that Soane sent home from Rome as his Royal Academy exhibit in 1779. Matthew Brettingham jun., although impressed by the scheme, questioned how practical the arrangements were.

24. The fourth Earl of Bristol and Bishop of Derry (the Earl Bishop) painted in Naples by Madame Vigée le Brun in 1790, well after he and Soane had parted company. When Soane met him in Italy he was, as his wife, from whom he would soon part, wrote in exasperation, 'everlastingly employed in buying ornaments for the Downhill', the house which he lured Soane back from Rome to redesign.

place upon arrival. From May to September 1778, the family took a house in the hills outside Rome at Castel Gandolfo but there, for once, the Bishop too was housebound for the family was struck down by malaria, Louisa only just surviving.

The Bishop led Soane to imagine that he was a potential patron, and quickly swept him, astonished by such good fortune, into his train. He became an ebullient *cicerone* for Soane and, presenting him with Palladio's *Quattro Libri* and a copy of Vitruvius,[25] set the tone of a pedagogical relationship. That winter he also introduced him to another Grand Tourist who had just arrived in Rome and whom he had himself met for the first time. The nephew of the late Earl of Chatham (a hero of the Bishop's) was someone he was eager to befriend.

Thomas Pitt (fig. 25) was a distinguished politician in his own right but undermined by chronic bad health. Now forty, he was on his second Continental journey, arriving in Rome in early December 1778, having progressed there in a leisurely manner from Pisa, where he had been taking the waters.[26] Pitt was travelling with a caravan; his aged father-in-law, his wife and two small children and an attendant doctor, William Pennington.

Pitt's youth had been an unhappy affair. After his birth in 1737 – a long-awaited son – his father, Thomas Pitt, almost immediately left his wife, born Christian Lyttelton. She returned to her family home at Hagley, in Worcestershire, and died in 1750. Meanwhile her spendthrift, rancorous former husband escaped his creditors to France, abandoning his Cornish estate at Boconnoc, only returning in 1761 to remarry and die almost immediately after. The young Thomas Pitt was supported throughout these difficult years by his uncles (on both sides of the family).

Young Pitt took a house in Twickenham, close to Horace Walpole's Strawberry Hill. He had spent long periods as a boy watching the transformation of his maternal home, Hagley, and its park by the pick of gothic revivalists – Sanderson Miller and Henry Keene – and the amassing of an enviable collection. Walpole was delighted at his new neighbour, such a knowledgeable architectural amateur. 'He draws Gothic with taste, and is already engaged on the ornaments of my cabinet and gallery'.[27] Nevertheless, in time Pitt would turn his hand with equal ease to a Palladian bridge (at Hagley), a Roman arch (the first of his several works at Stowe) or ornamentation ranging from the rustic to the authentically gothic. Walpole referred to Pitt's house as the 'Palazzo Pitti'.[28] Later the friendly neighbours fell out on political grounds.

Upon his father's death Pitt opened up Boconnoc again. The furniture had been auctioned off, the best oaks felled and the gardens ploughed up. Only some books and china remained. Despite the bad health that had dogged him since Cambridge and first had sent him abroad in 1760–1, he set about putting the estate, and the house, to rights. He also became a leading figure in the new Cornish china clay industry, fighting to keep its monopoly and beginning to restore the family fortunes after the depredations of his father. In politics he became an outspoken Whig MP, operating independently of the Grenville 'cousinage', although he had inherited the notorious pocket borough of Old Sarum in 1761 and, with a short spell at Okehampton, held it until he was made Lord Camelford in 1784, having declined the leadership of the House of Commons.

In 1771 the Earl of Chatham, his uncle, visited Boconnoc (his own childhood home) and was delighted by the scene, much as it remains, a gentle, undulating landscape marked by woods and water – 'full of repose, though not wanting spirit', as the earl put it.[29] That year Pitt had married the daughter and heiress of a Norfolk landowner, Pinckney Wilkinson, who was, in Horace Walpole's phrase, a 'great fortune'. Chatham had died in May 1778, encouraging Soane to design him a Mausoleum.

When Pitt and Soane met that December, introduced by the Bishop, one wonders whether Pitt was aware that he had already employed Soane, albeit as a lowly figure attached to Henry Holland's office. Despite the disparity in their ages and situations, Pitt and Soane quickly became on excellent terms and from then on Soane frequently turned to him as a sounding board for his ambitious architectural schemes.[30] Pitt, with his 'classical taste and profound architectural knowledge', as Soane put it, quickly became the mentor that Dance had been in London. Pitt may also

25. A drawing by Thomas Patch which shows Lord Camelford playing the flute. The former Thomas Pitt, a cousin of William Pitt the younger, was the most supportive of all Soane's patrons from Rome.

have warned the inexperienced young man against the foibles of the rich and high-born abroad, especially those for which the Bishop of Derry, a prince of the false promise, was becoming notorious.

The Bishop had a knack for casting aside family responsibilities, not to mention his ecclesiastical ones, and, unlike Pitt, he generally travelled solo and in rude health. When he first visited Naples in 1766 he had discovered an interest in geology and vulcanology, kindled by his meeting with William Hamilton, his old school-fellow and in April 1770 he embarked on an extensive Grand Tour with his thirteen-year-old eldest son, John Augustus, leaving the rest of his family in Suffolk and the Bishopric of Derry to do without him until autumn 1772. On that occasion he took a young Cork architect, Michael Shanahan, who was commissioned a few years later to build the Downhill, the Bishop's house in Ireland, from designs provided by James Wyatt.[31]

On 22 December 1778 it was Soane's turn to set off with the Bishop to Naples. At first glance they were an absurdly ill-matched couple: the Bishop, aristocrat and connoisseur, witty and outrageous, travelling with the awkward and somewhat obsequious Soane. At the last moment Robert Brettingham who was to have been of the party was persuaded not to join them by his friend Gavin Hamilton, the painter. His excuse was that there was little of interest for an architect in Naples but he may also have been warned off by a man who well knew the Bishop's reputation as a shameless exploiter of needy artists.[32]

The Bishop's growing reputation as a tricky patron may not have reached Soane but Thomas Jones had already found it exceedingly hard work to extract a £40 payment for a large view of Lake Albano. Despite that, hearing that the Bishop had just arrived in Naples from Rome, accompanied by 'Soane the architect', he hurried to his hotel to leave his card. 'I found him combing and adjusting a small single curl which was fixed by a string to his own short hair – "You see Mr Jones" said he, as I was entering the room, "I am my own valet – I am not like the generality of our noble families – poor half-begotten creatures who have not the use of their limbs and can not stir without a coach" – After a few minutes conversation, he mounted his horse, and attended only by his groom, set off, according to his usual custom on a ramble till dinner'.[33] Soane had fallen in with a most unconventional fellow.

Leaving Rome, the first stop for the Bishop and Soane had been at Velletri, in the Alban Hills, to view the treasures collected by Stefano Borgia (who became a Cardinal in 1789). In 1770 Borgia had been appointed the Secretary of the Congregazione di Propaganda Fede, responsible for Catholic missions around the world. On the pretext of discovering the current beliefs and faiths of those the Jesuits were seeking to convert, the missionaries were requested to send home representative artefacts from their posts, the rarest and most exquisite of which found their way into Stefano Borgia's already extensive private collection of local antiquities and implements.

What the Bishop and Soane saw was, in the making, an extraordinarily diverse museum of ethnography and fine arts, including Middle Eastern metalwork, oriental and European ivories and enamelling, Indian miniatures, as well as Greek and Egyptian objects and Christian icons and altarpieces. The collection is now a prized treasure within the

Museo Nazionale in Naples.[34] Such eclecticism was in the spirit of an exquisite cabinet of curiosities and perfectly reflected the wide-ranging interests and eccentric enthusiasms of Soane's travelling companion. Another visitor, a few years later, was Goethe who was struck by the variety in Borgia's collection, in which Egyptian idols, Etruscan terracottas and Chinese paintboxes were juxtaposed. On leaving, the local women called out to ask if his party would like to buy antiques and then, doubled-up with laughter, displayed a selection of old kettles and fire irons to the tourists.[35]

From Velletri, on its outcrop of the Artemisio range of hills, Soane and the Bishop dropped down to follow the Via Appia, running south-east and driven straight as a die across the featureless landscape of the Pontine marshes. Various papal attempts to drain the area with canals had made little impact on the dank, infested countryside. However, the current Pope, Pius VI, had initiated major new works, in particular the construction of the Canale Linea Pio which would run parallel to the Via Appia for many miles, a project which intrigued the Bishop.

Although progress on this occasion was not difficult, the roads in the area were generally very poor – a reflection of the run-down infrastructure in the papal states – and a number of visitors had had dangerous accidents. After the journey over the gloomy plain, at this time of year innocuous enough but in the warmer months a malarial trap, the travellers saw their horizon broken by mountains as they approached the Tyrrhenian coast at Terracina. Papal territory gave way to the Kingdom of the Two Sicilies. This was *Campania Felix*, a landscape blessed by a temperate climate, varied topography and favourable aspect and fertility, and the district chosen by the Roman élite for their villas and summer houses – a golden place immortalised by Virgil.

Soane's own familiarity with classical literature was brought to life by the Bishop's passion for the antique past, so evident and immediate in everything around them. The search for sites from the ancient pages, telling of, in Soane's words 'departed greatness', took on new meaning. A few miles on they stopped at some ruins, close to the coast, which the Bishop convinced Soane and himself to be those of the Villa of Lucullus, and the travellers settled down to an eccentric and delicious Christmas lunch, banqueting in the ruins on *spigola* (bass), fished from the nearby lake. It was an appropriate location for a feast, given their conviction that they were in the house of such a noted epicurean.

The evocative place and the delicious Roman meal prompted the two men to expand their plans for the Downhill, the Bishop's classical home in Ireland. Soane had already drawn on his memories of Claremont for a summer dining-room, and now he sketched a pair of alcoves from the villa which might make a pleasing detail in the new room. The Bishop also asked Soane to design a *canile*, a suitably neo-classical kennel, for his son's hounds (fig. 26). The confetti of commissions convinced Soane that he had secured a remarkable patron.

Meanwhile Soane eagerly soaked up the breadth of the Bishop's other interests, noting the profusion of oak and cork trees there as well as the sandy soil. His account of this idyllic day ended with a note that he and the Bishop had, on the basis of what they saw, mentally restored the plan of the villa.[36] The delight of discussing architecture, as an equal, with such an

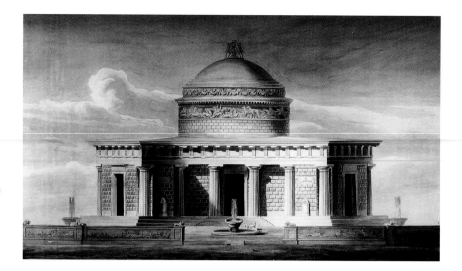

26. A later reworking by C. J. Richardson (*c.* 1835) of Soane's Design for a Canine Residence designed in Rome at the Bishop of Derry's request. Dogs ornament the classical 'kennel' from top to bottom, suggesting that the Bishop's commission was, at least in part, one of his famous practical jokes.

erudite and compelling man, still resonates in the account of this heady day in his *Memoirs* written fifty-five years later.

They travelled on to S. Maria Capua Vetere, the ancient Capua, where Soane considered the amphitheatre superior to the Colosseum in Rome. Second only to the Roman amphitheatre in size, the structure had lost almost all of its four storeyed walls, punched by eighty arches, and much of its Istrian marble masonry, following centuries of plunder. Nevertheless, the completeness of the substructure, especially the covered galleries and vaulted passages below the arena, meant that the structural evidence was (and remains) remarkably complete. Soane, always as fascinated by technological excellence as by architectural detail – ever the builder's son – stepped out the dimensions of the arena and mentally registered the configuration of complex space. Typically he noted the high quality detailing of the brickwork and the remaining sections of fine masonry and sketched one of the sculpted heads that remains *in situ*.[37]

They left the Capuan plain and arrived at Caserta, some 20 miles due north of Naples, where Vanvitelli's vast incomplete summer palace stood. Begun by Charles III in 1752, the works were continuing in the hands of the architect's son and for Charles's successor, that long-lived ruler, Ferdinand IV. Lacking the intended corner towers and dome that might have marginally lightened the effect, the palace was an over-scaled and elephantine construction, in a glorious setting. (In later years the grotesquely fat King of Sicily spent much of his time hidden at the furthest extremity of his park, in his 'English garden', enacting mock sieges and sampling dishes produced in a thatched kitchen on a lake.) The park was also designed by Vanvitelli, an almost entirely linear design, cutting through the surrounding town, its plan dictated by the water course which began high on the distant hillside and travelled down through basins, culverts, pools and fountains to the garden front of the palace below. The water was carried to its starting point by a massive aqueduct (fig. 27), also Vanvitelli's work, and it was to this that Soane and the Bishop returned a few weeks later. Where the palace was concerned, Soane echoed Chambers's judgement on Vanvitelli's work, regarding it as 'miserable in points of composition'. Spending little time at Caserta, later that day, 29 December, the party arrived in Naples. The journey had taken a week; one of the most extraordinary weeks in all of Soane's life.

He scarcely passed comment on Naples. Soane's silence is remarkable, compared to the young Goethe's first impressions. Arriving some ten years later, Goethe was bowled over by the city's natural site, the lazy arc of the bay, with Vesuvius rising beyond, and castles and villas wrapping the long, gentle coastline. He was also struck by the enormous vitality of the town 'gay, free and alive', even in the chill of February 1787.[38]

Soane's recorded Neapolitan enthusiasms were confined to a handful of buildings, in particular churches and monuments.[39] Soane apparently could not allow himself to look beyond buildings and taste the atmosphere and natural beauties. Probably the Bishop had left him to find his own quarters in the city, while he pursued a scintillating path through the fashionable drawing-rooms of Naples. Soane, left on his own, short of money and probably baffled by the dialect, may have been lonely and in some difficulty in those first weeks.

The blinkered view of Naples that Soane took – in marked contrast to his observations and evident enjoyment of the southern Italian excursions which he made, both before and after, with the Bishop – show him, left to himself, as narrowly focused and rigidly conformist. Goethe's infectious delight in everything around him only accentuates Soane's nervous immaturity and lack of response. Soane had to learn how to deal with wider cultural horizons, to use his imagination and to take pleasure in new experiences. Later friends made in Italy would teach him to unbend and introduce him to relaxed companionship, time spent away from the business of architecture. There was little or no spontaneity in Soane's nature, but he worked hard at it.

Towards the end of his stay in Naples, Soane joined two Englishmen, both of whom would play significant roles in his career, John Patteson, the inheritor of a family wool-stapling business in Norwich, and the older Richard Bosanquet, a City man who had been a director of the Bank of England and on the board of the East India Company and a member of a large and influential Huguenot merchant family. He had fled to France when his firm Bosanquet and Fatio failed in the late 1770s. The three men stayed at the Albergo Reale San Lucia, in which, Soane observed, 'the situation is most desirable, we had each a room in the upper storey'. Patteson did not reach Naples until mid-March, so Soane's earlier lodgings may have been distinctly less pleasant than this.

John Patteson had travelled slowly out to Italy, mixing business and pleasure. He made some trade calls in the Low Countries before travelling on to Leipzig, where he had been educated. In Hamburg, he had met up with a fellow Norfolk man, Charles Collyer, and his servant. Destined for the church, Collyer was a familiar enough model of the English traveller; he had no grasp of any foreign language and was entirely at sea. Patteson, trying to reach Leipzig in time for the annual Fair, became increasingly exasperated by Collyer who then fell ill, detaining him further. However, by mid-July 1778 he was enjoying Dresden and Leipzig without his 'burden'. As his widowed mother wrote, 'I am very sorry for him but think you have done all that friendship could possibly require'.[40]

Reaching Italy, Patteson found that the nobility was dismissive of busi-

27. The Acquedotto Carolino, designed by Vanvitelli in the 1750s and completed a few years before Soane and the Bishop of Derry visited it in early spring 1779 (see p. 40). The aqueduct brought water from the mountains to the famous gardens of Caserta and was a remarkable brick structure, a feat of both engineering and architecture.

ness and that those to whom he had letters of introduction were not people who would provide suitable amusement, being 'in the second and third class of those in trade'. However he was mesmerized by Siena, blessedly empty of his fellow Grand Tourists, and revelled in the beauty of the Tuscan language and the charm of the Sienese, 'my countrymen are no longer the only rational beings', he noted. However, he assured his mother, he would not fall prey to 'opera girls'. From Siena he went to Volterra, amidst its extraordinarily bare and sculptural countryside. He even finally acceded to his mother's requests for recipes, sending back to Norwich instructions for a complicated dish of pigeon, cooked with brains, truffles and mushrooms, in a rich sauce and topped with rice.

After this enviable introduction to Italian life, his arrival in Rome at the beginning of March 1779 was bound to be an anticlimax. He did not like the Romans or the Roman climate and lost no time planning a summer journey to Naples. As he wrote home on 31 March, 'pray don't be uneasy . . . I have formed a studious plan which I hope we shall not repent of 40 years hence'.

A more cosmopolitan young man than most of those on the route, Patteson was already struck by the rigid class divisions in the society of Grand Tourists. An acute observer, he saw that most English travellers continued their trail around the sites of antiquity 'spurred on by fashion and the fear of being laughed at' and he confessed that if it had not been for the 'tyrant fashion' he would not have spent more than eight or ten days in Rome despite being impressed by the scale and grandeur of its major Imperial monuments, while the gardens, vineyards and cabbage patches that interspersed the great sites of antiquity were eloquent reminders of the frailty of men and their empires.

Richard Bosanquet was some twenty years older than either Soane or Patteson and was, somewhat disturbingly to the ears of the latter's mother, known as 'Richard the Rake'. Patteson had told her some months earlier that he was looking forward to reaching Italy, where 'I shall see Mr Bosanquet at Florence who is a very good sort of a man, one who has seen and knows the world'. From Norwich came maternal warnings; 'you will excuse me if I tell you I have some fears at your being so intimate with Bozenquette [sic] the man who has conducted his own affairs so ill, is certainly not the proper person to take a young man by the hand whose good nature makes him sometimes too leadable'. He protested that he was not an innocent and why could he not 'do a friendly act and assist a deserving man although his imprudences may have led him into troubles, which of themselves are a bitter punishment'? Mrs Patteson cannot have been very pleased to hear that her son and Bosanquet were sharing lodgings in Naples.

Soane began to make a number of excursions, visiting the sites close to Naples, Pozzuoli and the coast of Baia and Cuma, enriched by their classical associations and the ruined sites of antiquity. In some travel hints for an unnamed friend,[41] Soane suggested that he visit the Arco Felice and 'several ancient temples' at Cuma but located the grotto of the Cumaean Sybil at Pozzuoli (later excavations sited the Sybil's cave at Cuma itself). Perhaps in response to more observant companions, no doubt including the Bishop, Soane's notebooks began to fill with a jumble of observations; points of local pronunciation, facts about climate and geology, rates of local pay, drawings of ornament, details of materials and construction techniques. He noted that in this southern climate the sheep bred twice a year and roses bloomed three times. Occasionally he breaks into a more expressive vein. His dictionary, at the back of the notebook, includes an interesting selection of phrases: the Italian for 'to vent one's anger', 'to assuage one's grief', 'she is a woman whose beauty obscures or eclipses every other' and 'to leap for joy'.[42]

One of the attractions of the volcanic region just west of Naples and inland from Pozzuoli, were the Campi Flegrei, an area of lakes, dormant cones and continuous subterranean activity, manifesting in jets of sulphurous steam and disconcertingly warm ground. At the Grotto dei Cani visitors enjoyed watching a dog become senseless as a result of the low lying gases in the cave, apparently to the point of death and then, released, bounding instantly back to life.

When, in his absence, Soane's elaborate design for the Bishop's classical dog kennel, discussed in Rome, was shown to the large party of 'Monsignori' around his dinner table,[43] the studied architectural witticisms were apparently well received. Soane's pavilion was loaded, ludicrously, with every conceivable version of canine ornament, from the summit of the dome downwards. The Bishop – a famously cruel practical-joker – may not have expected him to take the commission as literally and the party probably indulged in some sniggers at Soane's expense.

But if the Bishop may have used Soane as an occasional stooge, he also helped him gain access to a number of highly sought-after private collections, such as the palace at Portici just south of Naples where the king displayed the recent rich archaeological finds of the area. Such places could only be visited furnished with a pass or introduction from His Majesty's envoy Sir William Hamilton, but Soane does not record any direct dealings with him and perhaps the Bishop, an old friend of Hamilton's, asked for the precious document on his behalf.

In the city the San Carlo opera house, built in 1737 (and rebuilt after a terrible fire in 1816), was on every Grand Tourist's itinerary and Soane, all his life an enthusiast for theatre and theatres, went to a performance. He was struck by the splendour of the glittering interior but the acoustics were atrocious, partly a design fault but also because of the cacophany made by the Neapolitans greeting one another loudly throughout the performance.[44]

Beyond Naples, Soane began his excursions with the obligatory ascent of Vesuvius, climbing it for the first time on 20 January. Recently grown active (it would erupt again in August that year) the volcano remained accessible but pleasingly dramatic. Thomas Pitt was now in Naples and invited Soane to join his party, consisting of his doctor, Pennington, and a Cornish banker friend, Sir William Molesworth. It was an arduous journey, especially for Pitt whose knees were crippled and who must have been carried up in great discomfort. John 'Warwick' Smith, the watercolourist with whom Soane made another ascent, described the tough haul up the central cone, strapped to a local guide and sinking and slipping back with every step into the ash and cinders that rimmed the precipitous summit (fig. 28).[45]

With Pitt's party Soane travelled on to Pompeii,[46] first excavated in 1755 and offering a glimpse of real immediacy into the Roman world. Archaeological work was progressing but the site was treated somewhat as a bran tub, with tempting antiquities found by random digging.[47] Soane's

28. *The Ascent of Vesuvius* by Henry Tresham, a view from the late 1780s, showing the arduous business of getting Grand Tourists to the very summit of the volcano so that they can peer into the smoking crater. Local guides were employed to haul or carry them up.

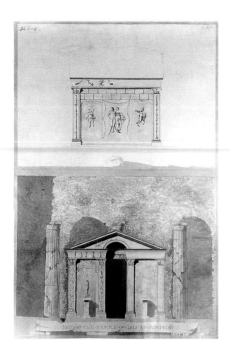

29. A lecture drawing of the Temple of Isis at Pompeii. Soane's memorable first visit had been by moonlight. The temple was reputed to have been the site of sacrifice but Soane's interest was in the ornament and the strong sense of antique mysteries.

first impression of Pompeii had been (by choice) in the moonlight, the perfect romantic introduction. Then he had thrillingly and illicitly (entry to the site was forbidden after dark) sketched the Temple of Isis (fig. 29), thought to have links to the Egyptian cults and which upon excavation had revealed the bones of sacrificial victims upon its altars.

Soane knew what he wanted to study at Pompeii; he drew a plan of the Via delle Tombe and sketched several monuments. He was mesmerised by the commemoration of death in classical antiquity and by then knew the Via Appia in Rome, but the paradox of a street of mausolea and tombs in a city itself buried alive was poignant. Pompeii led to Paestum, the outstanding site of Greek architecture in Italy.

Here Soane met another key figure for his future career. Philip Yorke (fig. 30), aged twenty-one, was the great-nephew of an important eighteenth-century patron, Lord Chancellor Hardwicke, and the nephew of an erudite bibliographer and one of the founders of the British Museum, the second Earl Hardwicke. Philip Yorke was, however, the first member of his family to take a Grand Tour, enthusiastically encouraged by his uncle. He had set out from London eighteen months earlier, in May 1777. The courts and diplomatic missions of Europe were full of his well-placed relatives and he arched well to the east, to Vienna and Buda (where he investigated Roman sites), before heading for Milan, arriving in a punishing heatwave in July 1778.

Philip Yorke's interests were wide; his notebooks record comments upon commerce, history, art and architecture and politics in equal measure. Throughout his life a conscientious and principled man, he had no sympathy for Italian high society and its nonsenses. The lofty Duchess of Parma, her head topped with a diamond encrusted toupée was, he considered, 'altogether one of the most ridiculous figures I ever saw in my life.'[48] Months later on his way home in Turin, he met the King of Savoy (and Sardinia) who impressed him by his policy of offering employment schemes to his impoverished people, such as a project to fortify one side of the city. This was in marked contrast to the Papal territories where constant changes of government had successively deprived the people of their living, leaving the streets crowded with beggars.

Arriving in Rome in November 1778, Yorke found the country in the grip of a terrible drought, the air laden with dust but piercingly cold. His regular letters to his uncle and patron are enthusiastic in his appreciation of Roman classical antiquity and art, seen in the company of James Byres, the Scotsman who 'professes architecture though he can scarce draw a line' as one visitor described him, who now acted as a *cicerone* to the nobility with a sideline as a purveyor of works of art, though his efforts were largely wasted upon Yorke.[49]

Philip Yorke's notes on Rome[50] were scribbled in pencil as he stood in the great treasure houses of the city – the palazzi Colonna and Corsini, the Capitol and the Vatican. Here and there are sketches; unidentified plans, drawings of an obelisk, a circular window, even of a king-post roof – suggesting he was thinking of building projects at home as well as imbibing Roman examples. There are pages in French, notes of the numbers of volumes in the great libraries, rough catalogues of the major art galleries. Meanwhile he dutifully wrote home, to his stepmother and uncle, detailing his visits.

30. Philip Yorke, painted by George Romney after he became the third Earl of Hardwicke. He and Soane first met at Paestum.

In early December he had an audience with the Pope, together with Lord Lucan (whom the Pope thanked for the favour that had recently been shown to the Roman Catholics in Ireland) and Lucan's son, Thomas Pitt and Pennington, and 'Messrs. Hailes, Bowdler and Freman'. Although obliged to attend *conversazioni* at the houses of the few Romans who cared to socialise with the constant tide of strangers that washed around their city, he was dismissive of Roman society with its fascination with 'cabals of priests and prelates'. Yorke was a serious young man who was travelling to broaden his interests and opinions, not his social circle. Nevertheless, while Soane was attempting to make do on an annual stipend of £60 from the Royal Academy, and John Patteson was attempting to keep his expenses to £500 per annum, Philip Yorke's expenditure for the months of January and February 1779 were, respectively, £204 2s 8d and £154 19s 8d.[51] Aristocratic Grand Tourists had different standards to uphold as well as company to keep. Meanwhile Soane had to try and make extra income by scouting for antiquities and had a commission from Pitt to find two female busts; such was the trade in these items that he wondered whether originals might prove cheaper than copies.[52]

Yorke, with his tutor and regular travelling companion Thomas Bowdler, left Naples on 27 January to visit Pompeii and Paestum. Bowdler was a Norwich man who had studied medicine in Edinburgh but did not pursue the medical profession and in later life achieved notoriety as the editor of the expurgated *Family Shakespeare*.

Pompeii had particularly seized Yorke's imagination (fig. 31). If there was nothing else whatsoever to see in Italy, a visit to the recently redis-covered city would still be worthwhile, he reported to his uncle. Scooping some ash into a paper, he noticed that it would not take much effort to clean the site from the volcanic residue, consisting of ash and small peb-bles. (Herculaneum, by contrast, was buried beneath solid volcanic lava.) He noticed five or six workmen 'who seem rather employed in watching strangers than clearing away the rubbish. It is impossible to see Pompeii without regretting that it is not in a country where the discoveries would be carried on with spirit.'

Yorke, like Soane, explored the Temple of Isis very minutely before pressing on to Paestum where he recorded his meeting with an English architect "by the name Soane who is an ingenious young man now study-ing at Rome'.[53] Yorke did not forget the youth measuring the temples of Paestum. Erudite and observant, Soane must have sensed that Philip Yorke would make an ideal future client. Yorke had already encountered, and dismissed, the posturing Bishop of Derry. The Bishop had invited Yorke and his companion to dinner but 'he talks so incessantly and is so decisive in his manner that he loses a great deal of his merit in my opin-ion'.[54] Nor did he rise in his esteem when a few weeks later the gossip went around Rome identifying the Bishop as the buyer, for £300, of a series of frescoes from a structure in the grounds of the Villa Negroni. (Later, prob-ably apocryphally, the Bishop was rumoured to be the purchaser of the Temple of Vesta.) It would, he wrote to his uncle, have been better to leave them alone as a rare and valuable example of an ancient house. (As the bricks were being taken to build the new Sacristy at St Peter's, the place was disappearing before their eyes.)[55] The hand-coloured engrav-ings of the frescoes made by Angelo Campanella in the late 1770s became an important reference for the strong colouring of interiors *all'antica* in the next decades; the Bishop's acquisition, however, was never heard of again. Shortly after the Paestum expedition, Yorke fell ill and it was many weeks before he had fully recovered. Bowdler, now acting as his doctor, became a companion for Soane and probably introduced him to another Englishman currently in Naples, Rowland Burdon.

Although the contact between Soane and Yorke was brief, they had obviously impressed one another. On his return home to England, Yorke was swept up in elections and parliamentary business, but before long, marriage and a young family would turn his mind to building improve-ments.

Soane had been, as no architect could fail to be, astonished by Paestum. Even today the three sturdy Greek temples appear to have landed by acci-dent upon the flat coastal plain of Salerno. Then, as now, the central struc-ture, dedicated to Neptune (Poseidon), retained its pediments and

31. Pompeii as depicted by Jakob Philipp Hackert. The painting shows the relationship of the newly excavated site to the Bay of Naples with the mountainous Amalfi coast rising over the plain.

32. An original drawing by an unknown artist of the temples of Paestum, seen in 1758. Thomas Major's volume *The Ruins of Paestum* (1768), consisting of engravings after these drawings, introduced the English to the most important Greek site in Italy. Soane bought the folio of drawings in 1800 for his collection.

elements of the pronaos and naos (the internal subdivisions of the temple). The other temples were dedicated to Ceres and to Hera. Their squat dimensions struck Soane as being 'exceedingly rude . . . they have all the particulars of the grecian Doric, but not the elegant taste; they seem all formed with the same materials, of stone formed by petrification'.[56] Familiar with engravings by Piranesi and Thomas Major (fig. 32), which tended to give a mainland Grecian elegance and grandeur to the temples, Soane found the reality took some getting used to.

Soane visited Paestum (fig. 33) again with the Bishop in mid-February. He continued his investigations of the temples, balanced for much of the time on ladders, while noting the amphitheatre and various fragments on the unexcavated site. In retrospect, Soane often harked back to his memories of Paestum and accorded Greek revivalism his close and continuous interest.

From Paestum, already easily 50 miles south of Naples, they left the well-trodden trail and went inland to the Cilento region, their destination the magnificent charterhouse of S. Lorenzo at Padula. Although founded in the fourteenth century, the extant buildings dated mostly from the sixteenth and seventeenth centuries and expressed the great wealth and confidence of the order. Soane sketched in plan the flamboyant double elliptical stair that had been recently added to the complex[57] as well as measuring the huge chiostro grande, to elucidate its rhythmic arcading (figs 34, 35).[58] A second stair, a simple curl of cantilevered stone leading up to the library from the main cloister, must have caught his attention too.

The sequence, starting with the church, entered through an enclosed courtyard, and leading to other rooms, small cloisters and courts and, finally, the principal cloister, off which the monks' accommodation opened, offered an oasis of calm and sophisticated architecture, enhanced by superb workmanship in every detail, from choirstalls to flooring. The

33. Temple of Neptune, Paestum, the central and best preserved of the temples, showing the pitted marine limestone and stubby baseless columns which Soane found surprisingly inelegant.

Carthusian monks were famous for their hospitality and travellers were made welcome. Soane was unusually expansive in his notes about the monastery. It suggested how an enormous site, with many varied buildings upon it, could remain coherent. The Certosa was finally suppressed in 1816 but the buildings survive to demonstrate their measured beauty.

Their way back led via Eboli and Salerno, with a visit to the cathedral there – although Soane reserved his comments for antique fragments and relics and remained apparently uninterested in medieval aspects of the building – as well as to new bridges and roads in the district. Another tour took them north-east of Naples to Benevento, with its Roman triumphal arch, and returning via Caserta the Bishop and Soane stopped to look at the nearby Acquedotto Carolino, begun in 1753 and inaugurated in 1769. This fantastic engineering feat, requiring tunnels through five mountains and three separate levels of viaduct, culminates at the Ponti della Valle where the aqueduct straddles the entire valley in a vast perforated wall of brick. Soane's observation, 'a great modern work and merits a peep',[59] somewhat understated the impression it made on him.

The structural possibilities of brick arches, first in the substructure (the cryptoporticus) at the Capuan amphitheatre and now here, were revelatory. The lessons lie buried but dormant; Soane was always interested in major engineering works, in France and elsewhere, but rarely included them in the 'polite' architectural discourse of his lectures, except by inference. Arches, he would later write,[60] were 'an invention which confers almost as much honour on the human intellect as the discovery of the laws of gravitation, of the circulation of the blood, or the successful labour of Galileo'. The impressions of this journey are there, indisputably, in his work at Chelsea Hospital, in the stable block and in the (lost) Infirmary.

As the Bishop and Soane travelled together in these weeks, far from the Grand Tourists' well worn routes, the conversation sometimes turned to Ireland. Soane carefully noted that during the winter months, the stone was laid in dry courses and only grouted after the frosts, with hot lime. These observations were worth recording for there was every sign that Soane would soon be working for the Bishop.

One last visit was to Herculaneum, still deep beneath a thick lava crust. Soane measured the seats in the buried theatre, to which visitors were taken by guides bearing flaming torches, a theatrical introduction to this evocative site. He had seen objects excavated from the site in the museum at Portici and now enjoyed an intriguing subterranean glimpse into cultured Roman life.

Mrs Hervey remained in Naples to nurse her still convalescent daughter Louisa but Soane and the Bishop set off north again on 12 March, taking almost a fortnight to make the journey back to Rome, a zigzagging progress to take in sites which appealed to the Bishop's passion for geology and engineering, as much as his knowledge of architecture and classical history. Soane's notes show him contrasting the daily reality with the evidence of the classical world. Back in old Capua, there were sarcophagi in every street. Two days later they were at Gaeta, noticing Greek lettering and a resplendent vase in the cathedral showing the birth of Bacchus.

The Bishop interested Soane in agronomy, geology, classical literature, botany and much else, with the result that his notebooks come to life with observations on ploughs 'as described by Virgil', the wheat fields sprinkled with olive trees, as well as, incongruously, the practice of manuring ground in Ireland with salted herring. As they crossed the Pontine marshes again, there were 4,000 men at work on the ambitious papal drainage schemes. Soane drew a section of the new canal, to compare it with that described by Horace. The Bishop was a master at linking the old texts to the new world.

After a number of diversions and about-turns, they headed back to Rome via Velletri, this time visiting Prince Angelloti's gardens, and on to Albano and Castel Gandolfo. Early spring must have made the journey through the Alban Hills particularly pleasant. Soane was impressed, on their visit to the Palazzo Barberini, at the sequence of rooms, those scarcely lit leading to others awash with light.[61] Again, he stored away the memory – images to be reused and adapted, over and over again.

After reaching Rome in time for the celebrations of Holy Week, in which the Pope went by a mule from the Quirinale to the Pantheon, an event which Soane witnessed twice, the Bishop and his family prepared to depart for home. In April 1779 the annual exodus began, taking, during the weeks leading up to summer, many of Soane's friends, contacts and even adversaries. Over the weeks both Hardwick and Henderson went, as well as the sculptor Thomas Banks (another of the Bishop's dupes and a man with whom Soane became very friendly), Philip Yorke, Byres (the ubiquitous guide and salesman) as well as the Hadfield family – resident in Italy since the 1740s as innkeepers for discerning English travellers.

Aged eighteen, Maria Hadfield, who had been destined for a musical career, was elected a member of the Accademia del Disegno in Florence.[62] She received encouragement from, among others, Zoffany and Wright of Derby and was an assiduous copyist in the Florentine galleries. During 1778 and 1779 she travelled to study in Rome and Naples, becoming a favourite with the English artist community who saw her as the next Angelica Kauffman. In Rome she lodged with Banks and his family and met his circle, including – as well as Soane himself – James Northcote, Henry Tresham and Prince Hoare, the latter falling unrequitedly in love with her. That summer the family, the recently widowed Isabella Hadfield and her children, including Maria and George who became an architect, left for England.[63]

Fascinating and extremely able, Maria (more Italian than English in her manners) was the first of several independent young women whom Soane met in Italy, apparently unconstrained by their sex or youth from pursuing successful careers in the arts. Maria, who married the ambitious painter and miniaturist Richard Cosway in January 1781 and became, in the mid-1780s, the hostess at one of London's most famous *salons* at their apartment in Schomberg House in Pall Mall, as well as a well-regarded painter, was to remain a lifelong friend of Soane's. Her life covered many personal vicissitudes, including the death of her only daughter aged six, long periods spent abroad and in convents, as well as intense friendships and affairs with many famous men, including the Corsican leader General Paoli,[64] the French painter Jacques-Louis David, the antiquarian Baron d'Hancarville and a short but intense dalliance in Paris with Thomas Jefferson.[65]

Soane, emerging from his straight-jacket compounded of frigid diligence and social unease, must have found her company heady and the

34. A recent addition to the Charterhouse of S. Lorenzo, from 1770, was Gaetano Barba's magnificent freestanding elliptical geometrical stair, which Soane carefully drew on plan.

35. The Carthusian monastery of S. Lorenzo, Padula which Soane and the Bishop of Derry visited on their journey beyond Naples. Soane carefully measured the huge seventeenth-century Grand Cloister and its arcading.

easy equality between herself as an artist and his fellows, a new experience. He must have been sorry to see her leave for London. In later life quaintly flirtatious and always fond of female company, he was beginning to notice women – and they him.

It was the end of one chapter in Soane's Italian stay and the opening of another. In the last months Soane had started to become more confident and independent; he spoke reasonable Italian, had met all manner of men and women, and he was ready for an adventure, away from the well-trodden path of the Grand Tourists.

3

SICILY, ROME AND HOME AGAIN

Following the annual April exodus back to England, a number of thoseGrand Tourists remaining in Rome began to hatch a plan. Thomas Bowdler (Pitt's doctor in Naples) and his friend from Durham, Rowland Burdon, together with John Patteson, from Norwich (all known to Soane by now, either from Rome or Naples), together with two others, John Stuart[1] and Henry Greswold Lewis, decided on a journey to Sicily. They suggested that Soane join them as draughtsman and they would pay his expenses. Two years earlier Richard Payne Knight, a wealthy young connoisseur, together with the landscape painter Jakob Phillip Hackert and his pupil Charles Gore, made the journey (intending to publish an illustrated account of it) but the path was not yet as well-trodden as that to Rome.[2]

Greece had been discussed as a destination but rejected.[3] Soane's position, as their dependent, meant that he could not dictate the route but he knew that they would not allow enough time for a careful survey of the major Greek monuments. Soane, subject as he was 'to their general wish and general habits', found – or so he later claimed – that the itinerary had been altered to a tour of Sicily and Malta. The journey proved far more valuable than he could have suspected.

The men were of an age, all in their early twenties. Bowdler, like Patteson a Norfolk man, was the instigator of the expedition, his second attempt at such a plan. John Stuart of Allanbank, just over the Scottish border, was travelling with his sisters, both of whom would marry during their time in Italy, and his own wife of a few months, Frances Coutts of the banking family. He and Burdon, from the English side of the border, Castle Eden in Durham, knew one another. Geographically, the odd one out was Henry Greswold Lewis who came from Solihull, in the West Midlands. He may also have been the last to join the party, since Patteson referred to a group of 'five in which number is a very clever physician and an architect' when he wrote to his mother from Rome, announcing the plan in early April.[4]

Soane had not fallen in with aristocrats or travelling artists or scholars like himself. These young men were the sons of merchants and landowners. He had every indication that they could become clients; even before they had left, Patteson was writing to his mother that they had been 'talking over plans for you' while Agnes Stuart (John Stuart's ambitious mother) was soon sending him a rough sketch of Allanbank so that he could consider improvements to the house before he returned from Italy.[5]

We know of the Sicilian tour in more detail than Soane provides because of John Patteson's letters home to his mother in Norwich. Soane, whose interest in the monuments was of a very different order from that of his companions, found that the pace of the journey would often irk him, but he was in congenial company and he made do with rapid observations. He set off from Rome on 11 April, and arrived in Naples three days later. While waiting for the party to assemble, and having bought a sun hat, Soane made another ascent of Vesuvius, accompanied by John 'Warwick' Smith, the watercolourist.

It had been decided that Bowdler and Stuart would take a shorter journey; Bowdler had himself been ill and Stuart, with his badly behaved sisters and new wife expecting a baby, had family responsibilities.

After eight days in Naples and a farewell day on shore with Stuart's family, they set off on 21 April on a Swedish vessel which managed to take a week over the journey (including another day back on shore), slowed by the lack of wind and a desultory captain who slept until daylight. They noticed that a small English sloop which had left harbour three days after them arrived at Palermo two days earlier. When they did reach Sicily they were subjected to a seven-hour wait to be checked by health officials and a battle with customs. Finally released by the authorities, they found Palermo, so romantically situated, almost paradisaical.

Their first night in the city reintroduced the party to beds with sheets (on board ship there had been a single hammock, the rest of the party slept on the floor) and was followed by a leisurely breakfast of fresh bread, oranges, strawberries and milk. Such luxuries allowed the young men, as Patteson wrote, to change overnight 'from brutes to civilized creatures'.

A continuing unpleasantness was the wind, for the early May *scirocco* was gaining strength and would dog their footsteps for much of the journey as Patrick Brydone,[6] the author of their 1775 guidebook, *A Tour through Sicily and Malta* had warned. Like Anna Miller's, Brydone's book included many tips on local food, climate and customs and offered advice on where to stay; Madame Montaigne, their hostess on the first night was, just as he had written, a 'noisy troublesome Frenchwoman' but she kept a comfortable, civilised house.[7]

Before leaving Palermo, and after Soane had bought himself a parasol against the roasting sun, they went to see the Villa Palagonia at Bagheria, an area peppered with country villas of the Sicilian nobility some miles to the east of the city.

The Baroque palace, begun in 1705 by Tommaso Maria Napoli for Ferdinando Francesco Gravina, Prince of Palagonia, was a bizarre creation, its gateways, walls and eaves crusted with grotesque sculptures of animals and people (or mixtures of the two) which had been added by the current Prince, his grandson, who was shortly to be incarcerated for insanity. Soane drew one of the stone caricatures and presented it to Burdon.[8] The house was approached by a lengthy, narrow avenue, walled to either side with its menagerie of horrible ornament, leading to a theatrical, open-air staircase up to the *piano nobile* and the effects within.

Brydone described the spectacular impression of the mirror glass which covered the vaulted ceilings, producing the effect of a 'multiplying glass', and extended to the doors, covered by smaller panes of glass (fig. 36). Fragments of broken porcelain were made into columns and pyramids. Coloured glazing in the windows intensified the effect. The principal rooms, including the grandest of all, the ballroom, were asymmetrical and focussed upon an oval entrance hall.

Soane never forgot the effects at the Villa Palagonia, referring in his printed 1830 description of his own house to 'the wonderful performances of the Prince of Palagonia in the decoration and furniture of his palace'. He had written to Rowland Burdon in 1819 to ask him to look at his notes again, to refresh his memory of it all.[9] Soane remained deeply fascinated by the way in which glass could be used, both to mirror, extend and play tricks with space and to throw intensely coloured light over the interiors.

On leaving Palermo, the six split into their two groups. Bowdler, a keen naturalist and geologist, ascended Mount Etna with Stuart; the others would do so at the end of their journey. Soane's party was embarking on what Patteson imagined would be 'a very romantic kind of journey', riding on mules and sleeping in convents or peasants' houses. The little difficulties 'will only serve as sauce', for the party consisted of 'four gentlemen who agree in everything and three servants . . . able to defend themselves'.

They hired seven horses and three baggage mules (and muleteers) as well as a uniformed guard and set a brisk pace. There was only time to spend two hours at Segesta where they admired the ruins of the remarkably intact Greek temple (fig. 37), 'which convinced us of the effect of proportion and simplicity'. Segesta, not mentioned by Brydone, was a complete Doric temple, its unfluted columns far more attenuated than the squat examples that Soane had seen at Paestum.

At Trapani, the travellers found themselves fêted. The city gates were opened for the 'English Milords' who were noticeable in their dress of 'long trousers and white slouch hats lined with green silk' and in their extreme youth, for none of them was more than twenty-five. For two days they were adopted and paraded around town, honoured guests of the governor.

After another dose of the *scirocco* and hospitality in a monastery, they arrived at Agrigento, probably via Selinunte. The temples of Agrigento (fig. 38) repaid study and the travellers were ready for a rest, with the sea nearby. On balance, the discomforts were greater than the pleasures. The four men were given a single room at the Franciscan monastery ('rather too close a stowage') and they all suffered from the heat, flies and fleas (which crept up into Patteson's white stockings, dozens at a time). All three plagues could be dealt with by plunging into sea water at every opportunity. As for the group, 'we never are together but we are as merry as it is possible, everyone has his hobby horse and whipping them now and then creates many a good laugh'.

Three of the four may have found the five days allocated to Agrigento excessive since, as Patteson wrote,[10] the remains of the old city were of little interest 'to any other than an architect'. Patteson was finding that the pace of the expedition, even at Agrigento, did not suit him too well, 'I can scarce steal five minutes for myself and am for the most part hurried out early every morning. All day I am employed in seeing and in the evening am generally so tired I am glad to get to bed.' Of the four, Burdon was the most sympathetic to Soane's point of view being 'quite an enthusiast after

36. The mirrored ceiling at the Palazzo Palagonia at Bagheria outside Palermo. The extravagant rococo detail of this palace, with its grotesque exterior ornament, made a great impression on all visitors but Soane was particurlarly fascinated by the inventive use of glass.

37. The Doric temple at Segesta, Sicily.

38. Thomas Hearne's 1777 watercolour depicting a temple 'said to be of Juno' at Agrigento, Sicily. Soane and his companions stayed there for five days but only Rowland Burdon shared his passion for antiquity.

antiquities, if he see four rows of stones the ruins of a Roman building it gives him infinite pleasure'. By contrast, 'Mr Lewis and myself see these venerable ruins with less passion and get many a good laugh . . . when they happen to admire a modern arch for an antient one'. It was all very good humoured.

For the non-architects, the fallen temples were less spectacular. Patteson's compensation was having the time to see the site in all its picturesque moods. 'The evenings are so serene and . . . the ruins rising so nobly from the tops of the trees and the sea from the background, afford such views as you may have seen in prints from Claude Lorraine's pictures.' Later in life Patteson became a knowledgeable collector of paintings.[11]

For Soane, time spent amidst the Greek temples and tombs of Sicily and southern Italy was invaluable and the scale of an example such as the immense Temple of Jupiter particularly appealed to him. Hollow, it could hold a man; perhaps the etiolated Soane was encouraged to test the fit by wriggling inside. The temples, their variations and individual characteristics provided a rich vein of material for his lectures, more than thirty years later, as well as in his work. He built only one classical temple, and that in brick, the Doric 'barn à la Paestum' near Solihull. His client was the same Henry Greswold Lewis who had laughed at Soane's passion for these antique structures.

John Patteson was an intelligent and observant traveller, interested in much beside the remnants of the classical world, reporting home on anything and everything that struck his attention. He revelled in the exotic and unfamiliar crops of carobs, pistachios, aloes, figs and pomegranates as well as oranges and lemons growing as plentifully as apple trees at home. Despite the fecundity of the place he was saddened by the signs of 'indigence and want . . . in the midst of plenty'. Though milk, bread and honey were available at meals, there was no fruit on the table and 'their meat and fowls would be thought unworthy Norwich Market'.

Patteson's mother wrote 'I durst not look into Brydone till I hear you are got back to Naples safe and sound and then I'll follow you through Sicily'.[12] Later she commented, 'I think your Sicilian tour will afford you more pleasing reflections than all Italy put together' but was eagerly saving her comments on it all for winter evenings on his return. She must have been entertained by his description of the proliferation of Sicilian princes and dukes, 'such Princes as in England would scarce pass for well dressed journeymen on Sundays.' She was glad, as the letters between them crossed Europe, that he had not got tired of her affection and anxiety as to his well-being, 'for I have known such things happen between mothers and sons'. Touchingly, she confesses 'I don't know how to live so long without you.' She hopes he will remember 'how to descend into a Norwich merchant' despite living so long as a fine gentleman. He bore patiently her constant references to marriage and old bachelors but describes the handsome, jolly, well-fed monks. He, like them, was enjoying 'sweet liberty'. Patteson's younger brother Henry (Harry) who had graduated from Cambridge and become a 'vast snuff-taker' in his absence filled him in with missing details from home from time to time; 'No chance of any alteration in our politics. Blood and desolation are become the favourite topics.'[13]

The relaxed camaraderie of this journey was something new in Soane's life. Their walk through the dirty alleyways and streets of Trapani or the uncomfortable nights spent stowed together in the tiny cell in the monastery at Agrigento were the stuff of which reminiscence is made. As Mrs Patteson wrote, 'I must congratulate you upon the harmony and felicity which has subsisted between you and your companions which is rather uncommon among four such young men, although you are four brave lads and had it been otherwise it would sadly have damped the pleasure of your expedition'. He had not, she added, mentioned 'your doctor' lately but she hoped to see him again sometime. Bowdler was, of course, on his separate shorter journey.

In late April Mrs Patteson had written to ask her son what he thought about a piece of ground that she had lately bought and whether he approved her building scheme. Soane and Patteson had already discussed it and in her next letter, she had a message for the architect in the party.

> I am glad you approve my purchase and I thank you for your schemes for me but please to remember that my aspect is east and west because I must have a parlour to each aspect . . . I want no entertaining rooms upstairs but a deal of lodging for selves and servants. I want a neat compact house with plenty of family conveniences, not omitting a powdering room and place for clogs and greatcoats, surely rooms of 20 × 16 would be large enough for me, with these hints I think you and your friend might make me a nice plan and I shall be much obliged to you for it.[14]

Here, hidden in an affectionate correspondance between mother and son, lies one of John Soane's first independent commissions. In 1774 John Patteson had inherited his uncle, and namesake's, Norwich house in Surrey Street, a street of substantial merchant houses, along with the family business, a partnership with the Swiss Iselin. Mrs Patteson's plans appear to have been for some land outside Norwich since Patteson refers to 'the country house scheme'.

From Agrigento, the four pressed on to Licata and took the local narrow boats, called *speronari*, prodigiously fast craft, across to Valetta. They did not linger in Malta, returning on 2 June, after a very rough passage, to Syracuse. Neither Patteson nor Soane recorded any comment on Malta (beyond Patteson's note of its conveniences and luxuries and the fact that Mount Etna could be seen from there). As for Syracuse, its Baroque splendours were not to modern taste but Soane brought home a drawing of the ruined Roman theatre.

The next destination in Sicily was Catania and Mount Etna and, for Soane's pleasure, a combined aqueduct and bridge nearby, newly built by the reforming Prince Biscari, who was a rare example of an enlightened Sicilian estate owner, a scholar and collector who published his own account of the island in 1781. Soane drew the bridge and illustrated it in his lectures, probably unaware of its subsequent collapse. The Biscari palace in Catania was, as described by Richard Payne Knight, 'a great irregular building, the ancient part of it in the barbarous taste of the Sicilians, charged with monstrous figures, and unnatural ornaments, but the part which he has built himself is simple, regular and elegant.'[15] Soane saw an unusual single-storey building with a memorable rococo interior in one room where two ceilings were superimposed, the lower stuccoed, the

39. Early nineteenth-century sketches by the architect John Goldicutt of Greek ('Sicilian') vases from Prince Biscari's widely admired museum in Catania, which Soane visited.

upper frescoed, with an intermediate level of windows providing an unexpected source of light. Soane stored the device away, together with his other examples of stolen light and *lumière mystérieuse*.

Biscari's palace housed a collection of antiquities (fig. 39), described by Brydone as second only to that of the King of Naples at Portici and much admired by Payne Knight ('we found the Prince in his Museum which is very rich and always open for the use of the studious') and by Goethe on his visit a few years later.[16] Patteson recorded their visit, and then described their ascent of Etna ('I don't remember ever being more tired'), first through a landscape reminiscent of English parkland and then up to the summit. It took them two days. The familiar-looking trees and woods had made Patteson homesick; he had had enough of travel.[17]

By 2 July, at the latest, they were back in Naples, having been to Taormina (where Soane was intrigued by the ancient theatre), Messina and two of the Lipari islands, as well as pausing twice on the coast of Calabria. Before leaving Naples Soane did some book and print buying, probably mostly commissions, and had dinner with the Stuarts. He also visited 'Mr P', no doubt Thomas Pitt who had been recovering from a long bout of illness at Lord Tylney's house. There was just time for a visit to Sorrento (the birthplace of Tasso) by boat before heading back to Rome.

In late July Patteson set off for home, having himself just recovered from a fever. Looking over the time away and despite the high points of the journey, he could muster little enthusiasm for Italy; he was not convinced that it was worth leaving England for, except to 'an artist or mad enthusiast after antiquities' but this was perhaps a jaded moment after illness.

John Patteson travelled with a Yorkshireman, Lees of Halifax, 'a brother shuttledriver'. It is clear from his letters that there was a crisp social distinction between those such as themselves, on what might be described as a working holiday, and the pleasure-seeking, spoiled young men of good families of whom he had seen all too much in Rome. His mother was delighted that he was mixing with his own kind again and being thrifty; economy, she observed, 'is a wise Dame'. The family business was in trouble, his brother had written earlier, and so he needed to be careful. Perhaps it was now that Mrs Patteson's plans for a country house foundered; no more was heard of them.

Patteson gave due credit for his new frugality, 'I have to thank one of my Sicily companions for my saving knowledge'. There can be little doubt who had introduced Patteson to the principles of good housekeeping. In the early days of his travels south he had been rather extravagant but promised to 'live all my days without pulling up the floors and will be contented with my house as I find it' – a resolution that Soane helped him to break. In one letter he told his mother that £500 per annum allowed a 'respectable footing' in the world of the Grand Tour. Soane himself was in financial difficulties; the Royal Academy stipend had proved entirely inadequate.

Summing up his time in Italy, Patteson was proud to tell his mother that the 'set of English' at Naples and Rome the previous winter, some forty, 'young and old', had behaved commendably. 'I did not hear of one folly being committed' nor of money wasted with 'lying antiquaries'. As for the famous Sir William and Lady Hamilton, they are 'like many, rather most other people' and had spent all winter in the country (at Caserta) with the king. He confessed that he had no portrait to bring home, but would have one painted for ten or fifteen guineas in London rather than the thirty asked in Rome.

Patteson returned to England from Venice via Turin, Vienna and Brussels, spending the last four months of his journey immersed once more in transactions for the family wool business. From Vienna Patteson sent Soane a present of a six volume edition of Laurence Sterne's *Tristram Shandy*. Since the Emperor's music master Anthony Salieri was travelling to Rome he was asked to deliver it to Soane at the English Coffee House. History does not record whether Soane, soon to meet Mozart's first Susanna, Nancy Storace, also met Mozart's arch-rival.

Soane had already chosen his favourite reading for his lifetime; his taste for the works of Sterne, Richardson, Smollett in English, those of le Sage and Rousseau in French, show him conforming to the literary tastes of his generation. On his journey out, Patteson had visited Vevey, in Switzerland, in the steps of Rousseau's Julia and her lover. It was a perfect 'sentimental situation' including a Lovers' Leap but 'this not being as yet my situation, I had not the least inclination to try the efficacy of it' he reassured his mother. Soane and Patteson appear to have shared literary tastes, in common with many of their generation, and it formed a good basis for their friendship, confirmed by the generous present.

Of the party in Sicily, it was Rowland Burdon and John Patteson who were to remain closest to Soane. Burdon shared warm memories of the journey almost fifty years later; 'Few expeditions have been begun, continued and ended with more uniform and satisfactory results than our visits to Naples, and its environs, our circuit of Sicily, our Maltese expedition, Syracuse, Messina, Trumboni and various *speronaro* adventures and the close of our travels in the classic cities of Lombardy.'[18]

Back in Rome again in early July, Thomas Jones met Soane a few days later in a party consisting of the Abbé Bellew, Rowland Burdon and John Coxe Hippisley, who was acting as a *cicerone*, more knowledgeable about Rome than the antiquarians, to the young Lord Herbert.[19] He was also carrying out some undercover work for the British government, pursuing his own efforts towards the cause of Catholic emancipation, and, after a bruising romantic episode,[20] was now actively searching for a wife. As Lord Pembroke commented drily on his son's companion, 'I remember Hippisley. Does he mean to practice Law or Gallantry abroad?' No man was to turn up with greater regularity throughout Soane's life than Coxe Hippisley.

Soane was systematically carrying on his studies (fig. 40) in these weeks but also apparently enjoying himself. Secure perhaps in the knowledge that most of his architect peers had left – borne out by Lord Herbert's list of artists in Rome which names but two English architects, himself and Brettingham – he was now mixing in a circle of artists including Henry Tresham and Nathaniel Marchant, men who would reappear in his dealings with the Royal Academy years later. Soane, unusually, was relaxing. He had established an enviable clutch of contacts, could sense the possibility of commissions on his return and was planning an architectural excursion north. Perhaps by now, too, his Italian was fluent enough to make life easier on a practical front.

40. A page from Soane's Italian sketchbook showing an elevation and plan of the Temple of Ceres or Athena at Paestum, 'the first temple you arrive at' coming from Naples.

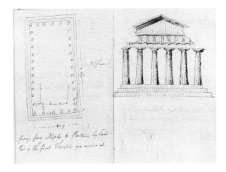

Soane had now begun to look at more recent buildings, such as S. John Lateran, having left the study of eighteenth-century Roman buildings until he had immersed himself fully in classical antiquity. Now his chronological journey could move forwards.

In August Soane and Burdon set out for the 'classic cities of Lombardy', crossing paths with Patteson in Brescia with whom they spent an agreeable twenty-four hours. Patteson was heading for Genoa where he was meeting Charles Collyer, his sickly encumbrance from Hamburg, who had been in the city for five months and was now a seasoned traveller.

The journey north was a pilgrimage to many of the major buildings by Palladio and included a visit to the Accademia at Parma, to investigate whether Soane might emulate Dance and bring home a medal. From the coast at Ancona and Rimini (where Soane was impressed by the triumphal arch) they turned back to Bologna, continuing north to Parma, possibly contacting the Accademia to find out the rules of the *concorso* which he proposed to enter, before travelling on to Milan. Their meeting with Patteson at Brescia was on the way back to Verona and Vicenza. Here Soane took his first brief look at Palladio's work, too closely identified with the Burlington school in England to offer the surprises and insights which he sought.

They continued to Padua, and from there Burdon and Soane probably approached Venice by boat along the Brenta, a route marked by Palladian villas, a memorable journey in the September sun. By the middle of the month, they and a servant were lodged comfortably in Venice, a notoriously expensive city for visitors. Burdon was leaving for home from there and Soane did not stay long.

Retracing his steps south to Bologna, Soane set himself a solitary academic exercise copying a set of projects for the west front of the church of S. Petronio, including work by Palladio (fig. 41), Vignola and Peruzzi.[21] He probably stopped in Florence to make contact with the Accademia del Disegno; in the following January he was elected a member. Honorary membership of one of the Italian academies had a lofty ring in England. In fact, the reality was less impressive and of the overseas members of the Florence Accademia some had never been to Italy at all, far less exhibited anything. In fact, British architects used the open doors of the Italian academies to confer status upon themselves, helpful self-promotion in an emergent profession.[22]

For all these travels Soane was heavily dependent on his friends for immediate financial help, which he intended to repay promptly, based on the promises of future clients, notably the Bishop of Derry. John Patteson had loaned him £40 for his expenses in Verona, which Soane repaid as soon as he possibly could.[23] He was punctilious in these matters. Intermittently he earned himself some small payments by purchases, for which he received a commission, or by arranging transport home for his friends' possessions, which could be a thankless task when things went missing – as did some of the Hadfield luggage in his care.[24]

Back in Rome, Soane made an excursion to the Villa Lante at Bagnaia, with its stupendous gardens of water, stone and orderly vegetation, and pavilions by Vignola. He also continued his exploration of Rome. Now he turned his attention to the Renaissance palaces of Rome – the Palazzo Farnese, the Palazzo Massimo alle Colonne and the Capitoline Palace.

41. Soane's copy of Palladio's façade design 'G' for S. Petronio, Bologna, one of many drawings which he made from the archive of schemes by various architects for this church, including some surprising efforts in gothic.

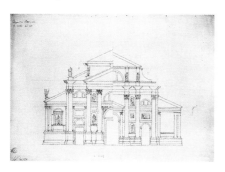

But of all the great Roman houses he was most intrigued by the Villa Albani (now the Villa Torlonia), completed for Cardinal Albani by Carlo Marchionni in 1764. The cardinal's treasures, a collection put together under the guidance of the Abbé Winckelmann, were displayed with great invention. There were marble reliefs set into the walls, niches for sculpture, even mirror glass placed behind the figures to display them fully.

Attached to the south wing of the Villa Albani was a modern 'Roman bath' complex and in the grounds stood a 'temple', an aviary designed as a Roman ruin. The connection between the Cardinal and Robert Adam, and between Winckelmann, the prophet of the Greek revival, and Albani, ensured that the curious combination of museum and pleasure villa was of extraordinary interest to Soane.[25]

As the temperatures dropped, the influx of Grand Tourists began once more. That autumn Soane met Henry Bankes, a rich young Dorset landowner who had just arrived in Rome. They must have become well acquainted for before long Soane produced two ground plans for the remodelling of his family home, Kingston Lacy near Wimborne, a solid country house built by Sir Roger Pratt in the 1660s.[26] Soane's relationship with Bankes did not lead to a commission – which went to Robert Brettingham who, having stayed on in Rome remet Bankes on his second visit to the city in 1782. The work on the house, less radical than Soane's proposals, continued for six years after Bankes's return to Dorset in 1784. Later, as MP for Corfe Castle, he was to have a baleful influence upon Soane's public work.

Meanwhile the larger-than-life figure of the Bishop of Derry was missed in the expatriate community but in January 1780 he was very much in their minds. English artists heard the news that he had very unexpectedly become the fourth Earl of Bristol, just before Christmas. Both of the Bishop's brothers had died, first George and now Augustus, leaving no legitimate children. As a third son, Frederick Hervey could hardly have expected to inherit the title. In the light of this news many artists were hoping that long unrealised promises might now come to fruition and Tresham gave a lavish party to celebrate the Bishop's elevation. No one could have more pleased with the development than Soane, remembering the many commissions that the Bishop had dangled before him.

That winter the English circle in Rome enjoyed a small scandal. Margaret Stuart, the red-headed sister of Soane's friend, had not always conducted herself decorously in Italy. John Coxe Hippisley had succeeded in at least one of his missions. He wrote to Lord Herbert early in March 1780: 'I must prepare you for *surprise* . . . In a word then I am *married* . . . the lady is no other than Miss M Stuart.' Her family, he reported, were not pleased but 'I did not know till the preceding evening that she was entitled to *sixpence*'. The deed being done, the family had conducted themselves with commendable *sangfroid* 'exactly as it had been the darling object of their Choice'. The letter continues at length, but finally Hippisley arrives at his point: should Lord Herbert find himself near Berwick, would he call upon her father, Sir John Stuart Bt, and 'assure him his daughter has not fallen into the hands of a highwayman'?[27]

Rowland Burdon, writing to Soane from Newcastle, reacted to the bizarre match, 'I never knew anything half so ridiculous as Margt. Stuart has been, of the two sisters I thought her the more sensible, but – I am glad you were so well with the family as to go almost every day, that looks as if you were upon terms with all the English this winter at Rome.'[28] At that very moment Agnes Stuart, mother of the bride-to-be, was writing from Allanbank, her house near Berwick upon Tweed, to her family's new friend, John Soane, with a rough sketch of her house 'which will no doubt receive much improvement by your corrections and improvements'.[29]

Early 1780 in Rome saw more English arrivals – among them Patteson's burden from Hamburg, Charles Collyer, now accomplished in Italian manners after his long stay in Genoa, and his Norfolk friend (and soon brother-in-law) Edward Pratt. Meanwhile Soane's immediate prospects had suddenly been transformed. Hardly had the news of the Bishop of Derry's elevation reached him, than a letter from the Earl Bishop arrived, full of commissions which had to be acted upon immediately. Soane had to weigh losing his last year in Italy against the prospect of a string of jobs and introductions to further important patrons. From the professional point of view he had no choice: he prepared to head home.

The loss of precious time in Italy was overshadowed by the excitement of what lay ahead. Soane's self-confidence had, against all the evidence, persuaded him that he would not be disappointed in the Earl Bishop. Possibly he felt that Hervey's increased wealth and lofty social position would make a new man of him. Soane was, after all, architect to the new Earl of Bristol, a nice role for a young man with big ambitions.

He began to organise his itinerary back to England and, perhaps, to reconsider the alterations that he had proposed to the Downhill many months before. There was the summer dining-room, the recreation of the Temple of Vesta, some work at his Suffolk estate, Ickworth, as well as possible commissions for the Earl Bishop's friends in Ireland. Soane's immediate plan was to visit Florence, Siena, Genoa and return through France, visiting Lyon and Paris.[30]

On 19 April Soane left Rome, travelling with the Reverend George Holgate and his pupil Michael Pepper (soon to ask Soane to design him a villa at Dunmow in Essex). After visiting Vignola's Villa Farnese at Caprarola and, perhaps on Patteson's advice, making a brief stop in Siena, he arrived in Florence four days later. There he was an assiduous tourist, visiting among much else, the Pitti and the Uffizi Galleries, Giotto's Tower and Brunelleschi's S. Spirito, which he considered the finest church in Florence.

Performing at the Teatro della Pergola in Florence at this period was a precocious English-born opera singer, the fourteen-year-old Nancy Storace. Although there is no hard evidence of a meeting, on leaving five days later he noted, with uncharacteristic detail, 'left Florence and dear Miss S' and immediately wrote to her. He had bought a pair of satin breeches, suggesting that he was moving in polite society and wanted to cut a dapper figure. As in the case of Maria Hadfield, Soane's meeting with the young singer led to a lifelong friendship.

For the moment their paths went in different directions; six years later, Nancy Storace was the toast of Viennese musical society, taking the role of Susanna in the first performance of Mozart's *Marriage of Figaro* and the singer for whom he wrote the concert aria 'Ch'io mi scordi di te' – Non temer, amato bene'. Her farewell concert in Vienna on 23 February 1787 is thought to have been attended by Mozart. On her return to London with her brother Stephen, a notable composer, and after a short, disastrous marriage, she became the musical partner and lover of the great tenor, John Braham, eleven years her junior, by whom she had a son.

Soane's own return to London, in the spring of 1780, was subject to a last minute alteration. Horace Mann, the elderly English envoy to the Tuscan court and a friend of the Earl Bishop, persuaded Soane to change his route home, following the Rhine Valley instead of trying the more uncertain journey through France. He went due north to Bologna, revisiting that quintessential city of brick of which he had become very fond. He took his favourite walk to S. Michele in Bosco and noticed that the women were all wearing Venetian dress to mark a festival. Once more he wrote to 'Miss S.'. [31]

He passed the castle of 'my friend the Marchese d'Olizzi' near Padua, but the family was in Venice. On the way to the city he drew the Villas Maldura and Morin, both now known to be by Scamozzi, rather than Palladio. In Padua he was impressed by (and sketched) the recently built Isola Memmia, a theatrical conceit consisting of an oval artificial island surrounded by a canal, crossed by a number of ornate bridges to the ancient university complex. From there he continued to Vicenza ('visited Palladio') and quickly on to Verona, travelling in a violent *scirocco* and on 'an infernal rough road', where he examined the work of Sanmicheli including his Lazaretto di S. Pancrazio, pursuing his interest in monasteries and institutions. After a few days, during which he did a great deal of drawing but also had time to note his appreciation of the style of older Italian women ('really the women have uncommon taste in putting on their clothes and setting themselves to advantage. I have been charmed with the grace and manners of many at 50'), he met up with Collyer and Pratt (who had been staying in Venice) in Mantua. There he sketched the Mannerist details of Giulio Romano's Palazzo del Te.

Soane, the confident traveller, able to fend off the irregular demands of the customs officers who 'frequently ask if you have contrabando to get a few baiocchi', was a very different young man from his self of two years before. But if he had become more independent as an individual, he had not become any more spontaneous in his design work.

Travelling home, Soane presented himself at the Parma Academy. He demurred from entering the Diploma contest, as Dance had done, and settled for a submission for honorary membership; his offering was a reworking of the old Royal Academy Gold Medal drawing, his Triumphal Bridge, this time using the Greek Doric Order.[32] Earlier, George Dance had explained to his father the advantages of a premium from Parma rather than Rome where 'judgement is so partial and protections of Cardinals, Princes etc. are of such consequence that in reality little honour is to be gained by it. Likewise no person can concur who is not in Rome at the time of concurrence, consequently the number of those who concur must necessarily be less in Rome than in Parma where all Italy nay all Europe may concur.'[33] If the last sentence suggests that a prize from Parma was more easily gained, it did give Soane the qualification he hankered after. Like many of his architect peers, Soane used these honorary memberships to underline his position in the profession – implying a greater sense of achievement than was the case even if the Parma establishment did not include 'dilettanti' among its honorary members as did the Florentine equivalent.[34]

From Piacenza he continued to Milan. There he went to the theatre (probably La Scala) and visited the Biblioteca Ambrosiana in which he admired both a portrait head and engineering drawings by Leonardo. Despite his altered itinerary, he was determined not to miss Genoa – even though it now represented a detour of some 200 miles.

On arrival he was not disappointed in 'the most charming city of Italy', where 'everything seems enchantment'. For five days Soane mingled in Genoese society, armed with useful letters of introduction. One from Thomas Pitt was to Madame Cileria and her two charming daughters who 'treated me with uncommon politeness and attention'. At last he felt, much as Patteson had done during his stay in Siena, that he was experiencing Italian life from the inside. He went to the Teatro Falcone and heard another celebrated English *diva*, Cecilia Davis, perform. He wanted to shine in Italian society and perhaps with an eye to impressing his female companions, Soane spent the considerable sum of 5 guineas on new clothes and an additional £1 7s on ruffles. Soane's recently acquired social polish, his smart introductions and his summons home from the Earl Bishop, payment from whom would repay 'all this cheerful extravagance' marked him out. He had aimed to meet the nobility and he had succeeded. To have to leave, when all was going so well, was a wrench. Before doing so he hosted a supper at 'the English house', on which he spent a guinea. In fulsome terms he wrote of his 'heartfelt sorrow' at leaving Genoa and his firm hopes of returning.[35]

After a couple of days in Milan he crossed Lake Como, to begin the journey up into the mountains. His misgivings over the lost French journey were forgotten in his excitement, faced with 'the beautiful Alps of which all descriptions must fall very short' (fig. 42). Now in Switzerland, he passed from Italian- to German-speaking cantons. As he headed through the Splugen Pass, the pines were clinging to the mountains up to a still perceptible snow line, even in late May. His time in Italy with English watercolourists and his geologist-naturalist friends had opened his eyes, and before that Thomas Sandby had introduced him to the powerful aesthetic and associational pull of landscape. More recently his reading of Rousseau's *Julie, ou La Nouvelle Héloïse* had infected his vocabulary and prompted his emotional and sensual responses to the dramatic scenery around him.[36] Romantic literature and picturesque theory between them allowed him to extract every nuance from his passage along a track which inched along terrifyingly sheer precipices, beside waterfalls, furious torrents and huge, disconcertingly balanced rocks.

On the other side of the vertiginous pass, Soane calmed himself down by carefully drawing and measuring, in great detail, several wooden bridges built in the middle years of the century by the brothers Grubermann. They had perfected a novel technique of overlapping and bolted timbers which allowed a much increased span, without piers. The self-imposed task was a last-minute decision on Soane's part, after the change of route home; he was now covering the same ground that the Bishop, his eldest son and Michael Shanahan had done in 1770[37] and perhaps hoped to outdo them with his efforts – a surprise to spring on the Earl Bishop when they met.

42. J.M.W. Turner's watercolour of the St Gothard Pass of 1804, evoking the agreeably sublime terror which late eighteenth-century travellers extracted from the precipitous landscape.

On reaching Zurich, he went in succession to Reichenau, to Wettingen, the location of the finest and most developed example of 'hanging work' as the technique was called, and to Schaffhausen, an earlier prototype (fig. 43).[38] The Bishop had for many years intended to build a bridge over the Foyle: having balanced the relative merits of stone and wood, in 1772 he commissioned a 19 foot-long model of a wooden bridge, constructed in a revolutionary fashion by John Conrad Altheir and pushed to Derry from Switzerland in a handcart, a six-month-long journey. Designed to be twice the length of the bridge at Schaffhausen, it arrived only to be rejected. [39] Now Soane was well enough informed to take part in the discussion, and its outcome, once he reached Ireland.

After this pleasant professional diversion, Soane went on to Basel. On the way, disaster struck. The bottom of his trunk had come loose and as the carriage rattled along the roads, the contents had spilled out behind it. The thin record that exists of Soane's Italian stay may, in part, be the result of this catastrophe. He wrote, in desperation, to report his loss to the authorities, listing the contents. There were many books of architectural studies, 'generalement avec les lignes seulement', notebooks and printed books in English, French and Italian. He had lost his Royal Academy gold and silver medals, 'quelques instruments pour un Architecte d'Argent dans une boite avec le nome [sic]', another set in copper, as well as clothes, 'quelques bijoux pour les femmes', important letters and the drawings he had prepared in the hopes of preparing an illustrated edition of Lady Miller's *Letters from Italy*. The letter is pitiful in its stilted French.[40] The contents were his memories of Italy as well as his *carte de visite* for his future career, including the 'repeated solicitations' of the Earl Bishop.

Having recorded his loss (nothing was ever recovered), Soane made his way home in disconsolate mood via Freiburg, Cologne, Liège, Louvain and Brussels, before embarking for England. The only occasion on which he observed the classical orders in use was on the gallows which, together with crosses, ornamented the roadsides in the Rhine Valley.[41] A more superstitious man than Soane might have found the various auguries distinctly unpromising.

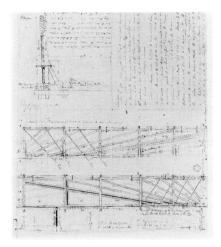

43 Soane's meticulous notation of the structure of Ulrich Brubenmann's wooden bridge on the Rhine at Schaffhausen, made to impress the Earl Bishop, on whose behalf he was hurrying home in May 1780. The remainder of the page is devoted to his unusually full diary entries.

4

RETURN

Back in England, Soane hardly had time to report the loss of his possessions before he rushed east to Ickworth, just outside Bury St Edmunds, to survey the site for the Earl Bishop's proposed new mansion on his Suffolk estate. Soane may have been surprised to find his patron and his wife living unostentatiously at Ickworth Lodge, a comfortable old farmhouse in which the Earls of Bristol had lived for the last fifty years.[1] Not surprisingly, the new earl's plans for Ickworth were for something altogether more impressive. But although he had the germ of an idea, and had summoned Soane to Suffolk to develop it, the Earl Bishop's attention immediately switched to his Irish country house, the Downhill, and Soane was quickly dispatched to County Derry.

The Downhill was the estate for which he and the Bishop had discussed exciting prospective improvements while travelling in Italy eighteen months earlier (fig. 44), especially the facsimile of the Temple of Vesta at Tivoli and a summer dining-room to remind them both of the Villa of Lucullus.[2] Then they had been playing a diverting game in the Italian sunshine; now Soane was confirmed as the Earl Bishop's chosen architect, a serious proposition.

Soane arrived in Ireland on Saturday, 27 July 1780.[3] After the months of anticipation he must have been taken aback to find the Downhill to be no mansion, but a large barrack-like house constructed from the dour basalt of the locality standing in a bleak, treeless landscape. Lord Bristol's 'Tusculanum' could hardly be more remote from the golden world of Mediterranean classical antiquity.

Soane found his patron at home but in disagreeable mood, suffering from a depressive illness. He was probably at his least pleasant that summer in Ireland, as he confronted his duties and the realities of his unpromising house after his long absence.

The Downhill's glory was its setting, perched high on the cliffs while turning its face inland from the Atlantic weather (and views). The coastal landscape, exposed and treeless, provided a vivid contrast to a heavily wooded valley below. By the time Soane arrived there was an immense compartmentalised walled garden and a copy of the Roman mausoleum of the Julii, at Saint-Rémy in Provence, built by Michael Shanahan, Soane's predecessor as the Bishop's tame architect.

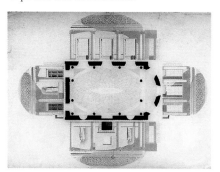

44. One variant of Soane's designs for the summer dining-room at the Downhill, the Earl Bishop's Irish house, conjuring up the ruined Villa of Lucullus where they had first discussed the scheme. The commission did not materialise, despite Soane's efforts over the summer of 1780, leaving him out of pocket and disillusioned.

The Downhill mausoleum was dedicated to the Earl Bishop's childless older brother George, the second earl, who had died in 1775. Although, for reasons of health, he had only been Lord Lieutenant of Ireland for a year, he had assured his brother's rapid passage up the ecclesiastical hierarchy. Having been recommended to George III for the bishopric of Cloyne in 1767, Frederick Hervey then became the obvious candidate for the see of Derry, the most lucrative of all, when it fell vacant in January 1768.

In the early days the bishop had been, when in the country, an enlightened and reforming cleric, taking on issues such as the tithe system and resolving to appoint no Englishmen to Irish livings. He pursued agricultural improvements and was a courageous and practical advocate of religious freedom, at one point presenting the Roman Catholics with a chapel, no longer needed when he built a new church. In 1770 the bishop received the freedom of Derry for his achievements.[4] As well as a church-building programme, from which Shanahan again benefited, he restored the Bishop's Palace and gardens in Derry together with the cathedral, adding a fine spire with money collected from local landowners. Unfortunately the subscribers were to see their money turn to dust when the old tower crumbled beneath its weight. The bishop had also instigated a major programme of road and, as we have seen, bridge building. In 1790 a wooden bridge was finally built over the Foyle at Derry, largely at the Earl Bishop's expense, transforming the port and its trade, while bringing in valuable revenue through tolls. It had been constructed in America and shipped to Ireland; the Earl Bishop did nothing by halves.[5]

Those who knew Soane and wished him well were convinced that he would profit by his stay in Ireland. Anna Miller, author of *Letters from Italy* which Soane had annotated and corrected during his time in Italy, and for which he had begun to prepare illustrations (now lost after the collapse of his trunk on the way home), had become a regular and effusive correspondent and friend. She wrote to say how envious she was: 'you daily enjoy the conversation, you possess the approbation and above all the friendship of perhaps the *most* learned, the *most* ingenious and the brightest ornament of the age we live in'.[6] The people of Ireland, Lady Miller considered, were fortunate in their new protector.

Others might not have agreed so readily that contact with the Earl Bishop was such a blessing; the painter Joseph Wright of Derby and the sculptor Thomas Banks were two of the most distinguished artists to suffer from his broken promises, so liberally scattered in Rome.

The Earl Bishop had architectural obsessions beyond his wooden bridges. The notion of an oval or drum-shaped mansion also possessed him. Michael Shanahan had built a prototype in Ireland, Ballyscullion on the shore of Lough Beg. In 1794, Henry Holland's draughtsman and protégé Charles Heathcote Tatham was approached in Rome by the drunken earl, who despite declaring all English architects to be rascals, commissioned him to transform Ickworth into an oval mansion, 500 foot wide. Tatham, who had fun toying with the preposterous notion, knew the Earl Bishop's reputation all too well, 'He took offence at my refusing to give him an estimate until my return home . . . I demanded only five guineas for my work before I began it . . . he was himself surprised and thought it much too reasonable – he has paid me that and no more.'[7] It was one of the crisper episodes in that patron's extensive and capricious aesthetic philandering.

Soane's commission back in the summer of 1780 started briskly enough. The Earl Bishop was eager to alter the approach to the house; he wanted to enter by the north, elaborating the 'cortile' with a colonnade and ornamenting the stable yard and the fronts of the stable buildings. Soane pointed out that the alterations would make for a disagreeable experience in bad weather and wrote in his notebook that it was '*absolutely* necessary' to enter by the south side.[8] The Earl Bishop could not fly in the face of the harsh reality of its site and the local climate.

Arguing his point and holding the attention of the Earl Bishop was wearying. Faced with the real deficiencies of the Downhill, as opposed to toying with a treasure-house for the acquisitions which were following him home,[9] the Earl Bishop was petulant. Soane was socially gauche and easily disconcerted by his client's razor-sharp wit and unpredictable moods.

On Tuesday 8 August, Soane took a day off and went to Newtown to look at bridges. In his absence, the Earl Bishop reconsidered his arguments and, encouragingly and surprisingly, capitulated to Soane's insistence on an entrance to the south. Soane's modest proposals and good sense were impressive; he must have been tempted towards something more flamboyant for his first major commission, especially given the nature of the client, but opted for a considered, practical approach.

A week later Soane had carried out a full survey and it was not reassuring. The house had been shoddily built. It had smoking chimneys, ill-fitting doors and windows and pitifully thin floors. There were no water closets and inadequate provision for the servants. The joinery in the gallery and circular drawing-room needed rehanging. Plastering was required throughout and some floors needed relaying. A great deal of essential work was required before the client and architect could indulge in the remodelling and redecoration of the house, the enjoyable part of the discussion.

Overall, there seemed to be work for about six men over a period of eight or nine months and, since his lordship wanted the work finished 'with all expedition' Soane had to find tradesmen very quickly, always difficult in an unfamiliar part of the country. He wrote to Richard Holland for a recommendation of a good carpenter and joiner; after so many months away his contacts were out of date and he wanted assurance that the tradesmen he employed on this job, upon which his future career depended, would be highly skilled and dependable. He also wrote to England for someone to paint arabesques on one wall of the long gallery. Soane was trying to build up momentum in the face of constant uncertainty.

Answers from London would take time and meanwhile Soane had to secure local supplies and labour. He offered to go to Armagh to enquire after tradesmen, or to Dublin, and in the meantime began to order materials. On 16 August he made an agreement with James Brown of the Ballycastle quarry for stone at 14 shillings a ton to encase the entire south front with a fine ashlar surface over the present rough rubble finish. The Earl Bishop was delighted by Soane's industriousness.

Soane began the drawings for the remodelled house. Hardly had he started than the Earl Bishop changed the brief. Rather than a rectangular room he wanted a gallery, 40 × 20 foot. Soane noted, with perceptible desperation, 'the whole house is an assemblage of galleries and passages. Surely if anything was to be built it should be a good room which would doubly answer the intention of room and gallery'. Twenty foot would be too narrow to see the Aurora which his lordship proposed for the ceiling. Nor did Soane agree with placing columns across the front of the house, given the hexagonal 'excrescences' already there. This interference did not bode well and indeed, it was the death knell for Soane's commission.

'Monday – Everything changed', Soane wrote. Hardly more than a month after his arrival, he departed in a mood of utter despair. 'Left the place on Saturday, the 2nd of September 1780 at half past 2 o'clock', Soane wrote in the little notebook that a few pages before contained the purposeful annotations of the most important commission of his career. Lord Bristol later claimed that Soane had left of his own will, but it had been his provocation which led Soane to take a step which looked very much like professional suicide.

Despite the Earl Bishop's long list of castles in the air, the commission dangled in front first, James Wyatt and then Soane, only Shanahan worked for him in Ireland. The Earl Bishop had no compunction in employing artists or architects, on little more than apparent goodwill and promises, and then disregarding their advice or abandoning the project in question. Shanahan had waited in the wings while Soane was tried and found wanting, returning in the 1780s to build the Mussenden Temple, a copy of the Temple of Vesta at Tivoli, the job Soane had so longed for. Shanahan, schooled on the same Continental route and in front of many of the same buildings as Soane, was patient and amenable in the face of his client's vacillation and whim as Soane never would be. Possibly, too, he was a more entertaining companion for the Earl Bishop, for whom that aspect of the relationship was also important. The Downhill was ill-starred; burned out in 1851, it was rebuilt and gutted once more in 1950.

Soane's mood as he crossed from Belfast to Glasgow must have been desperate. Not only had he lost the job at the Downhill (and with it, that which the Earl Bishop had intimated might fall to him at Ickworth) but he had not been paid more than a derisory £30 and a few expenses towards the £400 he was owed. Friends from Italy, such as John Patteson and Rowland Burdon, who had helped him out financially on his travels, had to be repaid[10] and his immediate prospects were negligible. He later told Farington that he returned from Italy 'about £120 in debt'.[11]

Soane approached Lady Bristol, the mother of the Earl Bishop's five children, who was now living at Ickworth under unhappy circumstances, facing the imminent collapse of her marriage. She waited until she had had a chance to ask the earl in person about the money his architect was owed; on Christmas Eve she replied, passing on her husband's response – 'you had dismissed yourself from his service and protection' – and she could get nothing for him though, she added kindly, 'I heartily wish it had been otherwise'.[12]

Soane spent a lifetime turning over in his head the events at the Downhill and regretting his unjustified faith in 'the magnificent promises and splendid delusions of the Lord Bishop of Derry', as he put it in his *Memoirs*. The most eloquent comment lies in his Account Book of 1781–6. The name of the Earl of Bristol is inscribed in a flourish of fine lettering;

45. Soane's rudimentary sketch for his friend John Stuart's house, Allanbank, near Berwick, showing his proposed new wings added to the existing house. At the last moment the family decided that they could not afford the planned improvements.

below it, the page lies completely blank.

From Glasgow, where he had disembarked from Ireland, Soane travelled east across Scotland to the Stuarts, the family he had met in Rome, at Allanbank near Berwick. Lady Stuart had already asked Soane to consider improvements to the house and now John Stuart himself wrote, to Derry, requesting some plans for a greenhouse (a conservatory in the modern sense) and for a lodge ('neat genteel and plain') and entrance gates.[13] Allanbank would be a distraction from his crushing disappointment in Ireland; Stuart of course as yet knew nothing of the *débâcle*.

Soane busily set about surveying Allanbank as a first step towards designing a sizeable extension to the mansion (fig. 45). He was well advanced in the scheme, after a second visit in October, mentally fitting out the house with doors covered with mirror glass. The client had told him he detested mahogany.[14] Soane suggested that Stuart spend money on 'conspicuous furnishings'[15] and make his savings elsewhere, such as using deal floor boards which could be covered. The mirrors would be cheerful and gilded drawing-room mouldings would add 'a grandeur . . . that carving never produces'. Stuart reined him in; cautious that the room should not be too elaborate in contrast with the rest of the house. Then Soane was brought crashing down to earth: the works he had authorised were to be stopped, the Stuarts did not have the necessary funds, even though John's wife was a member of the Coutts banking family. Soane was mortified and wrote pleading, revealingly, that 'a change would . . . deprive me of the credit'.[16] Stuart tried to reason with him; these were bad times and it had become almost impossible to raise money, 'Don't think me one of those people who have entirely changed my mind', he added in another letter, by now very mindful of Soane's terrible experiences at the Downhill.

Trying to placate Soane, he asked him for advice on a number of other projects. He wanted the name of a landscape gardener, had it in mind to build a new estate village[17] and was searching for a small London house. Soane helped him to find and alter, 42 Wimpole Street and, for his pains, had the alarming experience of being menaced by a money-lender who claimed the two £300 bonds he had been paid as his, in settlement of a debt of Stuart's. Soane – although merely caught in the middle – panicked, ignoring all advice, and threatened court action. It took weeks for him to calm down. In their dealings, Stuart was alternately supportive to Soane and maddeningly vague.

As with the Herveys, all was not as it seemed in this family. John Stuart had married Frances Coutts, his first cousin, in September 1778 against the express wishes of her uncle, Thomas Coutts. He was opposed on two grounds, those of consanguinity and money; her father, James, now dead, had not been 'always master of his words and actions' and had been taken on a last Continental journey in the care of Lady Stuart and her daughters, shortly after which the marriage had been announced.

In Thomas Coutts's opinion Lady Stuart was a scheming woman who had 'endeavoured to blow the coal of dissension between my brother and me for many years past from interested motives'. She and her daughters (in contrast to her husband, the baronet, Coutts's own relative) were 'a parcel of designing artful people' who had attached themselves to his wealthy niece in order that their brother might marry her as a way of 'repairing and re-establishing the fortunes of the house of Allanbank'. In fact, Coutts's fears were groundless; it was a successful marriage and the Coutts fortune was not squandered on the rescue of an ailing estate.[18]

Thomas Coutts held the Stuart's new son-in-law John Coxe Hippisley in equally low esteem. He wrote to a family friend, 'I see in the newspapers Mrs Stuart's [Frances's] confidante (and once, I fear, her director) is married at Rome to Mr Coxe Hippisley. I know him a little but not for any good. I fear he is but a bad subject, and no fortune. I suppose her £3,000 legacy from my brother will soon be applied to pay his debts.' He had heard that Hippisley's father had been ruined by meeting his son's extravagances.

Soane had discovered something of this unedifying family history and had apparently been gossiping. Unversed in the subtle boundaries between friendship and acquaintance in the socially unequal, Soane received a stern rebuke; 'you wrote a very extraordinary letter to Mr Hippisley . . . I am surprised you could be weak enough to write to a person who you well know does not conceal his bad opinion of you . . . I am extremely angry . . . It is the height of impropriety for any person unconnected to interfere with family affairs.' Stuart added a caution: 'I do assure you if you don't judge more wisely in future you will get badly thro' the world nor will you ever retain your friends.'[19]

Despite the difficulties, old friends knew and tolerated Soane's mercurial nature, his lack of judgement and the tenuous balance between light and dark in his temperament. Yet in Soane's defence, even Hippisley would become a lifelong friend. After the disaster with the Earl Bishop, Stuart and his north country neighbour and friend from Italy, Rowland Burdon, compared notes on what they termed Soane's '*Fancies*', agreeing that the condition was 'constitutional, therefore not to be helped'.[20]

Stuart's patronage proved hardly more substantial than the Earl Bishop's. Rowland Burdon, in happy contrast, offered no false promises. The Burdons, from Castle Eden near Durham, were an established and respected family and young Rowland, the fourth male to carry the name, was about to marry. That autumn of 1780 he too wanted to offer any support he could to Soane. However, Burdon had very limited resources since his father was still alive and living at Castle Eden and he had only just taken up a partnership in the family concern, the Exchange Bank in Newcastle, founded by his father and Aubone Surtees in 1768. The firm was involved in the risky business of lead mining and the establishment of turnpikes in the north-east. The best Burdon could do was to give Soane a welcome, a sympathetic hearing and a small commission for a porch, with the possibility of a more substantial scheme for a semicircular gothic stable.

The problem of Soane's friends as clients was not capriciousness but that in their eagerness to find employment for him, they tended to take an over-optimistic view of their own finances at a time of political uncertainty. The long running American war, into which Lord North's government seemed locked despite the shift in public and political opinion against it, was reflected in a jittery economic climate. Thomas Pitt had gained his political spurs by a furious attack on North's government in April 1780. Having returned from overseas he was horrified by the state of the country, so flourishing on his departure, so fallen now. Horace

Walpole reported the speech admiringly; he had never spoken so well before.[21]

Soane was at this point a slave to his professional ambitions. He had neither time nor inclination for the family life that his contemporaries from Italy had now embarked upon. For the present he was single-minded, eager to nudge any request for minor alterations into a substantial piece of architecture. In early December he had taken London lodgings at 10 Cavendish Street.[22] Both Thomas Pitt and Philip Yorke supplied him with modest commissions for repairs and minor alterations, keeping him going while he looked around for larger jobs.

Lady Miller, the friendly author of his Italian guidebook, seemed to be considering a commission for a copy of the Temple of Clitumnus at Foligno (the inspiration for the 'Temple' at the Villa Albani and which he had sketched for her) at her Batheaston villa. Soane had been assiduous in carrying out errands and commissions for her and she was eager to introduce Soane into her Bath literary *salon* – wickedly mocked by Horace Walpole and others.[23] Yet Anna Miller, while disguising herself in the vapid and effusive style expected of popular lady versifiers of the time, was well read and considerably tougher and more intelligent than she seemed.

Among the company at her gathering, she hoped Soane might find new patrons. At one o'clock on alternate Thursday afternoons, the guests congregated for a poetry reading. The 'contending poetical morsels' as she termed them, submitted earlier on a set subject, were picked randomly from the depths of a Roman vase, found at Frascati, and read out to the audience, who then chose a winner. From 1775 four volumes of these offerings were published as *Poetical Amusements at a Villa near Bath* and the proceeds contributed to a charitable 'pauper-scheme' for which her husband John Miller had been rewarded with an Irish baronetcy.

Although Lady Miller had been pressing Soane to visit her before his visit to Ireland it was not until a few months later that she invited him (or a friend with 'poetical talents') to submit a few lines of verse – the architect as poet would have been quite novel. The title for 8 March was 'Content', hardly the subject to suit Soane's current mood of angry dejection and there is no record of his reply. But Lady Miller was already ill and died that summer. His chance to lay siege to Bath society, or merely to design her a garden temple, was gone.

In these difficult months Soane's old masters, Dance, Peacock and Holland and friends such as Richard Holland and Edward Foxhall made concerted efforts on his behalf. Soane's vulnerability, unstinting effort and obvious promise encouraged such generous support. Dance gave him several measuring jobs, including work during May 1781 on the rebuilding of Newgate Prison (fig. 46), burned out in the anti-Catholic Gordon riots of early June 1780.

Fresh from that experience, Soane was encouraged to enter a competition in the summer to design two penitentiaries, one for women, one for men. It was his first encounter with his professional peers since his return. Thomas Bowdler, his friend from Italy, had become one of three supervisors of the Penitentiary Act through a family connection to John Howard, the prison reformer, and had already approached him. He hoped that the job might fall to Soane without a competition.[24] In fact, the winner for the male penitentiary, announced in March 1782, was William Blackburn, a

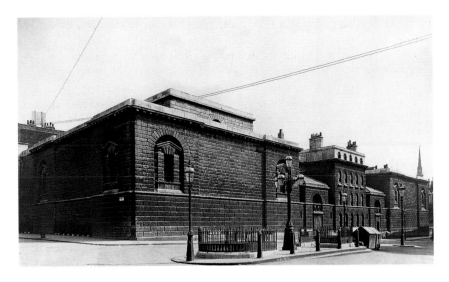

46. Photograph of Newgate Prison taken in 1900 prior to its demolition in 1902. Soane assisted Dance and Peacock in drawing up estimates for the rebuilding in 1781, following the enormous damage inflicted by the Gordon Riots.

Quaker, who in a short career (he died in 1790, as did Howard, aged forty) was to build a number of exemplary gaols in county towns embodying Howard's principles.[25] In later years Soane often went to examine his buildings, the most famous of which was in Gloucester. Gallingly, the winner of the design for the female penitentiary was Thomas Hardwick, also his companion in Rome, despite a tip-off from Thomas Pitt that he was the winner. Apparently there had been a last minute change. Soane was deeply disappointed and looked for someone to blame. He was congenitally unable to consider that any such failure was not a conspiracy. In the event the prisons were never built.

Pitt was, however, assuming the role of his patron and Soane's life immediately took a turn for the better. Pitt was an amateur architect of a very different ilk from the Earl Bishop. The latter unscrupulously milked his architects of ideas and then passed them back, as his own, to a willing local surveyor or builder. In the transaction, a great deal of money was saved and the process (inevitably very slow) allowed him to change his mind continually. Pitt, in contrast, was a decisive and erudite man, equal to any architect in his theoretical and historical grasp of the subject, but he also knew exactly what his limits were and when to hand over to a professional.

Pitt was an ideal patron, generous and knowledgeable, a man who paid his bills and ensured that Soane was introduced to anyone who might conceivably become a client. Like Burdon and others, he had come to understand the tensions of Soane's particular personality and at one point in the early 1780s offered him a peaceful stay in the family Thames-side villa, Petersham Lodge, where he could recover his spirits and good health after an especially stressful period.[26]

The connection with the Pitt family was to be central to Soane's career. Pitt personally provided commissions for Petersham Lodge, his wife's family home Burnham Westgate in Norfolk and the family estate at Boconnoc. He also introduced Soane to numerous clients; some belonged to a Cornish coterie of bankers, landowners and MPs of pocket boroughs, others were neighbours such as Lady Pembroke, but the majority came from the politically potent circles of the landed aristocracy, his relatives, who included the Lytteltons, Grenvilles and Temples. At the summit of this enviable pyramid of power and patronage stood his nephew William Pitt the younger who, in the final days of 1783, aged twenty-four, became First Lord of the Treasury, a post he would retain for the following seventeen years.

Yet ironically enough, behind all this prospective patronage lay the shadow of the Earl Bishop. Some years later Soane wrote to Pitt, by then created Lord Camelford, regretting that he had not been with him in Saint-Rémy, a journey that he had been cheated of by the Earl Bishop's peremptory summons. 'With your Lordship's observations it would have been a treat indeed – the Bishop prevented me [sic] many enjoyments . . . but as to him I owe your Lordship's friendship I readily forgive him everything and would as heretofore exert myself to please him.'[27] Pitt and Hervey had first met in Rome in the winter of 1778. The Bishop, a great admirer of Lord Chatham, was impressed by the similarities in his nephew whom Mrs Hervey described, 'he is much of his stature . . . a great deal of dignity in his manner, less fire, but all his sweetness'.[28] It was for Lord Camelford to point out, as Soane embarked on a commission for young William Beckford at Fonthill Splendens, the dangerous similarities in character between the two aesthete dilettanti, with their wild promises and their ability to seriously disappoint the vulnerable.

Like Pitt, Philip Yorke lost no time in supporting Soane after his return to England. Despite the pressures that descended upon him, he continuously supplied him with work. With the likely prospect of marriage (he married Elizabeth Lindsay in 1782) Yorke asked Soane to carry out a considerable programme of work at his estate, Hamels in Hertfordshire, in 1781. After the marriage Soane designed a rustic dairy at Hamels, complete with peeling bark on the tree trunk columns and a planting list of scented climbers, based upon one which he had already designed for Lady Craven at her Marie-Antoinette-like *hameau* in Fulham.[29] Adeptly jumping from fashionable primitivism, with its Rousseauesque touches, back to more mundane domestic alterations, he was soon working at the Yorke's London house on Cavendish Street. Soane was building up a versatile one-man practice and, reflecting the upturn in his fortunes, had now moved from his lodgings in that street to two floors nearby, in Miss Susannah Cecil's house, 53 Margaret Street. His rent of £40 for the year covered 'dinner and service'.[30]

Soane was soon working for other members of Yorke's family, especially his stepmother Agneta Yorke, at Tyttenhanger in Hertfordshire. Later he built her a riverside villa, Sydney Lodge on the Hamble in Hampshire. Throughout the 1780s Yorke kept Soane busy and finally, on his succession to the earldom in 1790, rewarded him with a major job, the remodelling of Wimpole Hall in Cambridgeshire.

Solid clients such as the Yorkes or Pitt used an architect such as Soane for a wide variety of tasks. The key commission might be years away, a reward for enduring a perpetual treadmill of small jobs: surveying property, arranging lettings, making minor repairs or alterations, even pursuing reluctant tenants for rent. As yet Soane had no underlings to whom he could delegate. Organising the emptying of cesspools and arguing with desultory building tradesmen were part of his daily grind of petty, time-consuming affairs, far from the delineation of fine ornament or finished

by an elliptical glazed oculus (fig. 57). The greater height of the new reception rooms meant that Soane had to juggle to deal with the connections and changes of levels between the 1720s house and his work, the kind of challenge that he rose to best. Upstairs he experimented with an arrangement that became a tried and tested favourite, a long low corridor punched by brilliant splashes of light, falling from two well-spaced glazed oculi – a memory of the subterranean passages below Roman amphitheatres. This was his most original interior yet.

He also designed a bridge for Giffard's park, maybe speculatively, since there was already a false bridge and Paine's classical version. Neither it nor a proposed chapel in the grounds materialised, but the bridge appeared on the walls at the Royal Academy in 1786 and two more views of Chillington the following year.

Soane's emerging circle of City contacts were very different men, some as newly arrived as the Giffards were long established. Most lived to the east of London, around Walthamstow and Leyton, the villages favoured as rural retreats for leading figures in the Bank of England, the East India, Levant, Turkey, Hudson Bay and Russia companies and other major institutions such as Royal Exchange Assurance or the Sun Fire Office. Soane seems to have found these businessmen straightforward and approachable, compared to the unpredictability of men such as Stuart, Greswold Lewis or, more dangerously, the Earl Bishop. Having made their fortunes in the last generation or two and in the case of the Huguenots as immigrant minorities, they must have presented a far less formidable social front. In several cases, they became close personal friends.

In the summer of 1783 Soane had combined a visit to the soap merchants and financiers, Richard and his father James Neave of Grove Lane, Walthamstow, with one to Samuel Bosanquet, first cousin of that charming reprobate Richard Bosanquet, John Patteson's friend with whom Soane had shared lodgings in Naples and who was still obliged to remain abroad. Samuel Bosanquet the younger was a director of the Bank of England and the Levant Company (fig. 58), positions which had come to him largely through his maternal grandfather's positions in both.[42] It may have been in connection with a project for a Lazaretto (a quarantine hospital) for the Levant Company that Soane visited the Bosanquet home, Forest House, in Leyton.[43]

A formidable Huguenot dynasty, the Bosanquet family and its connections by marriage could, at a stroke, provide entrées for Soane to almost all the bastions of influence in the City of London. Jacob, Samuel's cousin, had become a director of the East India Company in 1782 and remained involved for forty-six years until his death, rising through the hierarchy to become both Deputy Chairman and Chairman, keeping pace with Samuel's rise within the Bank of England.

Another Walthamstow contact was William Cooke, a Turkey merchant and a director of the Bank of England since 1780. Soane surveyed his newly acquired house, Rectory Manor, on 10 May 1783 and rapidly made drawings for the necessary works, estimated at £797. The following year Soane carried out some modest works on St Mary's church at Cooke's expense.[44] Before long the Cookes were regular guests at Margaret Street, as was Timothy Tyrrell, his old Reading friend and now a City solicitor,[45] who acted as his legal and financial adviser. Soane often

55. Malvern Hall, Solihull was remodelled by Soane for Lewis from 1783, and painted several times by John Constable from 1808 onwards. This version, showing the entrance front with some of Lewis's own adjustments, dates from 1821.

shared the use of his horse and borrowed small sums, quickly repaid. Now Soane bought his own mount, a grey mare, from Cooke for 15 guineas. Perhaps he felt it was a good investment, envisaging many such short journeys to the villages east of London as he built up his City contacts. Later, in 1791, Soane carried out more work on Rectory Manor. A few months after, William Cooke died aged fifty-two, the victim of 'a short illness, contracted by cold taken in looking after his workmen'. His building works seem to have been the death of him.

As a result of Soane's assiduity and professionalism, his growing reputation for completing jobs on time and to budget and his ability to choose the most reliable and skilled craftsmen, his name was being passed around a tightly knit circle of leading figures in the world of banking and commerce; all in their forties, they were well placed to advance Soane's cause.

Soane's own circle of friends from Royal Academy days was consolidated by the fact that several of them were now closely involved in his work. Edward Foxhall had worked on a number of Soane's jobs and in exchange he introduced Soane to his clients including William Beckford and Lord Arundell, of Wardour Castle, Wiltshire. Richard Holland and John Hobcraft regularly worked with Soane.[46] There seems to have been an easy reciprocal relationship between these young men all making their way in different, but complementary, fields and helping one another with money or contacts as needed.

On 10 January 1784 Soane had taken a Miss Smith to the theatre.[47] On 7 February she took tea and supper with Soane, the other guests being Tyrrell, Christopher Ebdon (another friend from Holland's office) and the Foxhalls. On 11 February Tyrrell lent him 10 guineas 'for my own use' and he purchased two sets of buckles, one for his shoes and one for his knees, together with some leather breeches – he always bought fine plumage when wooing. Soon his notebooks record his almost nightly attendance at plays and concerts.

Soane was in pursuit of the niece of the City builder[48] George Wyatt, an intelligent young woman who had kept house for her uncle for some years. Wyatt had, over the years, acquired a number of properties in Clerkenwell, on the western edge of the City, and had considerable interests on the Surrey side of the Thames. As a City man, the Surveyor of Paving, Wyatt had a foot planted comfortably, and profitably, on both banks of the river. He may have developed Albion Place, just south of Blackfriars Bridge, his home from 1781, and the question remains of his involvement in the Albion Mills, a revolutionary steam-driven corn mill powered by Boulton and Watt machines. Its huge capacity would have been the equivalent to fifteen conventional wind- or water-driven mills.[49] Since the promoter and builder of the Albion Mills was Samuel Wyatt, a family relationship has often, mistakenly, been assumed.[50] The mills were completed by 1787.

Soane must have met George Wyatt through Dance, certainly during the rebuilding of Newgate Gaol but possible earlier given their City links. Wyatt became his niece, Elizabeth's guardian, following the deaths of her parents. Jonathan Smith, her father died in 1763.[51] He was the licensee of The Castle, Cowcross Street on the edge of Smithfield Market (one of a number of properties belonging to Wyatt in this street).[52] The area was far from salubrious and in the early nineteenth century The Castle gained an unusual privilege, that of being an official pawnshop, following an incident in which the Prince Regent had been gambling in the area and

56. (below, left) Chillington in Staffordshire, where Soane added Ionic columns to screen the end of the entrance hall. Soane began work here for Thomas Giffard in 1785.

57. (below, right) Chillington, the oval oculus in the vast saloon, which stands on part of the site of an earlier, Tudor, mansion.

58. A portrait of Samuel Bosanquet of Forest Lodge, Walthamstow. Soane had met his cousin Richard in Italy and first visited the house in 1783. Samuel was an influential figure at the Bank of England, and became Deputy Governor in 1789.

had to forfeit his watch in order to continue to lay bets. The publican agreed and the honour was acquired.

Elizabeth (Eliza) Smith was a woman of her time. Independent, practical and educated, she also knew the world in which Soane moved, from her successful uncle's viewpoint. The eighteenth-century building trade was full of women, of whom Eleanor Coade was merely the best known; some were widows, some had inherited a business. Eliza Smith must have been familiar with several. Her uncle's business interests by 1784 were considerable, both in capital and property.

By April she was taking supper at Margaret Street most evenings; Soane's landlady Miss Cecil was presumably a suitably discreet chaperone. While Soane was away in Norwich on business he wrote to Eliza twice. On occasion he borrowed Tyrrell's maid to serve tea for them and by early May, Miss Smith was sitting for a portrait, accompanied on the second occasion by Soane – who had presumably commissioned the portrait of his intended wife and himself.[53] The portraits were an engagement gift. In the miniature Eliza is not conventionally pretty, but has a firm, intelligent look and a maturity beyond her years (fig. 59).[54]

Eliza Smith was a lively person who emerges in letters to her close women friends as someone enjoying herself unaffectedly and who inspired friendship. She also had an acute intelligence, an informed interest in politics, both domestic and international, and a shrewd head for business. Her loyalty was often tested, and friends sometimes lost, when Soane was prosecuting one of his own vendettas but she was always steadfast. Marriage to Soane would be anything but carefree.

On 12 July Soane confided in his notebook that he had 'cancelled his will and codicils' and in the last weeks of the month hired a coach on several occasions to take Miss Smith, by now 'Eliza', for several excursions. Perhaps they visited old haunts around Reading and paid a visit to Chertsey, perhaps they went wider afield – Soane sharing his favourite places and buildings, no doubt including his own work, with his future bride. Knowing that he would be immersed in a particularly busy time in late August, this was a kind of pre-honeymoon. On 21 August 1784 John Soane – the 'e' now firmly appended to his name – and Elizabeth Smith were married by common license at Christ Church, Blackfriars in Southwark, the parish church for Albion Place.[55] The licence suggests that she was over the age of twenty-one (below that age a special licence was required).

Eliza knew the life she was to expect. Two days after their marriage Soane set off to check progress on a job. The continuous travelling, long absences sometimes broken for just a day or two, the constant demands of clients, the endless meetings of exigent committees, the potential contacts and future patrons to be identified and courted, all contributed to the pressures upon him and, indirectly, on her.

Eliza was prepared and well able to play a central role in Soane's professional life; not merely as a socially adept hostess, but as confidante in his troubles. She moved effortlessly between the worlds of Soane's most important clients and that of his bricklayer brother. Her financially envious relatives would point out after her death that she had acquired 'superior address' to the rest of her family but she was, in reality, completely unaffected. From now on, few letters from good friends and patrons end without a fond message to Mrs Soane, far more than the simple observance of a politeness. She was an enormous asset to the frequently acerbic and irritable Soane.

As Soane's pupil George Wightwick would remark, many years later, the architect 'depends not more on his ability to answer the duties of employment than on the address and conduct necessary to form and secure a connection. Of all men engaged in the polite arts, he is the most frequently and continuously in personal communication with his patron'; indeed he might find himself 'the table guest and resident visitor of his employer'.[56] If Dance and Holland between them had moulded Soane into an accomplished architect, Eliza Soane brought Soane the personable architect into being.

59. Elizabeth (Eliza) Smith, soon to be Mrs Soane in a miniature probably by William Dance, one of George's brothers, painted just before her marriage.

5

ESTABLISHED

By early 1785 Soane's life had changed spectacularly for the better since the gloomy months after the *débâcle* with the Earl Bishop. With single-mindedness and ability he had built up a promising set of clients and equal resolution had secured him his eligible and delightful bride. Soane's financial prospects had also greatly improved. George Wyatt proved generous from the beginning; in March 1785 he gave the couple £1,000 and Soane asked his friend Timothy Tyrrell, who often acted for him in both legal and financial matters, to buy him 1,123 5 per cent Bank stock, amounting to £992 16s 3d.[1]

The urgency with which Soane pursued his profession in the late 1780s was driven by the birth of his first son, John, on 29 April 1786. Eliza must have been weakened by the birth and the child spent the first two years of his life with a wet nurse, Eliza Walker, wife of a 'first rate bricklayer'.[2] The practice was quite usual in well-off families.

John's birth gave Soane's life new purpose. The boy, and any children that followed would, he hoped, be the second generation of an architectural dynasty. Later that year, Soane bought the lease of 77 Welbeck Street – not far from Margaret Street and also on the Cavendish-Harley estate. Eliza's life was circumscribed by her pregnancies but she happily carried out commissions in London for Soane's clients such as the Pattesons of Norwich for whom she bought candles, lace, hats and bombazine for a gown (as well as arranging transport of the dress, costing 4s).

Soane was building up a small office. Sir Robert Taylor had instigated the practice of taking on pupils, assistants on the model of solicitors' articled clerks, for up to six years.[3] John Sanders was Soane's first pupil, introduced by Timothy Tyrrell,[4] who may have known Sanders's father, a tallow chandler, through the network of City liverymen. The sixteen-year-old boy lived as a member of the household at 53 Margaret Street from late 1784, as Soane had with the Dance family. The next year Soane encouraged him to became a student at the Royal Academy Schools and Sanders became a gold medallist three years later.[5] From now on Soane took on a new pupil roughly every second year and employed clerks of works and other assistants as required. Office hours were 7 a.m. to 7 p.m. in the summer and 8 a.m. to 8 p.m. in winter. By the standards of the time the routine was not harsh and the pupils treated fairly, with time off for study at the Royal Academy and for holidays.[6] There was usually a personal basis

60. The stables at Burnham Westgate, the north Norfolk house which came to Thomas Pitt through his marriage to the daughter of Pinckney Wilkinson. In the interests of economy Soane restricted the white bricks to the elevation only.

to the introduction of a pupil and both Foxhall's and Tyrrell's sons joined Soane's office.

Lord Camelford, the former Thomas Pitt, continued to keep Soane busy although his deteriorating health meant frequent travel abroad in search of kinder climates. For three years their exchanges took place largely on paper. In August 1786 Soane was working at Burnham Westgate (fig. 60), the north Norfolk house that Pitt inherited through his wife's family, the Wilkinsons. Just inland, at Burnham Norton, he could – had he been a church-going man – have listened to sermons delivered by Horatio Nelson's father.

Not all the work at Burnham was structural; diplomatic skills were required too. He was dealing with a particularly awkward tenant of Lord Camelford's, Mr Davis. Despite having his new barn 10 foot longer and the brewhouse detached 'this does not satisfy him, indeed his mind is never to be satisfied'.[7] At the opposite extremity of the country, Soane was embarking on a long programme at Boconnoc, in eastern Cornwall. Much of the work consisted of sorting out the after-effects of bad work-manship and replacing shoddy materials. His unfamiliarity with the local tradesmen made practical arrangements difficult. Apologetically, Soane wrote: 'your Lordship is too well acquainted with the plague of workmen and the difficulty of procuring good ones . . . to attribute the delay to any want of attention on my part'.[8]

The job involved extending the earlier house, re-roofing the old core and adding a new parapet, while the memorial obelisk in the park – designed by Camelford – needed repairs after being struck by lightning a few years before. All of this, if 'done in the most substantial and economical manner' would cost, at most £600.

But Boconnoc was in very bad shape. Gutters and roof timbers were completely rotten on the newer parts of the house and the woodwork on the south front had 'perished' under the plaster. Dormers and chimney shafts needed replacing and the structure depended on iron ties at many points. Arches in the areas needed strengthening and 'attempting regularity' on the cornices would be too expensive. The local clerk of works whom Soane had found, Cawley, suddenly demanded 24s per week but Soane assured Camelford that the work was going on fast and economically – so many men were working there that 'everybody in the country imagines themselves at work for me'.[9] No sooner was Soane back home from Cornwall than he received reports of water coming in under the sashes and fungus in the dining-room.

Soane's troubles followed him from Boconnoc. He had hoped for a rest but 'the Rowleys will take care I shall have but little. That unfortunate business continually harrasses my mind and will considerably shorten my days.' Camelford replied, 'There seems to be something ill omened to you in the whole of this Tendring Hall business.'[10] Among Soane's early jobs, few gave him more trouble. Tendring Hall, owned by an old landed family, the Rowleys, stood outside Stoke by Nayland, half-timbered and decrepit, overlooking the Stour Valley on the Suffolk–Essex border. Soane's first site visit had been on 8 May 1784, when he determined to demolish the old house and checked the quality of the local clay to see that it was fit for firing in the estate kilns. The son of a bricklayer, Soane knew the difference between suitable and unsuitable clay; good or bad bricks. George Wyatt accompanied him again in late May, to draw up estimates and provide a second opinion: he would act as subcontractor on the brickwork and masonry.[11] On a clear day they could have made out the rooftops of Dedham where John Constable was growing up.

The client was, nominally, Admiral Rowley but in effect Soane was working for the family trustees and it was there that the difficulties lay. The alteration of a trust established for a mentally retarded elder son was required, in order to release funds for building. This necessitated a private members' bill in the House of Lords. Lord Camelford had been involved in these proceedings and he may have been the original contact between client and architect. Soane's undertaking, to build the house for a fixed price (£12,050)[12] within a four-year period required him to act as both contractor and architect – a situation which became untenable. Counsel, John Scott KC, observed that because of an absurdly drafted clause in the bill Soane seemed 'neither Surveyor nor Contractor but both the one and the other and in that mixed character must endeavour by accommodation to do the best he can with the parties with whom he has to deal and whose situation is as awkward as his own'.[13] The episode informed Soane's insistence, from this moment on, that these functions must be entirely divorced.

Tendring, as built (fig. 61), shared elements of both the earlier Norfolk houses, Saxlingham and Letton, in their unadorned brickwork and generous bow-fronted rooms. The house was demolished in the 1950s, but photographs of the interiors (fig. 62) show that they were a development on those at Letton, a dark entrance vestibule giving way to the explosive effect of a full-height, top-lit stair punched through the core of the house and, beyond it here, a great bow-fronted living-room looking out over the park. While the ornament remained an Adamesque frosting of antique motifs, Soane's planning was becoming – house by house – more sophisticated and subtle.

Humphry Repton, the landscape gardener who would dog Soane's footsteps in coming years, was brought in to advise on the landscape in

61. The south facing garden front at Tendring Hall, Stoke by Nayland in Suffolk. Soane began the job in 1784 for Trustees of the Rowley family. The difficulties of the job helped form Soane's strong views on the proper and distinct role of the architect.

62. Tendring Hall, the staircase with Roman Doric columns marking the entrance from a low-ceilinged vestibule into a full-height, top-lit hall. The house was demolished in the 1950s.

1790 and criticised the site. Repton was nurturing architectural ambitions and remarked, with a certain cheek: 'had I been previously consulted the house would neither have been so lofty in its construction nor so much exposed in its situation'.[14]

But Repton was the least of Soane's troubles. The trustees were dilatory in paying his bills, questioning every aspect of the contractual arrangements and estimates, and upon his father's death William Rowley refused to pay: the story dragged on until 1791 when Soane was awarded a substantial payment by a board of arbitration. George Dance acted as his representative.[15] It had been Soane's largest commission (the estimates were almost double those at Letton), but also the most unpleasant. Tendring Hall was 'an explosive mixture, [of] restive owners, insubordinate workmen, suspicious trustees, and increasingly impatient creditors',[16] upon which Soane's iron views of the professional responsibilities of the architect, the necessary separation of the contractors' or builders' interests and, equally, the obligations of the client, would be formed.

Fortunately the only point of tension between Lord Camelford and Soane was the uncertainty of the post. The architect could not act until he received his instructions and the frequent loss of mail, either way, meant that communications tended to be staccato, 'I wish your Lordship could not only look from Montpelier to Boconnoc and see objects distinctly but also that it was possible to converse' Soane wrote plaintively.[17]

A convenient break in the journey to Cornwall was Cricket St Thomas, between Chard and Crewkerne in Somerset. Soane's first visit (and a frequent stop, too, for the Pitts when they were in England) to Rear-Admiral Alexander Hood (fig. 63) was on 7 May 1786 – a week after the birth of his son, John (later, Eliza often accompanied him to Cricket Lodge). The sixty-year-old Hood, Treasurer of the Royal Naval Hospital at Greenwich since 1766, was married to a relative of Camelford's, Mary West. After she died suddenly that September Hood remained close to his first wife's family who, after he lost his parliamentary seat for Bridgewater in 1790, helped him secure a pocket borough, Buckingham, under the patronage

63. Alexander Hood, the first Viscount Bridport and distinguished naval commander, by L. F. Abbott. Painted in 1795, some years after Soane had begun work on his Somerset house, Cricket Lodge.

of the Marquis of Buckingham. Despite their very friendly relations (Hood and Lady Buckingham had danced the night away at the Stowe Christmas Ball in 1790), Buckingham requested Hood to be prepared to surrender his seat should their political views differ.[18]

Later ennobled, as Lord Bridport (his brother, Admiral Samuel Hood, became Lord Hood), he would play a central role in the Napoleonic Wars, commanding the Channel Fleet against the French between 1797 and 1800. As a naval officer with increasingly onerous duties, he was rarely at home and it was, therefore, his much younger second wife, Maria Sophia, who effectively became the client. The two families struck up an easy friendship, encouraged by Lady Bridport's great liking for Eliza, and a series of cheerfully conducted commissions continued over almost thirty years, ending with Lord Bridport's wall monument in the church beside Cricket Lodge, the house that Soane had substantially remodelled.[19] As often with those Soane found sympathetic, he lavished great attention on the design of a fine library (fig. 64).

Another west country family with whom Soane made contact in the summer of 1786 was the troubled Beckfords. Young William Beckford was abroad, keeping a decent distance from the censure of English society following the scandal of his affair with Lord Courtenay, and it was his mother (Alderman Beckford's widow) who acted in his stead as he embarked on alterations to their Palladian house, Fonthill Splendens in Wiltshire. Soane's challenge was to transform an unsuitable second-floor passage into a top-lit gallery.[20]

Edward Foxhall was Beckford's agent, buying works of art for him at auction and bargaining with artists on his behalf,[21] whilst his firm, which became Foxhall and Fryer of Old Cavendish Street, was employed on the painting and furnishing at Fonthill Splendens. Beckford, who had a limitless stock of cruel nicknames, called Foxhall 'the Blockhead' or 'the Baldheaded Fool', but continued to employ him there and on Fonthill Abbey until his death.[22] Although Soane had recently begun work for Mrs Beckford's cousin the Hon. John Hamilton, later the Marquis of Abercorn, at Bentley Priory, in Stanmore, Middlesex and at the family's London house, everything suggests that Foxhall was the link to Beckford.

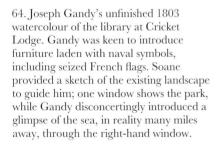

64. Joseph Gandy's unfinished 1803 watercolour of the library at Cricket Lodge. Gandy was keen to introduce furniture laden with naval symbols, including seized French flags. Soane provided a sketch of the existing landscape to guide him; one window shows the park, while Gandy disconcertingly introduced a glimpse of the sea, in reality many miles away, through the right-hand window.

Camelford wrote a letter of warning, on hearing that Beckford had approached Soane, 'I have seen the melancholy castle in which Mr Beckford lived with Ly. M [Lady Margaret Gordon his wife]; upon the banks of the Lake until she died. . .but I do not hear of any intention of building. He is I believe another Bp. of Derry'.[23] Camelford was paternally protective of Soane's fragile professional equilibrium and, considerably more worldly wise, did not want to expose him to another calamity like that at the Downhill.

Warnings ignored, Soane pressed on and designed the gallery in May 1787. Fonthill Splendens was a vast and secret treasure house, a huge house built thirty years earlier by Beckford's father. Soane's April visit, in Beckford's absence, was a rare chance to see the house[24] and within it, the prizes of the Alderman's collection – bought with a fortune founded on West Indian sugar plantations. Hogarth's *A Rake's Progress* had been bought from the artist in 1745 (the companion series *The Harlot's Progress* had been destroyed when the previous house burned down in 1755); many years later, Soane bought the series of eight paintings. The gallery at Fonthill that Soane designed would have been the first in a line of top-lit, canopied spaces – Soane's signature – in which a dome is placed directly upon the walls below, its sides sliced off to compress the space, the crown cut away to provide an oculus and the remaining surfaces made preternaturally thin by a skinny membrane of plasterwork. The very unsuitability of the mean, unlit space for its function provoked Soane to explore and develop a novel form, here multiplied. Despite that, the insuperable difficulties of displaying pictures in a cramped passage, however ingeniously lit, caused the scheme to be dropped.

The potential of top-lighting, in the variant forms of a circular oculus, clerestory or lantern, to utilise awkward space buried deep in the core of a site, was a theme he returned to endlessly. Soane had begun with a top-lit passage on a plan for a villa designed while he was in Rome and continually explored and refined the theme, until he achieved his own miniaturised and most exquisite version, the breakfast room at 13 Lincoln's Inn Fields.

Although the gallery was never built, Soane did undertake some minor works at Fonthill Splendens before its demolition in 1807. Beckford commissioned a spectacular state bed, incongruously modelled on the Choragic Monument of Lysicrates in Athens. Although Soane drew up schemes for it (no doubt executed by Foxhall) the project bore the imprint of Beckford's eclectic tastes and controlling personality as patron. Although Soane and Beckford remained in contact over the years – even calling upon one another in Bath in the late 1820s – his febrile personality does not suggest a congenial patron for Soane who (like any architect) preferred a decisive client who participated in early discussions and then allowed the designer to carry the results through, without interference or alteration.

Behind the excitement of new commissions and the possibilities which opened up with new clients, fell the mundane realities of professional practice. Soane could (with enormous, often unsuspected, effort) produce quite magical architectural effects but he also knew how to keep the wheels turning and the costs down. Working on Blundeston House in Suffolk for Mr Rix he noted that the library cornice was to be 'like Mr Branthwayte's

Eating Room [Taverham, Norfolk], base and surbase like Admiral Rowley's; architrave to doors and windows like ditto, door and shutter panels like Mr Branthwayte's Eating Room, frame to ceiling like Admiral Rowley's room. Chamber, cornice like Mr Gooch's Library'.[25] As he built up regular working relationships with tradesmen, he conveyed his instructions in a shorthand which they could immediately turn into the appropriate moulding detail. It also allowed him to make extremely accurate estimates. Before long, his best London men travelled to work on many of his country jobs: they knew his preferences and were becoming familiar with his approach. Elsewhere skilled labour was often hard to find. As his clerk of works at Piercefield later wrote to him from near Chepstow, 'here is not a good hand to be got in this country; I have got one good one out of Gloucestershire a man that worked under me. . .no person can tell what trouble I have had with country carpenters.'[26] He asked Soane to persuade the client, George Smith, to send him 'two good joiners from London, men that can work'.

Soane kept his established clients happy by his scrupulous attention to their affairs. In 1787 Eliza was expecting a second child and work on their town houses meant that he could spend more time at home. Lord Camelford wished to let one of his recently improved Hereford Street properties suitable for 'a single man or lady who likes space, a good air, easy outlets for exercise and no great expense'.[27] Soane apologised to Camelford that the house had been only yielding £700 in annual rent, the works having cost four times that, 'but then the immense load of Ground Rent is disheartening to adventurers' and, he added, 'you must . . . contrive a water closet'.[28] Soane was an excellent client for Joseph Bramah's newly patented system. On another occasion Soane entered, on Camelford's behalf, into a dispute with his neighbour in Petersham over a cesspool. His patron asked him to construct one 'to carry off what she is so good to pour down upon me'. No detail was too small for attention and Camelford had a light touch with his requests.

In February 1787 Camelford asked whether Soane had heard from Downing Street. But events had moved faster than he knew. Soane, thanks to his introduction, had been working for some months now for William Pitt the younger (fig. 65), at Holwood, his modest country villa, just south of Bromley in Kent and an easily accessible retreat from the pressures of his position. Lord Camelford retained an avuncular interest in his brilliant young cousin and knew that Soane, of whose qualities he was now entirely confident, was the ideal architect for him.

William Pitt's formality of manner was well matched by Soane's professionalism. He would not have been suited by the charming conviviality of James Wyatt. Pitt, an apparently haughty man, was perfectly amenable when considering improvements to his country retreat. He had bought Holwood in 1785 with large loans both from Coutts Bank and Thomas Coutts personally. It needed a number of alterations and small extensions (figs 66. 67). Pitt had not the time or inclination to become an architectural amateur in the family tradition, but he was an eager client. The following year, Soane made fifteen visits to the site, some on horseback, some by post-chaise.[29]

No other small commission required as many site visits but Soane could see his whole career resting on this job. Many of his journeys to Kent were

65. John Flaxman's posthumous (1812) statue of William Pitt the younger. Portrayed in marble, Pitt's famously unbending characteristics are emphasised.

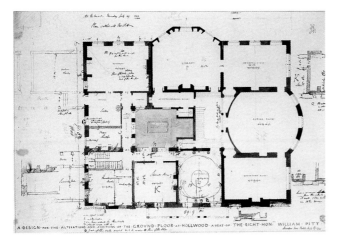

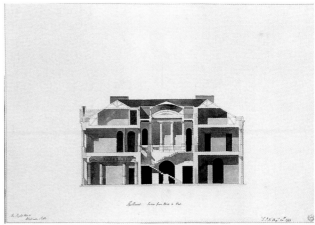

probably as fruitless as Humphry Repton's first few attempts to pin down his client, described in his *Memoir*. But when Repton did meet Pitt he found him both decisive and open to suggestions. Further, 'there was a degree of cheerfulness and lightness in his manner which no one could suppose from his natural formality and stateliness of person'.[30] Repton also discovered – as did Soane – that Pitt never answered letters on the subject of patronage ('he was better occupied in planning expeditions, establishing a sinking fund and devising ways and means than in corresponding about applications for appointments' he commented, somewhat spuriously) but was willing to consider personal approaches.[31] Soane realised that his visits to Holwood were an invaluable opportunity to secure Pitt's patronage.

From the beginning there were severe financial constraints on the work at Holwood. William Pitt's finances were already in bad shape and by January 1789 the family was rallying round. Camelford and Pitt's brother, the second Earl Chatham were concerned at rumours about his financial low waters,[32] 'He belongs to us, we all partake in his glory. It is not only just, but it is a *right* we *claim* . . . to share with him the inconvenience which that Glory may have brought upon him.'[33] The situation was not yet grave but Camelford, while relieved, signalled that he was always prepared to help his cousin financially: 'Assure him nothing would be more flattering to me than such a mark of his confidence and affection.'[34] Having been responsible for the Prime Minister's choice of architect and knowing Soane's experiences with deluded and profligate patrons, Camelford was concerned that he should not be dragged down by Pitt's miscalculation of his means.

The pace of Soane's life was unremitting. A few days after the birth of his second son George, just before Christmas 1787, Soane was off again to one of his most distant jobs, Mulgrave Hall in North Yorkshire: the bad weather and enormous distance made it a tedious prospect. It was his fourth visit since 1786 and he would be back again in February. Sometimes he took the coach to York, stopped in the city for a day or two, and then hired a horse for the onward journey. Even without a break, and travelling overnight, it took at least two days each way.[35] When visiting, he stayed in the house which cost just a tip of 5s 6d for the servants. Like Boconnoc and many other jobs, Mulgrave Hall had been a potentially

66. (above, left) A ground floor plan of Pitt's country villa, Holwood, in Kent, amended and annotated heavily by Soane, 'plan settled with Mr Pitt' Monday, 29 July 1799. Soane had been working there at intervals, proposing various alterations and extensions, since 1786.

67. (above, right) Soane's most elaborate scheme for Holwood, dated 20 August 1799, a section showing a cantilevered stair and full-height landing, marked by a screen of Ionic columns and lit by a broad lunette.

68. The walled garden at Mulgrave Castle, north Yorkshire, which Soane designed with flues at regular intervals to heat the glass houses, now gone. The bill for bricks and glass was enormous.

69 and 70. Repton's Red Book for Mulgrave. Left, before; right, after, showing that Repton planned to screen Soane's prominent additions to the rear of the house.

interesting commission which did not, in the end, allow Soane a great deal of latitude. Given a series of options for extensions to an existing house,[36] the client had unerringly chosen the dullest.

Constantine John Phipps, the second Baron Mulgrave, had been an intrepid explorer as a young man. When a captain in the Royal Navy he had, with young Captain Nelson, attempted to find the North East Passage and his portrait by Gainsborough shows him as a handsome venturer. Architectural decision making must have seemed a mild irrelevancy in a life previously determined by major naval engagements and adventurous journeys to the edges of the known world. Within the political sphere, he spent some years as an MP and became a Lord of the Admiralty. In middle age Mulgrave married Anne Cholmeley and it was in preparation for that event that he decided to modernise his family house. Although a Fellow of the Royal Society, a member of the Society of Antiquaries and a bibliophile with an unmatched library on nautical matters, his closest connection to architectural patronage (not perhaps a high recommendation), was that he was the Earl Bishop's nephew, his mother being born Lepel Hervey.

Soane added two useful new wings to the early eighteenth-century house, with large basement service areas. The interiors on which Soane could prove himself were confined to a rectangular dining-room with a niche for a bust of the Duchess of Buckingham, the builder of the earlier house, and a tiny oval anteroom. Soane earned £419 for the work at Mulgrave and a further £40 for unexecuted drawings and alterations to the family's town house in Harley Street.[37]

Soane's accounts cover work on the usual aspects of improving an older house, as well as a brewhouse and a massive brick-walled kitchen garden (fig. 68, 69, 70), with heating on all four sides (the chimneys and flues still remain) to serve the glasshouses which wrapped around virtually the entire perimeter, sheltering the peaches, vines and pineapples which struggled to flourish in the harsh north-easterly climate. A prodigious amount of very expensive 'best London' crown glass was needed, although glass now attracted heavy excise duties.[38] Twenty-eight feet of mahogany provided panelling and seats for three luxurious water closets, the height

of modernity.[39] The mahogany, the glass, the veined marble and all other special materials came in through the port at Whitby, one of the largest in the country at the time, from the quays of which Captain Cook had embarked some years before, in the *Endeavour*, partly funded by Lord Mulgrave.[40]

Hurtling from Yorkshire to Cornwall, Somerset to Norfolk, Soane unburdened himself to the always sympathetic Pitt: 'The constant and miserable whirl in which I live makes me unable to do at all time what my inclination most leads me to.'[41] Years later, Benjamin Henry Latrobe explained to his father-in-law the realities of an architect's life; the distances Soane travelled were nothing compared to those in America, 'How this *stationary locality* is to be effected without my throwing up my profession I do not see . . . in countries infinitely more populous, no architect nor engineer of any reputation could ever remain long in one place.' He cited Soane as his example, incessantly on the move supervising far-flung jobs.[42]

On the occasion Soane recounted to Camelford, he had travelled the 260 miles back from Mulgrave Hall to find a letter from Lord Fortescue, summoning him to Castlehill in Devon – an equal distance in the opposite direction – which 'forced me reluctantly to leave home the very day of my return. His Lordship had my plans and seemed to approve of them in May *1786* from which period to the present I had not heard anything of them.' On arrival he found very little done and that so badly 'that the greatest part must be altered and as much as possible to the first plan, this is flattering, but not profitable nor pleasing'. But his clients were too important to offend. Lord Fortescue was a brother-in-law of the Marquis of Buckingham and William Wyndham Grenville – the second generation of the 'cousinhood' or 'Cobham's cubs' as this ubiquitous political coterie had became known in the 1760s. They were all in Lord Camelford's outer family circle.

Despite the pull of such powerful clients, on this occasion he was 'absolutely obliged' to get back to town. George died aged six months that summer (later Soane noted a repayment of £2 16s 0d to Edward Foxhall for the funeral).[43] Just occasionally, he had to put his own family affairs first. Eliza provided the fixed point to which Soane returned, exhausted and often only briefly. Her life in these years, the late 1780s, was becoming an unhappy succession of difficult childbirth and infant mortality, endured for the most part without her husband. Another George was born on 28 September 1789. Eliza Soane was much weakened by her third pregnancy and the child was put out to a wet nurse, the wife of a journeyman bricklayer called Leake whose own baby had just died. However, Mrs Leake drank heavily, perhaps because of her own distress, and Mrs Soane decided to take the child away, to another wet nurse. Mrs Leake, however, resolutely refused to hand him back until ordered to do so by the Court of Conscience at Vine Street, Piccadilly. The episode might have been of little note, but later events caused Soane to return to it and make the story the centre of an elaborate fiction.[44]

Unlike the charming libertine James Wyatt, the acknowledged master of borrowed hospitality who 'when he liked his house he forgot he had other engagements',[45] Soane tried to head home the moment he had completed his business, particularly at this troubled time for Eliza. A fourth son, Henry, was born on 10 October 1790 but died of whooping cough six months later.

Perhaps, too, the elevated political circle around the Temple and Grenville families had less time for protracted hospitality than the scions of the landed gentry and aristocracy. Humphry Repton heard of the favourable impression that Soane made on their mutual clients, 'of his private character I have heard many incomiums [sic] which make me regret that we have not been more personally acquainted. In the little I have seen of him I was delighted with the animation of his manner.'[46] Soane's professionalism and architectural passion must have been much preferable to the social airs of those highly personable architects who settled in as house guests for the duration.

Soane certainly did not wish to confine himself to the design of country houses. He might be the Prime Minister's own architect, and thus supremely well-positioned for political patronage, but he worked just as conscientiously for clients such as the Bury St Edmunds yarn manufacturer turned banker, James Oakes. Appointed Receiver-General of the Land Tax for West Suffolk in 1787, a firm supporter of king and church, James Oakes was a leading citizen of Bury and a key figure in local affairs.[47] Although he was a landowner, he had no country house, did not pursue country sports (although his son, Orbell Oakes, did) and showed a lively interest in books, the theatre and paintings as well as in new industrial processes and scientific innovation. Soane was at ease with such men, the rock upon which provincial society was built.

Oakes wanted to expand his five-bay, early eighteenth-century town house (which in turn disguised an earlier timber-framed structure) in Guildhall Street in order to turn banker. The East Anglian textile industry was dying, his warehouses and sorting sheds in the yards behind the house fell empty. Oakes, like John Patteson to whose business he supplied yarn, was looking for new opportunities. Always cautious, Oakes gradually moved into brewing and banking, but decided against investing in local canal developments. The remodelling of his house may have been prompted by an inheritance. His mother had died in October 1788.

John Patteson had introduced Oakes to Soane and he called upon the family at breakfast in late November, on his way home from Norfolk. A week later, John Sanders came to draw up the plans. On 25 March 1789, a week after Bury had been convulsed by celebrations for the king's recovery from madness, Soane arrived, again at breakfast time, and spent two days finalising the plans with his client. A month later Oakes called upon Soane while he was in London.

On 31 July Oakes missed the ball at the new Assembly Rooms since 'Mr Soane [is] coming this evening to Bury to superintend my building'. Again, in late August Soane arrived by coach from London and the following day went over to the Reverend Henry Patteson's for dinner; he was the younger brother with whom John Patteson had corresponded from Italy.

The following March Sanders came back to measure the new building, in order to price the works, and plan the next stages of the job, probably the domestic improvements. Meanwhile, on 5 April Oakes noted 'Got into new Banking Rooms'. A week later, a Sunday, Soane arrived at seven in the morning on the mail coach. At three o'clock the next morning he was off in the Yarmouth coach.

Soane's work for Oakes was logical and elegant. Although Guildhall Street was still a mixture of town houses and their extensive gardens and meadows, where house cows and pigs were kept, Soane neatened the elevation and made it unmistakably urban (fig. 71). He extended the street frontage by adding to each side a two-storeyed wing joined to the main house by a narrow link section, with a door, and then attached a high screen wall, articulated by shallow brick pilasters and panels, to each of the adjoining premises.

The new accommodation provided a new banking office to the north, occupying the full depth of the building, with shuttered windows front and back, and above a formal dining-room for official entertainment (generally on market days), reached by a curved stair. The family dining-room was to the south, one end of the room marked by a segmental arch and columns. The town house with its counting rooms, combining the merchant's home and office under a single roof, was a contemporary model to which Soane would often return – more usually in the City of London.

Oakes's bank took some years to become established but it was his Bury and Suffolk Bank which helped to fund the Earl Bishop's extravagant building plans at Ickworth ten years later. Security against the 'considerable advances' that the bank had made was in the form of rents from the extensive Hervey estates in Lincolnshire. If the rents were not promptly paid, it was made clear, the arrangements would be withdrawn. James Oakes went out regularly, sometimes with friends, to see the model of the earl's grandiose scheme and to observe the progress of a house for which he had provided the mortgage.

The house that eventually rose at Ickworth, from 1795 onwards, was drum-shaped and based upon a design by an Italian architect, Mario Asprucci, the son of the curator of the Borghese collections in Rome. The dimensions, if not the detailed form, were close to Tatham's 5 guinea designs from Rome.[48] The Sandys brothers (who had also worked at Ballyscullion) supervised the job with, initially, a great deal of involvement by the client, whose letters rained down from the Continent. Yet the Earl Bishop was never to see the house, dying in Italy in 1803 and bringing construction to a halt. As James Spiller, Soane's surveyor friend wrote to him later after a visit to the still incomplete folly, 'Ickworth! Bears about the same proportion to the Coliseum [sic] as a currant dumpling does to the hunting pudding of the Pytchley Hunt boiled in a sixty gallon brewing copper! Verily the place deserves a better house.'[49]

As Soane tried to keep an equilibrium between his different jobs, site visits and the running of an office as well as his family life, Lord Camelford's warm letters from Rome prompted memories. Camelford wished he should share the city and 'all the glories of this place' with him, but 'a great many things however are gone – the Grand Duke and the King of Naples are removing or rather have removed everything that belonged to them. The Pope is erecting an obelisk at the top of the great staircase at the Trinité de Monte. I have not been here long enough to see his Museum which has been much enriched since I was here.'[50]

For all the goodwill between them, when Soane had not heard from his patron for three months he panicked: 'It appears to me really an age for the flattering hope of your friendship is a certain remedy for every dis-

71. James Oakes's house in Guildhall Street, Bury St Edmunds was adapted to accommodate his new bank alongside the house. Soane provided a uniform street front by adding marching pedimented wings and screen walls, alleviated by shallow blind windows and doors.

72. Boconnoc, the entrance hall at Thomas Pitt's family home in Cornwall. Soane repaired bad workmanship on the old house, altered the interior and extended the house. It is now an empty shell.

appointment of my life, indeed it is my only resource.'[51] Soane's insecurity was chronic. Contact was soon re-established; Camelford had been in Naples in March, moving to Florence. Now he wrote from Venice concerned that a new water-closet have a seat of oak or mahogany 'as it is intended for the ladies' and from Verona he wanted to discuss a thatched milk room. Lady Camelford, to whom Soane usually asked to be remembered, occasionally wrote on her own behalf on detailed matters. It is possible that she provided the very precise specification for the dairy. Sited in the flower garden, it must have 'gravelled walls', green trellis and be buried deep in roses and honeysuckle, Camelford reported, now from Neuchâtel. Almost a year later, from Lyons, he asked that all the best rooms be 'dead white'. The Camelfords were as attentive to such details as if they were on the spot.

Work on Boconnoc had continued throughout the period (Fig. 72); the application of roughcast to the exterior had been a success. Now Soane was considering the chintz room and the portico. He was excited by the possibility of building a mausoleum in the park (which came to nothing, although Camelford encouraged him to visit Lord Lansdowne's at Bowood for comparative purposes). Soane reported that the obelisk was repaired and looked magnificent. Nevertheless Soane continually pleaded for reassurance 'I beg your Lordship will never have any reserve in employing me in whatever I can be of the least use in, as it is the most flattering circumstance of my life to be honoured with your good opinion.'[52]

Working for Thomas Pitt, even given the frustration of conversing long distance on paper, with replies coming too late and queries going unanswered, was infinitely more agreeable than the difficulties of working for Rowley, Fortescue or any of the demanding, thoughtless clients that he was burdened with but dependent upon. On one occasion Camelford wrote to reassure Soane: 'never fear to enter into detail in business. There need be no apology for being circumstantial and writing long letters where the subject is interesting.'[53]

Over the last six years Soane had built up a solid *corps* of architecture and he decided that it was time to publish it. The initiative, and some of the financial commitment, were Soane's. He undertook to purchase a hundred copies from the Taylors, who had also produced *Designs*, which they now took the opportunity of reprinting twice, in 1789 and 1790.[54] For his part, Josiah Taylor 'bookseller' of Holborn proposed Soane at the Society of Arts, where he was elected a fellow on 29 March 1790.

Plans Elevations and Sections of Buildings, published as a folio volume in early 1789, showed a wide range of examples from Soane's country house practice. It had a lofty subscribers' list, including Sir William Chambers, Lord Chancellor Hardwicke and William Pitt and was dedicated to the king. Old friends and steadfast supporters were well represented: Bowdler, Burdon, Camelford, Collyer, Fellowes, Foxhall, Henry Holland (subscribing to two sets), Richard Holland, the future Lord Bridport, Patteson, Peacock, Tyrrell, George Wyatt and several other members of the Yorke family.

With the punishing experiences at Tendring fresh in mind, Soane carefully enunciated in print the responsibilities of the architect and defined the precise role that the professional man, without ambiguity, must play between the client and the builder. That definition was at the heart of his work. The honourable architect should never be tainted by his own financial interests; the developer and the architect should never confuse their roles. As Soane put it, in his classic, much cited definition of the architect's position:

> The business of the architect is to make the designs and estimates, to direct the works, and to measure and value the different parts; he is the intermediate agent between the employer, whose honour and interest he is to study, and the mechanic, whose rights he is to defend. His situation implies great trust; he is responsible for the mistakes, negligences, and ignorances of those he employs; and above all, he is to take care that the workmen's bills do not exceed his own estimates. If these are the duties of an architect, with what propriety can his situation, and that of the builder, or the contractor, be united?

The historical introduction to the volume invokes the names of Vitruvius, Alberti and the great masters of Italian Renaissance art and architecture. Soane then moves on to the practicalities. He nudges the potential client towards gaining his own expertise. 'Let him ... who intends to build take the opinion of his friends, as well as of professional men.' He should also look around him, at similar rooms to those he requires, noting the placing of doors, windows and chimneys for comparative purposes. After the architect has completed the drawings, Soane suggests the client commission a 'plain model ... free from all colouring, which only deceives the eye, and diverts the attention from scrutinizing the component parts.' Meanwhile, the existing house should not be demolished without careful study. Consideration must be given to ornament and thought given to other styles. Finally: 'unite convenience and comfort in the interior distributions, and simplicity and uniformity in the exterior'.

The practical section of the volume bears a close resemblance to the advice offered more amusingly in a little volume of measurements and plans for small villas, *Nutshells* by James Peacock, published three years

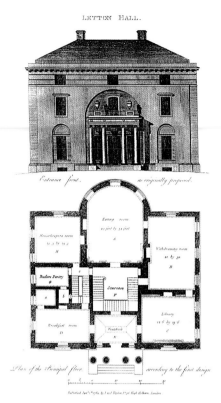

LETTON HALL.

Entrance front. *as originally proposed.*

Plan of the Principal floor. *according to the first design.*

Published Sept.1.1789 by J and J. Taylor N.º 56 High Holborn, London.

73. Letton Hall, Norfolk, as published by Soane in 1788 in *Plans, Elevations etc*. Soane used his folio volume to show future clients his range of work. In many cases he reverted to an ideal scheme or his preferred version, as here, rather than that built.

earlier. With the strictures against speculators, sensible advice on the testing of a design through plain drawings and accurate models, to avoid later mistakes, the setting up of contractual arrangements and control of costs, Peacock's text is the lively godparent of Soane's own introduction.[55]

Soane published the cream of his recent jobs (fig. 73). Of the eighteen illustrated, only three remained unbuilt (though he did not identify them). Of those built, few had taken quite the ideal form in which he published them. The volume was to commemorate the architect's best efforts, in purest form. The modest and dull option that the client might prefer was not for these pages although the sensible text would help to guide him through the unfamiliar process of commissioning a building. *Plans Elevations etc.* was a record of Soane's aspirations, as opposed to a fair copy of his work. The volume, with its eminent list of subscribers, helped to demonstrate his credentials. The timing is significant; the introduction is dated September 1788, just a month before Soane clinched the most important commission of his career.

Far-flung country house jobs were useful for building a reputation but they were not, either professionally or personally, ideal. Soane still hoped for the perfect country house commission, where he could place a mansion in parkland and surround it by the full complement of estate buildings, but his eye was on London and the most significant architectural position in the City of London. With William Pitt behind him and significant numbers of directors already clients, the niceties of selection might not prove too great an obstacle.

Soane claimed that his appointment as architect to the Bank of England following the death of Sir Robert Taylor succeeded a 'severe contest'[56] and in *Designs for Public Improvements* (1828) he claimed that 'my success on this occasion was regarded as a crime by some disappointed persons'. The final decision was made on 16 October 1788 and recorded in the minutes of the Court of Directors as unanimous.[57]

The only surviving record of these deliberations comes in a memorandum book kept by Samuel Bosanquet over a short period when he was a member of the Committee of Treasury.[58] On 30 September, three days after Taylor's death 'the following were offered for his place of architect. Mr. Soane, Holland, Leverton, Wright, Peacock, Reveley, Beazley, Cockrell [sic], Jupp. Afterwards Mr Wyatt, Mr Lewis. Postponed the considn. of their merits.' The meeting soon went on to discuss the likely income from the Walpole family sugar estates in Grenada, the Bank's security against large loans. Horace Walpole was taking a keen interest in the second discussion and must have been caught up in the other matter; he kept a newspaper clipping, published in *Anecdotes*, which listed nine contenders but not the names of Soane or Lewis. The order in which Bosanquet gave the eleven names is significant. Soane claimed that there were thirteen.

Many of the names on the list of architects for the job at the Bank were non-starters or unproven. Nathaniel Wright was more builder than architect, but with useful links in the City of London, while the much older Jupp was already Surveyor to the East India Company. Of the more serious candidates, Cockerell and Beazley had had the advantage of working in Taylor's office and young Charles Beazley (uncle of the better known architect-dramatist Samuel Beazley) was appointed steward of the Bank's estates, suggesting that he was valued but not considered quite the man for the major job. Samuel Pepys Cockerell, on the other hand, Soane's exact contemporary, may well have felt confident in his chances. On Taylor's death he assumed his posts as Surveyor of the Foundling and Pulteney estates but failed to obtain his more desirable positions. However, his pupil, Benjamin Latrobe, who left England for Virginia in 1795, had a remarkably close knowledge of Soane's early work at the Bank, suggesting that the Cockerell office and circle had looked hard at the new buildings. Eventually Cockerell's son, Charles Robert, succeeded Soane – though his father did not live to see him do so.

If Soane had planned from early days to achieve this job, he had been masterly in his strategy. Sir Richard Neave, son of his earliest Walthamstow client, was Deputy Governor of the Bank in 1781–2 and Governor in 1783–4 and remained a senior Director, while Samuel Bosanquet, by now both client and friend, became Deputy Governor in April 1789 and Governor two years later. On receiving a substantial legacy on his brother Claude's death in 1786, Bosanquet had bought Dingestow Court in Monmouthshire and simultaneously embarked on a substantial programme of works to dress up his seventeenth-century Essex property, Forest House, Walthamstow, in contemporary fashion. He had turned to Soane, whom he also asked to design his brother's monument at St Stephen's Coleman Street in the City of London. Later Soane redesigned the family grave in Leyton.[59]

Among the other members of the Court of Directors of the Bank of England in 1788, were William Cooke, Soane's friend and client from Walthamstow and Peter Gaussen, Bosanquet's brother-in-law. Beeston Long was Richard Neave's son-in-law and the brother of Charles Long, the rising Treasury star and close friend of Pitt and, later, the artistic adviser to the Prince Regent. Had the Prime Ministerial patronage been insufficient for the purpose, Soane had built up an effective reserve team in the Walthamstow and Leyton circle.

Through George Dance, who had worked closely with Sir Robert Taylor (they drafted the London Building Act in 1774), Soane had learned how his predecessor had established his network of contacts at the Bank and secured the job. It was a useful lesson. Dance himself may even have had a hand in Soane's appointment.

Camelford quickly wrote to Soane that he had heard of his success at the Bank 'from those who had contributed to it', suggesting that William Pitt's patronage had been decisive. Countering Soane's complaint that he had failed in his endeavours to get Taylor's other job, the Greenwich Hospital surveyorship, to which John Yenn, Chambers's man, had been appointed, Camelford commented tartly, 'Poor Revely [sic] would be glad to find himself in your situation'.[60] Soane had, perhaps, hoped that Alexander Hood, the treasurer at Greenwich since 1766, might smooth his path to that plum government job too.

C. R. Cockerell's unpublished architectural history of the Bank,[61] written when he was seventy in 1858, included memories of Taylor from his father, S. P. Cockerell. Taylor apparently was in the habit of visiting the construction site before the men arrived at work; finding anything unsatisfactory, he would 'push it down, and so leave it for them to reconstruct. They, observing this, and knowing who had done it, place [sic] some boards to act as a trap which should occasion him a fall'. Such retaliatory japes would not be countenanced under the new regime.

The first instruction that Soane received from the minutes of the building committee[62] was to convert the Old Pay Office into space for safe custody of the Transfer Office books. He had also conveyed his concern about the dome of the Discount Office and was instructed to lay a new slate roof. On 9 April, Soane's first half-year commission amounted to £117 11s 6d – a modest beginning to a job that would earn him many thousands of pounds.

Soane was directed to carry out his plan for lighting the Bank on public Thanksgiving Day, St George's Day – 23 April 1789 – when a service of celebration for King George III's recovery was to be held at St Paul's Cathedral. The authorities, poised to appoint a regency in the face of the king's illness which had unhinged his mind since the previous November, were relieved at the monarch's apparent return to health. The public shared that relief. The vulnerability of the monarchy and its pathetic, strait-jacketed king, had transformed public perception of a man who had been, just a few years before, vilified for the country's disastrous engagement in the American wars. Ironically enough, George III, with the young William Pitt as his first minister, would before long represent stability and reassurance amidst confusion and the menace of war.[63]

A huge London-wide celebration took place, requiring all public buildings to be illuminated with blazing crowns, 'GR' and 'God Save the King'. Houses without a display of candles in their windows ran the risk of being stoned. Soane quickly organised the illumination of the Bank of England, employing William Hamilton RA to design the transparencies (fig. 74). The artist took to his task with enthusiasm, depicting 'fame supporting the medallion of the King and immortality inscribing his name' and the 'Genius of Britain seated in her Triumphal car preceded by the City of London with her attendants, commerce and liberality'. It was the first of many such national festivities which Soane would be called upon to mark at the Bank.

Soane quickly embarked on a thorough structural survey which would lead to exterior and interior redecorations, repairs to stonework and iron, alterations to skylights and the siting of urinals in the lobby to the Stock Office. His report smacks of a building which had been inadequately cared for. On 18 June 1789, the building committee requested a clerk of works, 'a proper person to attend constantly at the Bank'.[64] Walter Payne, the man chosen, received £38 payment to cover the period 29 September to 25 March 1790: he was still clerk of works when Soane retired in 1833. Payne oversaw a team of artisans, some of whom would work at the Bank over the entire period that Soane and Payne remained there.

Soane's immediate clients were the members of the building committee. In 1789 this consisted of the governor (Weyland) and his Deputy (Bosanquet), with Payne, Beachcroft, Booth, Ewer, Neave and Peters – the same composition as for the previous year with the exception of Gaussen, who had died. The next year the committee retained the same membership, with the addition of Godfrey Thornton (for whom Soane started a major commission at Mogerhanger in Bedfordshire the following year).[65] In 1791 the treasury and building committees combined into one, to see through the heavy programme of property acquisition, prepared for in three separate Acts of Parliament, in order to expand the site. For the next

74. William Hamilton's sketches for transparencies, used when the Bank of England was illuminated on Thanksgiving Day in 1789.

twenty years, the architectural development of the Bank of England was Soane's main concern. It was the work he was known by, criticised and, less frequently, praised for and which gave him his standing and contentious position among his contemporaries and rivals.

The Bank of England was much visited and in 1782 a *vade mecum* was published, 'useful for all persons who have any money matters to transact in the Hall of the Bank etc., particularly to those who are not practiced in that business'.[66] Assisted by a plan of the Hall, members of the public (those for example wanting to convert 'common bank notes' into cash) were conducted from the cashiers' desks to the tellers' counters, in the appropriate sequence depending on their requirements, or to the accountants' office, to the dividend and transfer offices. Stock-brokers gathered in the Rotonda between 11 a.m. and 1 p.m. With this volume in hand, the reader has no need to ask for directions. The balance between accessibility and security – particularly following the Gordon Riots of 1780 – became a testing architectural conundrum.

In the early eighteenth century, the Bank, together with the East India and South Sea companies, was seen as the pre-eminent symbol of the seeping of power away from the landed interest. Through the National Debt, the Bank was seen to pose a threat to the traditional institutions. The solid assets of land and manufacture were menaced by the spectres of wide public credit, speculation and stock dealing.

Sampson's original Palladian building of 1731–4 symbolised in its classical, harmonious form, solid moral decorum (fig. 75).[67] Any hint of the Baroque (seen as capricious) would have undermined the strongly nationalistic (and anti-Catholic) statement. Sampson carefully divided the public aspects of the Bank's business from the private – as if to ensure that corruption could not take place.

With the end of the Seven Years' War in 1763 the National Debt became a secure investment. The major securities, Reduced Annuities and Consols (Consolidated Annuities Fund) were now managed by the

75. Engraving after Thomas Hosmer Shepherd's watercolour of the Bank of England on Threadneedle Street showing George Sampson's centre block built in the 1730s, flanked by Sir Robert Taylor's later wings. Both were demolished by Soane in the later phases of his remodelling of the site. The elder Dance's Mansion House can be seen on the left.

Bank on a fee basis. The Bank Directors worked at arms' length from the funds and the risk of corruption was lessened. Enlarged premises were required for their administration, both in taking in subscriptions and paying out dividends to the public.

In 1764, its Charter renewed by Parliament, the Bank was newly confident as a valued institution. It set about acquiring land and appointed a new architect, Robert Taylor. A late-comer to architecture from sculpture, he was fifty when he was appointed. He had no experience in the design of major public buildings but had an unrivalled grip upon the nexus of City contacts and understood their arcane ways. He had worked with George Dance sen. on the replacement London Bridge and his builder father (in 1733 the Master of the London Masons' Company) had worked on Dance's Mansion House. The two sons had drafted the London Building Act. More importantly, Taylor's clients over the previous twenty years had tended to come from the newly wealthy City classes and he was now rewarded with 'the principal architectural post in their gift'.[68] He was, in many respects, the ideal role model for Soane who had observed him, initially from the vantage point of Dance's office, as he picked off the plum jobs over the years: in succession, Architect to the Bank of England, joint Architect at the Office of Works and, in the very year of his death, Surveyor to Greenwich Hospital.

Taylor's East Wing and Bank Buildings, of the late 1760s, were followed by expansion west, providing premises for the Directors, private offices including the Court Room and the Committee Room. Taylor generally worked in a light neoclassical style although he used decisively Roman elements when necessary, for example when lighting the Reduced Annuities Office buried deep on the Bank site. A man of Continental interests and taste, he left his library to endow Oxford University's Taylor Institute for Modern European Languages. The Rotunda, which functioned as the Brokers' Exchange, was Taylor's major architectural statement. After the Gordon Riots, in which the Bank repulsed a number of waves of attack – while Newgate Gaol fell – Taylor was instructed to build a new west wing, to stand on the site of St Christopher le Stocks, which was summarily demolished despite strong protest from the Bishop of London and the parishioners.

Business at the Bank hinged on continual overseas hostilities, in the late 1770s those of the American War, but there was a sclerotic tendency. Many directors had been at the Bank for decades, many of the clerks were equally elderly. Taylor himself was approaching eighty. The Bank was battening down the hatches in the 1780s against the hostility of its immediate neighbours, the penalties of a lost war and the attrition of a poor financial climate.

The Bank directors were merchants, socially distinct from the landed classes, many of them with wide business interests. If by 1781 Lord North was able to refer to the Bank of England as 'a part of the constitution', it was also a private enterprise intent on profit and firmly anchored in London.[69] The next twenty years saw a revolution and by the end of the century the Bank was, as Sir Francis Baring said, 'the centre upon which all credit and circulation depended'. Gradually other banks ceased to issue notes and took to receiving their customers' deposits, while the Bank of England was the government banker, the store for the nation's gold and

76. Aquatint by J. W. Edy showing the Albion Mills on fire in 1791, five years after the corn mills, with their Boulton and Watt machinery, had opened. Built by the architect Samuel Wyatt. Although Eliza Soane's uncle, George (no relation) Wyatt, owned property in Albion Place, directly opposite and visible in this view, it appears he was never a proprietor.

the body which issued and honoured paper banknotes. The credit-worthiness of individuals and commercial enterprises, whose bills of exchange were accepted here, was largely determined within these walls.

In a brilliant strategy, easily argued as England teetered towards war and underwent huge domestic economic convulsions, Soane persuaded the Bank directors of their continual need for physical expansion to accommodate the Bank's altering and pivotal role. Starting with essential additions, the barracks for the Bank's own guard and premises for engraving and printing bank notes, approved by the Court of Directors in 1790,[70] Soane inched their plans for development forward – almost without them noticing. The moment had arrived for an architectural statement of his own. After five years in his post, Soane had won the right to create his own great public building. It would, incidentally, be a monument to his very particular genius.

Soane, for whom financial security was symbolic of so much else, became a rich man in his own right upon the death of George Wyatt in February 1790. The Soanes received both money and property,[71] the latter in Mrs Soane's birthplace, Cow Cross Street, and at Albion Place just over Blackfriars Bridge. It was in Albion Place, opposite the Albion Mills, recently built by Samuel Wyatt, that Soane set up a new office while he wound up Wyatt's estate and, simultaneously, expanded his own practice.[72]

The following year the terrace and Soane's office must have suffered enormous damage from the terrible fire which engulfed the mills on 2 March 1791, and burned on for three days, an effect intensified by its reflection in the waters of the Thames (fig. 76). A few days before the fire Humphry Repton had visited the mills and Samuel Wyatt had shown him an enormous fire engine and a 'tube' which Wyatt told him would pump up a vast column of water should there be a fire.[73] As one of the nearest buildings to the site, Albion Place must have lost its windows and been heavily charred and damaged by embers and other flying fragments of burning matter. One suspected cause of the fire was arson, given the threat the steam-powered mill posed to traditional millers, but John Rennie, the engineer who had assumed responsibility for the operation since late 1784, informed Boulton and Watt that the cause had been an overheated bearing on an upper floor. To make the mill profitable it had been over-worked and under-maintained, with disastrous effects. If George Wyatt had invested in the mills it would have earned him nothing.[74] His fortune had been built on more certain foundations than this brilliant but ill-conceived experiment.

6

LINCOLN'S INN FIELDS

Now independently wealthy, thanks to George Wyatt's legacy, Soane decided to make a domestic architectural statement of his own. He bought a freehold in Lincoln's Inn Fields (fig. 77), at the very heart of late eighteenth-century London.

Number 12 Lincoln's Inn Fields was to be a home for Soane's family, his wife and two sons, but also a show-case for his abilities; after all an architect's house is potentially his trade card. William Chambers built 13 Berners Street (with two adjacent houses for sale) in 1765 and much more recently, on his Hans Town development, Henry Holland had built himself Sloane Place, to include his office (to which, of course, his clients came) as well as the accommodation suitable to a family of considerable fortune.

Soane had chosen his location with care (fig. 78). A short walk from Somerset House, where the Royal Academy, the Royal Society and the Society of Antiquaries were all now installed, convenient for the Strand and its array of shops; not far from Paternoster Row and St Paul's Churchyard where the booksellers and publishers were concentrated, it was also equidistant between the City and Westminster, between commerce and government. An easy fifteen minute walk, past Newgate Prison and St Paul's Cathedral, took Soane to his office at the Bank of England. Equally, he could stride the distance to Great Scotland Yard, where in April 1791, the month of the Albion Mills fire, Soane had moved to accommodation provided by the Office of Works where he had been appointed a clerk of works the previous October.

To pursue wider professional concerns he could easily reach the coffee houses and inns where his peers met, in the many loosely constituted dining clubs which cemented the world of the arts and the professions before the foundation of their separate institutions. The Thatched House Tavern, the Globe Tavern and the recently built Freemason's Arms [1] were favourites.

Lincoln's Inn Fields, laid out in the late seventeenth century and for a time made disreputable as a haunt of prostitutes, was by the late eighteenth century a good address. In 1790 George Dance had moved to Upper Gower Street from Salisbury Street, off the Strand, an address unfashionably north, while Henry Holland's villa was well west of the focal points of London's social and intellectual life. Soane, by contrast, was ideally situated in the heart of the city.

77. The eastern end of Lincoln's Inn Fields seen from the top of Soane's house, drawn by one of Soane's pupils in 1813.

For Eliza Soane, whose voice is frequently heard in major family decisions and financial transactions, it was also a good location and may well have been as much her choice as her husband's. On 30 June 1792 Soane bought the freehold for £2,100 – a considerable sum, reflecting the increasing desirability of the area. Lord Mansfield, the Duke of Newcastle and other members of the nobility owned houses overlooking the Fields and Soane's neighbours included a number of leading doctors and lawyers.

Demolition of the seventeenth-century house was followed immediately by the construction of the new one. By August Soane was overseeing the installation of the copper and oven in the basement. In April 1793 he was spending long periods hanging up his newly acquired antique cast collection in the passage, the first items of his nascent museum. By May he was setting out the mirror glass in the drawing-room and by August 1793 he was indulging his favourite pastime, arranging and cataloguing books in his library.[2] From now on, the Soanes would frequent the auction houses and salerooms.

Friends rallied round. Edward Foxhall helped him find mirrors as well as many other items and Richard Holland's firm acted as bricklayers. The

78. Wallis's 1799 map of the City of London and Westminster, showing Lincoln's Inn Fields, almost equidistant between the City and Whitehall, an ideal central London location. Lincoln's Inn Fields are just west of the City boundary.

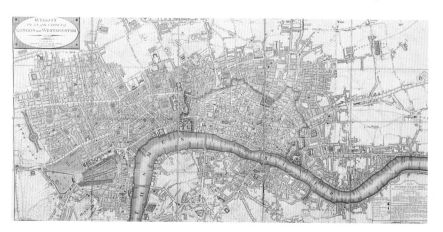

other artisans were his usual team. Soane understood that a tried and tested craftsman-builder was the secret of success, both in terms of the quality of the work and in keeping costs in check. As his own client on this occasion he was working in his best interests.

The impression given by Soane's notebooks over the period is that every spare moment from the remorseless round of meetings, site inspections and travelling was spent immersed in the new house. For a forty-year-old architect who had spent his career designing houses for others, it must have been a heady experience to be involved in a project on his own behalf. Nevertheless, the new house at Lincoln's Inn Fields was an expensive venture, some of his clients were slow payers and Soane's heavy load of major commissions required him to expand his office. Edward Foxhall and Richard Holland often provided short-term loans – as he often did to them during these busy years.[3]

A plan of the house into which Soane moved on 18 January 1794 shows a conventional enough arrangement for a late eighteenth century (fig. 79) London terraced house. In the basement a front and back kitchen, on the ground floor the breakfast room opening off the dining-room, and above that the drawing-rooms and bedrooms, with garret rooms in the attics. The stairs rose out of a long, full-depth hall. The slanting east party wall was a quirk which was to serve Soane's eventual scheme of extensions to the rear extremely well. The former stable area provided the space for Soane's drawing offices. It enabled him to move his practice back from Great Scotland Yard. The pupils entered from the separate, rear, door off

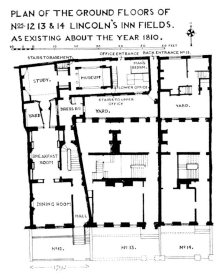

PLAN OF THE GROUND FLOORS OF Nos. 12 13 & 14 LINCOLN'S INN FIELDS. AS EXISTING ABOUT THE YEAR 1810.

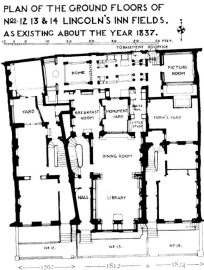

PLAN OF THE GROUND FLOORS OF Nos. 12 13 & 14 LINCOLN'S INN FIELDS. AS EXISTING ABOUT THE YEAR 1837.

79. (top) a ground floor plan of Soane's rebuilt 12 Lincoln's Inn Fields shown *c.* 1810, following the conventions of the late Georgian terraced house, but now spilling into the stableyard of No. 13; (bottom) ground floor plans of the three houses, *c.* 1837, showing the areas by then incorporated into the museum.

80. The Breakfast Room at 12 Lincoln's Inn Fields, the architect's miniaturised family under the trellising and open skies of the painted ceiling as depicted by Joseph Gandy, one of his first commissions for Soane.

Whetstone Park, the oddly named lane to the rear. Soane's house expressed the social hierarchies as clearly as any great London mansion.

Soane had built up a sizeable office by now; he had between four and six articled pupils, a paid assistant, the services of a surveyor and, for major jobs, a clerk of works on site. Given Soane's concern that his pupils should learn every aspect of architectural practice, he was actively collecting casts and fragments, and expanding his library, in order that the young men could measure and draw from the antique, learning the language of the classical Orders alongside the daily business of the office.[4]

The plan of the new house may have been conventional, but the decoration was not. Recent investigations have shown that the hall and stairs were painted stone colour, darkened with a grey glaze perhaps to give the impression of antique stucco rather than the more usual imitation masonry. The dining-room, on the ground floor at the front of the house, was a rich Pompeian red, varnished to produce the almost lacquered finish of some Pompeian interiors. The archaeological references would not have been lost on those chosen clients who came to the house. Their journey from the comparatively dark hall and stairway and dining-room into the sparklingly fresh decorative schemes of the breakfast room/library beyond was a typical Soane touch and an example of what they might expect from him.[5]

The vaulted, groined ceiling of the breakfast room was light and charmingly ornamented with a diaphanous, leafy trellis painted by John Crace, the decorative painting specialist whose family firm would work at Brighton Pavilion and prospered in the nineteenth century.[6] Interior landscapes were fashionable and at Norbury Park, the Surrey house of the connoisseur William Lock, an entire room had been painted to simulate the scene beyond the windows.[7] Soane's room could offer no parkland view but compensated with a small forest of potted plants, disposed on the roofs and around the lights to the drawing office below.

In *Nutshells* Peacock had recommended that such ceilings should take on 'the light, cool and delicately softened azure of the sky, diversified with such meliorated tints only, as the fleecy clouds produce when illuminated by the morning sun'. On one plan, from August 1792, Soane noted that the first-floor drawing-room ceiling be 'painted light blue sky, rays in the centre and a lustre'.[9]

The breakfast room (fig. 80) of sky and dappled foliage was a touch of *rus in urbe* and lightened a rather confined north-facing room, as did the mirror glass which helped dissolve the solid walls of the cube. Some years later, Joseph Gandy painted the family there; Mrs Soane and her husband sit at the breakfast table, on the carpet a diminutive John and George are playing. All the family has been curiously miniaturised as if they are tiny marionnettes within an elaborate doll house. The walls are covered by bookcases; Gandy shows a bibliophile's sanctum doubling as a family room.

Mrs Soane, apparently happy enough in Gandy's painting, was in reality very concerned about her small sons. The sheer unpleasantness of the London climate and conditions during much of the year, the fog, soot, coal smoke and blackened brickwork which struck out of town visitors so forcibly, threw the emphasis of life back indoors. In a letter to a Chertsey friend, Miss Smith (no relation), in early 1797 she confessed to being worried 'beyond bearing', a prisoner in the house in order to keep her sons

84. With the bath house at Wimpole, Soane reverted to an antique model. Water came from a (lost) reservoir or *castello d'acqua* which Soane built in the park. The tiny room with its paired round-headed doorways and stairs, discreetly top-lit, is one of his gems.

85. At Wimpole Soane's commission ranged widely to take in a farmyard, cottages and many other estate buildings. In 1793 he designed a range of hothouses, warmed by flues in the garden walls, so that the Hardwickes could enjoy pineapples, grapes and peaches on their dinner table.

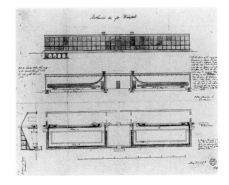

economies. Although Soane returned to work at Wimpole later, after the Earl of Hardwicke's return from Ireland, where he became the first Viceroy after the Union in 1801, the commission never gave Soane quite the intense personal satisfaction of two other contemporary jobs, an important town house which would lead to the most comprehensive country house scheme of his career.

The Marquis of Buckingham despite his tricky personality and 'proneness to take offence'[29] which meant that he did not long hold high political office, and watched his younger brother William rapidly overtake him, was a man of great influence and extensive connections. George Nugent-Temple-Grenville had became Earl Temple in 1779 and the first Marquis of Buckingham in 1784. His country house was Stowe in Buckinghamshire and the county his fiefdom.

His inheritance from his uncle, Richard Grenville, included a town-house, 91 Pall Mall, and a few years later he bought the adjoining house. Robert Brettingham, Soane's friend who had recently returned from Italy,

86. Soane had few opportunities to design London town houses, although he altered dozens. Buckingham House, begun for the Marquis of Buckingham in 1790, was a job of which Soane was particularly proud. The elliptical, top lit stairwell dominates the centre of the house and is ornamented to reflect its importance.

undertook some alterations in 1785–6.[30] Before long, the Marquis decided to transform the pair of houses into a mansion and turned to Soane – presumably introduced by Lord Camelford. In March 1790 he began the remodelling. Buckingham House took several years to build and cost £11,000.[31] It was, Soane remembered in his *Memoirs*, an entirely harmonious commission. Since no departures were made from the original designs and he had been allowed to carry his architectural intentions out fully, the estimates were completely accurate. It was to be Soane's only major town house and, with the work at the Bank, signified his arrival as an important architect in the capital. It too was demolished early in the twentieth century – for the Royal Automobile Club. In the Victorian period it joined the list of government departments designed by Soane, being used as the War Office.

As at Letton and Tendring, the house was dominated at its core by an oval, top-lit vestibule centred upon a stair which split to arrive at a first floor landing (fig. 86). There, the oval space was marked by a girdle of Ionic columns and, above them, caryatids supporting the elliptical ceiling and lantern. Soane was systematically developing a theme, the top-lit tribune, which would reach its apogee in his National Debt Redemption Office decades later.

In August 1792, the Marquis of Buckingham took Soane to visit William Praed[32] at Tyringham in Buckinghamshire. By now Lord Camelford had drawn Soane into an impressive political spider's web, centred on the two great Buckinghamshire estates of Stowe and Wotton – brought together when the Temple and Grenville[33] families intermarried in the early eighteenth century. Praed, a banker, had business interests and political ambitions – both of which involved the Marquis.

As Soane began to mull over the possibilities at Tyringham, Camelford was embarking on a last desperate journey to regain health. He had been in England in the summer of 1792 to see his daughter Anne, nineteen years old, finally married to her thirty-year-old cousin William, now Lord, Grenville.[34] Well-contented with the match, which brought two distant branches of the family together and proved to be a particularly happy marriage, he quickly returned to Italy, dying in Florence in January. His death was a deep personal loss to Soane, who had regarded him both as a father figure and an equal in architectural matters. He was profoundly indebted to him, for patronage, good counsel and for intellectual company. No one would take his place.

William Praed was a Pittite banker MP with interests in Truro and Falmouth,[35] who sat for St Ives until 1806, when he sold his property there. In 1796 he would try to obtain the parliamentary seat for Buckinghamshire but despite his personal friendship with the Marquis of Buckingham, he underestimated the grip that the family held in the area. Richard, Earl Temple, the Marquis's elder son, and later the first Duke of Buckingham and Chandos, held the seat from 1797 until 1813. Later, the family helped Praed take a seat for Banbury.

Praed was the moving force behind the new Grand Junction Canal, linked into the existing Oxford Canal at Braunston, making a direct route between the Midlands and London. He had been the promoter of the 1790 Grand Junction Canal Bill and became chairman of the Grand Junction Canal Company (fig. 87), which was founded in 1793 with a capital of

£600,000. The canal, over 93 miles long, and extended by a number of branches, was Praed's life passion. The board of the company united the Marquis of Buckingham, whose arms appeared on the company seal and the Earl of Essex and Earl Spencer (both of the latter owning property through which the canal would pass). In later years the board adjusted its membership to include more MPs, to ensure its continued political influence. Praed's obsession led to his parliamentary colleagues teasing him for having water on the brain.[36] In 1808 Praed chaired the preliminary meeting, studying surveys for the Grand Union Canal which would link the Grand Junction Canal to the Trent. Praed's ambitions were, for Soane, invaluable.

Tyringham was the Backwell family estate, centred upon an Elizabethan manor house, inherited by Praed's wife Elizabeth. For Soane this scheme consumed six of the happiest years of his working life – in his phrase. Things might have turned out very differently if Sir William Chambers's second daughter, Selina, had married Elizabeth's brother Tyringham Backwell twenty years before, for Chambers would have then been the obvious architect for a new house. In fact the engagement had ended abruptly and rancorously within two months of its announcement.[37]

In the early months of his commission, Soane made numerous site visits to discuss options with Praed, on occasion with John Haverfield, the gardener for the Richmond Pleasure Gardens at Kew, son of the vicar there and probably an introduction from Timothy Tyrrell, whose friend and neighbour he was on Kew Green. Soane enjoyed working with Haverfield and trusted his judgement. By introducing Haverfield to a number of his clients, he gained him patronage over the head of the assiduous Humphry Repton.

After seeing the final designs for the remodelling of the old house, Praed changed his mind – no doubt under Soane's persuasive powers – and in June 1793 he 'settled to have a new house.'[38] Obviously Soane wanted to give his client a full range of options and among the classical variants he dropped in a feeble gothic version.

On the evidence, William Praed was the epitome of the good client. At just this time, involved in an arbitration between an architect (S. P. Cockerell) and his client, Soane described the relationship between the architect and his employer; 'there ought and must be one common interest between both and fullest satisfaction and confidence in each other is requisite or the building cannot be conducted either pleasantly or properly'.[39] Praed and Soane struck a perfect balance.

For Soane this was the ideal commission; the sweep of the ground allowed for a substantial house set off by the slow curve of the river Ouse. The drive, off the main coaching route from Newport Pagnell, gave an opportunity for a gateway, with entrance lodges, leading on to a bridge positioned at an oblique angle over the Ouse. From there, the new house, on a slight rise, would come into view (the old house was well to the right of the drive, the church, ruinous, still further right). Nothing that Soane had been asked to do in his country house practice had offered a comparable chance to assemble the full estate complement of house, offices, stables, lodges and designed parkland.

The gatehouses, seamlessly linked by an archway in sternly Greek Doric, form a screen, framing the prospect of the house (fig. 88). Many

87. Through the Marquis of Buckingham Soane met William Praed, a banker and ardent promoter of the Grand Junction canal. In the summer of 1793 Soane designed a certificate, probably for those buying shares in the new company.

88. The entrance arch to Tyringham, with lodges to either side. Soane has reduced the classical ornament to an absolute minimum, giving the stonework a massive, elemental feel.

great houses had gateways marking an entry but without confining the vista or contributing to an architectural progression. At Tyringham, the gateway is massively solid in its construction, with hardly a mortar joint between each great block of stone and a bare minimum of ornament. It almost entirely masks what lies beyond, tempting and inveigling the eye onwards through the aperture and the landscape towards the house; it is a dark mass introducing the brightly lit park beyond, the frame to the picturesque scene. The staged approach through the park was a preparation for another sequence, this time within the house itself – again a dramatic, dark introduction to a space flooded by light.

The progression along the winding drive, over the angled bridge – offering its own subtle frame to the view ahead (fig. 89)[40] – lingering along the edge of the park and finally punctuated by the swelling exedra of the front elevation of the house, is taken at an appropriate, leisurely pace. The bridge itself owed a great deal to Haverfield; a letter from Soane to Praed refers to his wish to 'keep the bridge as low as possible (certainly better in point of general appearance) . . . I became a convert to the alteration'.[41] Built of Weldon stone, it was nearly complete by February 1794. It is rare to find Soane deferring to another designer but he respected the professional experience of his landscape gardener colleague and frequently turned to Haverfield for assistance in the siting and layout of buildings within the landscape, the planning of parkland settings, the use of water and trees and technical assistance in the fitting out and design of glasshouses.

On arrival at the house, the visitor was immediately drawn in through a dark entrance hall, a low heavily vaulted space with Doric columns in each corner (perhaps a memory of Moreau-Desproux's Parisian theatre), towards a vividly lit space beyond – the central tribune (fig. 90). The glazing was coloured, giving a constant glow to the core of the house. Soane's interior at Tyringham, lost in the major remodelling early this century, was organised entirely around this double-height, top-lit hall. Relatively subservient to these set pieces, the principal stairs were off-centre, while

89. Soane's bridge at Tyringham, leading to the house, seen in the middle distance. The dome is a later addition.

the drawing-room, facing the gardens, had a characteristic flattened bow-front – a motif which Soane used so often to catch the light and to give his interiors their characteristic sense of movement. There were, as usual, backward looks as well as glimpses of future work. In a note on the ornamental work to be carried out by the painter, John Crace, Soane wanted the central door of the tribune at Tyringham to be similar to that for 'Mr Dillingham's library at Letton'[42] – a commission of more than ten years earlier and Soane's first new built country house. Soane was always repolishing his gems.

The calculatedly theatrical device, of moving from dark into radiant, often coloured, light is one of Soane's favourite effects, recurring again and again in those commissions where he had been allowed his head. Years later, in one of the Royal Academy lectures, he would state that the object of architecture was to 'keep the imagination awake'. The sequences, exterior and interior, at Tyringham – an exciting, unfolding sequence of space and heightened experience – offered intimations of a romantic pulse beginning to beat in the heart of Soane's architecture.[43]

Realising that he had achieved a masterpiece, in June 1796 Soane proudly took George Dance out to see his work at Tyringham. Six years later, evidence of the amiable give and take between master and pupil, Dance asked Soane to show him the plan of Tyringham as a great favour since 'I want to steal from it'.[44]

Although Soane was able to further his exploration of architectural effects at Tyringham, he also bore in mind all the needs of the family and their large estate. As he planned, and replanned, the interiors of the house, he tucked the nurseries in neatly at mezzanine level, found space for a billiard room, and then produced a series of meticulous plans showing the whereabouts of drains, chimney flues and the other impedimenta of a large house. He introduced a steam-driven system of central heating. In the service courtyard, he sited Praed's office next to that of his steward and equipped it with ranges of sliding shelves and plenty of storage space. John Haverfield, the specialist, signed the drawings for the peach houses and a special stove for the vines.[45]

Unusually, we know a good deal about the organisation of the job at Tyringham from the correspondence Soane kept. He asked Praed to let him know 'if at any time the conduct of any of the workmen is not as it should be' but was also solicitous about them and their arrangements. He wrote to William Richards, his clerk of works, suggesting he stay in the millhouse, a farmhouse or even one of the lodges. Staying in the house was not an option. He would speak to Praed on his behalf but asked him to delay sending for his wife until these matters were settled. Joseph Parkins was working as a joiner under Richards but should he return to London then he could 'be in a position of trust as clerk of works'. Soane continued, much as he had to Robert Woodgate earlier, 'I wish to see you advanced in the world believing you to be deserving of encouragement . . . I wish you to do what you like. I shall be equally satisfied being . . . your real well-wisher.'[46] These exchanges show Soane at his best: equally thoughtful about his employees' comfort and advancement as about his client's convenience. He was also scrupulous about meeting his tradesmen's bills – 'no man makes a second application to me for any money he is justly entitled to' – but should he find evidence of shoddy workmanship, drinking on the job or any other failure, he was unswerving.

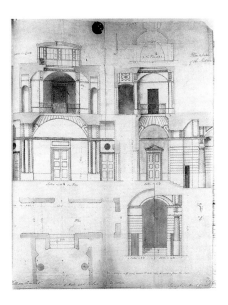

90. Sections through the tribune, or central hall, for Tyringham, William Praed's Buckinghamshire country house, dated March 1795.

As usual, when within reasonably easy reach of London, Soane used a well-tried team. Among the names in the accounts appear those of Richard Holland (responsible for carpentry and joinery), James Nelson (one of his regular masons, whose bill came to over £4,500), Daniel Mitchell (the glazier from Bentley Priory), Lancelot Burton (the plumber), Palmer, the plasterer, even his old friend the carver Henry Wood and a man who would become a close colleague, the surveyor James Spiller. Several had worked on his own house at Lincoln's Inn Fields.

The design process for Tyringham, a 'structure . . . completed in all its parts without any deviation whatever from the original plans', as Soane recalled, illustrates the way in which he worked up a major scheme. The drawings range from Soane's own fluent thick-nibbed ink sketches, which were then elaborated by the pupils into formal elevations or perspectives, to the bundles of plans, sections, details of construction and ornament, which were continually travelling between London and Newport Pagnell, where Richards would collect them from the Swan Inn. In the case of any uncertainties, the clerk of works drew the detail and asked Soane for his advice.[47] With a team of tradesmen already familiar with his working practice and detailing, Soane could keep a tight control over his estimates and the final costs.

On completion of the house, bridge and gatehouses at Tyringham, Joseph Gandy, who had joined Soane's office in 1798 on his return from Rome, was set to work to capture the result – the aspiration as much as the reality (fig. 91). His perspectives, watercolours fully worked up from earlier sketches, added picturesque flourishes to the setting (such as smoking chimneys at the lodge) and emphasised the dramatic transitions within the house, from darkened hall to brilliant centre. He applied his own idiosyncratic rules of perspective, bringing into view elements of the landscape that are, in reality, widely separated. Gandy's flourishes, as always, lent Soane's work another dimension. These perspectives were for posterity, for the walls of the Royal Academy and for Soane's reputation. For office purposes, often years later, drawings on a reduced scale were produced to form a visual record of the office output and Tyringham, the schemes proposed and the work as built, took its place among the eighteen folios that represent Soane's life's work.

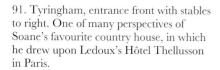

91. Tyringham, entrance front with stables to right. One of many perspectives of Soane's favourite country house, in which he drew upon Ledoux's Hôtel Thellusson in Paris.

Soane was continually on the move and Eliza found the hot summer weeks at Lincoln's Inn Fields depressing. As they grew up and needed more space, the boys spent their summers at Chertsey with Soane's family and friends but she loyally remained behind to act as Soane's hostess when needed, a stable presence amidst his preoccupations and absences. That summer she was particularly low and entreated their friend Mrs Smith in Chertsey to allow her daughter Sarah (Sally), to join the family for the summer holidays in Margate. She promised to take as much care of her as either of her own children and to take her up and down in the family carriage.[48]

Miss Smith, who must have been in her late teens, was to bring the boys back up to London; Eliza implored her to take care they did not lean against the chaise door, 'I have a great dread of the doors flying open . . . excuse the fears of a fond Mother!' In Margate Eliza was expecting her mother-in-law 'the Old Lady', as well as Mrs Flaxman and Mrs Spiller. 'Please bring my hat as I intend to shine in it at the Rooms.'[49] Away from home and the pressures of Soane's business and the obligation to appear in society on his arm, Eliza's youth and spirits easily returned.

Back at Lincoln's Inn Fields she betrayed her state of mind, writing to Sarah Smith in Chertsey who was having trouble with a young man, 'We are all in haste to put chains on – and as soon as we feel them, complain they are too heavy.' With the children gone, she was very down-hearted. John had been away at school since May 1793 and now George may have joined him (fig. 92). 'Had I kept him with me one other day, I had ruined his peace (perhaps) for ever. I am so low that I scarcely know what I write and my eyes are so bad that I cannot see the pen.' She ends with a report on her brother-in-law. 'Poor William is I suppose by this time dead . . . yet his mother is as calm as if nothing was the matter'. Soane's elder brother weathered his unspecified illness and lived into his mid-eighties, but the episode offers a rare insight into the tough personality of Eliza's mother-in-law.[50]

In Buckinghamshire the works continued. Two pupils had spent nearly three weeks measuring the work in order that the valuation could be made.[51] Quantity surveyors did not yet take this role. Soane's commission continued, now extending to the offices and, upon completion of the house itself in 1797, the building of the stables and demolition of the old house (its fine baroque door was reused, incongruously, in the stable yard). All of this, together with a walled garden, hothouses and greenhouses, was completed by 1800.

No client had before offered Soane a commission on the scale of Tyringham. The total cost of the work for Praed amounted to £40,623, of which Soane's fee was just over £2,000, well in excess of £57,000 in modern value.[52] During the job Praed's financial situation became difficult. The links between his banking and commercial interests were not always comfortable. In 1803 the Cornish Bank, in which he was no longer a partner, refused to take up Praed's offer of £5,500 of Grand Junction Canal shares, judging them an unsuitably speculative stock for a bank.[53] Soane was desperate not to jeopardise his first complete country house scheme and, confident of eventual repayment, entered into an arrangement. Praed paid him interest on what was, effectively, a loan; it was an

92. George Soane (b. 1790) aged thirteen, drawn by George Dance.

informal banking deal and, provided Soane's financial affairs remained in a healthy state, would be to his eventual advantage. Nor was it unusual. When pursuing Lord Arundell for the £208 16s 7d still owed from his work on the chapel at Wardour, a job from twelve years earlier and for which he had only received part payment, Soane assured him that he would be quite happy to take a bond, bearing interest.

Praed at this time was faced with the expense of setting up his London banking house (a commission of which Soane was confident) as well as the encumbrance of a massive and continuing investment in canal building – still not giving any financial return. When his father died in 1802, he owed £10,000 to the family bank. Eventually, Praed intended to repay Soane from the sale of his Jamaica property. In June 1807 the sale was revealed to have fallen through and it was not until 1817, twenty-five years after the first discussions about Tyringham, that Soane received settlement of the £13,000 outstanding.[54]

Only one part of the ideal set piece at Tyringham was dropped. In 1799–1800 Soane designed a 'Sepulchral Church' on a triangular plan, with which Praed intended to replace the ruinous parish church serving the non-existent village of Tyringham and neighbouring Filgrave. His son-in-law, the Reverend Henry Whinfield, had the living. The triangular plan was surmounted by a top-lit dome, with apses on the three points, each with a sanctuary and altar.[55] Laugier had illustrated such a church and Soane perhaps knew Thomas Tresham's three-sided lodge (symbolising the Trinity) at Rushton, in Northampton. However, the old church with its twelfth-century tower survived until a heavy restoration in the 1870s. Inside is an unusual and charmingly apposite wall monument to William Praed: a bas-relief showing a barge passing through a lock.[56]

As work at Tyringham came to a close, another job emerged nearby. William Ralph Cartwright MP had inherited the Aynhoe estate in infancy. He had recently returned from his continental travels and had taken up the county parliamentary seat for Northamptonshire, sitting as a steadfast Pittite.[57] Praed may well have introduced him to Soane.

Aynhoe[58] Park combined a late seventeenth-century central core with early eighteenth-century English Baroque additions, ascribed to Thomas Archer. At first the client asked for Soane merely to provide some sketches. 'I am not much accustomed to making plans to be executed unless under my own direction' Soane responded tartly.[59]

Although he was tempted to demolish Archer's two blocks, originally stables and kitchens, Soane compromised and linked them to the main house by placing a triumphal arch at each corner. Inside he transformed the *enfilade* of rooms by masking the full height of the windows, lightening the proportions of the high, boxy rooms with discreet and elegant touches (fig. 93), inserting columns, groin vaults and his characteristic ball mouldings and incised ornament. He carved an alcove, a vestibule, even a strong room, out of larger rooms and left-over space. On either side of the garden front he added upper storeys and low pediments to the single-storey wings (fig. 94), and above the library, with some deft alterations of level, provided a delightful, barrel-vaulted bedroom for Cartwright. He neatened off the work by a new west elevation.

At Aynhoe Soane shows, as at Chillington or at Wimpole, his growing ability to work with the existing fabric and, by tweaking at it, to achieve an architectural result which is fully his own. As George Wightwick later observed, Soane's planning was 'proverbially felicitous, especially as regarded the adaptation of such accidental divergences and by-corners, as the irregular form of the site might present'.[60]

In contrast to the pleasure of working with a receptive or at least compliant client, a Praed or a Cartwright, others meddled or failed to pay. Soane apparently never turned down a commission but he found ways of shaking off troublesome or unpromising commissions. Indecision was also a problem; he pointed out to Lady Pembroke that her wavering about chimney-pieces and staircase finishes at her house at Charles Street was bound to add considerably to the cost. She also had been altering details in the absence of the architect or his clerk. Her interference, he wrote frankly to her, made him 'truly wretched'.[61] Earlier he had remonstrated with her (as he also did with John Stuart) for dealing with 'Mr Holland the *Builder*'.[62]

On the whole Soane seems to have got on particularly well with his female clients. Philip Yorke's stepmother, Agneta Yorke, was a sympathetic woman and she had asked him whether she should tip the workmen. He suggests that she make 'some little compliment' to Pullinger, the clerk of works, or he would in her name, since 'I really believe his great object is, to give you satisfaction'.[63] Harmonious relations between client and tradesmen were in everybody's interest. When asked for his advice, he was firm and helpful, always mindful of good value for money.

As a scout for promising properties for clients, Soane was conscientious and dependable, often bringing in Foxhall or James Christie, the London auctioneer, to help with valuations. When Lord and Lady Bridport were considering a property in Grosvenor Square he firmly put them off a house he considered overpriced and 'indifferent'.[64] He offered Earl Fortescue, for whose town house he was planning alterations and additions, 'every exertion in my power . . . to lessen the expense'.[65] Having missed an appointment with the Earl of Shaftesbury, of which he had not been told, he was mortified since 'punctuality makes a part of my character'.[66]

93. The library, Aynhoe Park in Buckinghamshire. Soane transformed an existing single storey wing into an airy book-lined room with his usual subtle touches.

94. The south front, Aynhoe Park showing Soane's first-floor additions to the side wings. The library (fig. 93) is in the further wing, an orangery in the nearer one.

Rowland Burdon, his old friend from Rome and the Sicilian journey, had inherited the family estate at Castle Eden on his father's death in 1786 and from 1790 had represented Durham County in parliament. Despite the personal catastrophe of the death of his wife and daughter in 1791, the following year he promoted an Act of Parliament to carry out an election promise to build a bridge spanning the River Wear at Sunderland. This would link important commercial centres and together with new turnpikes, form 'a complete inland communication' as he put it. At 236 feet, it would be more than twice as long as the recently built, and internationally renowned, Ironbridge at Coalbrookdale. Originally a project in the hands of a committee, Burdon intervened to raise the full funds required for the projected bridge and took over the management. When Burdon drew Soane into the venture, certainly by November 1791,[67] he quickly offered support – moral, practical and financial.

The most advanced prototype bridge of which Burdon knew had been patented by Tom Paine in 1788, a system of iron ribs, based on the compartmentalisation of the spiders' web. His application stated that 'when nature empowered this insect to make a web she also instructed her in the strongest mechanical method of constructing it'.[68] In Paris Paine had discussed his proposals with Perronet, now in his eighties (and never a supporter of iron bridges[69]) and with Thomas Jefferson. In London he presented it to the Royal Society.

Thomas Walker and partners in Rotherham, cannon-founders with little to do between wars, were interested. Despite various difficulties and delays, in autumn 1790 they built a prototype section on Lisson Green, Paddington.[70] It attracted many visitors but failed to find a promoter – Paine's system was far from sound. Knowing of Burdon's plans, the Walkers took the model to Castle Eden but Burdon still favoured a masonry arch. In the summer of 1791 Soane returned from Ireland via Durham, he may have even seen the model. In the meantime Paine returned to America, more concerned with his 'political bridge', and left his patent to its own devices.[71]

Burdon had turned to Charles Hutton, the mathematician, and Robert Mylne, architect of London's newest bridge at Blackfriars, for advice. Mylne unhelpfully prophesied that Burdon's bridge would collapse but cited John Nash's 'now building' at Newport in Monmouthshire.[72] Burdon asked Nash for a proposal and he sent a design for a 200 foot masonry structure which he estimated at just over £17,000. It was immediately clear that it was neither structurally feasible nor economic. In 1793 Soane agreed to check the estimate and organised another independent opinion. They demonstrated Nash's figures to be laughable. Soane costed it at £65,680.[73]

For years Nash protested that Burdon had stolen his design and that the Wearmouth Bridge was in fact his (despite the fact that his own patented system was quite different and, probably, better).[74] After his experiences with Nash, Burdon never had a good word for him and was surprised by his subsequent success.

Soane was resolved that Burdon should consider an iron bridge. With a local schoolteacher and engineer, Thomas Wilson, Burdon went back to the Walkers and they erected a trial rib at the works and drew up a new iron bridge, which could be erected from scaffolding, a far quicker method than centring.[75] The only connection now to Paine's bridge was the probable reuse of iron straps from the Paddington model. Soane, who had told Burdon that he considered the work as 'a great public advantage' and would be happy to contribute 'any aid in my power whenever you think I can be of the least use', prepared a new estimate, in August 1793, at £23,414.

The foundations were laid on 24 September 1793, Soane having consulted Dance on whether piling or conventional masonry would be best. Soane reassured Burdon upon Wilson's skills; his 'caution and care ensure success, which I sincerely wish to attend every stage of this great undertaking'.[76] The Wearmouth Bridge opened on 9 August 1796 at the eventual cost of £26,000 (of which £22,000 was Burdon's personal investment).

In 1795 Burdon patented the new construction system, flat cast-iron voussoir blocks held by wrought-iron ties. The same year he commissioned a silver tureen from the silversmiths Peter and Ann Bateman. The Latin inscription translates as 'without your help I would not have achieved my fame. Let the iron bridge over the Wear bear witness to this. R. Burdon gave this as a gift to J. Soane, his well-deserving friend.'[77] In August 1796, their friend from Italy, Thomas Bowdler, forwarded a paper on the new bridge to Joseph Banks at the Royal Society, adding a postscript trumpeting its subsequent success.[78]

Burdon's bridge became an object of wonder, effacing the Ironbridge and illustrated on thousands of commemorative items as well as drawing visitors on an unprecedented scale. The bridge set Sunderland on the way to prosperity and gave Burdon a remarkable personal following in the region. When he stood down from parliament, giving 'no reason but a love of retirement'[79] he was prevailed upon to stand again. In 1803 Burdon's bank failed and despite strenuous efforts to save it, he was declared bankrupt in 1806. The year before, his bridge had begun to shows signs of weakness and it was considerably modified. The new adjustments solved the problems, but increased the financial burden upon its investors. Marc Isambard Brunel was highly impressed by the bridge in 1818 while Robert Stephenson pronounced it sound in 1846. It was rebuilt later in the century and again in the 1920s.[80]

Despite the bankruptcy (owing to the family firm's over-investment in the Tyne ironworks from 1797), Burdon's huge popularity in Durham gave rise to a campaign to reinstate him in his parliamentary seat – with his admirers paying his expenses. His status as certified bankrupt prevented this but his estates were saved by county subscription. Little of his dire circumstances emerges in his letters to Soane over the years (he died the year after his old friend) but a constant delight in his new family (he remarried in 1794) laced with a vital curiosity in everything about him – from politics and agriculture to the curiosities of a changing world – makes his correspondence unfailingly warm and lively.

Soane's personal investment in his friend's great enterprise brought him regular interest payments over many decades but Burdon, the most generous and tender of all Soane's old friends, never took his support for granted.[81] By 1818 the success of the bridge suggested that soon all debts would be paid off and it would become toll-free. 'I expect that this piece of news will not be unacceptable to one who had to do with the original idea, as far as a regular architect could venture to encourage an undertaking out of all regular rules of practice' he wrote.[82] In 1835 he was still confessing his weakness for new technology, 'I always had a hankering after projects of a novel description, for which you have occasionally rated me' and, the next year, recalled Soane's part in his great adventure, 'You my friend were the only person who whispered to me to "go on", which, amongst other acknowledgements, I am now gratified to make.'[83]

Soane's involvement in Burdon's venture is a reminder of the hold that pioneering engineering achievements always had upon him. Intrigued by bold projects and new technology, Soane enthusiastically embraced innovations such as Bramah's water closet or new heating systems (whether for forcing on fruit or for the comfort of clients). He was open to novel materials or applications, leading to lightweight or non-combustible construction. Sometimes it was the practices of the ancients which provided the clues, sometimes the inventions of the moderns.[84] His library, and his practice, are testament to this side of his mind.

Soane never forgot his meeting with Perronet, in Paris in 1778, introducing him to the notion of the far-seeing engineer as a major figure in the national life. While the men whom Soane came to admire in the field in England, in particular Joseph Bramah[85] and John Rennie, worked in a far more independent, entrepreneurial fashion than the functionaries of the *Ponts et Chaussées*, for Soane the role of engineering and its expansion of the possibilities, was crucial.

The arguments that had raged in France around the structural risks suggested by Perronet's new, flattened bridges or Soufflot's Sainte-Geneviève (later the Panthéon), where the piers were thought inadequate to support the drum of the dome, pitted the calculations of the engineers, the modernisers, against the French traditionalists.[86] Soane had admired both the Panthéon and the bridge at Neuilly (although judging it unattractive) on his first visit to France and returned to them in later visits and in the lectures.[87]

In Soane's work, function and utility could be made elegant. The apparent weightlessness and eventual near-abstraction of the classical orders and ornament in Soane's interiors was a celebration of sleight of hand, made possible by lightening the construction, using materials such as hollow terracotta cones and Coade stone ornament. On other occasions he improvised.[88] Soane's architectural language was liberated by his willingness to see the possibilities of new approaches, but always underpinned by the rules dictated by structural good practice and historical precedent. Modernity for its own sake – 'false economy, false mechanism, and great celerity' – was not at all to Soane's taste.

7

THE ASSAULT ON WESTMINSTER

The 1790s saw Soane move into his own house at Lincoln's Inn Fields and build up his private architectural practice at an astonishing rate. Above all, however, he was putting himself in pole position for public patronage; the Bank of England was just his launching point.

Back in 1789 Soane had the first scent of a commission besides which his work at the Bank would pale in importance. With twelve others, including Robert Adam, Dance and Holland, he was asked by a committee of the House of Commons to survey 'the several houses and other buildings immediately joining to Westminster Hall, and the two Houses of Parliament, and the offices thereto belonging etc'.[1] Many were in such poor condition that the inspecting architects noted that they were 'incapable of useful repair and improvement'; others were already derelict and had been disused for years. Restoration and alteration of the rest had done nothing to rationalise the arrangements and much to damage the fine medieval structures which stood on the site. Whitehall Palace had burned to the ground and the area remained a disgraceful mess; despite unbuilt schemes by most of the leading architects over the previous hundred years, including Wren, Hawksmoor, Kent and Burlington and the Adams, Westminster was a shambles.

The House of Commons at the end of the eighteenth-century was uncomfortably housed in the fourteenth-century royal chapel of St Stephen, members perching in choir stalls and the Speaker taking the place of the altar. The House of Lords sat in the Painted Chamber and the Prince's Chamber next door became the Robing Chamber. Both Houses offered the double discomfort of appalling ventilation and numbing cold. In and around Westminster Hall itself were the law courts. It was time to rebuild the Palace of Westminster. Soane's mind had been on the subject even before he had designed his ambitious Senate House while in Rome (see figs 16 and 23).

Soane was appointed Clerk of the Works with responsibility for St James's, Whitehall and Westminster in October 1790. This was a post answerable to Sir William Chambers as Surveyor-General at the Office of Works but its attraction for Soane lay in the area covered, with much of which he was, thanks to his survey the year before, now familiar. On receiving the clerkship, Soane wrote fulsome letters of thanks to both William Pitt and Joseph Smith, Pitt's private secretary since 1787.[2] With the post came an office at Great Scotland Yard; a convenient location for keeping in contact with his important clients and useful until such time as he could set up an office in his own house.

Soane's appointment coincided with an explosion in his private commissions and the first major works at the Bank. He had to perform a near impossible balancing act to juggle his obligations and build his house. For four years he exhibited nothing at the Royal Academy.

However Soane was conscientious in carrying out a continuous stream of mostly minor works at both Westminster and Whitehall and, infrequently, at St James's Palace, the home of the Duke of Clarence.[3] In April 1791 Chambers instructed him to assist Henry Holland by providing plans and sections and 'every assistance his leisure may permit after discharge of the duties of his place in his Majesty's Service' so that Holland might report to a committee on the 'improvement of the temperature of the air in the House of Commons'.[4] Although this was an uncomfortably subordinate role for the architect to the Bank of England, all set to embark on major works there, Soane's post had the great advantage of keeping him continually close to the heart of government.

While the Bank, like the East India Company, had a physical presence commensurate with its importance, the departments of state in Whitehall were fledgling bodies housed in private houses around the site of the ruined Whitehall Palace, of which only the Banqueting House remained. The physical condition of the Palace of Westminster merely reflected the wider chaos of the *ad hoc* arrangements of government. Meanwhile, the shambles that housed the departments of state had attracted a large number of whores to the area. Frederick Robinson complained to Chambers about the 'concourse of disorderly women' who overran Privy Garden and Whitehall but while acknowledging his problem, Chambers replied that there was nothing his office could do about it. He suggested that the residents appoint a 'stout watchman or two at the expence of the inhabitants'.[5]

After some years in temporary, domestic premises, in 1793 the expanding Foreign Office was rehoused in Downing Street, in a house on the south side, which had formerly belonged to Lord Sheffield.[6] Soane would find himself returning to these and the houses opposite at various times but his work there that summer, following the outbreak of war with France in February 1793, consisted of relatively minor adjustments. The job gave Soane regular contact with Lord Grenville, younger brother of the Marquis of Buckingham, who became Secretary of State at the Foreign Office from April 1791, remaining in post until the end of Pitt's first ministry.[7]

William Grenville, Pitt's cousin, was the coming man. Pitt had appointed him Leader of the House of Lords in 1790, aged just thirty, creating him Baron Grenville of Wotton under Bernewood. Grenville replaced the Duke of Leeds there, as he would do at the Foreign Office a few months later: his appointment conferred a new significance upon the post, as the government's chief minister in the Lords.[8] At the time that Soane began meeting him on official business, Grenville had just married Lord Camelford's daughter Anne and they had honeymooned at Holwood, at Pitt's invitation.[9] Despite all these connections, the Grenvilles employed Samuel Wyatt in preference to Soane; first, in 1792 at their country house, Dropmore in Buckinghamshire, and then at their town house, 4 Cleveland Row overlooking Green Park. James Wyatt's brother, 'the builder' was according to Humphry Repton a contrast to his sparkling, convivial sibling. Samuel, 'slow plodding, heavy in carriage [was] dull in conceiving the ideas of others and tedious in explaining his own'.[10]

In early autumn 1793 the Surveyor General, Sir William Chambers, asked Soane 'to lay before 13 architects therein named the Plan or Ground Plot of the House of Lords and Building adjacent' in order that they could begin to consider the reconstruction of Westminster Palace.[11] Because of his own responsibilities at the Office of Works, Soane found himself excluded from consideration for the one job he wanted above all else. It was a horrible turn of events. Soane seems to have decided to earmark for himself another position at the Office of Works, with no direct responsibility for Westminster. However the strategy backfired. The vacancy in question was for the job of district surveyor but Chambers appointed Charles Craig, a long serving Office of Works man, whom Soane described as 'brought up to measuring and accounts . . . not a person by whom any regular architect would submit to be directed'.[12] Faced with the failure of his scheme, Soane sulked.

In marked contrast to his earlier industriousness, by late 1793 Soane's desultoriness in his post had begun to try the Surveyor-General's patience beyond endurance. He cavalierly refused to meet Chambers to discuss complaints and told him that he was at home if he had anything to say to him.[13] Several weeks elapsed without another word. In fact, in late November and early December Soane was house-bound, probably with gout, but although he frequently used silence as a weapon in his disputes he never invoked illness as a defence. His absenteeism was seen by Chambers as insubordination and his abrasive cheek and spitefulness on paper were not well received.

On 12 December Soane visited Pitt 'by appointment on Office of Works vacancy' and spent three quarters of an hour arguing his case. Soane was confident that his special relationship with Pitt would overturn Craig's appointment in his favour. Pitt chose not to intervene. But the meeting apparently ended abruptly, the First Minister had more pressing matters than this to discuss.

Chambers too had lost patience and sent Soane a letter of stern rebuke. He was not prepared to enter an argument about the Charles Craig's suitability for promotion:

> which does not seem to me material to the business of this Office but am sorry to hear from you that his great inferiority and my violent resentment prevent, and will prevent, your attendance at this Office. I have already assured you that the latter never existed, and the dangerous consequences of the former might I think be very much alleviated by an expedient for which the world is indebted to German sagacity. In Germany when a great man connects with a Lady a few quarters inferior to him in rank, the great man preserves his own dignity, by performing on all connubial occasions with his left hand. The application is obvious[14]

Meanwhile Soane's list of tasks to be attended to at the Office of Works had lengthened alarmingly; by February there were nine separate jobs awaiting his attention.[15]

Chambers, Soane considered, had been obstructing him elsewhere. The new office for the Secretary of State (presumably, at the Foreign Office) 'might have been completed long ago if Sir William Chambers had not constantly altered my plans and uniformly done everything in his power to delay the business and to render my effort ineffectual'.[16] Then, early in January Soane was furious to discover that Chambers had told the king himself about his recent behaviour and requested him to pass on his justification 'in my own words'. Whether by accident or design, Soane's position had become untenable. In February he tendered his resignation and John Woolfe was quickly moved over to take on his duties.

Soane had thrown away his Office of Works position in order to gain the commission for the House of Lords. It was a dangerous gamble which he had reason to believe would pay off.

Instructions at the Office of Works had always come from one or other of Pitt's two key Treasury men. George Rose and his younger colleague Charles Long orchestrated political life around the First Minister; they were simultaneously whips, tellers and agents. They master-minded elections and dispensed patronage. Rose, who had been Secretary to the Treasury since 1782, and Long – almost twenty years his junior – often dealt with Treasury matters in the Commons on Pitt's behalf.

In the early weeks of 1794 Soane was working for George Rose at his country house, Cuffnells near Lyndhurst in Hampshire, refacing the south front and designing an orangery and a library (fig. 95).[17] The relationship was reciprocal. Going to breakfast with Rose on 4 February to discuss the job, he 'took papers on duties on tiles and slates'. Later the same day he worked out the duty paid on these items at the Bank and sent Rose the result.[18] Soane's information was of considerable interest at the Treasury, at a time when the government was reassessing taxes and duties, prior to imposing income tax in 1799. Rose and his colleagues experienced Soane's professional qualities and strengths at first-hand.

Charles Long had entered the Commons in 1789, moving rapidly to become Joint-Secretary to the Treasury two years later. He was one of Pitt's close circle from student days at Cambridge and thus was accorded the rare privilege of calling him by his surname alone.[19] Pitt had even entrusted Long with certain crucial negotiations with the French as the country inched towards war in the early weeks of 1793.

Soane rarely miscalculated someone's influence, but in the case of Charles Long he appears to have underestimated the man. His elder brother, named after their father Beeston Long, a West India merchant, was a director of the Bank of England. An amateur artist, Charles Long took a Grand Tour before entering politics and had drawn Hadrian's Villa at Tivoli 'like a madman'. Long could be mistaken for an insignificant figure. Pitt's sister Harriet described Long sliding in and out of the room: 'nobody knew where he went or when he came', he was so shadowy and unobtrusive.[20] Becoming Lord Farnborough in 1826, he remained at the core of government for the rest of his life, increasingly taking a leading role in artistic matters. Later, his and Soane's paths would cross with regularity. Although he nudged at least one official commission Soane's way, his extensive powers of patronage as friend of successive First Ministers and artistic mentor to both George III and the Prince of Wales seldom benefited Soane.[21]

95. A nineteenth-century engraving of Cuffnells, the Hampshire country house of George Rose, William Pitt's aide at the Treasury and a central figure behind the scenes in his administration. The king was a frequent visitor on his way to and from Weymouth. Soane worked on the house in 1794, designing the orangery and refacing the south front.

Both Rose and Long held their posts throughout Pitt's first administration, as did Joseph Smith, his private secretary and another Treasury man. The nephew of the Master of Gonville and Caius College, Cambridge, where Soane carried out substantial work in 1792, he also employed Soane on his house in Hereford Street that year.

Meanwhile none of the architects to whom Chambers had asked Soane to supply plans of the House of Lords the previous summer appeared to have taken the project further. He had, no doubt, confided his own hopes to some of his clients who sat in the upper House and they may have argued his case. As he put it, disingenuously, 'having been encouraged by many respectable Members of this House to consider plans for the improvement of the Chamber of Parliament and the Apartments adjoining it', he presented some 'general ideas' to the Lord Chancellor on 5 May 1794.[22] A month later Soane submitted a report, with sections and plans, on improving the ventilation and heating in the House of Lords (figs 96, 97). The drawings were exceptionally beautifully presented and the estimate £250.[23] He had taken his first step towards the prized commission.

The same month a full committee[24] was appointed to 'take into consideration the state and condition of this house; and by what means the same and the adjacent buildings may be rendered more commodious for the reception of the members – whose lordships having considered thereof are to report to the house.' The membership was the Lord Privy Seal (the Earl of Gower), the Duke of Leeds, Earls Spencer, Chatham, Camden and Mansfield, Lords Grenville, Amhurst, Harrowby, Thurlow and Hawkesbury. From the Bishops' side of the House, the Archbishop of Canterbury was joined by the Earl Bishop. If Soane was dismayed to see the Earl Bishop's name among the members, the fact that an attendance of only five constituted a quorum made it unlikely that he would attend. The committee met on 18 and 20 June and at a third meeting on 30 June, of which no minutes survive, chaired by the Duke of Leeds, it was agreed that 'Mr Soane (an architect lately belonging to the Board of Works)' be asked to consider over the summer what could be done to meet their objectives.

Despite the committee's apparently non-committal approach to their requirements, in its very vagueness Soane could see possibilities. Realising how many of his illustrious predecessors had prepared plans for the site – and all unsuccessfully – he was aware that he must try to nudge this into a full-scale job. Soane with his immaculate political instincts (and his Senate House scheme at the back of his mind) could do so, if anyone could.

The chairman, the fifth Duke of Leeds had, as Lord Carmarthen, been Lord Grenville's predecessor as leader of the House of Lords.[25] An ambitious man now without a role, he had already offered George III his services in forming an administration 'if his Majesty would remove Pitt and his friends'.[26] Soane had recently been working on estate buildings at the duke's country house, North Mymms in Hertfordshire, and before long was charged with remedying his friend Robert Brettingham's poor work on the elevation of 21 St James's Square, which did not worry Brettingham, who remained on good terms with Soane.[27] Major work was needed on the house and Soane and the duke went together to see the library at Spencer House, perhaps for ideas.

96. Section to show the heating system proposed for the House of Lords, hot air pipes leading into the walls close to the royal dais.

97. Soane's carefully drawn and lettered plan of the accommodation in the House of Lords.

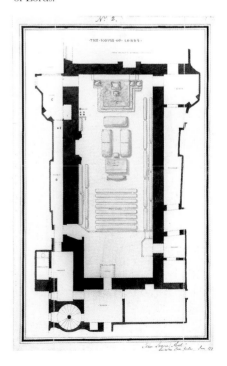

98. A freehand pen and wash drawing from 1799 showing Soane's design for the House of Lords, with the river in the foreground. Soane kept to a strictly Roman idiom for this commission and did not risk any of the 'fanciful' work for which he was criticised at the Bank.

Soane's invitation from the Lords' committee, gained on the back of the small job to improve heating and ventilation, but well and economically done, meant that he had catapulted over the head and authority of Sir William Chambers.[28] Over the coming months, well into 1795, Soane's office laboured on the designs for a new House of Lords, a great edifice on the banks of the Thames to rival Chambers' Somerset House in its reliance on a French academic classicism. It was a highly ambitious interpretation of their lordship's request to make their house more 'commodious'.

The difficulties dealt with, Soane's final solution was to wrap his classical building, topped by edifying sculptural groups and mounted on a massive rusticated base, around the sacrosanct core of the medieval St Stephen's Chapel and Westminster Hall. There were echoes of his Gold Medal Triumphal Bridge design and a dash of well-mannered Palladianism. His plan made excellent use of the riverside setting; from the Thames visitors to the House of Lords would approach up a flight of steps – a lion and a unicorn to either side – across a generous square (fig. 98). Internally he lavished great care on a new royal entrance, leading to the Scala Regia, a triumphal stair flanked by gigantic statues of kings.

Chambers, unassailably the senior figure in the architectural profession, cannot have been pleased. Soane had circumvented the selection process and so Chambers parried. Early in 1795 Soane complained that he had still not received necessary information: 'your people have refused to let my clerk copy the Drawing of Memorandum in your office respecting the two Houses of Parliament and the buildings connected with them. I am at a loss to account for this conduct but I have only to blame myself for I am persuaded the moment you know . . . the difficulty will be removed and no further delay occasioned.'[29]

Soane met the House of Lords Committee several times[30] and showed his scheme which included, for comparative purposes, modest conversions of both the Court of Requests and the Painted Chamber (but emphasising the unsuitability of these options), to his major clients in the House of Lords, the Marquises of Buckingham and Abercorn and Earl of

Hardwicke. His plans were circulated to a succession of royal princes, dukes, earls, bishops and others, and finally Soane went out to Windsor, to see the king.[31] George III, despite (as Soane claimed) praising the Scala Regia, had little power in the matter, on this occasion even less than Soane's friends in the House.

Despite his enviable network of contacts, Soane told the Marquis of Buckingham in June 1795 that he had heard nothing further but 'the moment anything transpires I shall beg to trouble your lordship'.[32] Soon after, the bad news came. Lord Grenville told Soane that the remodelling of the House of Lords was deferred due to the present state of the country. Soane's estimate of over £150,000 was expenditure that a country at war could ill afford. His attempt to lobby the king had been ineffectual in the face of the political realities.

In the circumstances, no return engagement could have pleased Soane more than another invitation from Pitt to consider improvements for Holwood. He carried out repairs to the roof[33] and roughcasting of the front and helped Pitt develop his own ideas for extensions to his house. William Pitt was happily following his cousins into the field of amateur architecture and became engrossed in improving his modest country estate, some 500 acres of woods with wide views from Sydenham to Knockholt Beeches.[34]

If Soane never achieved the easy friendship with the forbidding and increasingly strained Pitt that Humphry Repton claimed, the moonlit expedition into the grounds and overnight stay that he described in his *Memoir*, Soane had continuous and easy access to Pitt and his circle. On his first return visit to Holwood, in August 1795, he was carrying his plans of the House of Lords – 'by Mr Pitt's desire'. As ever, Soane's objectives were not social but determinedly professional and access to the Prime Minister at his most relaxed in his country retreat might, he believed, still procure him the prize.

Although Pitt had first envisaged a complete rebuilding at Holwood, Soane soon bowed to his client's financial limitations and settled for further improvements to the existing house. In August 1796 Soane took George Dance out with him to Holwood, perhaps to help him with a problem.[35] Dance found the situation beautiful but the house 'very indifferent

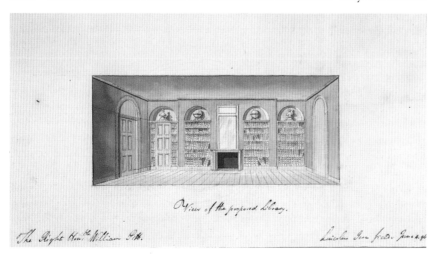

View of the proposed Library.

The Right Honble William Pitt.

99. The Library at Holwood, which Soane estimated at £1,270 and showed to Pitt in June 1796 who approved both design and estimate.

indeed and scantily furnished' and was surprised to find Pitt there on his own, until Lord Hawkesbury called in on business. Dance thought Pitt very pleasant and 'his deportment . . . quite free from hauteur'.[36] The ease with which his former pupil now consorted with the Prime Minister must have impressed Dance. In the end only the library was built (fig. 99).

Almost everyone within Pitt's close personal circle had become a Soane client by now. Robert Smith, the banker, had employed Soane on his London house in St James's Place in 1791.[37] In 1796 Pitt created him an Irish peer, Lord Carrington, and he was promoted to the English peerage in 1797 – the reward, it was said, for giving Pitt his personal financial assistance. Closer still to Pitt was his brother-in-law's family, the Eliots – William Praed's banking partners and a power to be reckoned with in Cornish affairs and far beyond.[38]

A new appointment in 1795 as Deputy Surveyor-General to the Office of Woods and Forests helped Soane swallow his disappointment at the deferral of the House of Lords decision and offered evidence of royal favour. The new position gave him a salary of £200 and responsibility for a number of incidental buildings in and around the Royal Parks, chiefly lodges, gates and other lesser structures. Here he would have regular contact with members of the royal family. He remembered Thomas Sandby's charmed life as a favourite of several royal dukes. That royal patronage could be something of a poisoned chalice did not deter him.

The Duke of Clarence, for whom Soane had already worked at St James's Palace in 1791 when Clerk of Works, had lived for some years with his mistress, the actress Dora Jordan, in Pitt's old house, Petersham Lodge, renamed Clarence Lodge. Soane already knew the house well and now the duke asked him to add a new wing to accommodate his rapidly expanding family of Fitzclarences. However, the king's placatory offer of Bushy House to the couple meant that Soane now transferred his attention there, starting the job with enthusiasm in early 1797, taking his instructions – as was his habit – over breakfast with the family. The duke wished for alterations to the stables, external steps and colonnades and Soane applied himself to the task in February and March.[39]

The job soon went sour. Since the duke was carrying out his improvements from public funds (topped up with a £2,000 loan from Thomas Coutts, his friend, and another from Dora Jordan for £2,400[40]), the Treasury wanted an explanation of the high costs and asked Soane to enquire into the bills. He unearthed a classic collection of sharp practices; reused items (iron and stone) had been charged for as new, while the bad workmanship, shoddy materials and overcharging were 'much beyond any experience of mine'. The duke's constant additions exemplified royal profligacy – admittedly on a very minor scale. Since Soane could not employ one of his own trusted clerks of works the supervision of the tradesmen on site had been non-existant. Soane's scrutiny saved the Treasury over £600 (from the original total of £3,789 17s 1½d)[41] and again demonstrated his professionalism to the watchful men around Pitt.

The architectural profession itself had been showing signs of a similar lack of control. Soane became an early member of the Architects' Club, founded in October 1791. Chaired by Henry Holland, architect members of the Royal Academy or any of the recognised Continental academies, met monthly for dinner at the Freemasons' Tavern to discuss common concerns. Each subscribed 5 guineas per annum (soon raised to seven). More often than not, the discussions became arguments.The club was set up to be a friendly society, along the lines of the Club for Doctors (which included physicians, surgeons and apothecaries) but it soon fell foul of a number of disputes, some based on professional issues, some on personality clashes. Farington recounts the blackballing of George Hadfield.[42] Either Soane or the mild Robert Brettingham was responsible, suggesting that the issue was some simmering quarrel from Rome. Soane was one of several awkward and intemperate members.

Soane's sporadic attendance at meetings depended on his travels. In March 1792, he was present when members determined to 'define the profession and qualifications of an architect', a discussion which inevitably, given Soane's proper and passionately held views on the subject, was to lead to dissension. On this occasion settling for a non-contentious issue, they decided to consider causes of fire and Richard Holland offered a pair of house 'skeletons' for trials at Hans Place.

The discussion of proper professional roles and appropriate fee levels was a subject on which Soane held the strongest views as he had already made clear in *Plans Elevations etc*. When the topic did come up, it was Dance and Henry Holland who fell out. By a majority, members of the Club wanted to charge an additional $2\frac{1}{2}$ per cent measuring fee above the standard 5 per cent for design and supervision.[43] Dance and Soane strongly disagreed with the imposition of an additional fee.

The man who had articulated all this most clearly was, however, not a member of the Club. In 1785 James Peacock had stated the standards expected of an architect with clarity and precision. In *Nutshells* he warned his reader, the client, not to buy a house built by a speculator any more than from a 'fan painter, toyman, laceman, paperhanger or undertaker'. Contracts should be firm and binding and made with a single individual, with no extras or variations, and a deduction made for the value of old materials. Dance and Soane had tough, unshakeable views and Peacock suggests himself as the man who formed them.

The row at the Club rumbled on for two years and when Mylne entered the fray as peacemaker he wondered sourly in a letter to Holland whether Dance who 'has a sensitive and generous mind' had been influenced unduly by someone. Without naming names, Mylne refers to the obstinacy of another member.[44] But in the discussion of professional fees, Dance and Soane stood shoulder to shoulder. Other members of the Club were, like Holland, involved in construction and speculative development; they could not apply the professional probity of Dance and Soane.

Holland told Mylne that his own disillusion with the Club went beyond personalities: 'Instead of professional regulations arising out of it . . . instead of order and harmony at the meetings the most indecedent blackguard and ungentlemanly language has been suffered to pass without censure, the most unexceptional candidates have been blackballed and nothing worthy of the Club is in my opinion left but occasional . . . conviviality.'

Mylne continued to argue for the benefits offered by 'the only meeting of gentlemen of the Art of Building' but the aged Sir William Chambers, who had declared his doubts upon the setting up of such a club (but was prepared to enjoy, when convenient, the monthly dinner) permitted himself to be wise after the event. Soane soon ceased to attend.

He had, in the meantime, joined a much more select club, having been elected an Associate of the Royal Academy on 2 November 1795, together with the Reverend William Gilpin, the watercolourist and picturesque theorist, and John Downman, the portraitist. Dance had used his influence as an Royal Academy elder statesman in Soane's favour and had hurried to give him the good news at eleven o'clock that evening with Thomas Banks and Farington. The Soanes were already in bed.[45]

Soane celebrated his election the following Saturday at home, by giving dinner to a select band of academicians. During the evening, Henry Fuseli paid extravagant attention to Eliza's plain cousin Miss Archbold – affording the guests much amusement at her expense after they had left Lincoln's Inn Fields.[46] Soane received his diploma at a small New Year's Eve dinner given for the new Associates. Lively talk ranged across animal magnetism, forgery of manuscripts and reminiscences of some of the elders of the profession and the evening lasted until two in the morning. It all seemed harmonious enough, even to Farington.[47]

At the time Soane joined the Royal Academy, architecture was accorded low priority at the institution. Chambers, treasurer since its foundation in 1768, had not taken an even-handed role in promoting his fellow architects into its ranks, passing over distinguished peers, such as his arch-rival Robert Adam, in favour of pupils such as the undistinguished John Yenn.[48] (After a furious row between Soane and Yenn, the latter had said he never wanted to belong to any club that would accept a man such as Soane; he cannot have been too pleased to find him joining the select ranks of the Royal Academy). The first Professor of Architecture, Thomas Sandby, although conscientious in the delivery of his lectures, was hardly a leading practitioner. In the beginning architectural entries to the Annual Exhibition could not compete with the paintings and attracted little interest. The difficulties led to a change in style and an emphasis on stronger draughtsmanship and colouring. Later Soane argued for showing architectural material in a separate room.

Four months after Soane's election as an Associate of the Royal Academy, Sir William Chambers died. Soane did not observe the niceties; within twenty-four hours he had called upon Farington to see whether he could stand for election as a full academician.[49] Farington said, carefully, that although Soane's chances were good for an early vacancy, his application was a little premature.

The same day Soane also called on his influential friends Joseph Smith and George Rose on another matter.[50] He hoped to be put forward by Pitt for the post of Surveyor-General, hoping that his unfortunate spell as clerk of works had been forgotten and that his current position as Deputy Surveyor of Woods and Forests would stand him in good stead.

In this case, Soane was too late and in any case Pitt had no voice in the matter. The king had already acted. Late on the evening of 9 March Pitt replied to his Majesty's commands and 'will give directions for the warrant to be prepared to appoint Mr Wyatt to succeed Sir William Chambers'. Pitt had been taken by surprise, having 'received no account of the vacancy; if he had, he would have taken the first opportunity of requesting your Majesty's orders on the subject'.[51] No wonder that Soane found the processes of patronage neither simple nor predictable.

The same month Soane was recommended for election as a Fellow of the Society of Antiquaries, his sponsors including the Duke of Leeds and the Earl of Hardwicke. On 21 May he was duly elected.[52] Other new Fellows in this period included William Beckford, Sir George Beaumont and John Carter the antiquarian.

As ever with Soane, his timing was strategic. On 11 June the first of a series of papers prepared by William Wilkins sen. on Norwich Castle was read to the assembled fellows by Sir Joseph Banks. He began by setting out the history of the site and its buildings but the second part, read on 18 June, included an account of the recent conversion of the castle into a gaol – described as a gross mutilation (fig. 100). The unnamed architect had 'entirely bereaved [it] of its antient beauty', both inside and out. It was the fiercest criticism of his architecture that Soane had ever received – but based upon antiquarian, not stylistic, objections.[53] In fact justifiable objections might have been made on humanitarian grounds; by confining the felons' accommodation so tightly within the twelfth-century keep, Soane's prison – a job which he had obtained in 1789 through the good offices of Robert Fellowes – was hardly a model of John Howard's ideas.[54]

Soane perhaps imagined that by becoming a Fellow of the Society of Antiquaries he would pre-empt this attack. He was furious and hit back, sneeringly referring to Wilkins as an 'able stuccatore', and, thirty years later, attempted to prevent the appointment of William Wilkins jun. to the Royal Academy by sending copies of the offending criticisms to all Royal Academicians. Justifiably outraged, Wilkins pointed out that his father had been dead eleven years and he had been just fifteen years old at the time of the dispute.[55]

Pressure of work was giving Soane bouts of ill health, physical and mental. Farington, who enjoyed domestic tittle-tattle, reported from the Soanes' own dinner table that both Soane and his wife had told him of his susceptibility to bowel complaints and that 'over exertion in his business frequently produces it. They have been married upwards of eleven years and Mrs Soane said he had seldom been free from some complaint of the kind for two months together'.[56] Soane also suffered from gout although one friend reassured him unscientifically but, as it turned out, accurately, that the affliction ensured the sufferer a long life. Soane may also have had the first intimations of eye problems but above all he was at the mercy of deep mood swings. Later in life he referred to the black depression that fell on him during the dark winter months.

Against the disputes and uncertainties in his official working life, Soane's work at the Bank of England was progressing with enviable ease. The Bank dominated his life throughout the 1790s and circumstances, in the shape of the increasing political tensions with France, transformed the status of the institution over these years. By the time that war was declared in 1793 the duties of a routine surveyorship had been transformed into an unparalleled opportunity for a major architectural undertaking. Soane's brilliance was to steer the Court of Directors and its sub-committee, the Committee of Building, into an enormous building programme but so subtly that he had their full compliance. Many of them had, by then, seen

100. Norwich Castle. Soane's conversion of the ancient castle to a gaol subjected him to strong criticism at the Society of Antiquaries.

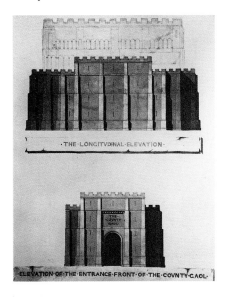

his professional reliability and architectural prescience first hand, on their own houses and business premises.[57] Some were close friends.

If Soane could sustain his argument for the structural unsoundness or unsuitability of an existing building, he was immediately given authority to commence work. Funds were released without difficulty for the imperatives were clear. In these years, Soane never had to argue with the directors. A private bill went to Parliament in 1793 to take in a considerable additional parcel of ground to the north-east of the existing site, on Bartholomew Lane and Lothbury. By 1795 it was cleared. Soane coped unfussily with the difficulties of the site, its changes of level and the main problem, the badly drained and boggy soil which needed great care lest the buildings settle.[58]

Soane's own position as a figure with influence and friends in high places in the City must have been reinforced by his childhood friend Timothy Tyrrell's appointment as City Remembrancer in 1793, a powerful office which put him in charge of all ceremonial occasions and made him the link between the City and parliament.[59] A Freeman of the City and a Chancery solicitor, he was a member of the Court of Common Council from the same date. Tyrrell supported Soane throughout his life with advice, contacts and practical help.

The Bank urgently needed barracks for its own Guard (with which Soane combined a Bank Note Printing Office) and offices for Bank officials, including Soane himself. These could be fitted within the existing boundaries and into parts of Sampson and Taylor's building: Soane's early work on the site was hidden and incremental, built behind existing walls (the soldiers had a separate entrance to their barracks through the Princes Street wall) or buried deep in the Bank's curious slab of a site. Increasingly the Bank became a fortress – for different reasons but with comparable architectural expression as the nearby Newgate Gaol – the exterior remaining entirely windowless. Getting light into the banking halls was the major design challenge.

The existence of the Bank Guard reassured neighbours in the City but proved, to their dismay, not to be at their disposal. In July 1791 a commemorative dinner held to mark the French Revolution at the Crown and Anchor Tavern in the Strand made the institutions of the City understandably nervous. The Lord Mayor asked for a detachment of the Bank Guard to protect the Mansion House, 'a Riot being apprehended', but the officer in charge gave a firm no.[60] Following the Gordon Riots, the Guard was unequivocally to be for the protection of the Bank of England itself.

From 1790 it was obvious that a number of key rooms from Taylor's day were in poor structural condition. The core of Taylor's scheme at the Bank, begun in 1765 after he had completed the Court Room and adjacent octagonal Committee Room, was the Rotunda (or the Stock Room, as it was then called) with the four Stock Offices off it.

The Bank Stock Office, which dealt with the Bank's own securities, lay north of the Bartholomew Lane entrance. It was deteriorating because of faulty leadwork – insect attack had led to water penetration and the timbers were rotting. After eighteen months of ineffectual repairs, Soane persuaded the Committee of Building to consider proposals for rebuilding. His ideas were sufficiently firm for him to produce a model for their meeting in early February 1792.[61] Soane's inheritance from Taylor was an

If Soane had been a little more intellectually nimble he could have defended himself effectively in Sir Joshua Reynolds' words from the second discourse. 'The more extensive . . . your acquantance is with the works of those who have excelled, the more extensive will be your powers of invention; and what may appear still more like a paradox, the more original will be your conceptions.'

Unfortunately Soane had no sense of proportion, while humour at his own expense was foreign to him. He treated the shallow barbs more seriously than they deserved, pursuing his case to the libel courts. He was fired by the shaming knowledge that *The Modern Goth* had done the rounds, entertaining the Fellows of New College, Oxford and published in the *Observer* on 16 October 1796.

Initially *The Modern Goth* had been drawn to Soane's attention by an elderly architect, Richard Jupp, as a clumsy diversionary tactic in a sour professional dispute at the East India Company. By the end of the century the East India Company had virtually become a branch of government. In a country now governed by a series of increasingly powerful ministries, it was effectively a Whitehall outpost in the City. The relationship with India was rapidly changing its emphasis from trade to administration, as commercial attention was drawn further east, through a massive expansion in the China trade in the late eighteenth century – partly brought about by Pitt's India Act of 1784 in which the heavy tea duties were lifted (the revenue replaced by that raised by the Window Tax).[76] From the moment that the Court of Directors had taken the decision to rebuild and enlarge their headquarters building, in 1794, Soane had been positioning himself, and organising a classic pincer movement, based upon his information about their intentions from friendly directors. In 1796 his name had duly appeared among the five architects shortlisted for the job, Jupp, Surveyor to the Company since 1768, Henry Holland, James Wyatt and George Dance. When the list was presented to the directors for their vote, Soane's name was missing.

Jupp soon confessed that he had suppressed it, explaining later: 'I was apprehensive that from his situation in the City, his activity, talents and perseverance I might meet with a formidable rival; but in doing this, I never meant to injure him, or to hurt his feelings.'[77] The combination of Soane's relative youth and his ability to use his powerful friends as lobbyists was a terrifying prospect for Jupp. When the two finally met, in Soane's office at the Bank of England, the old man was reduced to tears.

In a towering rage at his omission, Soane had disingenuously sent a note to George Dance asking him for the measurements of India House with which 'I should be tempted to amuse myself'.[78] Dance, hard to disconcert, was astonished. He advised Soane not to 'force himself into this business' and refused to supply him with the information. Soane's reply was of injured innocence; 'God forbid that I should wound the peace of any man.' Unless he should 'hear of the subject . . . from some of the directors', he would not pursue the matter. He then proceeded to design a new headquarters (fig. 104).

Dance was not up to Soane's manipulative skills. He was well informed on the internal discussions at the East India Company since his artist brother, Nathaniel (later Sir Nathaniel Dance-Holland), had been MP for East Grinstead since 1790, representing the company interest.[79] While he

104. Soane lost the opportunity to design a new headquarters for the East India Company in 1796 but continued to draw up variants long after, as this pen and ink drawing of October 1798 shows.

was in the habit of sharing his wide experience on many issues and was generous with advice to younger architects, Soane's request for privileged and restricted information crossed a moral line with Dance.

Dance's career had offered a foretaste of Soane's: his journey to Italy, marked by recognition at the Academy at Parma, his membership and professorship of the Royal Academy, his connections with Pitshanger Manor, his major commissions in the City of London, his involvement with the East India Company and much more. Through his dealings with George Wyatt, Dance had even introduced Soane to his wife. It was as if Soane had modelled himself, almost too literally, upon the man who had first offered him the opportunity to become an architect.

The difference between them came in their lives. Dance's ambitions and his work were well balanced. His equable temperament and effortless professional inheritance allowed him to remain uncompetitive and gentlemanly. On Saturdays and Sundays, he drew portraits, not ground plans. Soane, understandably driven by ambition, identified with uncanny precision those jobs which would advance his career and manoeuvered for them deftly. Thwarted, he became intemperate and his judgement was often weakened by his suspicion of other people's motives and behaviour. It was Dance who reminded Soane of proper conduct when his ambition overruled propriety and who concerned himself for Soane's health and state of mind when he suffered reverses.

Meanwhile Soane kept up the pressure. On 19 July 1796 he visited the chairman of the East India Company, David Scott, for whom he had, fortuitously enough, drawn up extensive plans for his Scottish house, Dunninald, the year before (fig. 105).[80] He apparently found a sympathetic ear; his omission had been 'no less a matter of astonishment to the Chairman than to myself', Soane wrote later in his outraged printed 'letter' to Earl Spencer in which he rehearsed his treatment at the hands of the Company.[81] After his visit to Scott, Soane then called upon his old contact Jacob Bosanquet who had been a director of the Company since 1782 and who was to become deputy chairman the following year and chairman in 1798.[82] Another supporter was Charles Mills MP, who wrote to his fellow banker William Praed agreeing that Soane had been wronged but adding: 'these architects have so much jealousy one of the other that I incline to think it may have operated here'. However, he added 'Soane shall not be passed by if I can help it.'[83]

A few weeks later Jupp wrote a pathetic letter to the Court of Directors asking if 'in the *decline of my life*' he could be chosen for the commission. As he wrote, 'there is scarcely any precedent where public bodies have resorted to the opinions of other architects than their own . . . I have Honble Sirs faithfully served the Company these twenty nine years and have erected for them many public buildings, and neither my skill in the execution of them, nor my integrity in the application of their money have been ever called in question.' He assured them that he had 'taken the judgement of those architects of eminence whom I know are my friends, that I might give to the designs that simplicity and dignity which a building of that magnitude demands'.[84]

Jupp threw himself on the directors' mercy and they responded honourably. On 22 September following a meeting of the Court he was asked to continue work on India House and to rescind instructions to the other

105. Soane designed Dunninald in Scotland for the Chairman of the East India Company, David Scott, in 1795. Soane was unfamiliar with medieval motifs as this unhappy 'castle' reveals; it was never built as Scott's fortunes fell shortly after.

architects. He was responsible for the execution of the building but it was, as has recently emerged (and as Jupp hints), Holland's hand that lay behind the design of the principal façade on Leadenhall Street, incorporating Theodore Jacobsen's elevation from the 1720s. Holland and Jupp's collaboration on the East India Dock warehouses quite naturally extended to the headquarters.

Two days earlier Dance had earnestly counselled Soane to stop his vendetta: 'as your real friend . . . I think I foresee more mischief as to the opinion of the world than you are aware of'. Dance advised him to rise above his troubles and quoted Hamlet, 'Oh Gentle Son, upon the heat and flame of thy distemper Sprinkle cool patience' and invited him to dinner.[85] Dance's good advice went unheeded.

The reverberations continued at the Architects' Club where the members censured Soane for his relentless campaign. Soane had told Jupp that as a proprietor with friends in the very highest places in the Company, he could make real trouble for him.[86]

But Soane laboured away on the lost commission; two years after Jupp's appointment, he was still obsessively turning out presentation drawings for the Leadenhall Street elevation. Fifteen years later he sent Jupp's letter to Isaac D'Israeli who replied that 'I have never seen the *naïvity* of a rival artist so clearly exhibit his secret motives'. Although referring to Jupp, his response equally applied to Soane – and to his extraordinary tendency to parade old grievances ever after.

At the Bank there was an alarming drain on the gold reserves in 1796 and the national mood became increasingly desperate with rumour of invasion.[87] In late December a Loyalty Loan was announced and was fully subscribed in four days. Offering a 5 per cent return, the target was to raise £18 million. The Bank itself subscribed £1 million and the East India Company double that. Pitt's banker friends rallied to the cause; Thomas Coutts found £50,000, Robert Smith (now Lord Carrington), £40,000. Most of the money came from the City and the lenders, but after the euphoria of such a rallying of public spirit had faded, the stock was soon discounted and investors were never fully compensated.[88] Soane himself had subscribed over £6,000.

The country's indebtedness to the Bank of England grew at a terrifying rate. Treasury bills were mounting and the permanent National Debt had reached almost £11.7 million. In February 1797 the first Restriction Act prevented the Bank from making cash payments and new Bank of England notes (nicknamed 'Newlands' after the Chief Cashier Abraham Newland whose signature was on every note) were issued. New £1 and £2 notes were issued, in addition to £5 notes and to provide domestic coinage the bank recycled their hoard of some two million Spanish dollars, overstamping them with the king's head and giving rise to the ditty 'The Bank to make their Spanish dollars pass, Stamped the head of a fool on the neck of an ass'.[89]

Further accommodation and expansion of the site was now a pressing matter; the staff, which numbered three hundred in 1792, doubled over the next five years.[90] By 1797, Soane was replanning the external spaces at the Bank, starting with Lothbury Court. The central courtyards of the Bank had a range of functions; the Residence Courtyard was home to key

106. A variant on Soane's designs for the Lothbury Court, designed in 1798–9, the heart of the Bank of England. The curved corner elements seen beyond the screen were, in the version built, squared off and topped with acroteria.

bank employees, their families and staff, while the adjoining Lothbury Court saw the movement of the nation's stocks of gold bullion, as it came in to be deposited in the vaults below the Bullion Yard. By the end of the rebuilding, there were nine courtyards within the site. The contrast between the domestic accommodation and the potent symbolism required for the premises where the nation's wealth was being handled, was not lost on Soane. The outer walls, with their impregnability and rugged show of strength, were to be the epitome of *architecture parlante*. (One observer, in the 1920s, compared it to a reassuringly solid cash box.)

Periodically, foreign dignitaries were brought to visit the Bank to glimpse British wealth and strength. Two Dutch Admirals, just defeated at the Battle of Camperdown, came in early November 1797 and were accorded full honours, the clerks even giving up a holiday to show them the operations. 'The brave strangers' were much impressed; the face of the Bank, expanding and magnificent, was becoming a metaphor for the nation itself.[91]

In deliberate contrast to the elemental simplicity of the interiors, in the Lothbury Court Soane used the Roman classical vocabulary at full pitch, a colonnade of giant Corinthian columns striding across the courtyard (fig. 106). Closing but not shutting off the adjacent spaces, the great screen gave a sense of occasion to what was, in reality, no more than a cavernous internal yard. This rich, conventional treatment was mirrored on the facing elevation on Lothbury Court. To the third side the route from Lothbury Court to the Bullion Yard was marked by a huge triumphal arch, inspired by the Arch of Constantine, complete with allegorical ornament. The loading and unloading of gold, the fuel in the Napoleonic Wars, would take place in a proud and resonant imperial setting; Soane's sense of classical history, his theatrical instinct and above all his adherence to the correct application, and associations, of the architectural orders rose to the occasion.

When Karl Friedrich Schinkel, the great Prussian architect, visited the Bank later he reserved his praise for the triumphal arch, which was in his opinion the best thing in the building. Otherwise he observed 'much that is useless'; he was unable to see the logic of Soane's planning.[92] Without experiencing the inspired internal planning of the enormous site, the impression was confusing. Schinkel, in many ways Soane's Continental counterpart, had little time for the apparently mannered approach of the older man.

Lothbury Court had to be seen in relation to the sequence of linkages woven around and off it (passages, lobbies, *loggie* and vestibules) with which Soane modulated the density of the island site, mastering his sprawling undertaking. Without any reassuring conventional symmetries to assist him on plan, there are echoes of Newgate, Ledoux's Hôtel de Montmorency (which was entered on a diagonal) and even the Palazzo Massimo alle Colonne in Rome, where Peruzzi's cranked elevation with its tapering internal courtyards had so intrigued him twenty years earlier.

Soane always responded best to the awkward; the piecing in of the Bank's unpredictable and expanding functions over the long years brought out his ability to cut and paste space – rearranging and disposing interiors and exteriors around the axes and routes as they opened up (fig. 107). There had never been, could never be a masterplan, hence Schinkel's dis-

107. Bird's eye view of the Bank, 1810. Seen from Lothbury, with the Tivoli corner to the right, this drawing clearly shows the courtyards which broke up the Bank site and allowed light and air into the buildings. This view also demonstrates how defensive were Soane's screen walls compared to the older sections, such as that in the eastern corner to the left.

quiet. The Bank would never, given its nature, be orderly or easy to read. From the outside it was essentially a symbol of power; the British Man of War rising above the seas, the dense medieval pattern of the city streets.

Soane's tasks at the Bank were varied but he took on an additional role as the threat of invasion became more acute and civil disorder was feared. The volunteer corps raised at the Bank in May 1798 consisted of 503 men and Soane was to be their Quartermaster.[93] He had to calculate the number of wagons needed to shift paperwork and other essential equipment in the event of evacuation; fifteen wagons would serve for 'books in use', one for Title Deeds, six for the printing presses. In 1802 the corps was disbanded during the peace but Soane reassumed his role thereafter, until the end of the Napoleonic Wars.

As the most important job under way in the office, most of Soane's pupils became familiar with the Bank, among them young Robert Smirke (fig. 108), the son of the painter and Royal Academician of that name, who had entered Soane's office in spring 1796. Smirke seems to have considered himself above the tasks such as the careful delineation of classical detail that Soane required of his pupils and was out of step from the beginning. Writing to his father in September to describe a typical day, he found Soane 'in one of his *amiable* tempers. Everything was slovenly'; he was forced to redraw a scheme on the back of an existing drawing, to save paper.

108. Robert Smirke jun. drawn by George Dance jun. in 1809.

More pleasurably, he had spent a morning at the Bank measuring carpenters' work and had a rare view of London, and the building itself, from the top of the Rotunda, 'the top of the Bank is a curious sight being entirely crowned with little domes, skylights. It is, I suppose, in the inside lighted by them alone. Mr Soane has added not a small number to them.' What a pity, he adds, that Soane was not responsible for Somerset House too 'for his name served as a passport for me over every place where they were building'.[94]

Now that Smirke was a pupil, two of Soane's worlds were uncomfortably close – his professional office and the Royal Academy. He had agreed to take him on a trial basis, free of charge, as a favour. Dance's high esteem of Soane and the logical argument that Soane would be unlikely to 'neglect the son of a man who he would be constantly in the habit of meeting . . . a young man also recommended by Soane's best friend Dance' persuaded Smirke that this was a good course of action. However, since the elder Smirke was a close friend of Farington, unflattering accounts of Soane's temperament and practice soon began to circulate around the Royal Academy: 'Soane does not conciliate the regard of his pupils, by a liberal conduct.'[95] On the other hand, Smirke's superior attitude towards his fellow pupils and particularly to tradesmen (in his own admission) was unattractive.[96] Young Smirke's 'ardent desire . . . to excel in his profession' which his proud father reported to Farington was evident, he said, in an extraordinary improvement during his brief months at Lincoln's Inn Fields. He was unwilling to credit Soane with the change.

By early 1797 Smirke senior was agitating to remove the lad, by now a Royal Academy silver medallist,[97] from his master's office. He did not feel that copying bills, about which Soane 'is childishly capricious and trifling' was useful and the shortage of work in the office – a surprising observation – made it an unpromising place to take up Articles.[98] Dance, according to Farington, agreed that instruction at home, helped by himself, might be preferable. Soane, hurt and insulted by Dance's involvement, from now on regarded the Smirkes, father and son, as enemies.

In the matter of professional advancement, as in other matters, Smirke had learned a great deal from Soane. He spent the months after he left Soane's office drawing up theatres and bridges and even delivered a set of drawings for a square and palace in Hyde Park to Thomas Tyrwhitt, the Prince of Wales's Secretary.[99] Youth and inexperience were no bar to his efforts to further his ambitions. Soane foolishly allowed his relationship with Smirke to become a major irritant in his professional life.

8

DISAPPOINTMENTS AND ACHIEVEMENTS

In July 1798 Soane paid for a certificate for his armorial bearings. He had adopted, without being entitled to do so, the arms of Thomas Some of Waversdon.[1] Eliza Soane, no doubt at her husband's instigation, also improperly adopted her uncle Wyatt's arms. So fashionable was the taking up of family arms, largely illicitly, that the government had decided to tax them and the payments appear in Soane's tax returns in later years. His armorial bearings on his book plate was a pleasing confirmation of his position in society (fig. 109).[2]

That December Lord Grenville called in the designs for the House of Lords and kept them for several months, raising Soane's hopes again. Less reassuringly James Wyatt, Surveyor-General at the Office of Works, had talked to the king about the new buildings at the Palace of Westminster and thought that Soane's position with Pitt (whether as his favoured personal architect or because of the king's uneasy relationship with his first minister is unclear) might add difficulties. George III had commented on Soane's designs, 'and knew his peculiarities well. If so', Farington confided to his diary smugly, 'there can be no apprehension of future works being trusted to a bad taste.'[3] Soane was not in favour with the king and, to compound his weak position, his staunchest advocate the Duke of Leeds suddenly died, aged forty-eight.[4] The Marquis of Buckingham had also fallen silent.

The signs were not promising but Soane heard no more until, he claimed, he read in the *Morning Herald* of 11 July that James Wyatt himself was to design a new House of Lords. His own scheme, so confidently put forward six years before, had finally been shelved. The high authority of his classical proposal had been lost in favour of a lightweight gothic solution which paid lip service to the medieval Westminster Hall and the Abbey, opposite. The king's views and Wyatt's persuasiveness had prevailed.

Delighted with Wyatt's work for Queen Charlotte at Frogmore, George III had the fullest confidence in his favoured architect and as a result was altering his architectural ideas, as he wrote in 1803 to his eldest daughter Princess Charlotte, now the Duchess of Wurtemberg, with whom he frequently exchanged news of their respective architectural and landscape improvements. Reporting progress on his current project, the castellated gothic Kew Palace, which despite slow progress because of a 'certain want

109. Soane's armourial bearings, appropriated from a Suffolk family in 1798.

of diligence in Wyatt' and a shortage of workmen, was delighting him, he admitted: 'I never thought I should have adopted Gothic instead of Grecian architecture, but the bad taste of the last forty years has so entirely corrupted the professors of the latter, I have taken to the former from thinking Wyatt perfect in that style.'[5] There was a new general on the battlefield of the styles.

Years later, Martin Archer Shee expressed his indignation at Soane's treatment and the substitution of his scheme by 'the miserable erections which have since disgraced . . . a situation so calculated for impression and effect'. He echoed the general bewilderment. 'Surely your friend Wyatt could never have been the author of such *designs* nor of the intrigue by which they were preferred to yours' he wrote.[6] But it was not by machination but by royal infatuation that Wyatt gained the commission at the House of Lords. All that was left for Soane to do was to try and extract payment.

Soane, possibly unaware of the deep partiality of the king for Wyatt and his works, convinced himself that Lady Grenville (Thomas Pitt's daughter Anne) was the person responsible for his failure. Beyond the Grenvilles' patronage of Wyatt's brother Samuel, he had no solid grounds for this notion. However, Soane's sense of becoming marginalised was heightened by the Marquis of Buckingham: he owed Soane money and for more than a year failed either to pay or respond to his bad news – an object which 'you pursued with so much ability and zeal'. When he did, he was keen to point out that he had had no voice in the decision but admitted that he would favour a gothic solution to the new House of Lords where it confronted Westminster Hall and the Abbey although he was 'not sure whether I should not have preserved a grecian front to the River'. Soane endorsed this weasely response with an angry 'So much for Buckingham!'[7]

Soane could only fume and extract the £445 15s 10½d he was owed. In 1801 he petitioned the House of Lords[8] and reminded them of their instructions in June 1794, at which he had 'laid aside other important concerns and professional employments and employed the greatest part of the years 1794 and 1795 in the execution of the orders of this House'. The results of his efforts were shown 'to many most respectable Members of this House who were pleased to express their fullest approbation and to recommend from time to time alterations in the minuter details on which the petitioner was laboriously employed and at length completed the same'. He then ran through the subsequent history of the project, including its presentation to the king at Windsor, and 'presumes to hope and trust, that their Lordships will direct for him such remuneration for the very great expence he has incurred by employing surveyors, measurers, draughtsmen and others, in obedience to their Lordships' commands; and also for the labour and professional talents'.

His petition was referred to committee, which reported on 29 April. The committee noted that Soane had produced 270 plans, elevations and designs and had estimated the works at £154,600. It examined his pupil Henry Hake Seward who confirmed Soane's version of events. The members felt that Soane had employed 'great labour, talents and industry' in his preparations. On 26 June 1801, the order address and copy of the Lords' Committees was presented to His Majesty by the Lords with White

Staves and his answer, that 'he would give directions accordingly', recorded. Soane finally received £1,000, the double-payment a sop to his pride, on 30 July 1803.[9]

Farington reported an odd remark by Mrs Soane who had told him over a dinner at Lincoln's Inn Fields that 'Mr Soane was not to be compared with Mr Wyatt as to ability, but had taken more pains than Mr W would do.'[10] She was, perhaps, playing a rogue card for the notorious gossip to pass about, evidence of Soane's modesty and respect for the most powerful architect at the Royal Academy, at a moment when he was busily soliciting votes for the Royal Academy election.

Soane comforted himself by printing a lengthy account of the entire episode.[11] Like many that followed, the pamphlet was sent to friends and influential people to set the record straight but tended merely to cloud the picture. Soane's career from now on took place amidst a flurry of printed accusation, self-justification and anonymous detraction. 1799 saw his first outing in the libel courts.

On the death of Richard Jupp that spring, the surveyorship of the East India Company fell vacant. Soane found himself on the shortlist together with S. P. Cockerell and Henry Holland. He pursued the post strenuously, calling once again upon his many patrons and contacts with East India Company influence. The ballot on 1 May recorded a negative vote against all three candidates and disagreement among the committee members. Yet the following week, behind the closed doors of the Court of Directors, Henry Holland was comfortably elected. Soane suspected the intervention of the President of the Board of Control, Henry Dundas MP, a close associate of Pitt's, along with Earl Spencer, a long-established and faithful client of Holland's.[12]

The vote (according to Soane, but not minuted) was fifteen for Holland and nine for Soane. To secure nine votes in the face of such opposition says much for Soane's lobbying abilities but the votes of the Chairman and those representing the City interest were not enough to tip the balance in his favour. He must have been sure of some votes: in addition to the Chairman, David Scott, whose house he had pointedly shown at the Royal Academy in 1798, and Jacob Bosanquet, Soane could depend on Charles Mills, who would replace Scott as Chairman in 1801, since he was working on Mills's London house, 1 Mansfield Street in 1799.

Soane had struggled to obtain the commissions for India House and the East India Company surveyorship. Scott was astonished at his double failure.[13] Without any hint of deference (or tact), Soane wrote an injured letter in May 1799 to the Prime Minister, his solid patron until recently. He had 'flattered myself from your kindness that the result would have been otherwise' and he chose the moment to resign his position in the Woods and Forests which, he complained, 'is so very unlike what it was represented to me that it is impossible for me to do justice to the appointment'.[14] In early June the king instructed Pitt to offer the post of Deputy Surveyor of Woods and Forests to James Wyatt.[15] Perhaps Soane felt that Pitt's indebtedness to him, as the bills mounted for Holwood, gave him a privileged position. He wondered if he had lost Pitt's patronage – as some said – because he had been 'ungrateful' and voted against the Court of Directors who had agreed to pay the creditors of the Nawab of Arcot, a heavy burden on the proprietors (share-holders). Something had gone badly wrong and according to Wyatt, 'Soane has lost all footing with Pitt – who wishes to see the lines on *The Modern Goth*.'[16]

As usual Soane too unwisely resorted to print. He circulated a letter to Spencer, pointing out that 'the Company has not bought good value with Henry Holland'. Disingenuously he argued that he was concerned as a proprietor (which, he pointed out, the earl appeared not to be), then gave himself away with the suggestion that 'my own disappointment has wholly resulted from your Lordship's strenuous and repeated interference in favour of Mr Holland'. Returning to the economic argument, he made a hypothetical case. Were Lord Spencer to appoint a surveyor to 'a great national debt', would he choose a man who stood 'in the closest relation of blood and domestic intercourse with the tradesmen whose work and supplies were to constitute the heaviest charges of expenditure – of that expenditure which it was the chief province of the Surveyor to control and audit?' It was clearly different, he added cheekily, from the appointment of an architect at Althorp or Wimbledon, two of the three important commissions Holland had carried out for Spencer. 'God forbid, my Lord,' he wrote, unconvincingly, 'that in supposing a possible case, it should be considered as obliquely reflecting on the reputation of the successful candidate under your Lordship's powerful protection.' He was only worried having heard that the accounts in the Surveyors' department over the past seven or eight years showed expenditure 'not greatly short, as I have heard, of a million'. So the concerned proprietor ended his letter.

Despite everything, Soane was eager to keep his relationship with George Rose sweet, for he, jointly with Charles Long, continued to hold the key to patronage through the Treasury as well as that of personal access to Pitt. Soane immediately wrote thanking him for his consistent support and his 'extraordinary zeal and kindness on this occasion'.[17] He also pursued his grievance against the author of *The Modern Goth* and on finding the name of the author, the surveyor Philip Norris,[18] he took the advice of leading counsel that the case would stand up in court and issued proceedings for libel.

The judge in the King's Bench, Lord Kenyon, on hearing the evidence on 17 May 1799, took a very different view. After an entertaining discourse by Mr Law, counsel for the defence, who provoked laughter in court when he likened the Bank with its 'Egyptian hieroglyphics' to a 'Hall for Buonaparte' and wondered whether the Governors and Directors of that institution knew the difference between 'the figures of pounds, shillings and pence, [and] those of Hercules or Adonis',[19] the judge, himself citing Pope and Dryden, brought the whole sorry business to a rapid close. It was an expensive mistake; a sledgehammer approach to what had been little more than a puerile slight. By continuing to prosecute the case, Soane had drawn the attention of everyone, from the Prime Minister downwards, to a glancing satire. One or two papers published extracts from the offending verses, which now were guaranteed notoriety. Within his own peer group and at the Architects' Club, Soane's standing was now very low: even Dance was wearying of his behaviour.

Soane now realised that he had been wrong in assuming Pitt to be at the root of his troubles at the East India Company. He wrote desperately to him in the summer of 1799.[20]

As my mind was not quite satisfied with the drawings I had the honour to submit to you at Holwood, I have made more drawings for the improvements . . . which I hope and flatter myself will meet your approbation; be assured, Sir, no exertion on my part shall be wanting to make the house as worthy the possessor as I possibly can, for I can safely say it is, now, almost the only wish of my life to see the whole building completed.

He requested an appointment, so that no time be lost, but it was too late; the problem turned out not to be *The Modern Goth* but the state of Pitt's finances.

After Pitt's resignation, which took place on 3 February 1801, the list of his debts drawn up by the Bishop of Lincoln and sent to George Rose showed an £11,000 mortgage on Holwood (in two sums of £7,000 and £4,000) and the immense sum of £2,098 owed to Soane.[21] The sale of Holwood, his only realisable asset but also a 'sink of expense' had been proposed as early as 1800 but the house was not sold until October 1802, for £15,000.[22] It was a terrible blow to Pitt.

Bitterly as Soane took setbacks such as those at East India House and the House of Lords, he never lost momentum as a result of disappointment – rather the reverse. He merely fine-tuned his political contacts. During 1801, with Pitt out of office, Soane started work for Robert Banks Jenkinson MP, Foreign Secretary in Addington's new administration.

Jenkinson, who became Lord Hawkesbury in 1803, had entered the House of Commons in 1790, serving on the India Board and becoming Master of the Mint in Pitt's administration. His new acquisition, Coombe House at Kingston, about an hour from Westminster, was by coincidence familiar to Soane, who had worked there for Wilbraham Tollemache in 1782.

The rural atmosphere of a comfortable estate, just by Richmond Park, provided necessary relaxation for the Foreign Secretary and his wife, pottering around amongst ther pigs and turkeys before hurrying back to the ministerial round. The rutted lane and woodland setting failed to enchant one guest some years later. 'Coombe par ci, Coombe par la: nous avons été par tous les Coombes d'Angleterre' exploded Madame de Staël, two hours late for dinner. Soane paid many visits to Coombe over a long period, during which his small improvements to the house gradually made the Hawkesburys' haven more and more agreeable.[23] Lady Hawkesbury was Louisa Hervey, the Earl Bishop's youngest daughter whom Soane had met convalescing in Naples and, recovered, at Ickworth.

In 1808 Hawkesbury became the second Lord Liverpool and in 1812 the Prime Minister. Soane would work for him in Walmer when he became Warden of the Cinque Ports and later, in his official capacity, on Fife House in Whitehall. If Soane could not foresee that Hawkesbury would become Prime Minister, he had shrewdly ascertained that he was a young politician with good prospects. As the man who reconciled Pitt and Addington, Hawkesbury was in a strong position to lead the faction-ridden Tories through the harsh post-war years, with their problems of unrest, royal misbehaviour and economic crisis. As Pitt's star descended, Soane presciently identified a key new political client.

Royal favour still eluded Soane. Henry Holland remained securely – if frustratingly, given his client's ability to change his mind at every turn –

positioned in the royal favour, having worked for the Prince of Wales from the mid-1780s onwards, first at Carlton House and then in Brighton. For Soane, George III, with his close interest in the Royal Academy, had once seemed in some respects a more promising patron but James Wyatt was the king's man. Royal patronage was as distant a prospect at the end of the 1790s as ever. So far alterations for the Duke of Clarence had been the zenith of his work for the royal family.

Another prong in Soane's attack on the various 'Establishments' was to become one of the original proprietors of the newly formed Royal Institution. Set up with wide aims – loosely termed 'scientific philanthropy' – by Count Rumford, just arrived in England from Bavaria, in the autumn of 1799 a London mansion in Albemarle Street was purchased as headquarters. By May 1800 Soane was one of 280 proprietors, the body from which the ruling council was elected, paying 50 guineas for the privilege (soon to rise to 200 guineas). Soane may have become involved through John Coxe Hippisley, from Rome, who had resurfaced as Treasurer.[24]

Fortuitously for Soane's professional practice, in the late 1790s a young man applied to him for work. Joseph Michael Gandy, just returned from a turbulent visit to Rome, curtailed by his patron's bankruptcy[25] and the advance of the French, was a former Royal Academy student of great promise – he obtained the Gold Medal in 1790 – who had been in James Wyatt's office from the age of fifteen (fig. 110).

Gandy, who had travelled out to Rome with C. H. Tatham, already showed originality. The emotive language and the vivid, pictorial descriptions in his letters were those of a painter, even a dramatist in search of incident, but hardly of an architect following the path of classical antiquity. He revelled in the sublime landscape of the Chigi park, the monumental grandeur of the sequence of mausolea along the Appian Way (which he thought might well form a model for principal roads into London), and the catacombs, where he spent seven hours (taking string and bran to scatter behind him, Hansel and Gretel-like). He was thrilled by the illuminations at St Peter's.

> All night the Cathedral is illuminated by a cross of twenty five feet high and two broad, on all sides filled with lamps suspended from the dome. You must conceive this cross how brilliant it must appear to the eye for there are no other lights in the church, this giving sufficient light for the whole, the great depth of the aisles behind, the height of the dome above, forms such an amazing contrast with the illumined cross, as to give the effect I suppose that the sun would have were it to issue from the sky . . . in the dead of night.[26]

He witnessed a fantastic firework display on the Castel S. Angelo, the rockets being fired simultaneously and forming 'a beautiful fiery circular canopy [which] overspreads the whole heavens'. He had seen 'nothing to exceed it except Mount Vesuvius without those terrible emotions which that mountain gives you'.[27] Gandy liked to be in the thrall of his emotions and took a lugubrious delight in public hangings which were a regular feature of life in Rome, heightening the tension which the approaching French armies were inducing.

110. The Arch of Septimus Severus, Rome attributed to Joseph Gandy

The panic spread to the English community; he wrote home on 5 October 1796 'we English are in a state of war among ourselves which grows worse every day. As to myself I keep at home . . . I wish I was in England.'[28] Although he bought a selection of marble vases, Etruscan pieces and even Poussin paintings, his patron's failure meant that all his purchases were repossessed before he could leave Rome. Despite the difficult times, Gandy travelled to Naples, and Mount Vesuvius erupted, as if on cue.

Returning to London in 1797, he cannot have hoped for much. 'Oh Joseph,' his father had written that April, 'the distress this country is in I cannot describe'.[29] Two months later, the scene was worse still:

the sailors [are] in a state of mutiny, marines also, and the Government is in continual alarm for the soldiers. Disaffected people are endeavouring to throw their allegiance away. For some times past Plymouth, Portsmouth, Sheerness, and places adjacent have been in a state like siege, and by our own shipping, in fact the shipping has fired balls at other ships that were not mutinous, and at different places on the coast, furnaces for heating balls are prepared to fire our own ships . . . The French are preparing to invade, having no other enemy now to cope with . . . Ireland is under martial law. Civil war and rebellion in that country. This is very alarming and yet John Bull is but just wagging his tail, and pawing the ground, bellowing a little and tossing his head . . .[30]

As his father wrote, Gandy was hurrying home, travelling from Florence with the King's Messenger, Hunter.

As an unknown architect without patronage, Gandy could hardly have returned at a worse moment. He had no chance of setting up in practice on his own account and, having failed to find a post as a district surveyor, in his view a dull job ensuring that buildings did not infringe any Act of Parliament, there were no obvious prospects. When he solicited employment in person, 'Soane was the only architect who answered his wishes . . . for him he bent the whole of his genius in that line of direction which forwarded his views' as a family source put it, tortuously.[31] Soane, immediately spotting his extraordinary abilities as a perspectivist, employed him as a draughtsman.

Gandy added a dimension to Soane's work which his own and other careful, but dry, hands could not. The combination of rich coloration, theatrical light-effects, an exaggerated perspective and an inventive use of small touches – an open architectural folio, a scene glimpsed through the window – gives the interiors a remarkable sense of movement, unfolding spatial effect and illumination. Out in the landscape, evening light, seasonal colouring and, when needed, thundery effects replace the ubiquitous pale blue cloudy skies of standard renderings. It is as if Soane's architecture had been waiting for someone to translate his buildings from pleasing fair copies into a continuous narrative – a visual argument with which to confront a critical world.

Gandy became the inspired interpreter of Soane's work, offering an idealised architectural vision. Soane immediately set him to work on his proudest achievements; the breakfast room at No. 12, at Tyringham and the Bank. Gandy freed Soane from the confines of his tight, troubled personality and put himself at the service of Soane's suppressed romanticism

111. Joseph Gandy's 1830 cut-away perspective shows the Bank as a Pompeii-like survival. However, the only ruins are those to the right of the ornamental frame, there is no decay and it offers a detailed record of Soane's entire building programme at the Bank of England, a kind of cumulative construction drawing. Clearly identifiable is the Rotunda, in the right foreground, the Bullion Court in the centre of the site, leading to the Lothbury Court (resembling the Forum Romanum) behind it.

(fig. 111). As the two men worked together each seemed to offer the other wider and more exciting possibilities. What Gandy might have achieved as a painter, rather than as a minor architect and supreme architectural draughtsman, is perhaps suggested by the career of his near contemporary J.M.W. Turner (fig. 112).

The recent heady experiences in Rome and Naples gave Gandy his ability to translate Soane's flights of architectural imagination vividly. Gandy worked for Soane very much as a modern architect might employ a trusted photographer to convey the idealised image of his building, perfectly lit. Gandy's characteristic high viewpoint and altered perspective achieved a magnification of space, accentuated by the miniaturised figures. He ensured that Soane's interiors were a picturesque journey; the succession of brilliantly lit and profoundly dark spaces was, in his hands, a validation and evocation of Soane's intent. The great theatrical swags that framed many of the perspectives helped to signal that the norms and conventions of architectural rendering had been relaxed.

At the Royal Academy, where Soane had scarcely exhibited lately, there was suddenly a flurry of his work on show. Gandy's interpretation of Soane's schemes, built or unbuilt, were eye-catching in the Continental fashion of Grand Prix and Diploma works. He employed theatrical presentation (increasingly literally) and strong colour; there was no danger of overlooking Gandy's work (and, therefore, Soane's) even in the darkest, highest corner of the Royal Academy galleries.

After Gandy left Soane's office around 1800, to start his own architectural practice, much of which was based in the north-west of England, he continued to undertake work for him for another thirty years. Gandy's involvement in the presentation of a Soane building or project was, by definition, proof of its importance.

Gandy's highly coloured, dramatic view of the world made its own impact upon Soane, much as his equally theatrical ideas did. Although we now see much of Soane's work (especially that which no longer stands or which was never executed) through Gandy's eyes, it is tempting to wonder whether Soane had begun to see his buildings as they might appear to Gandy, before he had himself laid a line on paper.

Soane backed Gandy's campaign to be elected as an Associate of the Royal Academy in 1802 and later Gandy used the Royal Academy to display his own, increasingly fantastic, architectural fantasies. Some of the later commissions that Soane supplied to Gandy were a way of disguising charity for patronage (he supported Gandy and his family steadfastly, all his life) but they never failed to glorify Soane's achievement. Gandy admired Soane the architect unreservedly, writing many years later: 'you are the only one . . . [to] show that architecture is not an imitative art, whose models must be formed in the mind, because there are none in nature'.[32]

Soane's trust in Gandy later led him to place his son John in his office and his dependence on Gandy's ability to present his achievements to a wider world grew over the years, far more than it did upon the writings of John Britton or John Taylor, the two men who most faithfully represented his interests, and opinions, in print. Gandy, a man as much at odds with the world as Soane often saw himself to be, helped to give him the confidence to express his individuality – now that he had achieved a position of professional strength and financial independence.

Soane's relationship with Gandy was assisted by his understanding of his quirky, possessed mind – unstable in a way Soane could never admit to being but oddly similar in its obsessive, persecuted manner. Their relationship was symbiotic and central to Soane's career. He owed him far more than has been acknowledged. Sir John Summerson in his essay on Gandy[33] saw him as a tough romantic in a literary tradition and in his radical rustic designs he found 'a frustrated Wordsworth of architecture'. Gandy combines the functional, the abstract, with the symbolic in a way which has more than a hint of Ledoux and Boullée.[34] It was Gandy, far ahead of Soane in the breadth of his interests and references, who released the latent romanticism in Soane's work. He teases it out, introducing a narrative element (there are often clues for the initiated in the work) and by the end, in the great 'catalogue' pieces, takes Soane's work to a crescendo – adding a sense of fantastic melodrama, teetering on the line where popular panoramas, dioramas and theatre met the work of painters such as John Martin.[35]

Correspondingly, Soane also acted as the brake on Gandy's fantasies. Left to himself, Gandy's fervour became unchecked and his tumultuous mind lacked discipline and, later, any sense of its limits. His final project, interrupted by his death, was to have been a view, in one thousand drawings, of the history of the world's architecture.

In 1798 a twenty-two-year-old topographic painter called William Turner had applied for Associate Membership of the Royal Academy. He was unsuccessful but the following year he did become an Associate. His ambitions and abilities as a lobbyist in his own interest were little short of Soane's own. When Gandy was elected an architect Associate of the Royal Academy the year after himself, Turner objected that he had not yet built anything. He may have felt that Gandy was a rival but he had little to worry about on that count.

At the time that Gandy entered his office, Soane was attempting to become a full academician. In February 1799, his first try, he received just one vote on each ballot, the successful candidate being William Daniell of Chertsey, with Joseph Bonomi (an Italian-born architect) four votes

112. George Dance's drawing of a very young William (J.M.W.) Turner, from August 1792 when Turner was seventeen, when he worked with Thomas Hardwick among other architect contemporaries of Soane's. It may have been then that Soane first met the impressively able young draughtsman.

behind. Over the coming months Bonomi and Soane fought it out. Soane applied his formidable skills to lobbying, holding dinners for men such as Farington, Smirke and Tyler – powerful Royal Academicians who would need considerable persuasion to vote for Soane. In the meantime, with Wheatley's death came another vacancy.

By February 1802 there was a strong core of promised votes for Soane and a campaign orchestrated by Thomas Banks, as Soane himself was in bed with gout (although discussing a commission with a client when Farington, who was following his efforts with interest, called).[36] There were three vacancies and the favoured candidates were Soane, Turner and Rossi, with Bonomi as the outsider. The favourites won.

Soane remained confined indoors and immobile, although that evening he happily received a deputation of congratulatory artists at his bedside – including Dance, Lawrence, Richard Cosway, Daniell, Flaxman and Banks.[37] The following day Eliza Soane did the rounds on his behalf, conveying thanks to those who had supported his candidacy. By the end of the month he was better but it was Mrs Soane who had been to Christie's auction house to bid for Beckford's memorable series of *The Rake's Progress* by Hogarth. The series of eight paintings cost Soane 570 guineas. The previous year Beckford was already deep in a prolonged and costly court case and began to readjust his possessions to better reflect the gothic setting of Fonthill Abbey, and to bring in some necessary funds. James Wyatt's gothic 'abbey' replaced Fonthill Splendens where Soane had first seen the Hogarths eighteen years before.[38]

A few days later the new Hogarths were on display over dinner at Lincoln's Inn Fields to a select group of Royal Academicians, Farington, Smirke and Westall. Gratifyingly the connoisseur Sir George Beaumont was eager to purchase the Hogarth series and had asked Farington to offer Soane 600 guineas, to which the response was that if he was to part with them 'it must be at a high price'.[39] A 30 guinea profit was hardly Soane's object in his grandest purchase yet.

In this spirit of reconciliation Soane even commissioned Smirke sen. to paint a vast transparency for the illuminations at the Bank, celebrating the Peace of Amiens.

Soane and J.M.W. Turner, as he now styled himself, proudly attended their first Anniversary dinner,[40] a fine meal with distinguished guests and 'considerably heightened by several excellent glees and catches'. By December 1802 Soane and the other new members had joined the Council, on the rotating system that was operated at the Royal Academy. There are grounds for speculation that Turner and Soane had already been acquainted for some years before meeting at the Royal Academy, despite the considerable difference in their ages. In his late teens Turner had followed a course of lessons on perspective with Thomas Malton jun. and worked in the office of Thomas Hardwick, whom Soane had known from Rome. As long ago as March 1792 Soane had written in his notebook against the name of Turner, 'To define the profession and qualifications of an architect'.[41]

That June, Soane had laid on a large, four-oared boat to row his Royal Academy friends to Osterley down the Paddington Canal, linking the Grand Junction Canal to Brentford. At three o'clock they dined in the Menagerie on a meal brought from the inn at Ealing. It was, Farington wrote, very agreeable and the weather was delightful. The President, Benjamin West, was of the party and so was Dance.[42] Turner was not there; it was his season for travelling. Soane was jointly lobbying for his next strategic move at the Academy and helping his good friend William Praed by drumming up interest in and, perhaps subscriptions to, the Grand Junction Canal. Soane had recently subscribed £3,000 himself.

On this occasion the guests did not visit, but no doubt knew all about, Soane's new project nearby in Ealing, his almost complete country house, Pitshanger Manor.

9

THE PITSHANGER DREAM

While the boat-load of Royal Academicians was rowed along the canal past Osterley that summer's day in 1802, work on Pitshanger Manor (fig. 113), the house in Ealing, was continuing. Soane's country house project had already engrossed him for two years. It would take another two to come near to completion. Finally, on Sunday, 29 April 1804 Mrs Soane recorded that the family had 'dined at Ealing on a hot dinner for the first time'.[1] The rebuilding of Pitshanger Manor, scene of Soane's early work with George Dance, was complete for the time being. Displayed in the house, the prize in his growing collection, was Hogarth's tragic story of the decline of a young man, *The Rake's Progress* bought from the Beckford sale.

In May 1800 Soane had purchased a plot of land in Acton for £500 and set his draughtsmen and model-maker to work on a proposed villa. Hardly had the plans been completed than Soane, possibly tipped off by Thomas Dance (George's son and a trustee of the Gurnell estate during the minority of Gurnell's daughter), discovered that Pitshanger was about to be sold. Given the memories that Pitshanger held, it was extraordinary that fate should have seen it fall into his hands twenty-five years later. Fortunately, John Winter, solicitor to the Bank of England, who was involved in Soane's recent libel case and had been his client for a house nearby, bought the Acton site from him, allowing Soane to seize the chance of purchasing the house from which his entire professional journey had begun.[2]

Having to raise a considerable sum, Soane made a careful calculation of his means, to the very penny. In 1799 he itemised his holdings: Bank stock at £4,000, East India stock at £6,000 and 5 per cent Loyalty Loan at £6,025. In addition he held £6,285 8s 4d in 3 per cent consols and £1,000 in 4 per cent consols. He had ten shares in the London Bridge Waterworks and some in the Westminster Annuity Office, one City bond, five Grand Junction shares (which paid no interest) and £4,750 in Grand Junction Bonds, paying interest. There was a £1,000 mortgage out to James Spiller and £500 in the British Fire Office. Soane's holdings were a remarkable spread, many of them concerns in which he had a professional interest. That year his unearned income was £1,792 6s 2d. 'For business done but not all in the present year' he had earned £2,419 9s 8d.[3] Rents from various properties amounted to £600 in 1804, although two were being rebuilt.

113. Pencil view of Pitshanger Manor, as it was in 1800 when Soane bought it.

In 1800, an exceptional year, his expenditure was £12,088 19s 5d which included the £4,500 he paid for Pitshanger. His income was £11,695 0s 5d – equivalent to about £350,000 in modern terms. He had sold his Loyalty Bonds (to which he had subscribed in 1798) to raise the funds for buying Pitshanger and the remainder went towards a massive loan of £2,900 to his client at Bentley Priory and Baronscourt, the Marquis of Abercorn. Soane's business affairs were a formidable operation aimed at balancing the advantages of advances, bearing interest, made to important clients against the return on numerous small speculations including turnpikes, wet docks and an East Indiaman.

Soane bought the Pitshanger estate for £4,500 on 1 August 1800[4] and set Henry Seward to work on the following day. Soane's object was, in retrospect, to 'have a residence for myself and family, and afterward for my eldest son who . . . had also shown a decided passion for. . .architecture, which he wished to pursue as a profession . . . I wished to make Pitzhanger Manor-house as complete as possible for the future residence of the young architect.'

Currently the 'young architect', now aged fourteen, was being educated, with his brother, at a school in Moorfields (just north of the City of London) run by the Reverend Charles Applebee. Their previous schoolmaster, Mr Wicks had proved wanting – Soane grumpily paid his bills 'for *not* teaching the boys' and, six months later, 'for keeping the children in ignorance'.[5] By the time that Pitshanger was nearing completion, in September 1802, the boys had moved to the Reverend William Chapman's school in Margate, in the hopes that John's worryingly weak chest might respond to a seaside climate.

The immediate function of Pitshanger Manor, though, was to provide a fitting stage for John Soane RA, as he had become in 1802. His house would become a place in which City financiers, aristocrats and landowners, artists, writers, medical men (but few fellow architects) could meet at his invitation. Chambers had bought Whitton Place in Hounslow, a Palladian villa by Roger Morris, and James Wyatt nearby Hanworth Farm, but no other of Soane's architect contemporaries could boast such a backdrop. Pitshanger would be like Reynolds's studio or the Cosways' *salon*-cum-concert room at Schomberg House or their subsequent house at Stratford Place, an artist-collector's house.

Richard Cosway, like Soane, knew and was inspired by both Horace Walpole's Strawberry Hill and Beckford's Fonthill Abbey. After Maria Cosway (Soane's friend Maria Hadfield from Italy) had returned to Paris in 1801 Soane was a regular visitor to Stratford Place.[6] The Cosways' own works mingled with Old Masters on their walls in what Hazlitt described as 'a fairy palace . . . specimens of art, antiquarianism, and *virtu* jumbled all together in the richest disorder'. Soane's advantage over Cosway was that he (like Walpole and Beckford) had designed the setting of his collection.

Ealing was, like the neighbouring parishes of Hanwell, Greenford and Perivale, a rural area with an economy dependent on the city. In 1799 a large amount of the farmland, some 1,400 acres, was put down to grass providing hay for London's horses and dairy cows. Almost 300 acres was devoted to market gardening. A walk from Brentford in the 1770s, a distance of some 2 miles, passed five gentleman's seats as well as the houses of a bishop, a duke and a princess. John Yeoman wrote 'I leave the reader to judge the pleasantness of our walk and where there was no gentleman's seat, it was gardeners' gardens with fruit trees all in full bloom which makes it like the seat of Paradise.'[7] The princess in question was George II's youngest daughter Amelia who lived at Gunnersbury Park from 1763 until 1786. the year that Soane began his remodelling of Pitshanger, the house was demolished. The rebuilt house became the banker Nathan Mayer Rothschild's mansion.

The parish of Greater Ealing consisted of around 250 houses. Brentford, where the Grand Union Canal joined the Thames, was a growing town with new docks and warehouses but due north Ealing remained undisturbed until the coming of the railways. Only the hugely popular annual Ealing Fair, held in late June on Ealing Green just in front of Pitshanger Manor, broke the calm of the village. The lordship of the manor was held by the Bishop of London; the fishing rights in the sub-manor of Pitshanger remained in the hands of the Gurnells. Soane made good use of the latter privilege.

Soane's opposite neighbours were Edward Payne and Lord Kinnaird at, respectively, Ealing House and Ealing Grove, while the Hall or Red House was still the property of Mrs Peyton, the remarried widow of Jonathan Gurnell, his immediate neighbour. The family, wealthy from the commercial success of Gurnell, Hoare and Harman, also owned farms in and around the parish. The sale of Pitshanger represented the beginning of the break-up of their considerable holdings of land and property.

The medieval church had been rebuilt as a modest early Georgian structure while Rectory House, a moated Elizabethan building, was run as a well-regarded school by the Reverend Dr Nicholas; among the teachers for a few years was Louis-Philippe, Duc d'Orléans, later to be proclaimed the French king on the crest of republican hopes – soon dashed. Ealing was, conveniently for a frequent traveller like Soane, on the turnpike to the west country. The New Inn was a stage-post, also offering a regular coach service into London, less than an hour's journey along the Uxbridge Road.

It was, then, a predominantly rural scene that met Eliza Soane and her cousin Miss Levick when they went out to Ealing in August 1800 to see the house for the first time. This venture had clearly been Soane's decision alone. Plans and designs for the Acton site were adapted. Soane experimented; he pulled rooms out into curving bow fronts, into ovals and ellipses. In one plan the ground-floor was dominated by a 24-foot-long oval dining-room. On several plans 'John's study' is marked (fig. 114), replacing the earlier 'boys' room'. For the exterior, early drawings show that he intended to use flint and brick; even the pilasters were of flint (fig. 116). A shallow, circular lantern breaks the roofline, almost the only characteristic Soane hallmark at this stage. There was, as yet, no indication of his decision to retain the Dance work in the south wing.

With only himself to please, Soane was uncertain. He explored divergent options, toying with the materials of his youth, the flints and clays of the Thames Valley and the Chilterns, a reflection of the retrospective mood in which he had bought the house. Tempted as he was to delve back into his memories, in the end he confined the use of flint to a rusticated entrance arch and an ornamental bridge. Among the many schemes for

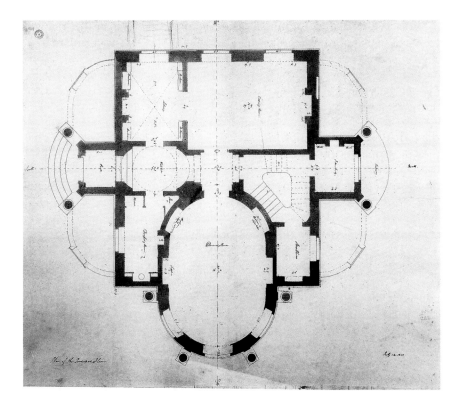

114. Ground floor plan of Soane's planned villa at Acton, dated July 1800 and showing 'John's study' to the north (right of the picture). A month later Soane had finalised the purchase of nearby Pitshanger Manor instead.

the entrance gate, one shows a pair of lodges, with flint pilasters employed as they were on the early versions of the main house.[8]

When built Pitshanger Manor was of white London stock brick, dressed with Portland stone. On 6 October, his clerk of works from the Bank, Walter Payne, began to supervise the demolition of the old house – his instructions being to retain the south wing and George Dance's elegant rooms. Soane claimed there was nothing sentimental in this decision, but that he had drawn these rooms when he was first in Dance's office.[9]

115. Soane's elevation of Pitshanger, dated 4 September 1800, in which he toyed with using flint as an ornamental feature. Dance's wing is to the left.

By October the drawings show Soane had now finalised his thinking for the front elevation; the visitor's first impression of Pitshanger would be a triumphal arch. Four giant Ionic columns mark the entrance, a version of his hidden Lothbury Court gateway at the Bank. The parapet is accentuated by urns and a sarcophagus, sculptural panels are set into the masonry and each column is surmounted by a Coade stone statue modelled upon those at the Temple of Pandrosus in Athens. Soane had travelled full circle and returned to the scheme for the Acton house, as worked up in his models. While for his country-house clients he usually offered a menu of options, frequently paring them down to match their finances, here – as his own client – he is working through the possibilities to a climax, a memorable personal architectural statement (fig. 118).

By 1801 the designs for the exterior were largely resolved, apart from the ornamental details which he was still refining. Soane threw all his efforts, and his best colleagues and tradesmen, into the job, as evidenced by Walter Payne's division of his time between here and the Bank. The excellent John Haverfield provided advice on the planting and layout of the grounds. A mulberry tree and strawberry beds were to be retained and a circular grass 'plat' formed the principal feature in the main garden, with flower borders along the Mattock Lane perimeter.[10] As his attention turned to the interiors, he brought in his friend and Beckford's wealthy agent, Edward Foxhall, now also a neighbour in Ealing, and the auctioneer and estate agent John Robins, for whom Soane was rebuilding nearby Norwood Hall at this period, to advise and provide furnishings, upholstery and ornament. Mrs Soane was fully involved, buying at auction, organising the numerous tradesmen involved and choosing items. Money was no object; by 1801, a year of national financial calamity with rising prices and bad harvests, his half-yearly commission at the Bank had risen to an astonishing £1,032 5s 9d. As demolition progressed, he meticulously accounted for any materials he was able to resell at the standard $2^{1}/_{2}$ per cent commission.[11]

In autumn 1801 Soane had moved on to the layout of the service wing at Pitshanger. In a series of rough plans, the functional elements, the washhouse, bakery, wood and coal stores, formed a block to the north. Soane designed a stable block with one of his favourite screen walls, marked out with shallow blank arches – little deeper than the grooves and incisions into plaster and wood that increasingly served him as interior mouldings. As the scheme developed, a full-width, top-lit, north-facing gallery for plaster casts and models was added on this side. Soane noted 'ruins of a temple opposite this window'.

The idea of a fragmentary classical landscape glimpsed outside a gallery filled with casts of antique statuary was a bold notion. Evocatively caught, it would be the punctuation mark in a sequence which began as the visitor passed through the triumphal arch into the house.[12] Thomas Whately extolled the effectiveness of ruins. 'All remains excite an enquiry into the former state of the edifice, and fix the mind in a contemplation on the use it was applied to . . . they suggest ideas which would not arise from the buildings, if entire'. If such effects 'properly belong to real ruins . . . they are produced in a certain degree by those which are fictitious . . . the representation, though it does not present facts to the memory, yet suggests subjects to the imagination'. Soane had bought Whately's *Observations on Modern Gardening* in 1778, a very early purchase.[13]

Vanbrugh had been an early exponent of the emotive, associational aspects of a ruin, arguing that Woodstock Manor should be preserved, merely to be glimpsed across the park at Blenheim (a view of which Soane was particularly fond). From then on, the eighteenth century had seen a rage for mock castles, eye-catchers and *fermes ornées* such as Wooburn Farm near Chertsey which Soane knew. Many estates with which he was familiar – Hagley, Wimpole, Chillington, Painshill – had a ruined castle outlined on a knoll or nestling by a lake for double effect.

Ruins of a fictional classical antiquity were more *recherché* and Soane's exchange of space, between the windows of his house, its antique contents and the classical ruins beyond was both deft and original. In the final arrangement the gallery was attached to the north of the house, no longer linked to the ruins, and a 'rude' colonnade ran from the house to the service wing. The interplay between the contents of rooms in the house and an area for display was, however, to linger in the conservatory/gallery that Soane added in 1802, running along the entire west front, a brick pillared loggia with coloured glass inserted in the full-height glazing.

Soane was suffering from the effects of chronic overwork and in early October he had a bad attack of gout, a pain described by the Reverend Sydney Smith as like walking on your eyeballs, and was confined for several days. He hated illness and was an irascible invalid and difficult patient, cancelling appointments and operations and disregarding medical advice. He later told Timothy Tyrrell that 'to a mind naturally active, no torture is like the pain of idleness'.[14] Recovered, he began to take close friends, such as William Praed, out to view progress at Ealing. In early December, the house was sufficiently advanced that he could concentrate on building his ruins.

Supervision of Pitshanger meant countless journeys to Ealing. Generally he used his own carriage for the journey but in good weather he sometimes went on foot, a distance of around nine miles from Holborn. In May 1802 he walked to Pitshanger with Thomas Banks, in July with Thomas Leverton, later on he returned to town on foot with Turner. The long walk on light summer evenings allowed for the discussion of Royal Academy, architectural or business matters. By this summer, the main burden of design and execution was complete (fig. 115). On rare occasions he spent a relaxing day at home with his rod and soon he was stocking the waters with fish.

Long before the house was ready for occupation Soane had written a lengthy, clumsily ironic description of Pitshanger.[15] 'There has lately been discovered in the Manor of Pitshanger at Ealing the remains of a very ancient building of Greek and Roman architecture.' The visitor would come upon a motto 'et fillii filiorum'[16] which would show 'that not only some private person had occupied the site, but also that he had fondly flattered himself with the hope of its remaining for ages in his family'. The manuscript is dated 1802; Soane was optimistic about John and George, the eventual inheritors of his fine mansion, as they neared university age. When he printed the account in 1833, he had abandoned all but the faintest hopes of a family succession.

Soane also set Gandy to work. As early as November 1800 he had spent almost a fortnight on a perspective envisaging the house as it was to be

116. Rear elevation of the rebuilt core of Pitshanger Manor, showing Dance's wing retained to the right. In 1802 Soane added a conservatory along the length of the principal floor.

(including the retained Dance wing but excluding the service wing and gallery to the north), set in well-planted, mature grounds in which a bevy of 'fashionables' are promenading (the wispy figures, in this case, added by Antonio Van Assen). In 1802, when the decoration of the rooms had yet to be finalised, Gandy visualised the library and breakfast room, fully furnished and decorated. Upon consideration, Soane abandoned the delicacy of the aqueous colours and light panelling of a scheme based upon Roman frescoes for his breakfast room and turned to something altogether more structural, coloured in strong, dark simulations of marble and bronze, and overwhelmingly classical.[17] In his own house he could develop schemes too bold for even his most accommodating clients.

Increasingly, Gandy's spectacular renderings of Soane's work incorporated plans and designs for lost projects, the visual counterpart to his pamphlets of self-justification. If his House of Lords would never be built, then his perspectives and plans would reappear over and over again in Gandy's paintings. Thus, visitors to the Royal Academy in 1803 saw in Gandy's perspective of the Pitshanger library the designs for the House of Lords unrolled, casually, on a table. (They also saw the House of Lords itself exhibited in its own right, year after year. Soane believed in hammering points home.)

Eliza was not prepared to sacrifice her summer holiday by the sea for Pitshanger. In 1803 she tried to tempt Soane to take some time off to join her and Mrs Wheatley in Margate. Francis Wheatley RA had died two years before, leaving his widow in financial straits and the sympathetic Mrs Soane had taken pity on her. Soane consented to join them; it was never wasted time to be seen in a fashionable resort; a good slice of the influential and fashionable society of London could be found in the triangle of Thanet resorts, Margate, Ramsgate, Kingsgate and Broadstairs during the season – offering strong possibilities for meeting old clients or finding new ones.

In 1803 Mrs Soane gave a grand supper in honour of the celebrated musical partners, their friends John Braham and Nancy (or Anna –

Mozart's first Susanna from Florence) Storace who were appearing at a benefit at the Theatre Royal. As that year Eliza did not have a cook with her, she sent the haunch of venison round to Kidman's Hotel to be prepared. She told Soane 'We sat down *21* – without the boys – and a very jolly dinner it was – I assure you we have had full credit for it – for it has been as much talked of as any Cabinet dinner in town – your friend Mr. R. Bosanquet is here, I invited him, but he is too ill, or fancies so, to dine out.'[18]

Soane, when of the party, was always eager for architectural excursions and over the years he visited Minster and Pegwell, Rochester and Cobham Hall and rarely missed a visit to Canterbury. Nevertheless in 1803 his mind was much taken up with the completion of Pitshanger and the continuing dramas at the Royal Academy.

In August 1804 Mrs Soane was on the north Kent coast again, but this time in Ramsgate and once more with Mrs Wheatley. Farington met them at the Margate Assembly Room one evening. (The two towns were sufficiently close for such excursions.) Soane's health was a topic of conversation: Eliza had told Mrs Wheatley (who had told Farington) that he was in pain and sleeping badly. She suspected 'a stomach & bowel complaint; an apprehension of some ossification'.[19] Given Mrs Soane's consistent kindness to Mrs Wheatley she might have been unhappy to discover her gossiping about her husband's intestines. Later in the holiday, Soane, presumably now recovered, joined them.

Although the family had already spent many summer days at Pitshanger, it was in the summer of 1804 that the social launching of Soane's great enterprise took place. The house became the backdrop for what Soane, gilding the lily, remembered as a succession of 'Gothic scenes and intellectual banquets'.[20] Britain and France may have been at war, for in May 1803 hostilities had resumed, but that was no reason to forego offering hospitality on a grand scale. Pitshanger was on view to clients who had become friends such as the Simmonds, a Reading family for whom Soane had designed both a house and a new brewery, the Collyers, Pattesons[21] and Pratts from Norfolk, Lord and Lady Bridport from Somerset and the Samuel Thorntons from the City. Other regular guests were close personal friends such as Robert Pennington, Mr and Mrs James Peacock, John Taylor – the editor of the *Morning Post* and (incongruously) the royal oculist – and the antiquarian John Britton and his garrulous wife. Others included Braham and Storace, friendly academicians and their families, such as the Flaxmans, the de Loutherbourgs and the Beecheys, Sir Francis Bourgeois and, most frequently of all, J.M.W. Turner, the latter as enthusiastic a fisherman as Soane. Selected friends came to dine and stayed the night. The constant stream of visitors and the congenial summer parties ensured that the beautifully appointed villa would be talked about in the highest circles, bearing witness to Soane's abilities, his originality and, self-evidently, his extraordinary success.[22]

Pitshanger, completed, was an assembly of Soane's ideas and his visitors were taken on a tour of house and grounds. Visitors entered the forecourt through the flint and brick arch and past a lodge, neatly tucked back against the wall, a curving corner rendering it almost unnoticed. The archway offered a taste of the rustic – Pitshanger, the rural villa – ornamented with the symbols of hospitality, pineapples. The short drive took an oblique approach to the house – a memory of the corner entrance to Ledoux's Hôtel Montmorency and a reworking of the oblique approach to Tyringham – maximising the small forecourt, and approached their host's grand homage to Rome and the Arch of Constantine.

On entering the hall, through the temple front and its carefully chosen antique ornament, visitors would be bathed in golden light, coming from the internal fanlight and the amber glazing which pierced the full height 'tribune' or vestibule, its walls painted to simulate veined marble of various colours.[23] From that point they could immediately see, through the windows of the small drawing room ahead, the interior landscape of the greenhouse and beyond Soane's carefully planted gardens. On the walls of the drawing-room or 'retiring parlour', the first room that any visitor would enter, hung Soane's finest trophies from Beckford's Fonthill Splendens: *The Rake's Progress* and his Canaletto.

Beyond it, the conservatory-gallery extended across the full width of the west-facing garden front and was filled with antique fragments, urns and statues peering out between the vines and heavily scented plants. Soane had envisaged a theatrical effect, with the conservatory ideally lit by the moon or a careful arrangement of lamps. Beyond, the gardens would be 'enriched with company enjoying the delights of cheerful society'. The picturesque interplay between the exterior and interior was continual. Turning right from the vestibule or inner hall, visitors found themselves in the library, again with a window looking into the dense vegetation of the conservatory gallery.

The library and the east-facing breakfast room off it were the most refined version to date of Soane's domestic interiors; a linked pair of canopied rooms, their walls punctured by niches and dissolved by mirrors, their ceilings defying the ostensible restrictions of a small cube, peeling back to reveal a simulation of summer skies, or thrown open as if under a shady pergola at Pompeii. In the library – which may have been more of a study, since most of the books were upstairs – Soane had returned to the decorative theme of the breakfast room at 12 Lincoln's Inn Fields, painted trellis-work. The walls were grained to look like golden satinwood. Doors and shutters were of fine, inlaid wood.

The sternly classical scheme of the breakfast room came as a complete contrast (fig. 117). There were bronzed caryatids in each corner, marbled panels, winged victories in the spandrels of the ceiling and, on the canopy, Soane's favourite flattened and optically adjusted Greek Key ornament, pierced by an oculus to reveal a *trompe l'œil* sky. These were domesticised and miniaturised versions of the grand rooms at the Bank or at Wimpole, which few of his friends and clients could have seen: Soane's hand was becoming increasingly assured. As at Lincoln's Inn Fields, he was his own ideal client.

As if to set his innovations in context, visitors would be taken down a few steps to the south wing, and back three decades in architectural thinking, to George Dance's eating-room, with its lacy, compartmentalised ceiling decoration set squarely upon an ornamental cornice and frieze. It, and the drawing-room above, had little relation to Dance's own current thinking and less still to Soane's. They were a distant milestone along Soane's professional journey. But he chose these rooms to display some of his finest acquisitions to date, for a visit to Pitshanger was also a visit to a private gallery. His collection of architectural folios and his prized library were kept in the large drawing-room. Until 1807, all his important purchases were displayed at Pitshanger.[24] The huge *Merry Wives of Windsor*, a suitably convivial Shakespearean scene and Owen's feeble pair of portraits, showing Soane in one, his sons in the other, hung in the dining-room.[25]

The latter portrait, first shown at the Royal Academy in 1805 and then taken to Pitshanger, shows John, looking mournful and distracted, holding his mortar board, proof of his entrance to Trinity College, Cambridge in March 1804. George, behind him, has a spark of liveliness in his sidelong glance and a fresh, rakish air about him. Soane's younger son was already showing signs of independence (fig. 119). Soane's unrealistic aspirations for his sons were already marking their demeanour.

For those who wanted to complete the tour, there remained the basement monk's dining-room, which lay below the west front. In June 1804 'Monk' Lewis, the eponymous author of the 1796 novel,[26] was among his visitors. Intriguingly, the arch-populariser of the literary gothick craze had come to Pitshanger, an early guest to the finished house, to view Soane's built exercise in gothick fantasy downstairs.[27] Another visitor was James Boaden, whose *Aurelio and Miranda* of 1798 was based upon *The Monk* (as were countless popular entertainments of the time, ranging from opera to pantomime).[28]

The room that these priests of the current literary fad visited was encrusted with actual gothic fragments, lit by stained-glass and inhabited, Soane liked to tell, by a resident hermit.[29] Lewis laced his immature tales with a salacious dash of illicit passion played out by friars and nuns in catacombs and poorly lit crypts. Varying the genre, Beckford's *Vathek* had introduced a note of oriental mystique, an eclectic mixture of medievalism and the eastern suiting Beckford's picture of himself as the abbot of an exotic cultural order. Soane was no Beckford, nor a Walpole, although the latter's gothick cabinet of curiosities, seen under a shaft of golden light at Strawberry Hill, played its part in forming his tastes. Nevertheless Soane was as ill-suited to facetiousness as to gothick revivalism, either in prose or architecture.

Soane's own preferred reading matter was solidly that of the Enlightenment and he remained entirely unreceptive to James Peacock's advice to study Macknight's *Truth of the Gospel History* and 'burn Voltaire, Hume, Gibbon and the rest of the infidel rout'.[30] In 1802, the young Reverend Sydney Smith, an exemplarily broad-minded cleric, referred to the 'shallow impostures, and the silly ignorant sophisms of Voltaire, Rousseau, Cordorcet, D'Alembert and Volney[31] and . . . Hume . . . While these pernicious writers have power to allure from the Church great numbers of proselytes, it is better to study them diligently, and to reply to them satisfactorily.' Some years before, that 'complete original' and most unclerical figure the Earl Bishop had pressed a collected edition of Rousseau on the agricultural observer (and future country parson), Arthur Young.[32] Soane was no proselytiser but the Enlightenment was his creed and classical antiquity his church.

Outside, to the north of Pitshanger Manor, a colonnade, built of 'mutilated trunks of ancient columns', linked the main house to the service wing and gallery. From there, the visitors could glimpse, framed by Soane's cast collection (to which he was continually adding), his final master-stroke, a

117. Detail of the breakfast room at Pitshanger Manor, a marked departure from the earlier one at Lincoln's Inn Fields (see fig 80). Soane used dark, classical ornament for this east facing room and gave the library, beyond, a lighter decorative scheme.

miniature ruined forum, half-buried as if excavations had scarcely begun (fig. 118). In various drawings he pictured them 'restored' and 'excavated'. In 1806, two years after John had begun his studies at Cambridge, Soane set him to work to 'restore' them in a futile exercise, aimed both at educating his son in the architecture of classical antiquity and at pouring scorn on over-jealous antiquarians. Pitshanger had become an uncomfortable forcing house for his son's tentative move to an architectural career.

John Haverfield, who had worked to such good effect with Soane at Tyringham, reorganised the setting. To the rear he had the advantage of several mature cedars. Earlier formal layouts gave way to a large lawn edged by a path and shrubs. A walled vegetable garden lay to the south while to the west was a pond and a rustic bridge, apparently an earlier structure which Soane had refaced with stone and flint, adding carved heads to give it an air of greater antiquity. Beyond, the gardens gave way to 28 acres of pasture, which were let for grazing, and a stream for Soane's fishing.[33]

Furnishing and equipping the house from scratch was prodigiously expensive: Mrs Soane's account books show several hundred pounds' worth of goods purchased in 1804 alone. Three years later she was still buying Turkey carpets and Spode china. Eliza shared her expertise gained at Pitshanger with Lady Bridport, by now a close friend, and won a personal commission to dispose of the furniture from their Harley Street house.

In 1801 Soane had spent time at Cricket Lodge in Somerset, carrying out the considerable programme of alterations upon which the Bridports

118. A bird's-eye view of Pitshanger, drawn to be engraved as the frontispiece to the 1833 printed history of the house, showing the flintwork entrance gate in the foreground and the approach to the triumphal front of the house (Dance's retained wing beyond, to the left). The service wing and the ruins extend across the site with generous gardens and park beyond.

119. William Owen's portrait of John and George Soane, exhibited at the Royal Academy in 1805, the former bearing out his Cambridge tutor's observation that he has always the appearance of being dissatisfied, the latter looking restless.

161

had embarked once the admiral had retired from his post as Commander-in-Chief of the Channel Fleet. Eliza had joined him there. The Soanes returned through Bath where she could not resist 'the temptation of a sip in the Pump-room, though perhaps had I confined *my sips* to the *good bottle* my kind friends had given me, I should not have been so tormented with the head ache.' Her letter of thanks to her hosts continues to discuss the political situation, the government see-sawing between peace and war, and being satisfied with neither. 'How is it possible to reconcile such inconsistency . . . surely no good will be done till they chuse a female Parliament, for the males talk so much, and do so little, and that little so badly, that they all appear to belong to the family of the *Wrongheads.*' Eliza was obviously well at ease in this politically well-connected family, moving in and out of the houses of Pitts and Chathams. Back at Lincoln's Inn Fields she envied the Bridports their 'charming retreat'; for 'at Cricket all nature seems at peace . . . here all is confusion, extravagance and folly'.[34]

Pitshanger Manor may have been an escape from 'the noise, dirt and bustle of this filthy Town' but it brought more domestic responsibilities and expenditure. There were staff to organise, a resident cook and maid, gardener and one male servant. Eliza even had to purchase peafowls for the grounds though her own preference was for dogs, a number of which joined the family in these years. This was an establishment of some scale and the organisation and continual entertaining took its toll on her.

Despite that, Eliza enjoyed London in season. One busy week in the summer of 1805 shows her enjoyably combining business and pleasure. On Monday 13 May she visited Turner's gallery and a concert: the following day she and Soane visited the Pantheon to see Lunardi's hot air balloon. On Friday she and Mrs [John] Taylor viewed Boydell's Shakespeare Gallery, its contents about to be dispersed, and on two evenings running she went to an unnamed Shakespeare play, the second time with Lady Bridport. On Sunday there was a small party at Ealing, with William Praed and J.M.W. Turner, who spent the night at Pitshanger. On Monday Eliza was in town, bidding for James Durno's *Merry Wives of Windsor* at Boydell's auction.[35]

From the winter of 1804, as he began to plan his assault upon the professorship at the Royal Academy and as his workload fell away due to the stringencies of war-time, Soane embarked on his own further education. The evidence lies in twenty volumes of manuscript and a vast accumulation of loose sheets of notes, translations and extracts. Continually building up his libraries (that at Pitshanger the gentleman's folio collection, that at Lincolns Inn Fields the working tool),[36] Soane wove his way unsystematically through an enormous theoretical literature. David Watkin has divided the quest into three strands: the search for origins, the architecture of appropriate character and the application of meaningful ornament.[37]

Absorbed in the statements and theories of Vitruvius, Laugier, Blondel, Chambers and others, Soane's own architecture was now being forged against a theoretical background, offering him confusion, contradiction and uncertainty. The architectural eloquence he longed for on the page and as he lectured was often equally elusive in his design process, and is exemplified by his struggles at the Bank, trying out variant after variant for the Tivoli Corner and the Lothbury Court. Rarely citing his written sources for his lectures (any more than he cited his design sources for buildings) he repeatedly circled his objectives, finding it desperately hard to reach a conclusion. Soane, contradictory to his core, was often confused and inconsistent in his judgements and had the disconcerting habit (especially so for someone who brooked no criticism by others) of criticising his own work as well as things that he had previously praised.[38]

Soane's immersion in theory at this date may have helped him face a number of commissions in the gothic revival style – in which he was never happy although he may have taken comfort and ideas from Wren's only City gothic church, St Mary Aldermanbury. In early 1805 he began designs for the Marquis of Buckingham's library for his 'Saxon' manuscripts at Stowe. The marquis wanted to house the collection in suitable style and suggested that Soane take advice on the 'various Gothicks' from John Carter, the most scholarly of the antiquarians.[39] Concurrently Soane's alterations to Ramsey Abbey, near Ely, for Robert Fellowes's nephew were dressed to suit the existing monastic buildings. Lightweight gothic did not suit Soane. Drawing up new designs for Brasenose College at Oxford at this period (another contact made through the marquis) he offered Roman and Greek Doric alternatives while Philip Hardwick offered a 'perfunctory' gothic variant.[40] None was built.

On 3 May 1804 Eliza Soane had purchased two watercolours from Turner's gallery. One was a dramatic landscape of the Val d'Aosta in the Savoy, the other of the ruined chapter house of Kirkstall Abbey (fig. 120), exhibited at the Royal Academy in 1798, a low vaulted space suffused with shafts of light, the effect intensified by the reflections from a pool of water lapping around the columns. Soane enjoyed true gothic architecture for its associations and its detail: he hated meaningless revivalism.

No one was a more frequent or welcome guest of the Soanes over this period than Turner. The two men's shared love of fishing offered long companionable hours passed together on river banks. Neither man a natural intellectual, they found common ground in their dogged investigations of architecture.[41] Soane periodically lent Turner money – always a sign of friendship with him (although failure to repay a debt, or at least interest, was a sure way to lose it). Turner was scrupulous in this respect, as careful with his growing wealth as Soane himself. They also introduced each other to patrons; through Turner, Soane met Dr Monro and surveyed his Bushey house in September 1805, borrowing some drawings by Paul Sandby. Later, Lord Egremont, one of Turner's major clients, commissioned some designs for Petworth Park from Soane. In his turn, Soane introduced Turner to Lord and Lady Bridport.

John Britton, James Spiller and J.M.W. Turner all shared architectural interests and obsessions with Soane. All three friends were on the fringes of his professional world but not too close for comfort.

A passion for books, topography and antiquarianism ensured that Britton and Soane would become friends. By his own account, John Britton was self-taught; his father was a Wiltshire baker and maltster whose business failed during Britton's childhood. He had started in life as a clerk to a London wine merchant, but his horizons were expanded by meeting a watch-face painter who became his mentor.[42] Through him, he met E. W. Brayley the elder, the librarian of the Russell Institution, with whom he was to collaborate on dozens of volumes on the antiquities of

120. J.M.W. Turner's 1797 watercolour of the ruined chapter house at Kirkstall Abbey near Leeds. Painted in 1797. Mrs Soane bought it and a second painting from Turner's Gallery in 1804. The play of low light shafts, water and the vistas beyond the ruins were all appealing elements to Soane, evoking poetry in architecture. From now on Turner and Soane were to be close friends.

Great Britain, an encyclopaedic exercise with much of the research undertaken on foot.

Britton and Soane met some time in the late 1790s. Britton was impressed by Soane while Soane soon accorded to Britton the role of *cicerone* to the cathedrals and ancient treasures of the country that he discovered on his travels. Despised by John Carter for the shallowness of his scholarship, Britton was prolific and energetic. Many of Soane's side-trips on his professional journeys were the result of tips from Britton or Gandy. During the Pitshanger years Britton was immersed in preparing the early volumes of his five volume series *Architectural Antiquities*. In Volume I (published in 1807) he dedicated a plate of Great Maplestead church in Essex (a round church belonging to the Knights Templars) to Soane.[43]

Britton was a tireless fixer, promoting useful networks of contacts, both on his own account and that of others. By 1810 the Brittons were holding Sunday evening *conversazioni* for artists, bringing together the society that revolved around the Royal Academy, the theatre, the publishers and booksellers of Paternoster Row and the leading journalists of the time. Soane benefited greatly from Britton's support and counted him among his closest friends, even patiently bearing the cloying attentions of Mrs. Britton. Despite great strains on the relationship later, it nevertheless endured.

The surveyor James Spiller, Soane's exact contemporary, had been a pupil of James Wyatt's and though not enrolled as a student at the Royal Academy, may have attended some of Sandby's lectures. Spiller became Surveyor to the Royal Exchange Assurance, for which Soane had carried out work in 1786, at around the time that Soane was appointed to the Bank of England and they were also both involved in the Eagle Insurance Corporation, of which Spiller was surveyor. Around 1799, Soane offered Spiller a mortgage of £1,000.

The two men became boon fishing companions with common friends and links to Reading and the Thames Valley. Spiller, at his best, was witty and good company. Soane regarded him as a professional partner, with his skills as a surveyor, and began to employ him on certain commissions.[44] They were in complete agreement on the evils of speculative building and the temptations afforded by vested financial interests: later, Spiller often drafted papers for Soane on these issues. A persistently quarrelsome man, Spiller had no patience with trying clients, notably Thomas Horner of Mells Park in Somerset whose father-in-law, John Coxe Hippisley, passed the job on to Soane in 1810.

Given their personalities, the relationship between Soane the architect and Spiller the surveyor would never quite mirror that symbiotic one between Dance and Peacock. Despite Spiller's steadfast support in Soane's family dramas, eventually the friendship foundered – seemingly because of Spiller's failure (or inability) to repay his mortgage. As Soane's eyesight deteriorated so Spiller's hearing, which had long been a trouble to him, failed completely, causing him acute distress. It was a sad and terminal falling-out.

The third of the triumvirate, Turner, although a far younger man, was in social background, ambition and personality the most similar to Soane himself. Becoming pre-eminent in their respective arts, both men had the enquiring minds of the self-educated but lacked intellectual rigour, failing to assemble their conclusions to good effect. They felt at ease with one another and confident in exchanging the fruits of their reading and thoughts.

In 1805, Turner rented Syon Ferry House at Isleworth.[45] He had a small sailing vessel and began to use it for expeditions on the river, often combined with fishing. For his major upriver journey he waited for the calm weather and continuing warmth of early September. On 8 September Soane and Timothy Tyrrell were in Pangbourne (a favourite haunt) and remained there or in Goring for several days. Everything points to the trip being organised to coincide with Turner's; he had dined at Ealing the week before and the idea may well have taken shape then. In addition Flaxman and Miss Denman (his sister-in-law) had also been at Ealing with Soane and Tyrrell a few days later. Flaxman's monument to Sir Francis Sykes, the nabob who had built Basildon Park in 1776 and who had died in 1804, had been recently installed in St Bartholomew's church, Basildon.[46] Soane's and Tyrrell's familiarity with this stretch of the Thames made them valuable guides for Turner, for fishing as for sketching, and all of them would have been interested to see Flaxman's new monument.

Turner sketched Reading from upper Caversham, his view taken from the churchyard of St Peter's, but along the stretch between Mapledurham and Pangbourne, where the trout fishing was famously good, the drawings are minimal (fig. 121). Turner's oil sketch of Goring (fig. 3), the church and watermill seen over the meadows on a summer evening, stands out from other work on this journey. A 'portrait' of Soane's home town would be an appropriate gesture of thanks to his guide – although it was never finished and never became his.

Since 1802, the Soanes had been more than summer visitors to Margate. The Reverend William Chapman, whose school in St James's Square John and George attended, was a key figure in the life of the town.[47] He had eight children, six sons and two daughters – to one of whom Laura, John, aged twenty-four, became secretly engaged in 1807,

121. Goring seen over the water meadows. A page from Turner's sketchbook, kept during his journey to the stretch of the Thames between Reading and Pangbourne in the early autumn 1805, in company with Soane and his old friend Timothy Tyrrell, the City Remembrancer. Most of the time was spent fishing – a passion shared by all three.

after a carefree summer holiday spent riding donkeys, shopping and buying lottery tickets. His irate father quickly broke the liaison. Although he was of age his father did not judge him ready for marriage. Architecture was the next step – not matrimony.

Union Crescent, Margate, where the Soanes stayed in 1805 was described in the local guidebook as 'a handsome row of good houses and by far the most regular and uniform of any in the town'. The description holds good today, despite their dilapidated appearance. Like the crescent, Cecil Square, Hawley Square (to provide lodging for the Soanes in 1809) and Addington Square were developed from the 1760s largely to accommodate the influx of London gentry, as were the Assembly Rooms, the Theatre Royal, the two subscription libraries (Bettison's and Garner's), seven bathing-rooms, hotels and fashionable chapels.

Throughout the holiday period, the sailing boats or 'hoys' came from Billingsgate loaded with passengers – 20,000 a year in these peak years. Eleven boats ran daily in the high season and their arrival was known as the 'hoy fair' – hundreds of people crowding to see who was coming in. A journey on the Thames was cheaper than by coach, which took a long day (or night) to cover the 72 miles, but less certain. In good conditions the passage took eight or nine hours, in bad, far longer.

The temperament of the sea was a major subject of discussion as everyone gazed out over the horizon toward France and the Low Countries, distant countries while England remained at war. In 1808 a terrible storm broke the jetty to matchsticks and washed away the bathing huts as well as Garner's library on the harbour: John Rennie was brought in to construct a handsome pier to provide protection. In 1809 there was another disaster, this time, man-made. Visitors watched in horror as the dead and dying from the disastrous Walcheren expedition (the failed British exercise to seize Antwerp from the French) were brought ashore. Nine were buried at Margate one Sunday alone and as many again at Ramsgate. A number of distinguished London surgeons were there to assist with the wounded, including Thomas Keate, the doctor from Chelsea. 'What do those deserve who were the promoters of the business?' Mrs Soane wondered.[48]

A detailed account of the holiday in 1805 survives in Mrs Flaxman's letters home to her husband, who, like Soane, had remained hard at work in London. She and her sister, Maria Denman, arrived in early September and found the town 'pretty full, the large houses in particular are all occupied'. The sisters had found lodgings near the Soane family and were just off to join them for dinner. 'You must contrive to come for a day or two,' she wrote to her husband, 'if it be only to make studies from the brawny shoulders of the bathers, fine muscular motion I assure you'. She ends her letter with a message for Soane who had been ill with a fever ('I have said nothing of it here') and she hopes he has recovered. Eliza would be writing the next day but 'he must write a better character for it was with much difficulty she could make out his late Hieroglyphics'. Soane's terrible writing and unpredictability as a correspondent were an endless source for complaint by his family and friends.

By the next letter, Mrs Flaxman reports that they have moved lodgings, 'I no longer sleep in the same garret with Sir W.B. [William Beechey] – I have never yet seen him', and that the holiday is going well. 'We are going this evening to meet a large party of *Margrites* [persons visiting Margate!]

at Mrs Soane's – Braham is to treat us with a song – on Sunday I heard a good sermon from the village parson. I believe he is to be of our party also for he is an old acquaintance of Mrs S. and her son George is with him for education.'

Mrs Flaxman wonders how her husband is passing his time 'that I may (in idea at least) hop in your walks and gambol in your paths'. A few days later she berates her husband for his failure to join them. 'We are much vexed at the *assured* impossibility of your coming and a little disappointed at Mr Soane's delay, for we fully expected him tomorrow indeed I had laid a bait for him in my own mind, but I shall keep it fresh till Thursday which will be the 20th – where he again promised to be with us.' (That time, Soane kept his promise). She found Mrs Soane unfailingly kind and John was 'a young man of excellent dispositions and loves his little Toby [their dog]'.

122. Thomas Rowlandson's view of Summer Amusement at Margate.

The September weather was usually clement and designed to improve the health; 'the sea air braces and strengthens one prodigiously',[49] Mrs Flaxman commented. The bathing-rooms offered sitting-rooms, with daily papers and grand pianos for those who did not wish to go into the water. Those who did inscribed their names on a slate and then were driven, in horse-drawn vehicles, into the sea 'under the conduct of careful guides'. At the back the bathers modestly descended the steps into the water under cover of a canvas umbrella. The precaution was introduced after ladies, who were not always clothed, complained of prying eyes. Usually, modest flannel undergarments were worn but not in Rowlandson's drawings which show buxom women bathers piling naked into the water (fig. 122). Eliza Soane's party were indulging in sea bathing in different measure. 'Maria went in for the first time!! Mrs S. bathes like a Naiad. As yet I have only taken the dry bath.'

One day they had seen the India Fleet pass the north Kent coast. 'Several of them anchored off our bay – the poor sailors many of them having been pressed for the King's ships.' To speed the fleet back to London, fishermen had been taken on as temporary hands leading to a great scarcity of fish in the market. 'You see I begin to enter into the gossip of the place', wrote Mrs Flaxman.

The Soanes had more than a passing interest in the fleet. A proprietor of the East India Company since 1795, John Soane had invested in an East Indiaman, the *Earl Camden* (formerly the *Lord Camden*), captained by Nathaniel Dance,[50] George Dance's nephew, and owned by John Pascal Larkins. (A few years earlier, George's sixteen-year-old son had sailed to India on her.) The contract for Soane's share in the rebuilt vessel was signed in July 1801 and Soane's one thirty-secondth of a share had cost £1,325.[51] He quickly insured his investment. She set out from Torbay on 8 January 1803[52] with a 1,200 ton chartered load, 130 men and 36 guns. Her outbound cargo value was valued at an astonishing £79,705 19s 2d.

The captain's journal, which he was obliged to keep throughout the twenty-month voyage, offers evidence of the miserable conditions of the crew. Many absconded when they made land, others drowned or died; many were Lascars and Chinese by birth.[53] On Tuesday, 17 May 1803 Dance noted that they had sighted land and arrived in 'sultry Bombay' where they took on cotton and carried out 'some private trade on behalf of the officers'. The vessel went on to Whampoa, in Macao, where the cotton was unloaded and a cargo of tea taken on. William Harrington, seaman, died there and was paid his wages for ten months' service. His effects were sold for seven shillings. The *Earl Camden* sailed on to St Helena where, on another voyage, Nathaniel Dance had been reimbursed for victualling prisoners of war on the island. He was knighted as a result of an event on this voyage: joining a number of other merchantmen, he successfully headed off a French squadron under Admiral Linois near the Straits of Malacca. The shareholders in the vessel had come perilously close to losing their investment.

Since her husband could not join them in Margate, perhaps, Mrs Flaxman suggested that they could all meet at Canterbury Cathedral. The excursion took place, but without Flaxman. 'I shall never forget the beauties of Canterbury nor the satisfactory pleasure of seeing it with such company', wrote Mrs Flaxman later. Soane had been their guide. He returned to London while the ladies returned safely to Margate at half past eight and hurried to Bettison's Rooms where they enjoyed themselves until later, '"like Cymon thinking of nothing at all"'. The end of the holiday was approaching.

10

THE ROYAL ACADEMY
AND
OTHER BUSINESS

Buying and rebuilding Pitshanger had satisfied some of Soane's aspirations, but his desire for advancement, recognition and status remained as fierce as ever.

Soane's dive into the choppy waters of the Royal Academy showed naïve disregard for the complex politics of the institution, which hinged upon its relationship with the king. George III's mercurial state of mental health was an added complication; in early 1804 he had suffered a serious relapse but recovered sufficiently to receive graciously William Pitt when he returned to office in May, although he was showing signs of irrationality which did not augur well.

Later in the year, Sir William Beechey had the shock of meeting the king who accused him of having no colour sense and dismissed him with the outburst 'West is an American, and Copley is an American, and you are an Englishman, and were you all at the Devil I should not care.'[1] The king who had pledged to be 'patron, protector and supporter' of the Royal Academy was hardly in a state to deal with their squabbling.

Soane was eager to have a voice in any dispute but, political only in his opportunism, did not fully understand the history of the tense political divisions between the various camps. Ten years earlier Farington had met the Smirkes, father and son, together with Banks at a meeting organised by the Whig Club to campaign against the Sedition Bill 'who I joined, telling them as they were crops and democrats, I should be safe under their protection'.[2] Such a stand, and the significance of their bare heads, marked Smirke out as something of a republican and francophile. By 1804 he had moderated his stance sufficiently to be elected Keeper of the Royal Academy only to have his appointment overruled on political grounds by the king and given to Fuseli. Soane voted for Thomas Banks, a reciprocal gesture for his support in his own recent campaign.

Although many alliances between Royal Academicians were temporary, the friendship between Robert Smirke sen. and Joseph Farington 'the Dictator of the Academy' was a close personal one and the much younger Thomas Lawrence was friendly with both men. All had come to share an extreme wariness of Soane when crossed, intensified in Smirke's case by a mutual distrust following his son's short stay in Soane's office. Meanwhile, gossip regularly filtered back from Chertsey via the Daniells, their family still the publicans of the Swan Inn.[3] Farington passed on everything, suitably embroidered. His treatment of Soane in his diary was rougher even than that accorded to other Royal Academy dissidents and Soane did nothing to help himself. He was becoming ever more unpopular 'being desirous to take the lead in everything', but 'has not a head or temper for it' as Farington reported.[4]

1803 had been the most turbulent year in the Royal Academy's existence. The president, Benjamin West, was accused of re-submitting his painting *Hagar and Ishmael* which he had previously exhibited in 1776. Soane who sat both on the council (through the rotating system by which newly elected Academicians served) and on the hanging committee with Turner, Bourgeois, Rossi, Richards and Wilton, took an unusually placatory view, blaming the dispute upon the press.[5]

Earlier that year, the French Ambassador, General Andreossi, attended the Academy dinner in recognition of the Treaty of Amiens. The previous summer many Royal Academicians, including Turner, had seized the interval of peace and hurried to Paris, and beyond. Now the signs were that hostilities could reopen at any moment, with French troops reported to be massing on the coast around Boulogne. Since the Ambassador spoke no English, the civilities were courteous but necessarily formal. War within the Royal Academy was, however, already engaged; a procedural dispute hinging upon the relative authority of the general assembly (the full body of the Royal Academy, forty members) and the council (eight, plus the president) caused five members, Soane, Copley, Yenn, Wyatt and Bourgeois, to be suspended by the general assembly in May. George Dance had moved the motion for their suspension. In November, the king intervened, and reinstated them. In the meantime the five penned an anonymous pamphlet, in which Soane's voice could be spotted behind the hand of Copley.[6]

Eliza Soane had been heartily sick of it all from the beginning: 'I hate the Academy – and all belonging to it – they are a lot of ungrateful hypocrites for Godsake, think of yourself and let them go to the devil' she wrote loyally in the summer of 1803, chiding her husband for keeping ridiculous hours which, she knew, would sooner or later lay him low.[7]

By December 1804 Soane – despite his support for West the previous year – was one of the coterie of Royal Academicians pressing for the president to resign, which he did in December 1805. West realised that Soane was an arch trouble-maker in the internal politics of the institution and resented his chameleon-like behaviour and lack of personal loyalty. James Wyatt took West's place as president.[8] He was characteristically desultory during his year in office and made no effort to resolve the divisions or to improve the position of architects within the Academy. After a year, the Academicians asked the king for his preferred candidate for president. Despite Wyatt's favoured position at court, there was no reply, and Benjamin West was re-elected president.

A week later Edward Edwards ARA, Teacher of Perspective, died. he had been the first student of the Royal Academy Schools in 1769 and had dutifully carried out his task in the form of private lessons. Joseph Gandy, although only recently elected as Associate, put himself forward for the Professorship of Perspective, perhaps hoping that Soane would argue his case. A call for volunteers among the full Academicians produced just one name, that of J.M.W. Turner and so his election in December 1807 was a foregone conclusion.

Meanwhile Soane had his sights set on the Professorship of Architecture. George Dance had failed to deliver a single lecture since his appointment in 1798, a reasonable argument for his replacement. However, Soane's intrigues did not make the succession a clean affair. His personal loyalty may have been weakened by Dance moving the vote to suspend the five dissidents eighteen months earlier but in December 1804, Dance was taken aback to receive an anonymous letter informing him that Soane was plotting to wrest the professorship from him.[9] Their relationship could not withstand this act of disloyalty.

Pitshanger completed, Soane had begun an ambitious preparatory exercise in the hopes of obtaining the professorship: reading, note-taking and translating (from Italian as well as French which he continued to learn, and practice, throughout adult life) innumerable architectural treatises and sources. Within the Royal Academy Sir Francis Bourgeois, Sir William Beechey and Henry Tresham were leading the campaign on his behalf. That summer, the two Soane family portraits by Owen hung in the annual exhibition as if to underline the point: typical Soane gamesmanship. In November 1805, Dance finally resigned the professorship.[10]

Soane gained the professorship, according to his own account, unanimously on 28 March 1806. Turner wrote quickly to congratulate him with two snippets of verse – one of which alludes to professors who are paid to read lectures which they never deliver. Henry Holland also wrote a generous letter of congratulation.[11] Six weeks later a pupil, Henry Seward, had already begun work on the first lecture illustrations.[12]

It was an interesting moment; society was being tempted into the lecture theatres of London and the major cities to hear (and see) demonstrations of new scientific phenomena and to hear literary and moral disquisitions (fig. 123). What had begun in small and exclusive literary and scientific institutions was becoming popular entertainment, widely emulated in provincial Britain.[13]

At the recently founded Royal Institution the lecture theatre was steeply raked, admitting an audience of several hundred men and women and soon the London, Russell and Surrey Institutions[14] were offering similar programmes. Newspapers and periodicals announced the forthcoming lectures and reviewed the events. The presentations were designed to be lively; a Voltaic battery could produce dramatic effects to show the characteristics of an electro-magnetic field, while discussion of optics was aided by a plethora of mirrors, prisms and coloured glass. Medical topics were illuminated by skeletons, écorché drawings, living models and even dissection. 'Star' speakers such as the Reverend Sydney Smith caused traffic to block the streets.

Lectures at the Royal Academy were open to interested outsiders and non-professionals, but only to men. Presentation (as much as the content) needed improvement. Henry Fuseli, Professor of Painting from 1799 to 1805 (and again from 1810 onwards), spoke in a thick Swiss-German accent, without any illustrations, but published his lectures (as, later, did John Flaxman, Professor of Sculpture). In 1805 the Somerset House lecture theatre was rearranged so that speakers could at least see all their

123. Thomas Rowlandson's depiction of a lecture in chemistry at the Surrey Institution, founded in 1808. Public lectures on a wide variety of subjects became popular in these years and later Soane gave a version of his lectures at the Royal Institution.

124. Joseph Gandy's compilation of views of the Bank of England (exhibited at the Royal Academy in 1822). The 1797 Consols Office is second from the left, top row, and the Accountants' Office (1805) bottom row, centre. The Five Per Cent office (1818) ia second from the right, top row. A German visitor in 1826 described 'the beautiful, gigantic building . . . a maze of large and small rooms lit from above . . . Hundreds of clerks work here, crowded together, and mechanically transact the colossal business.'

audience, sitting on three sides of the room. A tiered layout would have been far more practical but in the Grand Room there was no option for such an arrangement.

Turner and Soane, once appointed, were eager to improve the lighting and sight-lines, given that their lectures would be heavily dependent on their illustrations – as Sandby's had been years before.[15] Without good visibility for their drawings, scaled up to be seen by the more distant members of the audience, neither the professor of architecture nor of perspective could have held the attention of the room, given the shortcomings of their spoken delivery. The preparations of text and illustrations occupied Turner and Soane intermittently over several years.

One job that eluded Soane at the beginning of the new century was the Bank of Ireland; the Act of Union in 1801 had rendered the enlarged institution that he had begun to design irrelevant. But he continued to be heavily engaged at the Bank of England (fig. 124). In the late 1790s he had added domestic accommodation for the accountant, the famous Abraham Newland after whom banknotes were nicknamed, and his deputy (the Bank's most senior officials), the doorkeeper and an office for his own clerk of works (and, therefore, himself). The Accountants' Court (later called the Residence Courtyard) marked the move of the Bank site towards a self-contained settlement – on the lines of the Tower of London.

Also in these years, the three per cent Consols Transfer Office – the office to which most visitors came, including Mrs Soane who collected her own dividends from time to time – was rebuilt, the largest yet. Completed in 1799, it was another variant on the sequence that had evolved from the original Stock Office and the first banking hall which directly reflected the new activity in business which had been brought about by the wars with France.

However, it was a relatively minor phase within Soane's largest proposal to the directors thus far, the first one to which they showed some signs of resistance to the pace that Soane was setting.[16] He wanted to replan the Bullion Court, add further offices and to gain access to it from Lothbury. In October 1797 the directors approved, in Daniel Abramson's phrase, his scheme 'for making the Bank's private backyard into a monumental public court'. Soane divided the Residence Courtyard from Lothbury Court with a monumental screen of Corinthian columns. Continually altering the triumphal archway up to early 1800, adding appropriate ornament, the classical emblems of commerce (caducei) and the four continents, as well as Thomas Banks's variants on allegorical renderings of night and day from the Arch of Constantine, Soane was offering his riposte to Lord Chief Justice Kenyon. The Lothbury Court was intended to be the public entrance to the Consols Transfer Office but by its completion the plan had changed; to quote Abramson: 'A daily public audience never arrived to enliven and give meaning to the colonnaded courtyard.'[17]

In 1799 the Bank took responsibility for collecting the new Income Tax; the huge National Debt, managed by the Bank, was rising steeply all the time. By act of parliament, passed in June 1800, the Bank was allowed to continue Princes Street in a straight line to Lothbury,[18] leading to an extension of the north-west corner of their island: the final shape of the 3-acre site was now determined. The piecemeal way in which the land was assembled had meant constant uncertainty as to where the entrances and axes were best located. Now, once the purchases were settled (not always easily)[19] the jigsaw could be completed.

Soane had marked out the extremities of his site and envisaged the acute north-west angle, the Tivoli Corner (fig. 125), as his eyecatcher in order to benefit from the line George Dance's intended (but unexecuted) City improvements. Its design preoccupied Soane constantly in 1804–5 and intermittently the previous year. He prepared alternative models and played with varied sarcophagus forms on the skyline. Prominent on the north-west corner of the Bank site, it signalled to the passing public the quality of the architecture within but did not link to either of the main public entrances (Threadneedle Street and Bartholomew Lane). Soane saw it

125. Joseph Gandy's watercolour of the Tivoli Corner evokes Soane's favourite Roman building, the tiny Temple of Vesta at Tivoli with its distinctive version of the Corinthian order. The curved treatment emphasises the acute angle of the north west corner of the Bank site where Lothbury and Princes Street meet, and would have been a prominent feature in Dance's unfulfilled plans for the north of the City. Soane showed alternative models of the Tivoli Corner to the Building Committee and spent much time on the design.

126. Photograph by Frank Yerbury from 1923 showing the extremely stylised treatment of the pilasters, capitals and cornice of the north facing loggia in the Governor's Court – a strong contrast to the imperial Roman and full Corinthian order of the adjoining Lothbury Court.

127. Yerbury's photograph (1923) taken from the Princes Street vestibule looking towards the loggia of the Governor's Court; another instance of Soane's brilliance in transforming incidental left-over space, small passages and lobbies, into great architecture.

neither as entrance nor passage.[20] Although his early designs favoured a triumphal arch form, by 1805 Soane had arrived at a pure evocation of the circular Temple of Vesta at Tivoli, one of his favourite memories of the Italian journey, the complex and particular Corinthian order of the original making a perfect refulgent culmination to a rounded corner.

At the same time he designed the north-facing loggia to the Governor's Court (fig. 126), a stark elevation of four huge paired pilasters, scarcely ornamented – a hint of things to come at 13 Lincoln's Inn Fields. The elevation facing it offered the strongest possible contrast with its rich Corinthian columns with heavily rusticated bases. Soane enjoyed such unlikely juxtapositions.

Between 1805 and 1808 most of the remaining building work on the site was completed, the south and eastern perimeter walls and two remaining Taylor halls apart. On the north-west corner new barracks for the bank guard were begun in 1805 while Soane's Greek Doric vestibule to the Prince's Street entrance connected the core of the site and the outside world (fig. 127). From it, the dominant north–south Long Passage could be reached.

Soane delighted in such 'lesser' spaces – vestibules, corridors, lobbies and alcoves – a pleasure abundantly evident at the Bank (fig. 128). By offering incident, with ornament and illumination from hidden sources (harking back to the Roman subterranean regions that he had been so excited by), Soane's passages were always memorable. At the Bank they were highly important adjuncts, conducting the traffic between the major offices and courtyards. Finally, a new Bullion Office, with three transverse barrel vaults, was added to the east side of the Bullion Court and in 1808 the entire banknote printing operation was brought on to the site.

On 29 September 1808 New Princes Street opened to traffic and the New Bank Buildings (to be distinguished from Taylor's Bank Buildings which stood opposite on Threadneedle Street) were soon ready for letting at the north-west end of the street. He fitted out premises for Thellusson and for Morland (one of his own bankers) and the London Wet Dock Company among others.

Soane's experience in commercial street architecture was gained at 90 Fleet Street, where he had designed the headquarters of Praed's Bank in 1801. Its bold arcaded elevation heralded his own house. The *Times* of 5 January 1802 reported on the 'elegant new building' just opened as the banking house for Praeds Digby Box Babbage & Co. Their eyecatching headquarters were far removed from the polite domestic dress of James Oakes's Bury New Bank or from the discreet City counting houses which Soane had designed for a number of his banking clients.

His clientele exemplified the way in which the merchant classes had swiftly, and with foresight, changed direction in the late eighteenth century; embracing new opportunities in banking, turnpikes and canals, brewing and manufacture. Praed's Bank (fig. 129), newly arrived on the edge of the City from its provincial roots, represented an image of enterprise and modernity and Soane responded.

The Bank of England was now a destination for dignitaries. Queen Charlotte paid a visit on 12 June 1805, accompanied by several of her sons and daughters. The governors and directors wore full court dress for the occasion and the grenadiers of the Bank Volunteers formed a welcoming guard of honour. 'Mr Soane, the architect, led the Royal Party with a plan of the Bank in his hand . . . In the Bank Stock Office, the clerks were all at their desks, and Mr Newland, with the most respectful attention, explained the business to the Royal Party.' The visit took two hours and on departure, some 557 clerks gave three cheers. The royal party were greatly impressed both by the banking operation and by the magnificence of the building.[21] Soane liked guiding visitors around his work at the Bank, some had been the beneficiaries of massive loans: emperors and lesser royalty, diplomats and ambassadors came in succession to see the most important public building of the time.

On all occasions of national joy or solemnity, the Bank now stood centre stage. Two and a half months after the Battle of Trafalgar, on 9 January 1806, Nelson's funeral cortège wound through the City (the catafalque having journeyed up the Thames from Greenwich to the Admiralty the day before). Soane and Spiller went to St Paul's Cathedral to witness the most heroic public send-off staged in years.[22] Soane asked Gandy to include Nelson's funeral procession in *Architectural Visions of Early Fancy and Dreams in the Evening of Life*, the compilation exhibited at the RA in 1820. This evocation of a major ceremonial occasion may have been the germ for Soane's theoretical royal processional route from the west of London to the heart of Whitehall – marked by his own unbuilt public commissions and other dreams – which so occupied him in the 1820s.

Lady Hawkesbury had been surprised by Nelson's diminutive coffin when she went to the lying-in-state at the Admiralty and was greatly affected by the silence of the black-draped room, lit by flaring torches. The day of the funeral she spent six hours watching the immense procession wending from Whitehall, through the Temple Bar to St Paul's.[23] Meanwhile, Pitt was making a slow invalid's progress back to town. He had been in Bath for some weeks when confirmation of the defeat at Austerlitz and illness closed in on him in fatal combination. Hawkesbury had invited him to Coombe on his way back, assuring him he would find a healthy combination of good air and (thanks to Soane) a comfortably warm house. His invitation was not accepted and there were to be no more letters between them; Pitt died on 23 January. His funeral, at Westminster Abbey, took place a month later. Soane was not present and did not remark upon it in his notebook. He carried on with a busy schedule, only varied that week by a succession of early morning appointments with Mr Stott for treatment by the latest medical cure-all, galvanism – electrical shock treatment being used at this period as much for physical as for mental ailments.[24]

The near-blind king had tried to persuade Lord Hawkesbury to take Pitt's place but it was Lord Grenville who headed the Ministry of all Talents, together with Fox (who died later that year) and Sidmouth, a ministry which continued during 1806 and until March 1807. With Grenville at the head of government, the man who, directly or indirectly, had been the cause of his failure at the House of Lords, Soane could expect no special favours.

Soane's work at the Bank of England continued to attract more than its fair share of criticism. One publication entitled *A Treatise on forming, improving and managing Country Residences* referred to the Bank as 'that huge mass of deformity'. The author, a twenty-two-year-old Scot lately arrived in London, John Claudius Loudon, could claim greater authority on the planting of parkland, even on agriculture, than on architectural style. Yet the Bank of England is one of the few modern examples he cites, and cas-

128. Prince's Street vestibule of the Bank, also by Yerbury (1923) showing Soane's masterly treatment of intermediate spaces, and his liking for low Greek Doric entrance halls, preceding top lit larger spaces, a device he had already introduced frequently in his domestic work.

129. Praed's Bank on Fleet Street, a design dated 29 September 1801. The bank was for Soane's client William Praed from Tyringham and his first exercise in the type of stone elevation he would later refine for his own house, 13 Lincoln's Inn Fields.

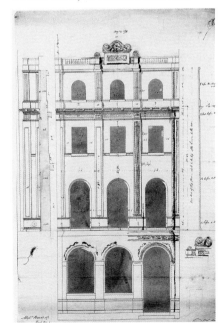

130. The ground plan of the Bank of England, as completed. A comparison with the cut-away (fig. 111) shows the principal areas.

tigates, particularly for the mannered use of sunken pilasters and attached columns. If a still unknown landscape gardener, whose architectural experience to date consisted of one design exhibited at the Royal Academy in 1804, chose to single out the Bank for criticism, it spoke much for its notoriety and the perception of Soane as a maverick.

Humphry Repton supports the impression that Soane's best clients remained solidly behind him in the face of the criticisms.[25] Repeating the usual remarks about his desire for novelty at all cost,

> by reversing or turning things topsy turvy – for instance the rustic storey such as we see at the bottom of buildings he placed at the top over the Corinthian entablature! In the library at M [Mulgrave] Castle he arranged the shelves for large books at the top – and small ones at the bottom! And those mouldings which are usually raised and embossed he sinks . . . but every innovation will have its admirers and I have heard one of the Directors of the Bank of England assert that at their Board he had obtained the name of the 'Fanciful Soane' by which they meant to do him honour.

The committees, governor and directors could not fail to be impressed by his achievement in remodelling the enormous site piecemeal, an unfolding plan of immense complexity but following an underlying logic (fig. 130). The Bank, and the complexity of its operations, had made it a city within the City, and its growing self-sufficiency was expressed in a concrete form by its buildings. Soane was fashioning a small metropolis for the directors and they, as a group, represented an élite society in which he was uniquely well positioned.

At Mogerhanger in Bedfordshire, where Soane had been called back, this time by his previous client Godfrey Thornton's son Stephen to remodel the house, he was happy to be working again for a family for whom he could do no wrong. In 1791–2 Soane had made a modest addition to an earlier house: hot on his heels came Repton, whose *Red Book* judged the remodelling as too insignificant for its park setting. He also was concerned that Soane's full-length drawing-room windows revealed the messy state of the gravel after coaches had turned, not to mention 'the occasional defilement of horses waiting at the door'. Such deficiencies, he added, were 'unavoidable where Genius is confined to the altering of an old house instead of having full latitude to plan a new one'.[26] Unintentionally he had planted the seeds of Soane's commission.

Soane's skills and his confidence as a designer had developed enormously since the earlier job. In 1806 he began with the stables, starting work in earnest on the house in 1809, swivelling the entrance to the north, retaining certain of the earlier rooms but burying them within an ostensibly new house. Comparison of the two phases is very revealing of the distance he had come in the last twenty years; from the details, inverted mouldings now chiselled deep into the wainscotting or even marked as parallel incisions alongside the sweep of the new main stair, to the use of blind windows to skilfully mask the junctions and adjustments. Now quite substantial enough to earn Repton's definition of a 'country-seat', it had a new upper storey, an impressive Doric porch (fig. 131) counterpointed by the fretwork of double height verandahs to the south and east and a kitchen block separated from the main house. It was rendered in Parker's cement the colour of Bath stone and the window-frames were painted

131. The entrance front of Mogerhanger in Bedfordshire, the Thornton family house to which Soane returned, having originally carried out work in the 1790s. The Greek Doric portico and attic storey seen in the photograph were part of Soane's substantial remodelling around 1809.

black. Soane – much immersed in the preparation of his lectures – poured time and effort into Mogerhanger. Some of the results reappear at 13 Lincoln's Inn Fields, such as the panelled dining-room ceiling which he adapted for his own library.

Stephen Thornton, a director of the Bank of England from 1802, his father Godrey and his brothers William (who took the name of Astell) and Claude George, both of whom became clients, were cousins of Samuel Thornton, for whom Soane worked at Albury and at St James's Square. Of them all, Samuel was his closest friend, becoming a trustee of 13 Lincoln's Inn Fields after the 1833 Act of Parliament. The Thorntons were important figures within the Clapham Sect and leading City merchants – their fortune coming from trading in Russia and the Baltic – and when they faced difficulties during and after the Napoleonic wars, Soane was happy to extend loans to both Samuel and Stephen.

Soane's friendship with clients occasionally led to conflicts of interest. In the run-up to the 1806 elections he was asked to vote for both Patteson and Fellowes in Norwich. The two men were standing for the constituency and both counted upon Soane, who had purchased property in order to have voting rights, as he also had in Buckinghamshire, Reading and Caterham. In this case he acted in the only proper fashion, writing 'I am fearful my professional engagement will not allow me the pleasure of attending the election of members of the county of Norfolk.' It was an unusually diplomatic move although he did, finally, cast his vote. On the fringes of the Norfolk election was, yet again, the ubiquitous Sir John Coxe Hippisley who offered to lend his voice 'cheerfully and loudly' to the matter.[27]

Soane himself was never persuaded to stand for election to Parliament but he was a vestryman at St Giles in the Fields and became a Justice of the Peace for Middlesex in 1810. There were, over the years, numerous elections at East India House and the Royal Academy. In the routine way, loyalties were called upon and old moral debts resurfaced. Anyone thought to have influence was involved in a continuous round of solicitation and lobbying. Soane could not always excuse himself but more often now he took a conciliatory line, what he termed the middle course, and abstained. He could always plead the pressure of business.

Professionally Soane remained as insecure as ever. Despite his enviable clutch of patrons and public offices, younger men were snapping at his heels and no one represented a greater threat to his position than Robert Smirke jun., just back from four years in Italy and Greece. George Dance introduced his friend's able son to Sir George Beaumont, who in turn introduced him to the Lowther family. In December 1805 Farington was already reporting how pleased Lord Lowther was with the young man, 'so ingenious, – modest and gentlemanly in his manners'.[28]

George Dance was as generous to Smirke as he had been to Soane many years before. Farington noted that Smirke's design for Lowther Castle was heavily dependent on an idea of Dance's.[29] George Dance knew the site well, having drawn up some designs for it earlier, and Smirke, as yet unversed at working on such a scale, was happy to discuss his proposals with such an experienced architect. His commission at Lowther ran for many years, interrupted by major jobs in London and elsewhere, but it led to Smirke's appointment as surveyor to the Royal Mint. Before long, he became the preferred architect to an inner circle of landed aristocrats, the new Tory power-brokers.

While Soane's contemporaries Samuel Pepys Cockerell and, to a lesser extent, William Pilkington and Thomas Hardwick occasionally trod on Soane's professional toes, he had had no serious competition from members of his own generation of architects. Of the older men, Samuel and James Wyatt had taken their share of the desirable jobs but it was at the mention of Henry Holland's name that Soane became most defensive. Holland, with the family building firm behind him, and no compunction about engaging in speculative development, was a wilder card, unbound by the professional rules to which Dance and Soane both subscribed. With Nash, Soane knew his weaknesses; with Holland, he feared his strengths. Then, in June 1806, Holland died, aged sixty.

Among Robert Smirke's own contemporaries, Charles Heathcote Tatham, Holland's protégé, built himself a house in St John's Wood but showed no inclination to fish in political waters, while the younger Charles Robert Cockerell, Smirke's pupil, did not return from his prolonged Grand Tour until 1817. None of Soane's other pupils showed Smirke's combination of ability, tenacity and privileged access to key patrons. He was active and adept on Soane's home ground, high-level political patronage, before long taking on one of Soane's own trickier clients, the Marquis of Abercorn, as well as eventually securing a Prime Minister, Sir Robert Peel.[30]

The combination of powerful advocates, social polish, professional diligence and dependability, with the engine of thrusting ambition, was achieving for Smirke in a handful of years what Soane had diligently built up over decades. Soane continued to work for influential patrons, many of them, gratifyingly, satisfied former clients or their relatives returning with new commissions – such as Port Eliot, the Cornish seat of the Eliots at St Germans, or Mogerhanger, mentioned earlier – but he could see that his circle of influence was no longer expanding exponentially.

11

'THE ROUGH STORM OF LIFE'

In November 1806 a Colonel Drinkwater asked to visit Pitshanger Manor. It appears that the colonel was interested in purchasing the house. 'I know not how to answer your question' Soane wrote, 'I am delighted with the place and if it depended on me no money would tempt me. I yet hope the other parts of my family will be induced to think of Ealing as I do.'[1] At heart, Soane already knew that the venture was failing in its purpose. The boys had not responded to the house as an architectural object lesson while the social side of life at Pitshanger Manor was proving to be an exhausting parade for Eliza.

While Robert Smirke, with the instincts of an engineer and the careful business methods of a clerk, his father and his influential friends behind him, embarked on his relentless rise up the architectural profession, Soane's misfortunes seemed to be multiplying. Two of his most important patrons, William Pitt and Samuel Bosanquet, had died in 1806. The directors at the Bank had, for the first time ever, questioned and curtailed his programme of works.[2]

Worst of all, Soane's relations with George Dance had broken down finally and, possibly irrevocably, because of the underhand way he had schemed to take the professorship at the Royal Academy from him. By 1809, relations between them were so poor that when the Speaker of the House of Commons asked S. P. Cockerell, Soane and Dance to survey the buildings around Westminster Hall, Robert Smirke replaced Soane because it was thought Dance would not now work with him.[3] Soane had to face a terrible truth: he and his architectural mentor and revered teacher were now distanced almost as terminally as if by death. It was a deep personal tragedy for Soane. As professionals, with great mutual respect, the two men had traded ideas and, in recognition of their old master–pupil relationship, Soane had regularly taken Dance to the buildings of which he was proudest. Dance tested out his own architectural conundrums on Soane, trusted his judgement and was delighted by his 'favourable acceptance of my twin bridges' – his competition design for a replacement for the old London Bridge (part of improvements to the Port of London).[4] Dance had confessed to 'stealing' from Soane's Tyringham plan while Dance's ideas had sparked off Soane's solution at the Bank Stock Office.

Adding to his troubles, Soane was now seeing his domestic commissions tailing off to a steady trickle. The renewal of hostilities with France after the breakdown of the Treaty of Amiens had made private clients nervous of heavy expenditure and to see Smirke's meteoric rise, promoted by the good offices of George Dance among others, was upsetting. Only the professorship at the Royal Academy could re-establish his standing as the wide-ranging intellectual that he so wanted to be, a model for future generations of architectural students. But settling down to an academically respectable middle age was not for Soane; he wanted both roles, to be both the intellectual and the professional leader of architecture.

There was no established route, no formal application procedure or selection process, by which architects could obtain key jobs. Even when a limited competition was held, old habits of patronage, nepotism and favouritism reared their heads. After Pitt's death the political scene had shifted and Soane was no longer at its epicentre. Only Lord Hawkesbury continued at Cabinet level, returning to the Home Office in 1807. After his father's death, the new Lord Liverpool commissioned Soane to embark on more work at Coombe House, beginning with a library.[5]

Opportunism and contacts were all. Smirke, as ambitious as Soane, missed no opportunity to advance himself. So eager was he to replace Samuel Wyatt as the surveyor to the Royal Hospital at Chelsea that he applied before the incumbent's demise. After Wyatt's death, Smirke tried again but on this occasion Soane trumped him and was appointed to the post in January 1807.

Soane had several contacts at Chelsea, a nest of sinecures. George Aust, the Paymaster of the Forces, whom Soane had known when working on the Foreign Office, became secretary and registrar at the Hospital in 1795 while Joseph Smith had been paymaster to the out-pensioners since 1794. In pole position was the paymaster general, whose official position made him *ex-officio* treasurer. Charles Long was appointed (jointly with Lord Charles Somerset) on 4 April 1807 and remained in the post for ten years. Their immediate predecessors from February 1806 had been Lord John Townshend and Richard, Earl Temple, the eldest son of Soane's patron, the Marquis of Buckingham.[6]

The new position, at the heart of the military establishment and thus close to government, was prestigious but it brought Soane considerable worry and only a modest salary, £220 per annum. Nor, at the beginning, did it appear to offer much architectural opportunity. Sir Christopher Wren's masterly buildings dominated the site and the memory of his grand, but unfulfilled, plan to connect the Hospital with Kensington Palace was still evident in the odd axis of the plan.

The Royal Hospital was to all intents a defence installation and since 1793 a telegraph had been housed on the roof, one arm directed at the Admiralty, Wimbledon and thence to Portsmouth, the other, via the Admiralty, at One Tree Hill in Hampstead and to Yarmouth.[7] Its maintenance was among Soane's duties.

Most usefully, with the job came a small house on Paradise Row and Soane slept there for the first time that June. It was, like the Bank, a village with a variety of residents. Dr Charles Burney had been comfortably installed as organist there since 1783.

In 1807 Soane also purchased the freehold of 13 Lincoln's Inn Fields, for £4,200, from his next-door neighbours and friends the Tyndales. Mr and Mrs Tyndale continued to live at No. 13 but Soane may have already envisaged the house as more than a mere investment. As Pitshanger increasingly began to look like a failed enterprise he was reconsidering his options, but in the event of having to sell the house he wanted to ensure its memorial. George Richardson was preparing a second volume of his prestigious folio *Vitruvius Britannicus*. Soane supplied text and plates, showing the plan, front and rear elevations.[8] The engravings were dated 7 July 1807 and publication was in 1808. Soane subscribed to two sets. 'The country residence of John Soane Esq.' was the only architect's house in either volume and one of very few villas to be illustrated, along with Sydney Lodge, Soane's house for Agneta Yorke. Contemporary guide-books also began to note Pitshanger Manor. Hughson's *Circuit of London* (1808) referred to Soane's transformation of the house into 'a retirement from the fatigues of the metropolis, a dwelling equally classical and convenient'. The account had no sooner been written than it became an epitaph on Soane's project.

In the meantime he was offered an intriguing distraction. Soane had quickly found common cause with Sir Francis Bourgeois at the Royal Academy, who introduced him to a circle of theatrical figures including John Philip Kemble whose portrait as *Coriolanus* (exhibited at the Royal Academy in 1797) Soane owned.

Sir Francis Bourgeois and his friend Noel Desenfans were central figures in the late eighteenth-century art world, distrusted and admired in not quite equal measure. They commanded the heights of artistic politics, rather than those of artistic excellence. Neither was English, neither was quite what he seemed. Bourgeois was a second-rate painter, although Desenfans applied all known devices to propel his protégé on to the top rung of Royal Academicians. He had been trained by Philippe de Loutherbourg, the artist and theatre designer from Alsace who had worked in London since 1771. Bourgeois took a Grand Tour in 1776. Desenfans, like Bourgeois, had influential friends but lacked *bon ton*. In early July 1807 Noel Desanfans died and Bourgeois commissioned a mausoleum, an unlikely rear extension to the London terraced house where he and the Desanfans lived, together with their collection of paintings.[9]

Desenfans, diplomat and picture dealer, was a man ahead of his time. Fifty years later London art dealers such as Ernest Gambart amassed fortunes and became society figures. Desenfans, viewed against the familiar model of the often unreliable agents who operated in Rome, appeared a gadfly figure rather than a great collector, yet he had, assisted by Bourgeois, amassed a spectacular, if conventional, collection of paintings for the King of Poland in the early 1790s. The abdication of the king and political paroxysms in Poland left the pair with a national gallery for which they had not been paid and for which they had no home.

Paul Sandby's undated portrait of the pair shows the highly conventional Sir Francis Bourgeois (his knighthood was Polish), in wig and boots, dozing on a sofa while Desanfans, a little monkey of a man, in turban and tunic, feet on the furniture, holds forth gesticulating (fig. 132). Mrs Desenfans remains unseen. Absent at the couple's dinners, she was considerably older than her husband but had brought him a private income. Mrs Soane liked her and on hearing of her death, in 1813, was puzzled

132. Portrait attributed to Paul Sandby of Sir Francis Bourgeois (left) and Noel Desanfans, behaving true to character.

that she had left her affairs in such confusion. 'I think she was a *just* and good woman and meant what was right.'[10]

Bourgeois lived in the Desenfans household, as protégé and friend. The Desanfans' collection hung throughout the house and the idea of a link between their collective burial place (as it was intended to be) and the gallery endured. The original plan, to open a public art gallery, foundered when the Duke of Portland refused to sell Bourgeois and Mrs Desanfans the house. Where the mausoleum was concerned, the site in a tiny cramped yard dictated a scheme with no elevations. To the rear of 36 Charlotte (now Hallam) Street, it was hardly in the tradition of those dignified and hermetic memorials in the landscape such as Hawksmoor's for the Earl of Carlisle at Castle Howard. The private celebration of death in a domestic setting was normally confined to the aristocracy, the irreligious or the eccentric – Beckford planned to be entombed in the gallery at Fonthill Abbey. Soane's pocket version of the genre in the terrace off Portland Place was a domed 'chapel' with a top-lit alcove for the three sarcophagi (fig. 133).

Soane had long been interested in the mausoleum as a building type, both for its classical antecedents and modern interpretations of the form, and had designed his share of academic versions looking back to work by Piranesi and Chambers. To date he had never had the chance to build one, despite those promised him at the Downhill, at Boconnoc and even the church-mausoleum at Tyringham. Mausolea remained of constant interest to Soane and he himself may have planted the unusual notion in his friend's mind.

On his summer visits to the north Kent coast Soane visited James Wyatt's Darnley mausoleum at Cobham and through Turner he knew Wyatt's Brocklesby mausoleum in Lincolnshire (fig. 134), a top-lit drum flooded with coloured light. Progress from a darkened lobby or vestibule towards a luminous space beyond was, as we have seen, a favourite effect of Soane's and the chance to extend the dramatic possibilities without being hampered by the domestic considerations of heat or direct light was liberating.

A later remark of his friend Richard Holland offers a tantalising hint that Soane at some point also entertained such a scheme for himself at Lincoln's Inn Fields. In the end only Eliza Soane's dog Fanny was interred there.

There is no sign that Eliza Soane ever fully warmed to the Pitshanger project; as hostess she had to organise all the domestic arrangements and the constant entertaining was arduous. 'Bottling cherries all day' is a rare domestic note – though whether a pleasure or a chore we cannot tell. By contrast, the winter weekends out at Ealing, with the boys away and Soane engrossed in business elsewhere, weighed heavily. Many evenings she found herself alone.

Now in her mid-forties, Eliza was worried about John's health and her sons' failure to meet their father's high expectations. Her preference (and clearly theirs) remained for the pleasant routine of a low-key social life at Chertsey, where keeping an eye on Soane's elderly relatives could be combined with visits to old friends and occasional outings in the vicinity. She usually stayed with the Smiths, a couple with several daughters and a son.

133. The Desanfans mausoleum, of 1807, designed by Soane to fit into a tiny stable yard behind a terrace in central London. This unusual domestic burial place was the prototype for the Dulwich mausoleum.

134. J.M.W. Turner's watercolour of
James Wyatt's Brocklesby Mausoleum in
Lincolnshire, a lecture diagram based upon
a building to which Turner introduced
Soane, lending him a print in 1804.

Richard Smith, the father,was a surgeon-apothecary. Richard Clark, a
former Lord Mayor of London and now Chamberlain in the City, and his
family were also friends as well as the local solicitor, confusingly also called
Clark.

In 1801 William Soane is listed in the freeholders' list as a bricklayer but
by 1803 (aged sixty-two) he appears as a gentleman.[11] Financial support
from his brother and moral support from his sister-in-law seem to have
been welcome; the boys were fond of their elderly uncle. In later life he
retired and cultivated his allotment at Addlestone and the garden around
the cottage at Goosepool, a hamlet just beyond Chertsey in the direction
of St Anne's Hill, where he and his wife Mary lived, possibly with their son
Francis.[12] William's eyesight was failing by now and his health often gave
cause for worry although he inherited the iron constitution of his mother
and younger brother and lived into his mid-eighties, dying in December
1825.

As well as the time spent in Chertsey, there were regular summer holidays in Margate or Ramsgate (the latter thought to be more socially select). The family, often with friends or relatives (in 1805 Mrs Flaxman and her sister Maria Denman made up the party, in 1806 Soane travelled down with Foxhall and William Beechey, in 1809 Miss Woodmeston, a cousin of Mrs Soane's, kept her company) took rooms in the late eighteenth-century fashionable 'new town' which had developed to reflect the leading bathing resort that Margate had become.

George joined his brother up at Cambridge in the spring of 1806, going up to Pembroke College: John transferred from Trinity to join him later that year. During term-time they communicated only rarely with their father. Since most holidays were spent in Chertsey or with their mother by the sea Soane was becoming increasingly unfamiliar with his sons.

George had told his father that his true interests lay in literature. Soane's response was to put him to work to catalogue his library (no mean task) in the summer of 1808, while his mother and brother were already in Ramsgate. George completed the long job but signed off with a violent tantrum, throwing the ink and inkstand on the floor. Recently, over dinner at Pitshanger, he had met James Boaden (fig. 135) and his family. Boaden was a prolific playwright and Shakespearean scholar (he identified WH, the dedicatee of the Sonnets, as the the Earl of Pembroke – an attribution accepted by scholars for many years) and as the future biographer of Dora Jordan, Sarah Siddons and John Philip Kemble an intimate of many leading figures of the theatre.[13] George gravitated towards those, such as Boaden, who might help him achieve his objective to become a writer, especially in the theatre.

135.Portrait of James Boaden by Samuel de Wilde (a student contemporary of Soane's at the Royal Academy). Boaden, a respected figure in the theatre world, would become George's father-in-law.

At four o'clock in the morning of 20 September 1808 the Theatre Royal Covent Garden exploded in flames, perhaps a victim of the Georgian delight in pyrotechnics on stage although the cause was never determined. James Boaden described the scene in his biography of J. P. Kemble, the actor-manager of the theatre, 'within less than three hours after its commencement, the whole of the interior was destroyed: nearly all the scenery, wardrobe, musical and dramatic libraries, and properties of all kinds, were a heap of smoking ruins'. Twenty men died, including three from the Phoenix Fire Office. Handel's organ and manuscript music, an enormous number of play scripts and stage sets were lost and there was little more than the £50,000 insurance to pay for a new building. After the initial shock, the theatre world rallied round and the search began for an architect.

Hardly twenty-four hours had passed before the portrait painter Thomas Lawrence, moving into centre stage at the Royal Academy, was writing to Farington about Robert Smirke junior's suitability for the job. He wanted to recommend him to Kemble; it would be 'a bold enterprize for him and will try his powers severely but if they are equal to it, perhaps no work is so well calculated to produce a powerful impression and fix him in public opinion'.[14] Three weeks later Lawrence wrote again; he did not want too much credit for gaining their young candidate the job, it had been an act of friendship. Smirke's father, a second-rate painter but a first-rate manoeuvrer with influential friends, was serving him well.

Soane's own elder son had recently come down from Cambridge without a degree – probably because of his chronic health problems. To keep

John's education moving, Soane arranged that he become Joseph Gandy's pupil in June 1808.[15] Almost immediately Gandy formed a partnership in Liverpool with George Bullock, better known as a furniture-maker and brother of the entrepreneurial William, and they moved north.

Gandy had been working intermittently in the north-west since 1801, taking on Thomas Harrison's job of remodelling Lancaster Castle to incorporate the county courts and gaol. The additions to the massive medieval castle were in the Gothic Revival style: the court-house interior was fitted out in a filigree of plaster and carpentry. Neither Harrison nor Gandy had used the style elsewhere; Gandy's known domestic commissions are loosely Greek Revival while the designs in his remarkable pattern books veer from visionary geometries to a wide-eaved, italianate style.[16] Gandy's architectural instincts were both eclectic and novel. He may not have been the steadiest guide for an uncertain architectural pupil to follow.

While Soane's son, frequently in bad health, showed little energy or enthusiasm for a lifetime's architectural project, Robert Smirke's son was flourishing. Before long he was consulting George Dance about the designs for Covent Garden. In fact, Thomas Lawrence reported that Smirke had resisted Dance's advice to apply more 'theatrical fancy' along the lines of his own Theatre Royal in Bath, opened in 1805 and decorated by the Royal Arms and masks of the tragic and comic muses on its capitals.[17] His next goal was the Royal Academy and Thomas Lawrence was busy canvassing for young Robert's election as an Associate of the Royal Academy, 'I ventured to recommend that he call on all, even on Mr Soane; because a candidate should come into a society without resentments: but his father has so strong objections to him that I suppose he will not.'[18] But even without Soane's help, Smirke's election was assured.

London now waited to see what form the rebuilt Covent Garden would take. On the last day of the year an elaborate masonic ceremony marked the laying of the foundation stone.[19] The Grand Master of the premier Grand Lodge, the Prince of Wales, assisted by his brother the Duke of Sussex and attended by Kemble and Smirke – both of whom had rapidly been admitted as freemasons – prepared the site according to masonic rite. Life Guards (all masons) lined the approach. The builders watched from a high scaffold as the Grand Treasurer placed a bronze box in a cavity in the massive foundation stone and the prince, to the accompaniment of martial music, set the stone in place with a silver trowel. He was then presented with the plumb level and square and

> pronouncing the work correct, he gave the stone *three* knocks with his mallet . . . *Three* cups were then given to his Royal Highness, containing corn, wine and oil, which he scattered and poured upon the stone; then placing a plan of the building in the hands of Mr Smirke, the architect, he desired him to complete the structure, according to that plan.

After the playing of 'Rule Britannia' the party dispersed, the masonic brothers to Great Queen Street, having formally minuted the proceedings. The proprietors, their friends and a crowd of fashionable actors and actresses ended the day with a grand dinner.[20]

Meanwhile on 23 October 1808 after dining at home with Sir Francis

Bourgeois, their doctor and friend Robert Pennington and Gandy, with the Flaxmans joining them for tea, the Soane family settled down to a 'council of war', a serious talk to John and George 'about their prospects'.[21] John's architectural pupillage was progressing in fits and starts and Pennington may then have offered to provide George, still at Cambridge, with a period of medical training.

Soane had recently learned about a number of debts incurred by his sons at Cambridge and asked Robert Fellowes, whose own sons were up at the university and who knew the Master of Pembroke, to make enquiries about their reputations. The reply was not reassuring; the master saying that he did not tell tales out of college and Fellowes telling Soane that the college, so proudly associated with William Pitt, currently had a very low standing within the university.[22]

Fellowes, who possibly did not realise that John had already left without a degree, tactfully nudged Soane: 'I conclude you do not stint them in your allowance – with every attention to economy they must cost you about £250 each. I have mentioned this matter of expence, because I am convinced nothing improves a young man more and rubs off all rust and awkward habits and absurd if not positive opinions so much as mixing in a variety of company, which must be attended with expence – it is as necessary as books.'[23] The most that his informants could discover was that the younger brother was still at Pembroke 'but secludes himself from the rest of the college'. Fellowes continues 'he may be naturally studious . . . [but] great allowances are to be made for young men – they see what they think fault in old ones and by avoiding them run into the contrary extreme. We must take the world as we find it and endeavour to make the best of it – we must expect to meet with what we do not like in as well as out of our family and we must reconcile ourselves to it.'

Soane can have had little idea of the reality of university life; pupillage took the place of higher education for architects, apart from that offered at the Royal Academy (though Wren had Cambridge, even Pembroke connections). Soane's experiences were as an outsider, working as an architect for the vice-chancellor on his Senate House proposals and for the Syndics at Caius and St John's Colleges years before. Soane's eagerness that his sons should go up to Cambridge was, presumably, for social reasons and the signs now were that he had, again, miscalculated badly. Universities were closed establishments, overseen by clerics, who often exercised no personal supervision over the undergraduates who were, as a result, left to their own devices. The only obligations upon them were to attend chapel daily and to deliver a small portion of classical translation weekly. Most students idled away their years at university in entertaining and being entertained, generally in the lower aspects of city life.[24] For John and George, without the social connections which many parents could provide, but with the unrelenting pressure of parental ambition upon them, it was an indeterminate form of education, from which it was alarmingly easy to drop out or deviate. John and George Soane just disappeared from sight.

As always, personal and professional difficulties brought bad health for Soane. Increasing concern about his sons' future employment as well as professional pique as Smirke's Covent Garden rose at breakneck speed, with all eyes on it, exacerbated his state. As the pressures built up, John

136. Thomas Cooley's drawing of Soane delivering his Royal Academy lectures in 1810, shortly before he suspended them for some years. John Flaxman, his colleague as Professor of Sculpture, looks considerably more relaxed in his task in the lower sketch.

137. Turner's lecture drawing (*c*. 1810) of the Temple of Neptune, Paestum. Since Turner did not visit southern Italy until 1819, it is likely that he turned to Soane for help with the subject.

Britton wrote to chide Soane for his 'symptoms of hippishness, arising from too great irritability of the nervous system: with a feverish thirst for fame, in yourself and family'.[25] Few but Britton, who managed to both flatter and instruct Soane in a naïve, but affectionate, fashion, could have got away with such frankness.

Three years after his appointment as professor, Soane finally delivered his first Royal Academy lecture on 27 March 1809. It seems to have been an experiment and he gave no more that year.[26] He had been heavily immersed in the practical elements of preparation in the preceding weeks and it was, perhaps, to test the acoustics and sight-lines of the room, and his own delivery, that he made this dress rehearsal. Turner and he had by then substantially reordered the Great Room at Somerset House.

It made good sense for the two fellow professors to work together. In 1809, with the sculptor Francis Chantrey, they also constituted the hanging committee for the annual exhibition. Both men were planning to use large numbers of drawings to illustrate their respective lectures.[27] Turner's treatment of the orders and architectural terms (in lectures 3 and 4) (fig. 137), his quotations from du Cerceau and his choice of buildings to illustrate such as the Temple of Neptune at Paestum or the screens used both in front of Holland's Carlton House and Robert Adam's Admiralty building, suggests reciprocicity between the two. Soane would pay close attention to Turner's fifth lecture with its ideas on reflection, refraction and light sources. Logic suggests that Turner would have turned to his colleague for corroboration and discussion of architectural matters. The process was a stimulating exercise with shared enthusiasms and insights. Delivery was another matter: both Turner and Soane struggled with their texts, diligently assembled but confusingly expressed.[28] Turner prevaricated and did not present his first lecture until January 1811 but Soane's series started in earnest in 1810 (fig. 136) with Turner in the audience.[29]

In 1809 Henry Holland's Theatre Royal Drury Lane also burned to the ground, in one of the most spectacular fires London had ever witnessed. Among the losses detailed by Boaden were William Capon's superb gothic stage sets including a view of New Palace Yard, Westminster and a reconstruction of the Palace of Westminster. The evidence of a rich seam of theatrical antiquarianism went up in flames – just a few hundred yards from the rising walls of Smirke's new theatre. Benjamin Dean Wyatt's replacement would see both Soane and his son George working there.

Meanwhile hardly were the ashes cold at Drury Lane than Covent Garden reopened, a year to the day after the fire.[30] Everybody had their views about the new Theatre Royal, the first Greek Revival structure in London. Smirke's real achievement, to design and build a huge new theatre within twelve months, went largely unmentioned. *The Covent Garden Journal* offered an unctuous welcome; 'The classic genius of the architect, as carried into almost instantaneous effect by the builder, equalled, in the eyes of many, the executive power of Aladdin's lamp.' Others were more concerned with the choice of the Greek Doric order, unusual for a building of this nature, given the classical hierarchy. Smirke's father had proudly discussed it with Thomas Lawrence, agreeing that grandeur of effect such as the Doric would possess ought not to be sacrificed in a building which might be considered national, for a fanciful notion that something lighter in style would alone be appropriate to a theatre. On the contrary [Smirke] thought a building of this kind should have a graver character. Who he said in thinking of the plays of Sophocles and Euripides being acted at Athens, would think the taste of a building improper if it was in a style of dignity and gravity?.

A solemn theatrical style would be preferable to much of the 'light trash' in existence. 'Dress a man well, and you elevate his sentiments', seemed to Farington to be a suitable maxim.[31]

A Swedish visitor to London, Eric Gustaf Geijer was more critical. 'People made a great fuss about this building. It was said to combine elegance with simplicity. It is at least not *grata simplicitas*. I think it is heavy. The windows are too much like slits. The whole building does not rise happily and openly to invite the onlooker in to take part in public amusement. It is too much shut in and too much like a *warehouse.*' Judged from the Continent, with models such as the Théâtre de l'Odéon or Victor Louis' much admired theatre in Bordeaux, Covent Garden was nothing special.

Geijer was astonished by the next act. The theatre opened to a nasty smell of fresh paint on the first night but also to a riot, due to the proprietors' decision to raise ticket prices drastically and to set aside many boxes for private use. The building had been prodigiously expensive and the theatre-goers had to help pay for it. The Old Price (OP) riots took place nightly (fig. 138):

> A contest began between the general public and the management of the theatre, which lasted for months. There is no kind of noise for the expression of disapproval – shrieking, whistling, howling, bellowing, crowing – which was not there heard in the most infernal symphony that ever tormented mortal ear . . . They brought rattles, trumpets, posthorns . . . Contrary to the usual custom, the public stood up, with hats on, during the piece; as soon as the curtain fell and between the acts, they sat down to rest from their labours.[32]

Those who were arrested and prosecuted were supported by public subscription, OP commemorative items were made and sold and there was an OP dance with its own music. John Philip Kemble, the actor-manager, hired boxers, including Daniel Mendoza (the most celebrated prizefighter of the day) and fought back. For sixty-seven nights the riots continued but in mid-December after a respectable lawyer had been arrested, acquitted and then successfully sued the police for wrongful arrest, a meeting was arranged between the OP protesters and Kemble, representing the proprietors. Compromise on all counts brought peace and matters returned to normal.

The opening of Smirke's Covent Garden Theatre had not pleased Soane. Smirke had succeeded in designing and building a key London building in record time and to considerable, if not unanimous, praise. In so doing, he had inched himself closer to court circles and had added his membership of London freemasonry to that of the Royal Academy.[33] By contrast, his former master's work at the Bank of England was widely criticised and largely unseen, his House of Lords unbuilt and his dealings with the Board at Chelsea a permanent headache.

138. Thomas Rowlandson's cartoon of the Old Price Riots at the just reopened Theatre Royal Covent Garden, in which George Soane became involved.

Nor was Soane's unhappiness with the newly built theatre simply a matter of professonal jealousy. The OP rioters were hard to characterise as a group. Some were practised trouble-makers but others in the crowd were respectable young men who simply objected on principle to the way the theatre was becoming priced into exclusivity. On 16 October the *Morning Chronicle* published the name of one John (in error for George) Soane as a rioter, while the *Covent Garden Journal* reported that 'the son of Mr Soame [sic] the architect in Lincolns Inn Fields was ordered to give sureties himself in 50 pounds to answer a charge of riot and disturbance by hissing and hooting during the performance'. Soane's notebooks show him apoplectic with fury; equally at the mistaken name and at George's involvement. John Britton, writing two days later, tried to calm him down,

> I write to . . . assure you that there was nothing in the papers, for I believe I saw them all, nothing has occurred in conversation, even among those connected with the theatre, that can at all attach to you, professionally, or morally: nor will the conduct of your son be found reproachable at all. He was very moderate, and was very *unfairly* brought into notice.[34]

George, hardly off the packet-boat home from Margate, had become an indicted OP rioter and his father was asked to find bail. Aged just twenty, George had been swept along with a gang of friends for it was all little more than horseplay in a good cause. As Britton predicted, the affair passed quietly and the Bill of Indictment was 'not found' by the Grand Jury.[35] Soane was not prepared to leave it there; to forgive and forget was not his nature. George's name had been in the newspapers, not for some prize or accomplishment, but as a defendant in a court case.

At Chelsea Hospital, Soane was having continuous difficulties with the commissioners, a particularly prickly set of clients drawn from both the military and the government. The governor, General Sir David Dundas, was a man who ruled his small empire 'with an excess of regimental zeal'. It came as a shock to Soane to be subject to strict rules, extending to the keeping of animals and other minutiae, and to have to deal with a frigid and largely uncongenial Board.

A new infirmary was needed but no one could agree on anything. Currently sick pensioners were housed under Wren's high roofs at the top of the courtyard ranges. The medical men, the physician Dr Benjamin Moseley of whom Soane noted 'it is to be hoped that Dr Moseley is better acquainted with his duties as a physician than he seems to be with those of an architect' and the surgeon, Thomas Keate, could not agree on the brief – a matter in which Soane had no authority or knowledge to intervene but the resolution of which determined his architectural solution. In addition, the Board was at odds with its paymaster, the Treasury.

The location and site for the infirmary engendered another tedious official row, not of Soane's making. Walpole House, which stood to the west of Wren's main group of buildings, was not suitable for conversion (either functionally or economically) and its demolition became inevitable, despite its traditional association with the name of Vanbrugh – of British architects, with Wren himself, the man Soane admired most. In the meantime, a considerable portion of its land (with a river frontage) had been sold to provide a site for Thomas Leverton's house for Colonel Gordon, a functionary of the hospital. The curtailed area of Walpole House was, Soane knew, inadequate for the drying grounds and other service buildings needed for a sizeable hospital.

His early vision of a spreading three-storey, arcaded block (fig. 139) – with the strong rhythmic articulation of the great aqueduct that he and the Bishop had seen near Caserta – facing the unembanked river, flanked by the ornamental canals of Wren's scheme and ventilated by river breezes, was curtailed to become a modest structure built in yellow stock brick and 'in the same unadorned style as the rest of the hospital, so as to make a part of one great whole' as he told the board.[36] It was a far cry from the Hôtel des Invalides in Paris, the prototype which both Wren and Soane held as their ideal.[37] The infirmary, the first substantial job that Soane had received at Chelsea, where he had been doing little but essential maintenance work after Samuel Wyatt's sluggish years in the post, would earn him only a paltry additional £100 above his salary. There was no commission. Parsimony dogged Soane at Chelsea, just as it had Wren who had produced a masterpiece in modest dress.[38]

When it suited them, the Board accused Soane of failure to attend meetings or to communicate information, but the members frequently acted without his advice or simply ignored it. Farington reported 'He was required to attend the Board at a time appointed, instead of which a letter was received from him stating *that he was going to the Bank* and could not attend.'[39] It was, apparently, only Charles Long's intervention which prevented Soane's dismissal.

The working atmosphere was unpleasant, comparing unfavourably to his usually excellent relations with the Court of Directors at the Bank. Because of the public nature of the commission, the Board at Chelsea was continually in search of economies. Required to use the hospital's own tradesmen, Soane had to endure their often poor, over-priced work in

139. Soane's elevation for the Infirmary at Chelsea Hospital, drawing on his memories of the rhythmic brick arcading of the Caserta aqueduct (fig 27). He wanted the hospital to overlook the Thames, a healthy setting for the invalid pensioners who can be seen taking the air in the drawing. The reality was a cramped site well away from the breezes.

contrast to the excellent workmanship and moderate costs which his own proven team could have provided.

The arguments at Chelsea rumbled on over the summer of 1809. Mrs Soane, responding from Margate to his fears that the commissioners might dispense with his services, counselled 'surely they dare not? They may try to provoke you to resign, but depend, they dare not go farther.' By the end of September Soane's determined stance had paid off and Mrs Soane wrote with justifiable pride 'you have gained great credit in this part for your spirited conduct at Chelsea and I had the pleasure to be pointed out as the wife of an honest independent man'.[40]

By the summer of 1809 it was clear that the great Pitshanger venture was over. Soane rationalised his intense disappointment. 'Mrs Soane never liked the country. I had hoped however that prejudice might have been overcome.'[41] Given her long and happy stays in Chertsey and her pleasure in the beauties of Cricket Lodge, Eliza's problem lay elsewhere, in her dislike of her role as hostess of a *salon* in a house which had never been a family home. The house and 30 acres, only 6½ miles from London, was advertised by James Christie in the *Times* on 21 June 1809, extolling its elegance, its pleasure-grounds, walled kitchen-gardens, two coach-houses and stabling for seven horses.[42]

Showing her usual acumen, Eliza advised her husband to hold out for £10,000 and not to accept the £7,000 suggested by James Christie, the son of the famous auctioneer and family friend. 'I consider it as an affront . . . you are not distressed for the money'[43] she wrote, asking him to convey her opinion to Christie. They had bought the house for £4,500 and spent prodigious sums on it: she wanted a fair return. When it was eventually sold at the higher price to General Cameron a year later, Soane noted that Eliza was well-satisfied.

As Pitshanger Manor first went on the market, the summer of 1809 in Margate offered, as usual, entertaining distractions for Eliza Soane: four music meetings, with Braham and Storace in town, little Fanny – the family dog – scampering around and spilling the ink over one of her letters and her cousin Miss Woodmeston proving a pleasant companion. Late in the stay she met the de Loutherbourgs. George's journey had been uncomfortable, he had been forced to spend the entire night on board the London packet boat to Margate owing to the rough seas. Once he was safely disembarked he and his brother indulged in a little light gambling, winning 5 guineas on a stake of 3 shillings. His father cannot have been so amused by their choice of recreation in view of George's recurrent debts to booksellers and others at Cambridge.

Eliza wrote to her husband: 'I shall be glad to hear you have begun your alterations, as I think it will be an amusement for you'. She knew very well that building work was Soane's own prescription for recovery during periods of trial. His current project at Lincoln's Inn Fields was to improve the office/museum arrangement to the rear of No. 13. Mrs Soane must have suddenly worried that he would go further and they would return to a building site at No. 12. 'Do you mean to make improvements in the house?' she wrote, 'don't mistake me, I by no means wish to urge it'. Then, following his long silence, she relents slightly, 'pray if you do anything, do not forget to *paint* the Eating Room and Library' which are 'in such a bad state they make the whole house look shabby'.[44] Later in September she sympathises with him over servant problems, adding 'I expect to see the house very complete for I know your taste and expense you do not consider.' He must be very tired; why does he not relax with 'one of your long journeys'. 'Mr. Putt [in Devon] wants you and *that* air always agrees with you – besides . . . *I* should like to stay here a few days longer.'[45] Warm weather into early October pleased Eliza, 'how nicely it will dry the paint'.

The new 'Plaister Room' or 'Model-room' – he referred to the space now known as the Dome by both names – was rising on the site of the stables at No. 13. Though not literally a dome, but a square encircled by pendentives, the summit surmounted by a skylight, it followed Soane's favourite model, that of the tall, top-lit 'tribune'. As he began to shift his creative and exploratory focus from Pitshanger to Lincoln's Inn Fields, it was here in a space modelled to full height, a dramatic vortex to his house, that he displayed his growing collection of antique fragments and sculpture (fig. 140). Soane's model for the house/museum was an accumulation of impressions. In 1804 he had visited Thomas Hope at Duchess Street. Here, in a more conventional house than either Walpole's or Beckford's, Hope displayed his collection, which was – as Strawberry Hill had been – open to a self-selecting public, who bought tickets or who were invited. Soane kept a close eye on Duchess Street through John Britton, who catalogued Hope's books and later published a description of Deepdene, his country house.[46] There were other connections; Hope owned a pair of magnificent Gandys, one showing the scene from Milton's *Pandemonium*.[47]

Behind No. 12, across the yard outside the breakfast room windows, Soane converted the old office into his new study/library. The library, the plaister room and the new offices, on two levels, were aligned along the rear boundary, west to east. Soane, often working late at night on the lectures, complained of the poisonous smell of paint. It was not a comfortable house in these months, nor were Soane's spirits lifting.

In early January 1810, it was John and his father who had reached loggerheads over his extravagance. 'As I find from the dissimilarity of our dispositions that it is impossible for us to live together without materially injuring the happiness of either, I think it best we separate', he wrote.[48] He proposed returning to Cambridge, to take a degree and Orders, and imag-

140. One of Gandy's several resplendent views of Soane's new 'plaister room' to the rear of 13 Lincoln's Inn Fields, the core of his growing museum. This version depicts it glowing from an unseen light source below.

ined that with economy he would be able to live on his allowance from his father.

But virtually overnight Soane relented. John's willingness to follow an architectural career was rewarded by the transfer of the interest on £5,000 3 per cent stock. He also made over £6,500 in Bank stocks to Eliza.[49] There was no mention of George who continued to receive a minimal allowance.

In fact George was showing signs of responsibility. Robert Pennington entered George that month at St Bartholomew's Hospital, of which he was a governor. When he left, nine months later, Pennington testified that 'he does not owe any one a single farthing: his general conduct since he has been in my house has been perfectly correct: he deceived me with respect to his attention to his profession but I trust he may still produce some effects worthy of your notice.'[50] George had attended three series of lectures, those on physic and materia medic, physiology and surgery, and chemistry but he had given up the unequal struggle. Pennington charged £78 15s for nine months' board and lodging; the experiment was over. Whatever the serious defects of George's character, Pennington retained some affection for him and even in the 1820s offered him support in the face of his father's implacable hatred. George's period toying with medicine was the equivalent to John's pupillage with Gandy, but an unsuccessful diversion given his single-minded ambition to write.

Smirke's inoffensive Greek Revival building at Covent Garden caught the full brunt of Soane's accumulated bitterness, in the fourth in his opening series of Royal Academy lectures, delivered on 29 January 1810.[51] By now the building had come to encapsulate his miseries, professional and personal.

The lecture, accompanied by a total of seventy illustrations, opened with a discussion of the correct use of columns and pilasters, the appropriate treatment of façades and 'the abuses of the pediment and balustrade . . . serious and growing evils'. Then Soane turned to another 'fatal' practice. 'It is no uncommon thing to see one of the fronts enriched with columns, pilasters, and other architectural ornaments, whilst the flanks are left plain, as if belonging to other buildings, or erected by different persons at different times.' This, he continued, 'is to be seen, not only in small houses where economy might in some degree apologize for the absurdity, but it is also apparent in large works of great expense, both public and private, even in works where in a great degree the national taste is implicated'.

Soane illustrated two town houses, Adam's Lansdowne House and Leoni's Uxbridge House and then continued with 'two drawings of a more recent work [which] point out the glaring impropriety of this defect in a manner if possible still more forcible and more subversive of true taste. The public attention, from the largeness of the building, being particularly called to the contemplation of this national edifice.' The audience registered shock as the two illustrations of Smirke's new theatre were pinned up, one of which showed none of the neighbouring buildings, which in reality largely hid the bald side walls (fig. 141). Some people claimed that the building was unrecognisable from the lecture drawings. Soane had broken a taboo, never to criticise the work of a living fellow architect.[52]

141. One of Soane's two lecture drawings of Robert Smirke's Covent Garden theatre, of which he was highly critical (largely because of the bald side elevation) causing an outcry at the Royal Academy and the passing of a rule to forbid criticism of a living artist.

He continued: 'It is extremely painful to me to be obliged to refer to modern works, but if improper models which become more dangerous from being constantly before us are suffered, from false delicacy, or other motives, to pass unnoticed, they become familiar, and the task I have undertaken would be not only neglected but the duty of the Professor . . . becomes a dead letter.' The laws of the institution required him, among his other tasks, to offer students 'a critical examination of structures'.[53]

Obliquely, he had already fleetingly criticised aspects of several works by living architects; he touched upon the Auction Mart, Bartholomew Lane by John Walters[54] and John Nash's first London building on the corner of Great Russell Street and Bloomsbury Square.[55] The latter, a large double house, exemplified the careless conjunction of a heavy entablature with slender pilasters and continued with 'this strange and extravagant absurdity which is daily increasing' as in two of George Dance junior's buildings, the elevation of the British Institution (formerly the Shakespeare Gallery) and the Portugal Street front of the Royal College of Surgeons.[56] He also discussed Dance's St Luke's Hospital and offered 'high praise' to Newgate. Finally he turned his guns on Smirke.[57]

Soane's remarks about Covent Garden Theatre caused an uproar, some listeners hissing as he spoke, others clapping.[58] The audience included some who felt that criticism of living architects was perfectly valid. James Wyatt, for example, had told Sir Francis Bourgeois (who was ill and had missed Soane's lecture) that there was 'no place so proper as the Royal Academy for remarks to be made on works of art, ancient or modern, for the improvement of the student'.[59] It earned him Soane's undying gratitude.

Lawrence reported back to Farington: 'That rascal Soane commenced in his public lecture on Monday night a direct personal attack on Robert Smirke producing a distorted drawing of the theatre. . .One can never be prepared for the insanity of such *venomous malignity* but the Academy hear this, the Council hear it . . . I am going with Smirke to Mr West to try to move him. He has been to George Dance but he declines it.'[60] George Dance had no heart for the prosecution of vendettas.

On 6 February a unanimous resolution was passed in the Council 'That for a Professor in any department in the Royal Academy to criticise the works of living artists, particularly of members of the Academy, was highly improper.' Soane as a consequence 'expressed to the President that his 5th lecture not being conformable to that Resolution he should not proceed at present'.[61]

Despite suspending his lectures, Soane decided to argue his case against his fellow academicians. Bourgeois was impressed by his self-defence: 'I think you answered yesterday . . . in a manner that must give you great pleasure this morning when you reflect on it. Sir W [William Beechey] said he never heard you speak so well.'[62] In the vote on the criticism of the works of living artists seventeen were against, just two (Bourgeois and Beechey) supported Soane's stand.[63] A few days later, Soane again read the offending lecture to his friends at home; John Landseer, the engraver, thought if Fuseli could praise Benjamin West's *General Wolfe* there was no logic in ruling out criticism.[64] The following Sunday Farington reported that Soane had been at one of John Britton's regular evening parties for artists, 'railing at the Royal Academy'.[65]

Although it seemed that Soane had decided to martyr himself on what was, on the face of it, an academic point of dispute, there were hidden issues on both sides. Wyatt's support was a significant chink in the Royal Academy's united front but, for the moment, the academicians had found a way to control their unruly and ungovernable Professor of Architecture. Soane retreated; first to brood and then to compose an appeal. On the walls of the Royal Academy that year hung his dusted-off scheme for the Leicester Square Opera House, twenty years old.

In the autumn, curiosity finally got the better of him. On 14 September Soane went to Covent Garden, to examine the huge interior with its central heating, modern stage technology and strongly coloured decoration. 'First time of my seeing interior of Covent Garden Theatre, better than the outside, but bad indeed!'[66] he confided in his notebook.

Richard Holland, one of Soane's oldest friends and John's godfather but long out of touch with him, had a solution to Soane's travails. He suggested that he retire. 'I think at a certain time of life the more we *can* divest ourselves of . . . cares and anxieties . . . the greater will be our enjoyments.' Holland had done so, and was enjoying the fruits of leisure. Soane could hand over 'the great labour' to young John Soane 'to qualify him to succeed you in any appointment you hold'; if his godson's view of architecture was modelled on his father's, 'what may not be expected?' But despite the attraction of the 'tranquil shades' that Holland described, Soane claimed that the offer of the professor's chair had 'destroyed all my plans of retirement'. Unusually frank with his old friend, he confessed that the 'only half extinguished embers of ambition' had been easily rekindled since 'my unfortunate attachment to architecture is as difficult to be extinguished, as a passion for play in the mind of a professed gambler'.[67]

As for George, Holland carefully advised Soane not to despise his efforts and his 'passion for dramatic writing' which Soane so denigrated and to encourage him to 'give nature its course, he *may* excel and his success would be very flattering to you'.[68] That George was not quite the black sheep that Soane chose to make him was apparent from Pennington's practical support.

John's pupillage in Liverpool continued, punctuated by frequent visits south, on health grounds, but in the autumn of 1810 the practice collapsed following an acrimonious dispute, in which Soane was called to mediate. The following year Soane wrote that he was anxious to see all Bullock and Gandy's differences settled 'when I hope they will be as good friends as ever'.[69] Gandy's 'impracticable disposition' as Soane described it later was already proving a difficulty; his life was subsequently marked by financial crises and incipient mental instability. Soane remained sympathetic and steadfast towards him through many vicissitudes.

Gandy, despite his need for the welcome £100 that he received annually for his pupil (the same sum that Soane had paid Gandy himself), tactfully indicated John's unsuitability as heir to Soane's architectural practice. 'Mr Soane's constitution does not seem calculated to bear with the rough storm of life, nor can it go through the incessant fatigue with which you have overcome difficulties on the road to fame more successfully than many others, a road which lengthens with each generation.' When under pressure, working 'a few days together without interruption, makes him exert himself beyond the powers of nature, the consequence was a nervous headache, I should take care not to repeat this experiment'.[70] Soane was not disposed to listen to Gandy's advice.

12

PLEASURES AND TROUBLES

Towards the end of the calm months of 1810, during which George was under Robert Pennington's supervision at St Bartholomew's Hospital, John and Eliza Soane used their elder son's stay in Liverpool as an excuse for a tour together. The thirteen-day journey on which they embarked on 6 August was unique in their marriage. Apart from visits to the Bridports in Somerset and a few days snatched during the family summer holidays on the Kent coast, they very rarely travelled as a couple. Eliza knew little of England beyond the southern counties.

Their itinerary, carefully planned by Soane, with some help from Gandy, was packed with interest and Eliza's spontaneous comments on the buildings and the countryside they saw finally puts flesh on the bones of Soane's travels. His own notebook entries are unfailingly unrevealing (except in rage) but her observant diary[1] provides a different insight and also underlines Soane's energy – they were up most mornings at five or six, often to visit three or four different towns or monuments and then travel on to their inn. They were taking one of his regular routes, which led to several clients in the west midlands.

From Oxford, which impressed Eliza although they had only time to see 'King's' (New) College where Mr Wyatt 'has placed the organ so as to hide a beautiful painted glass window', and Merton College with its fine garden, they went on to Woodstock where they stayed overnight. Before settling down the Soanes walked by moonlight in Blenheim Park, a memorable introduction to Vanbrugh's impressive mansion and landscape. They returned at 6 a.m. the next morning – perhaps to compare Eliza's daylight impressions with those of the night before.

They hurried on to Stratford upon Avon, to visit Shakespeare's birthplace and tomb – even then much-visited. In the churchyard the trees were 'very curiously arched . . . so as to prevent the rain coming through' and an ancient crone appeared to show them the church. Eliza was much struck by the stark black and white of the rectangular Warwickshire timber-framing. It was, like the stone walling that she noticed replacing field hedges from then on, quite new to her – very dissimilar to the close studded Kentish framing with which she was familiar. Their next stops were at Kenilworth Castle and Warwick Castle, the latter with its 'awfully' grand approach cut between two sheer rock walls. Inside, shown around by a well-informed and 'very ladylike' Scottish housekeeper, Eliza was impressed by the furnishings, the armour, and a Rubens. After a quick professional call on Lord Hood at Whitley Abbey[2] they headed for Coventry, admiring the three spires of the handsome church and, equally, the steam powered ribbon factory employing 500 men and women. Via Lichfield and a night at the Crown Inn, Stone, 'a dirty place, nothing interesting',[3] they arrived in Liverpool at 9 p.m., the last few miles in extreme discomfort, 'the spring of the carriage having broken . . . we were in jeopardy for seven miles'.

Liverpool in 1810 was a city and port of immense size (fig. 142), almost five thousand ships used the port each year, and the numbers were still rising. Although the slave-trade had been abolished in 1807 Liverpool's trade with the Americas remained buoyant. Their hotel, the Liverpool Arms, where they spent four nights was large but 'with not *every* accommodation that could be wished for the traveller'. They had, in Eliza's phrase, an 'invisible landlord'. From it they had a splendid view, both of the shipping and the major buildings, including the Town Hall and Exchange, built by John Wood the elder of Bath and, following a serious fire, remodelled by James Wyatt. There was also a play house, presumably the Theatre Royal.[4] Architecturally impressive as its centre had become, Liverpool also offered, among many entertainments for the visitor, 'bathing machines as at a watering place'.

In Liverpool too Eliza was up by six o'clock, and walked down to the pier on her own, to wonder at the enormous quantity of shipping and the sheer energy of the place. The crowds were mostly sailors and 'rich dirty looking merchants very forbidding in their appearance'.

The Gandys were attentive hosts. That first morning Gandy and his sister called, walking with them out to St James's Walk, which gave a view of the Mersey to one side and open sea to the other. Cotton was lying out to dry in the fields. They visited the fort and the bathing-rooms before joining Mr and Mrs Gandy for dinner and the theatre, George Frederick Cooke playing Iago in *Othello*, one of his set-piece dramatic roles. Eliza, with an acute eye for these things, was impressed by the theatre-going crowd. 'Ladies very smart and flimsy.' They were back at midnight after a 'most delightful day'.

On the Friday, they explored the town further and visited an exhibition. At the Billiard Room, a building designed by Gandy,[5] the men struck Eliza as impolite with, her favourite term, 'money getting' faces. John's lodging on Brownlow Street, in the desirable Mount Pleasant area[6] was small, but neat and comfortable. His bedroom looked into the stone quarry, a massive cave entered by a dark archway bored through the stone. That evening the wives dined together, while Soane went out with Mr Foster, another 'great money getting man'. This was John Foster, senior, the Corporation Surveyor who, with his son, was responsible for much new development in the city. Back at the hotel Eliza packed for the next leg of the journey.

Once again they rose at dawn and found their dog Titus asleep in the carriage. They crossed the Mersey to the Wirral in Cheshire and went straight to Chester and the Rows; 'a very curious old town – where it appears you walk through the people's houses'. They saw the great Greek Revival Shire Hall and gaol complex, 'built by a Mr Harrison and does him great credit. The hall built in the form of an amphitheatre.' (figs. 81,

142. The Prince's Dock at Liverpool (1831). Eliza Soane who took an early morning walk to the harbour on her 1810 visit was amazed by the activity. Thousands of ships used the docks annually.

143. Plan of Chester Gaol by W. J. Donthorn (after 1820).

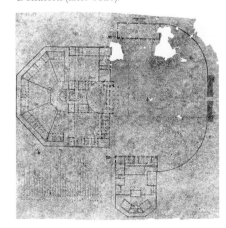

143). Soane was eager to show her this building which he so particularly admired for its pure and uncompromising use of the style and form of a Greek agora, forming a civic centre-piece. He had regularly revisited it, as it slowly took shape, over the years since 1791. Then they walked around the town on the walls and enjoyed market day.

From Wrexham the Soanes continued to Ellesmere, Eliza commenting on the lake and 'curious tomb stones in Ellesmere church yard the first place we saw the graves dressed with flowers'. From the Bowling Green, thirteen counties could be seen. The journey to Shrewsbury was 'a most enchanting drive the Welch [sic] Mountains on one side the Wrekin on the other'. They arrived at one o'clock on Sunday and went immediately to the pleasure gardens, laid out early in the century with fine lime avenues. The setting was familiar to them from Farquhar's *The Recruiting Officer*. At the end of one avenue, 'a ferry takes you to the Poor House, a girl ferries you over in a very curious manner by means of a rope and pulley, she using a hook'. Another led to St Chad's, built twenty years before by George Steuart 'and we were Christian enough to walk through it being Sunday'. Eliza had long ago grown used to Soane's distaste for church services. 'After dinner although very wet, Mr Soane and myself walked down to the bridge[7] and round . . . the town, the castle and house of correction, [John] Howard's bust over the door.'[8] The Wrekin could be seen, with the clouds below it.

On Monday morning they left Shrewsbury for Coalbrookdale,[9] walking to the Iron Bridge and on to Buildwas Abbey, 'a most romantic place, part of the building converted into a farmyard a very pretty farm house adjoining and a small iron bridge over the Severn'. The latter, Thomas Telford's first iron bridge, was considerably wider and lighter than its famous and older near-neighbour. It was an exact contemporary of Rowland Burdon's Sunderland Bridge.

Mrs Soane was stunned by the furious activity in Coalbrookdale (fig. 144). At the factory visitors could follow the manufacturing process all the way through, from the arrival of the local ore to casting. Founded in 1708, the Coalbrookdale company dominated the valley and the contrast between the beauty of the natural setting and the belching furnaces, well known from paintings by de Loutherbourg, Wright of Derby and others, was highly impressive, 'much beyond any thing I could imagine wonderful' as Eliza put it. She had a moment of vertigo on a dangerously steep flight of stone steps down into the valley, 'the only place where an accommodating gentleman was wanted'.

Their journey continued down the Severn to Bridgnorth and then Ludlow. The final 20-mile stage was on terrible roads and the carriage trace broke. 'A wet day and in sad plight slept at Ludlow.' The sight of the splendid castle wiped out the bad experience, and she was surprised to find a poor family housed there 'on condition they keep a place for playing fives'. Their premises were the tower 'where Lord Mortimer was confined no light a square place from the top which conveyed his food down to him'. Nevertheless, Ludlow was prosperous, chiefly inhabited, wrote Eliza, by 'persons who live on a small fortune'.

Beyond, the roads became even worse. 'From Ludlow to Leominster most execrable infamous roads obliged to walk in the rain up all the hills.' Wednesday found them in Hereford, where they visited the Assizes (she

144. J.M.W. Turner *Limekiln at Coalbrookdale* (*c*.1797). One of many dramatic images of this most impressive of modern industrial landscapes. When John and Eliza Soane visited it in 1810 it fully lived up to her expectations.

may have meant John Nash's prison, built between 1792 and 1797). and met a Mr Wightwick, probably the father of Soane's future assistant George.[10] At the cathedral, where the west tower had collapsed specacutularly in 1786 and been rebuilt by James Wyatt, launching his career as a cathedral destroyer, they admired the fine organ and tombs as well as 'curious old cloisters round which the gentlemen belonging to the foundation lodge' and, despite Eliza's vertigo, ascended the west tower, 'very narrow and dangerous'. From Hereford to Ross was 'a beautiful drive had we not been sadly incommoded with a jibbing horse traces broke wet day thunder and lightning'.

The foul weather frustrated their next plan which was to have been a memorable journey, taking a boat along the Wye to Chepstow, passing Tintern Abbey and perhaps glimpsing Piercefield, Soane's unfinished house for his ruined client George Smith, high above the gorge. Instead, they stuck to the muddy, rutted roads between Ross and Gloucester where they spent the night and saw another 'handsome cathedral and fine old town with three churches'. After Gloucester they went on to Cheltenham 'just in time to see the company go to drink the waters dressed very smart although not eight o' clock in the morning'. They returned through the Cotswolds via Northleach and Witney 'a very curious town blankets on cloth[s] out bleaching'. After a last night on the road, they hurried quickly through High Wycombe ('nothing remarkable') back to Uxbridge, where they met up with their horses and went to Ealing, for a day of fishing. They were home in Lincoln's Inn Fields by nine o'clock that evening 'after having a most delightful journey and what I hope never to forget being out 13 [underlined three times] days'. Soane's notebook entry for 17 August was gnomic as usual: 'back in Ealing. £69. 4.0d for trip'. Two days later he recorded 'conversation respecting G and Miss B'. George was expert at spoiling his parents' pleasures. Miss B was Agnes Boaden, the daughter of James Boaden and a regular visitor to Pitshanger.

To add to their troubles, on 1 September Gandy wrote to the Soanes to tell them of the difficulties in his professional life; although John's intermittent months in the office had not been a resounding success, Gandy offered to prolong his period of study. John remained in Liverpool until February 1811[11] but soon after both he and Gandy were back in London. Gandy now increasingly worked as a topographical draughtsman for John Britton and others, and travelled widely. Young John Soane was again unoccupied.

The king's health was, like John's, a worry. George III's Golden Jubilee celebrations in 1810 had turned out to be no more than a popular distraction, the elderly king had a very tenuous hold on events of state and he was vulnerable to any shock or upset. When his beloved daughter Princess Amelia fell ill with galloping consumption, his fragile sanity was lost. Her death, aged twenty-seven, revived his worst symptoms. On 6 February 1811, the Prince of Wales finally became the Prince Regent. John Nash was firmly established as the court favourite, not a good development for Soane. Nash, his exact contemporary, had been appointed architect to the Department of Woods and Forests in 1806. He used the opportunity to embark on the largest public project ever seen in the capital.[12] The potential of Marylebone Park, which returned to Crown ownership in 1811 and thus became Regent's Park may not have been immediately obvious, but Nash's wizardry, less contrained by professional ethics, was still a threat to Soane's pole position in his profession. Nash's scheme rankled away in Soane's head for almost twenty years until he drew up his own proposals for a triumphal route through London, an old man's unrealisable post-script.

In the spring of 1811 Eliza Soane and her elder son (showing worrying symptoms of his illness) spent some days in Brighton. The much-loved family dog Fanny was with them, unwelcome in their over-priced lodgings and being led miserably about on a black ribbon, the result of a public ord-nance introduced 'on account of mad dogs' – presumably an outbreak of rabies, making Eliza feel like a 'blind beggar'. John would have liked his father to join them and in an uncharacteristically ebullient postscript to his mother's letter, assured Soane that the sea air and the sound of the waves 'will be of infinite service to the active Professor of Architecture; leave, leave those active members of rebellion and fly to your most affectionate son'.[13]

John was using the holiday to confide in his mother about his attach-ment to Maria Preston, whom he had met on his previous visit to Margate, and hoped he could soften up his father by introducing some architectural news. He had been weighing up the new Prince Regent's contribution to the resort. To Henry Holland's Royal Pavilion, the Prince of Wales had recently added the Indian-style riding house and stables by William Porden, marked by a huge oriental dome, but John was unim-pressed: 'I saw not the great convenience of the plans. The building raised for Chinese Baubles and not to live in.'[14] Nash's tinselly transformation of Holland's sober pavilion was still in the future.

Soane failed to respond to the news of John's intended marriage to Maria Preston. Eliza was angry with him, for this and other reasons. 'It is very troublesome to be continually writing to an Old Woman – bad enough to be plagued with such a one at home, particularly when we have kind friends always at hand, to point out the evil.'[15] The cheerful, com-panionable mood of their previous summer's journey had been forgotten. Someone had been gossiping about the company Soane kept in her absence and Eliza wrote, in undisguised fury, that she was reviewing 'the many *pleasant occurrences* of the last twenty six years of my life'. As she drily commented: 'I . . . find it is from home I can learn the concerns of my fam-ily. Tomorrow probably . . . we shall learn more. I hear town is very gay – as are *all my friends* in it . . . Adieu, farewell.' Soane, stung by the unchar-acteristic sarcasm and the valedictory note, replied that if she had not signed the letter, he could never have guessed it was hers. She replied that her letter was written 'on mature consideration and conviction'.[16]

Soane had not told them that he was a candidate for the surveyorship of St Paul's Cathedral, following the death of Robert Mylne.[17] The surpris-ing news had reached them on the grapevine. Soane's hopes were dashed when S.P. Cockerell was appointed, an obvious candidate since he was already Surveyor to the sees of London and Canterbury.[18] Again Soane was mortified; he found himself 'opposed' to 'the architect who planned and erected the steeple of . . . St Ann's Soho'. This unsuitable man (a par-ticular enemy of his friend James Spiller after their confrontations over the poor quality development of the Foundling estate) 'was appointed Curator and Conservator of the Glory of Architecture – the Cathedral of St Paul's'.[19] Soane never succeeded in gaining the patronage of churchmen, whose world represented as complex a political structure as any of those he had conquered. But despite his lack of sympathy for clerics, he resented his failure to achieve a professional foothold in their sphere.

Trying to re-engage her husband in domestic matters, Eliza told him that John's proposal had been accepted by Maria's family. Mr Preston was pleased with the match – as was she. But Soane had no welcome to offer Maria, although she had once sat beside him at dinner at Pitshanger and was no stranger to the family, as Eliza reminded him later when relations worsened. Soane apparently considered that John should follow his own example, deferring domestic pleasures until he was professionally qualified and established but his views had not prevailed and he retreated in pique.

However, on the day of the marriage, 6 June, Soane made a brief appearance at Sewardstone, and sent on a draft for £500[20] to the honeymooners in Tunbridge Wells from where John sent his thanks and expressed his hope that his parents would be able to visit them shortly.[21] Soane, while already enquiring whether Maria's father had provided the £2,000 settlement promised, then made a tempting offer to the couple, the use of the Clerks of Works' house at Chelsea. John could have 'the profits of my situation at Chelsea Hospital and at the Bank *as soon* and for as long as you are willing to discharge all such parts of the duties of these situations as can be done without my attendance. Happiness I most sincerely wish you – it is within your reach – it depends on yourself, but no man can truly possess it, who does not employ his time and talents usefully.' He closes, emotionally and portentously, 'I have done my duty and if the sun ever clouds your prospects it will not be imputable, to your affectionate father. PS I write under some agitation and I regret to say in haste.'[22]

John knew well that he was unfit to be Soane's clerk of works – which was what the offer amounted to. He had exhibited two works at the Royal Academy that year but he was far from ready to assume day-to-day responsibility for a major public building.

Relations between his parents were becoming difficult again over this period. Soane was angry that Eliza condoned John's marriage and could not bring himself to feel any affection for his daughter-in-law, who looked upon Eliza as an adopted mother (her own being dead). Eliza also realised John's desperate need to escape from his father's remorseless pressure to join a profession for which he appeared so wholly unsuited.

As if to spite his family, Soane took himself down to south Devon immediately after the wedding for an uncharacteristic week of roistering with his old friend Richard Holland and a group of young girls to whom the middle-aged bachelor seems to have acted as a kind of flirtatious uncle.

To judge from the reverberations of this week at Coombe Royal, a house just outside Kingsbridge, Soane also must have acted the buck and soon the attentions of Miss Eleanor (Norah) Brickenden (fig. 145), the silliest if not the youngest of the company, became fixed warmly upon him. Soane, always susceptible to flattery and attention from women, was superficially ensnared by the impressionable vicar's daughter from Hereford.

145. Clara Maria Pope's portrait of Norah Brickenden, a Herefordshire vicar's daughter who developed an attachment to Soane. Her attentions were not welcomed by Eliza Soane who broke off her friendship with the painter of this portrait, the former Mrs Wheatley.

On the way back from this hedonistic interlude of beach picnics and festivities in the pretty seaside house surrounded by orange and lemon trees, Soane called at Cricket Lodge. He was relieved to find the Bridports 'tête-à-tête'. Soane had taken three of the girls shopping in Exeter on the way home, sending them back loaded with packages. He had been, he confessed to Holland, 'near falling into the lions' den'. He enclosed, without fee, a sketch for his library; 'I think yours is a very good idea, but you must let me tickle it up a little. This you will say is vanity. Be it so: – it is my way.'[23]

Soane returned to London, out of temper because of John's failure to respond to the offer of the Chelsea house and employment. Soane was also increasingly agitated about Mr Preston's failure to answer letters. In July they met and Preston reiterated his promise to invest £2,000 for the young couple. In the autumn Maria's father asked if he might call again. Soane replied that he did not wish to see him, but to hear from him. Menacingly he adds 'I begin to know his character. I felt much agitated.' The dispute spluttered on and in years to come, long after her father's death, Soane would continuously blacken Preston's name to his daughter – referring to his 'wickedness and imbecility' in one letter. His irrational behaviour towards her father further poisoned the relationship between Maria and her father-in-law.[24] Yet, after Preston's death, Maria was able to buy a house in Brighton costing £2,450 which, as she pointed out, if not exactly to the letter of her father's promises, certainly kept the spirit of the agreement.[25] Soane's sour implacability was mystifying to Maria and infuriated Mrs Soane.

Eliza was always eager to offer John and Maria her friendship. She and Fanny settled into lodgings at 11 Harbour Street, Ramsgate in September 1811 while the young couple stayed nearby. Both Ramsgate and Margate were short of visitors: 'it may seem ill-natured to say I am glad of it – but really the inhabitants were so saucy that it was time they should be lowered'. John had not been well but was improving. She, too, had been feeling better and

more quiet in my mind than I have been for months but unluckily for me there always starts some demon to make me wretched and which I am now sure will shortly bring me to my end. Yesterday I met by chance a person who reported some conversation you had about your family 'at the same time pitied us both for having a son who was so incapable to taking care of himself'.

Deeply wounded that he should gossip outside the family about his private disappointments, she continues, 'I must say, people are not very tender of you as a father who would speak thus of a son, for people in general are anxious to make the best of their own and particularly when that own is all affection.'[26] She accuses him of self-pityingly telling tales to anyone who will listen and hopes that young John will not hear of this. Soane replies that he has no one to tell his tales of woe to, and asks her to name the source. It is the bitterest exchange between them yet and shows how Soane's obsession with his sons' faltering careers was poisoning their marriage.

But now both the Soanes were reeling from a bolt from the blue. George, the Cambridge graduate with mounting debts and no visible means of support, had married Agnes Boaden in July 1811 despite his parents' plea that the couple wait two years.[27] Eliza blamed Agnes's parents for promoting the match – 'so advantageous a bargain'. In a bitter letter later she blamed Mrs Boaden for surreptitiously bringing her daughters round to George's lodgings and encouraging the girls in 'eternally coming after you'.[28] George's marriage was as great a disaster for Mrs Soane as for her husband. Although she pleaded with George to treat his new wife with kindness, given his 'ungovernable temper', she would send him no more than the quarterly £50 that he might expect as a single man. 'You being unfortunately of an obstinate, violent, self-willed disposition and having fallen into *bad* hands' she could do nothing further for him.[29] The 'bad hands' were his theatrical and literary friends.

The events of 1811 had taken their toll on Mrs Soane: 'Good God, how am I changed. A few months back and I had courage and spirits to face any difficulty, now I tremble and shrink from every trifle. The postman's knock puts me in a terror.'[30] Week after week she extended her stay on the coast, pleading John's bad health, which took the form of consumptive spasms and coughing. While Soane was busy at Lincoln's Inn Fields, broken only by three days' fishing at Pangbourne and a period in Cheltenham, Eliza kept at a comfortable distance. In September he sent her a plaintive message via John. 'I begin to fear she has forgotten there is such a place as Lincoln's Inn Fields and what is, I admit of less consequence, such a person as John Soane.'[31]

Eliza's mood lightened when she learned that Maria was expecting a child. She made her way back from Ramsgate via Chertsey, happy to hear that her husband planned to join her there. She asked for replenishment of the wine stocks: 'What you get here is too bad to drink.' Further 'I have been to a sale and bought something for you, as I never forget anything that I think will contribute to your happiness.'[32] Nevertheless, a gulf had opened between them. In November he tetchily quoted Eliza: 'wishes to know when I go into the country – want a small party which always puts you out of humour – I must therefore have them when you are from home! – indeed'.[33] His continued depression mirrored the crisis in the national mood, lowered by many years of war and a royal family in difficulties, exacerbated by years of bad harvests and leading to rising prices and popular unrest.

During 1811 Soane had been distracted by a major new commission. Following the death of his friend, Sir Francis Bourgeois, after a riding accident, he had another chance to explore the curious notion of a gallery-cum-mausoleum, which he had already tried in miniature in the yard behind 36 Charlotte Street.

Bourgeois had willed the picture collection that he and Noel Desanfans had built up for the king of Poland at Dulwich College. He knew the college through his friend, the actor John Philip Kemble, and considered that 'the Institution is for an excellent purpose, the distance from London moderate, and the country about it delightful.'[34] It also already owned at least a hundred paintings from the Cartwright and Alleyne collections. The offer of another major collection of pictures and the funds with which to rebuild the ruinous west wing of the college, where the almswomen were housed, came as a timely helping-hand to the governing body. Soane's commission to design London's first purpose-built public art gallery to house a permanent collection came as Bourgeois lay dying.

Lancelot Baugh Allen, the recently installed master of Dulwich College (all masters had to bear the name of Allen) had taken Bourgeois' last testament. They discussed Soane's adeptness in turning a tiny coach-house, just 25 foot long, into the Charlotte Street mausoleum. Allen confessed a preference for a gothic building at Dulwich and wondered if Soane was the man for the job, given his objections to the style. Bourgeois had a strong card to play: 'Soane is a man of fortune who has only two sons who will be most amply provided for . . . you may depend upon his treating you as a friend and that he will not make it an expensive business'.[35] The master could scarcely object to Bourgeois' choice of architect if Soane was himself prepared to underwrite the project.

Soane hurried out to Dulwich the day after Bourgeois' death on 7 January 1811 secure in the knowledge that the job was his. He began by trying to retain part of the old Jacobean collegiate quadrangle, awkwardly balancing an uncharacteristic timid classicism against the seventeenth century features. He struggled on, juggling different plan forms, and finally in mid-May sent his clients five different designs and an estimate of £8,000.

It took months more hard work to achieve a solution within the stringent budget and to juxtapose the three disparate elements: picture gallery, mausoleum and apartments to replace the existing almshouses for six 'Poor Sisters'. Although Soane took no payment, the master was demanding and required endless alterations and changes to the design.

Work at Dulwich finally began in late November 1811 but the mausoleum designs were still in flux the following spring. Soane walked there to set out the foundations in April and by late June the office was preparing drawings of the timber framing for the rooflights, the main innovation in Soane's new gallery. George Basevi and Charles Tyrrell, among other pupils, sketched the builders at work (fig. 146). They show the paraphernalia of the trades and lively glimpses of construction detail – a remarkable snapshot of the building industry of the time as well as the skeleton of one of Soane's major buildings. Sometimes the young men portray each other, as they sit at their drawing boards or clamber about on site. The days out may have been a pleasant relief from the rigours of the office. After receiving a sick notice from Charles Tyrrell, Soane was furious to chance upon the young man in rude good health. Soane's mood at this period must have made him a man to avoid where possible. The Dulwich job did nothing to improve his spirits and would run on for several years.[36]

James Boaden had offered George an invaluable introduction to the theatrical world and it pained Soane to have to admit that George had met him under his own roof. Boaden was a well-liked, honourable man, but through him the families became ensnared in a spiralling tragedy. George, following his marriage, sent his father his first published 'literary trifle' in August[37] but receiving no response he disappeared from view, resurfacing a few months later with a completed novella, *The Eve of S. Marco* 'a romance in three volumes', a tale of the Inquisition, set in Italy, with a puff for himself as a suitable translator of Schiller's plays (some of which he did, later, adapt and translate).[38]

He again sent his father a copy of the work, but was dismayed to have received no acknowledgement to his letter of mid-April[39] by the beginning

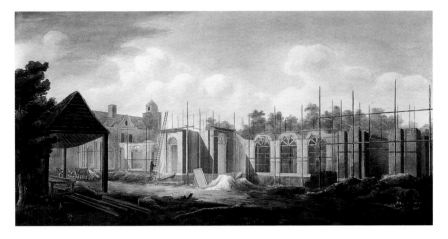

146. Dulwich, work in progress. The mausoleum for his three friends is the structure which projects from the gallery, in the centre foreground. In these years Soane often asked his pupils to record buildings under construction, drawings which are revealing of early nineteenth-century building methods as well as of his architecture.

of May. 'It is not in human power to create talent and therefore the absence of it is not to be imputed as a fault to anyone' he wrote, 'no price can be too dear, *no exertion too great* to regain the esteem and affection of a father'.[40] Reading the volume, it may have occurred to Soane that his son's efforts at gothic literature were as unconvincing as William Capon's elaborate stage sets or even James Wyatt's new work at Westminster.[41]

George's appeal brought a response; if he would take up 'some rational pursuit' and begin to support himself 'you may *then* find a friend in an injured and insulted father'.[42] George welcomed the contact; seeing this 'as the pledge of revived affection'. Letters passed to and fro, Soane asking for conditions, in particular that George discard his 'treacherous' friend Mr Lewis. Given the Boaden connection, this was probably Matthew 'Monk' Lewis, another visitor to Pitshanger – of whom an aunt said that he had a new friend for every month of the year. Following the enormous success of *The Monk*, written when he was twenty, Lewis wrote seventeen more theatrical adaptations and plays in fewer years. In 1812 Lewis (according to Byron 'a damned bore') ceased writing altogether on coming into a comfortable inheritance with the death of his father, deputy secretary at the War Office.[43] He sent his final volume *Poems* to Walter Scott who remarked that there was always a violet among his weeds.[44]

George, in his best literary style, continued to argue his case with his father, proclaiming, 'I would do anything to gain your affection . . . you were once my dearest friend'.[45] He claimed that he was earning something from his writing, looking out for pupils and waiting for an engagement on the *Quarterly Review*.[46] Despite that Soane's prejudices were set hard as he revealed to John. 'I was never fond of romances and novels; such works I was early taught to look upon as trash for silly girls.'[47]

Any glimmer of rapprochement between Soane and George was short-lived; on 18 May Soane wrote 'I have read your two publications [the two volumes of his novel] – such productions will neither add to your fame nor . . . your fortune'. Soane had spotted, on page 243 of Volume I, a telling, if somewhat gothic, portrait of a hated father.

'But this ONE was my father!'

'In name indeed, but not in reality. Has he not abandoned you to the world?'

'He has! He has! And dreadful to me has been the consequence. He has driven me to desperation, to be – but no more – no more – *He is still my father* and cursed by the *son who would avenge his wrongs in word or deed upon a parent's head!*.'

Soane's copy is emphasised as above and anotated with the words 'base young man, your father never injured you'.

The *Eve of S. Marco* was typical run-of-the-mill gothick fiction, the staple fare of popular publishing, available in the blue-backed volumes of the Minerva Press. George's novella was as over-stated on the page as Fuseli's paintings were on canvas and equally hard to evaluate. No author could touch 'Monk' Lewis for his macabre succession of titles, from *Tales of Terror* onwards, but he had imitators everywhere. One, the author of *Zastrozzi*, was an eighteen-year-old schoolboy, Percy Bysshe Shelley. George's liking for Schiller, Goethe and Italianised gothic horror tales was in the van of fashion. Typically, Shelley had spent considerable thought on how to gain entry to the church next to his Sussex home, in order that he could spend an entire night in the vaults 'harrowed by fear'.[48] Life was threatening to outpace fantasy.

The best escape from it all was through satire or saturation. Only the sprightly touch of Jane Austen and Thomas Love Peacock, Shelley's friend, could manage to wittily reanimate the genre while a glut of titles from George Soane and others finally drove the gothick novel into extinction. With humour, George might have gone far, but he had inherited none.

Soane was still not despairing of nudging George towards more gainful and respectable employment. Suiting the family's social status nowadays he suggested the army or the Church. 'As to the Army', George replied the same day, 'I do not profess myself a warrior', while the church was 'not exactly consonant with my wishes . . . I would enter it were I *certain* of church preferment'. He wanted a quiet, unassuming life 'dedicated to literature . . . which is my delight and for which nature I think certainly intended me'.[49] Agnes was expecting a child but Soane chillily denied reponsibility for both, unless George be ordained. Then the correspondance petered out until the autumn, when George mentioned that 'what I had saved from my uncle's legacy' had been helpful in supporting them. He was later to assert that his father had cheated him of this money.

It cannot have escaped Soane that an art gallery, designed in memory of Sir Francis Bourgeois, was a suitably defiant gesture towards the artistic establishment from two of the Royal Academy's least compliant members. He had spent his time in the wilderness 'correcting' the lectures and perfecting his 'farewell address'[50] but if he was planning to give a last series of lectures and then bow out he was taking his time. Curiosity had drawn both Soane and Gandy to Turner's 1812 lecture series. Soane's criticism wounded Turner and caused him to heavily revise the series and change the illustrations before delivering them again in 1814.[51] As a result John Britton received a rough welcome when he attended the Academy dinner that year on Soane's ticket. 'Mr. Turner accosted me, and said there was no plate or seat for *me* . . . I concluded . . . that I was an improper person to be admitted . . . Much chagrined I was going to leave the room, when the same gentleman told me I might take a seat at the *bottom of the table* . . . I consented to remain and take my humbled station.' He remonstrated but to no avail. 'It only remains to ascertain if Mr Turner meant to insult you, or myself *individually* or both jointly.'[52]

The Prince Regent was not present on the occasion but had presented a massive bronze chandelier to improve the lighting in the Great Room. During the first toasts a sinister rumbling began, suggesting an imminent earthquake, and the vast 'beastly lump' dropped on to a tiered table, shattering every glass in its path. Miraculously the chain still supported the several tons of chandelier, preventing the entire room and some 150 guests descending to the cellars. British phlegm saved the day and the banquet continued.[53]

Only in rebuilding 13 Lincoln's Inn Fields did Soane find complete distraction from his troubles at the Royal Academy and from his sons. As he had done next door in 1792, he levelled the front part of the existing house and began again from scratch. He asked the Tyndales to move out. The stables had already been transformed into the 'Plaister Room' (fig. 148) but since 1809 he had been ruminating on retaining No. 12 for his own house and using the site at No. 13 as a series of architectural galleries, on a conventional L-shaped plan around a courtyard. It smacked of Turner's arrangements in Harley Street. In a lecture draft prepared in 1811 Soane described the 100-foot-long gallery in which he planned to display his drawings and prints, with another above it, to house models and 'parts of buildings ancient and modern'.[54]

That idea had been entirely set aside by 1812. Nevertheless the notion of a museum was central to Soane's scheme; in that year James Perry's *European Magazine* described it as 'an Academy for the study of *architecture* upon principles at once *scientific* and *philosophical*'.[55] No. 13 was to be a combined home, office and museum, completely separate from its neighbour.

Eliza spent long weeks that summer in Chertsey and remained there for longer than usual, avoiding the building works until well into the autumn. Her friends were being very kind 'and make little parties at home to amuse me'.[56] On 4 July she sent him a note, 'I thought on you all day – *for this day you begin your house*'.[57] This was no joint project.

On 13 July 1812 George Tyndale, the forbearing solicitor who had been his sitting tenant since 1807, gave up possession of No. 13[58] (fig. 147). When the Tyndales returned to No. 12 in October 1813, in what was effectively a swap, the two houses would be entirely separate – the 'Plaister Room' to the rear of No. 13 was connected through to his study (his old office at No. 12) but it was all walled off.

By 1 August demolition was complete. Early August was very wet and Eliza wrote, worried that the bad weather might have delayed work (it had). Mrs Soane could not have guessed at the efficiency of Soane's building team and for a moment sounded a despairing note, wondering if she might not be able to return until the winter 'till the dirt and noise is over'. But by the middle of the month the brickwork was completed and floors were being inserted. The workmen were well rewarded for their hard work and on 17 August Soane gave them each 2d to 'drink the health of Lord Wellington and his brave Army' after the victory at Salamanca.

The pupils and assistants continued to work as best they could, in the

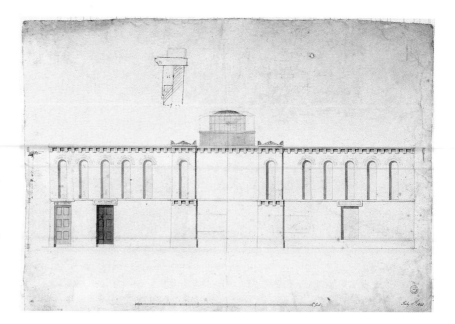

147. Soane's drawing of July 1808 showing the rear wall of numbers 12 and 13 Lincoln's Inn Fields, off Whetstone Park. The doors to the left of the picture, are marked for himself (to the right) and, to the left, for his neighbours, the extremely long-suffering Mr and Mrs Tyndale who continually swapped houses with him. The rooflight of the 'Plaister' room can be seen in the centre.

midst of a building site. Only once, surprisingly, did Soane ask a pupil to record progress. In August 1812 George Basevi drew a section through the dome at No.13, from skylight to crypt, complete with its encrustations of sculpture built into the walls, and ranged on every surface.

Eliza, hearing of the excellent rate of progress, was delighted that 'your building goes on so much to your satisfaction'.[59] As an aside, she wondered if her husband had been able to organise John's accommodation at Chelsea 'for I own to be a little anxious on that business'. But Soane was still prevaricating about the arrangements. John was showing interest in the project at No. 13, perhaps in the hope that the cottage at Chelsea would finally now be theirs. He wrote sarcastically from Tunbridge Wells where he was again taking the waters: 'Having kicked out the Half-bred Attorney or non-descript, I suppose you will soon be plunged in all the glorious confusion of dust and brick and mortar . . . you have another opportunity of adding to your Architectural fame.'[60] A fortnight later he wrote, 'I congratulate you on the good sale of the old materials and hope that the workmen keep pace with your wishes.'[61]

There was no answering reassurance about Chelsea since John had not concurred with his father's unrealistic conditions. However John's health was better and in his letters to his father he attempted to placate him with morsels of gossip, politics and even flattery. 'I have heard that No. 13 promises to be the first specimen of Architecture that the Metropolis can present to the eye of the enraptured artists and I am certain to find the internal equal to the external.'[62]

Soane had turned his full expressive powers into transforming a narrow site – no different from hundreds under development in the late Georgian expansion of London – into a memorable gallery-cum-house. As John observed: 'you have an advantage of which few can boast over those who have employers of whim or caprice or want of taste'.[63]

13 Lincoln's Inn Fields was far bolder than anything Soane had designed for even his most compliant or adventurous clients.[64] Portland

stone gave way to brick on the second floor, the three principal floors breaking forward in a projecting loggia, the parapet marked by Coade stone figures (fig. 149). The stone was cut, as if by a scalpel on stucco, by shallow, but sharp, indentations denoting 'pilasters', horizontal mouldings and frets. The ornament on the new house was both discreet and outrageous. No. 13 was a most improbable version of the Georgian terraced house.

While the new façade stood brazenly among its conventional terraced neighbours, it was particularly addressed to the south side of Lincoln's Inn Fields, from which Soane's house could be easily seen above the shrubs and young trees of the square. As John put it 'will not the patch-work on the opposite side frown? . . . let it do so, the very thought does me good'.

The Company of Surgeons had moved to 41 Lincoln's Inn Fields in 1797. Soon after, George III granted the Royal College of Surgeons its charter. In 1799 they decided that a new building was needed, particularly to house William Hunter's bequest of anatomical specimens.[65] In July 1800 they asked their own surveyor, Neill, as well as George Dance and James Lewis to provide plans for a new headquarters and museum. Soane was not considered for the commission although Charles Long was the chairman of the Building Committee, and he found his omission galling. Perhaps he was hoping that he would inherit the job but Dance gently put him straight: 'I like your reflexion on the vanity of life and your advice to me to quit the *turba insana* – surely you take a pleasure in mortifying me – but it won't do', he had written to Soane in 1802.[66] By 1803 Dance and Lewis were working in partnership on the proposals – 'the patchwork on the opposite side' in John's phrase.

By 1805 Dance and Lewis still had not provided the Surgeons with even a model, although they did have drawings.[67] Slowly and provokingly the building took shape in front of Soane's windows. Dance and Lewis, who spent eight years working on the building, received their commission, split between them. Dance had been uncertain how to charge since it was 'perfectly new to us to be jointly employed' and, to his cost, left the decision to the Surgeons, as Soane would never have done.[68]

Hardly had the façade of No. 13 been completed than William Kinnard (or Kinnaird), the District Surveyor, lodged a complaint, claiming that it projected beyond the rest of the terrace. Soane, of course, saw Kinnard's actions as personally vindictive rather than bureaucratic.

> Praise is however due to this dapper animal on this occasion – he had been taught to believe that the two *old women* in the front were *intended* to ridicule the infantile idea in the great architectural work opposite where two old men with Greek names on their skirts are represented embracing or rather hugging a sort of shield which they display to the public view, thereby to *attract notice* and to direct the multitude to contemplate the beauties of that great work.[69]

As John had also realised, the elevation of No. 13, with its dominant caryatids, was an audacious riposte to Dance's newly completed north-facing portico with its figures of the surgeon sons of Aesculapius, supporting an escutcheon with the college arms (fig. 150).

Soane mustered his forces, representing himself at the court hearing in October, and won the case. He also ensured that Perry's *European Magazine*

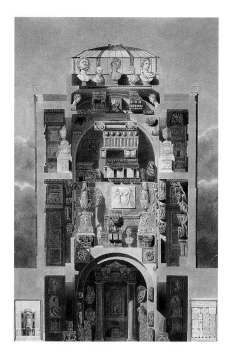

148. A section through the Dome (or Plaister Room) at Lincoln's Inn Fields drawn in 1810 by Soane's assistant George Bailey who had joined the office in 1806 and became the first curator of the museum after Soane's death in 1837.

149. One of several designs for the façade of 13 Lincoln's Inn Fields; Soane settled for a different treatment of the upper parapet in the elevation as built.

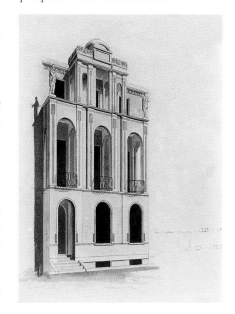

150. The inoffensive portico of the Royal College of Surgeons which George Dance jun. and James Lewis added just as Soane began his own façade. He could see it through the trees of Lincoln's Inn Fields as a provoking reminder both of a lost job and the lost friendship between himself and Dance.

carried the full history. In January 1813 Gandy drew an elevation of the north side of Lincoln's Inn Fields, from numbers 13 to 15 (fig. 151). The architectural treatment of No. 13 spread across all three houses, extended to almost the dimensions of the Royal College of Surgeons. It was a great conceit, emphasised by the figures of Mr and Mrs Soane standing on the first-floor balcony.

Inside No. 13, rather than the conventional eighteenth-century compartmentalisation of space within a slice of terrace (here deepened by incorporating the yard and stables into the house), Soane contrived a flowing sequence of rooms. The stair wound sinuously up to the top of the house, on each turn a rounded corner, niches and alcoves occurring at intervals. For the visitor, entering from the hall, painted to simulate marble, the first impression was of the dining-room and library, a rich Pompeian red with patinated bronze ornamental effects. The room was conceived as a single space, divided only by piers which doubled as bookcases, the effect enlarged by generous mirrors. From the dining-room (the back room of the two), two routes were offered, wrapping around either side of the internal courtyard. From here, any similarity to a standard house type vanished. The spaces became miniaturised, intricate. One passage led to Soane's tiny study (also red), with an internal window on to the courtyard, and, beyond it, a dressing-room. From there Soane could reach his office. The alternative route led to the breakfast room, the most exquisite version of Soane's floating 'saucer' domes to date, its pendentives punched through to add another source of light. Eventually the room would glitter with over a hundred mirrors, mostly convex. The walls and ceilings were grained to simulate a light-toned wood. Beyond it was the old office, turned into a library and study.

On the first floor, in his drawing-room, Soane used a sharp, strong yellow paint, long a favourite colour and already used to resplendent effect in silk covered panels in the great drawing-room at Wimpole. He varnished all the painted walls in the house to produce an impeccably Pompeian effect.[70] Red and yellow remained his preferred colours, despite many other alterations in the house.

Soane was also busily considering practical matters in his new house. Natural light could be amplified by mirrors which he used whenever and wherever possible. His continual exploration of heating methods is a reminder that Soane was always excited by, and open to, technological innovation but liked to place it in an historical context. He bought numerous books and introduced the subject in the lectures, quoting Senaca. He was interested in Benjamin Franklins's stove and intrigued by the latest patented central heating systems.[71] In the basement of No. 13 he installed a bath for the servants in addition to a second-floor bath for family use; there were several water-closets.[72]

As Soane laboured away on No. 13, Turner finally began to build his own small house in Twickenham, Sandycombe Lodge (fig. 152).[73] Although he had owned the land since May 1807, he was slow to take an architectural decision. In contrast to the failed enterprise at Pitshanger, Turner's house was to be a modest retreat for himself and his elderly, but energetic, father. For the exterior Turner took endless trouble, producing many sketches, drawings and plans before determining on a symmetrical small villa with deep Italianate eaves. The two-storey centre was flanked

151. Gandy's drawing of numbers 13–15 Lincoln's Inn Fields which imaginatively extended the architectural treatment across three houses (two of which were not Soane's). Mr and Mrs Soane can be seen standing on the centre balcony of No. 13, to the left.

by a single storey to either side, the ends cosily rounded off.[74] (Soane's farmhouse for Thomas Swinnerton at Butterton in Staffordshire, commissioned in 1815, had similarly deep and prominent eaves and every right-angled wall was chamfered.)

Turner had been saddened by the demolition of Pope's Twickenham villa in 1807 and the English classical villa and its Claudian setting on the Thames was an imagery that may have influenced him. There is, however, no evidence for the genesis of Turner's ideas for the interiors beyond a single chimney-piece. As a subsequent owner, Anne Livermore, wrote, the interior of Sandycombe Lodge gives every sense – but no evidence – of being Soane's, in particular the hall, a miniaturised version of that at Pitshanger, with the familiar pair of compressed segmental headed arches and the small winding stair, top-lit with a round-headed niche on the turn.[75] Although there were no grand dinners, no gatherings of his patrons in Twickenham, Turner frequently invited his close friends and fishing companions, such as Francis Chantrey, to Sandycombe Lodge.[76] Once matters resolved themselves at the Royal Academy the disagreement between Soane and Turner was soon forgotten.

152. Turner's italianate cottage in Twickenham, Sandycombe Lodge, in an engraving after William Havell. The curving side 'wings' are a favourite Soane motif but it is the interior which bears his imprint most clearly.

While George embarked on his literary career in the teeth of his parents' disapproval and John drifted, in search of health and purpose, from resort to resort, the signs were that the end of the Napoleonic Wars might be in sight. Even without an invasion, the unnerving threat from across the Channel, the Continental blockade and a succession of bad harvests had been economically and politically destabilising as well as generally demoralising. Widespread uncertainty about events added daily anxiety, euphoria alternating with despondency, as news of victories and defeats trickled slowly home.

Political events were proving punishing for some, rewarding for others among Soane's merchant clients and friends. Samuel Thornton, the inheritor in 1790 of an estimated £600,000 from his father John

Thornton who had been second only to Henry Hope of Amsterdam among the great merchant princes of Europe, was forced to sell Albury House in Surrey (where Soane had worked from 1800 onwards) as the combination of wartime trade difficulties with the Baltic states and domestic bank failures came home to roost.[77] Soane, whose own finances remained sound, with his interests well spread, and of whom it was later remarked that he had great business acumen, saw a succession of bankruptcies, actual and rumoured, among his friends – George Smith's in the early 1790s, Rowland Burdon's (as a result of over-investment in the local iron industry) in 1803, and in 1819, John Patteson's. There was a moment of panic about his Betchworth client Henry Peters's solvency in 1812. As an architect and as a successful financier, Soane had benefited enormously from the Napoleonic wars. Many others were feeling the chill.

At the Bank he had to organise illuminations speedily as news of any major victory emerged. On 18 and 19 August 1812 there were official celebrations for Wellington's victory at Salamanca, which had occurred in late July. A collection of patent lamps, quickly garnered from various offices, were placed on the inside of the windows facing Threadneedle Street, suggesting that the Bank had been caught by surprise. The next day the governor quickly ordered a double row of lamps and a big 'W' picked out in lights.[78]

This rudimentary effort was useful practice for Soane during the spate of celebrations over the following two years. At their most elaborate, the entire Bank was opened up until midnight or later and dozens of house porters and messengers were drafted in. The successful conclusion of the Battle of Vittoria on 21 June 1813 was marked by three nights of illumination in early July. The opportunity to present his great arch and the succession of interior courtyards, passages and ante-rooms in dramatic chiaroscuro was not to be lost; the flickering lamps, throwing dark shadows or pointing up details with a carefully directed wash of light, could be used to paint the architecture in a Gandyesque drama seen by thousands. On 5 and 6 November there was a repeat, this time to celebrate the victories of the Allied Armies in Germany. Soane was becoming a master of these theatrical and evanescent displays – experience which he would use on the permanent lighting arrangements at Lincoln's Inn Fields and elsewhere.

Soane ensured that his work at the Bank was also seen annually on the walls of the Royal Academy. In 1810 and 1811 he showed his designs for the north front 'as originally intended' and in 1812 for the new entrance hall. In addition a steady trickle of invited visitors came to look at the Bank for themselves. One critic, writing in 1809, had linked Thomas Hope's Greek revival interior at Duchess Street to Soane's work at the Bank of which Lawrence had earlier reported that Hope did not approve:[79] 'As little good taste is manifested in overloading our walls with the symbolical images of antiquity, as in making our national Bank resemble a Mausoleum.'[80] Of all Soane's work it was the Bank that attracted the highest praise and the most sustained criticism.

In his family life Soane was finally facing the obvious, that neither son would follow him into architecture. That realisation, together with the continuing Royal Academy dispute and the rupture with Turner as well as other pressures, real and imagined, as he started the reconstruction of

No. 13, left him seriously unstable. He spent early September consigning the torrent of his misery to paper, in *Crude Hints towards the History of my House* and in the *Appeal*, another pamphlet which he circulated to his friends.[81]

Crude Hints is a tortured and bitter lament about failure – at the hands of others. As personal as anything he ever wrote, less contrived than the self-justifying pamphlets or the later *Memoirs*, Soane's misery at the failed dynastic enterprise is raw. Written in three weeks it was an epitaph to the hopes built into No.13, which he envisaged revisiting in 1830. He imagined finding 'a miserable picture of frightful delapidation'; a metaphor for the disaster that had overcome the ambitions of a man who hoped to found a 'race of artists'.

Despite its manic tone and its tortured, gothic style, *Crude Hints* is revealing of the man Soane believed himself to be, 'a mere child in the world – he was indiscreet where policy is wont to impress restraint . . . he never gave himself a moment's time to reflect on who was the author of the works he criticised'. He had not shrunk from declaring 'open war' on those who transgressed the 'laws of nature and the practice of antiquity', regardless of such practices being 'protected or hallowed by high nay even Royal patronage . . . until at last he had raised a nest of wasps about him sufficient to sting the strongest man to death'. He alluded to his domestic troubles and disillusion: 'he saw the views of early youth blighted – his fairest prospects utterly destroyed – his lively character become sombre – melancholy brooding constantly over an accumulation of events brought him into a state little short of mental derangement'. So it continues until the 'anonymous' subject dies of a broken heart. 'The subject becomes too gloomy to be pursued – the pen drops from my almost palsied hand.'[82] The sudden introduction of the first person is a shocking moment in these fevered ramblings, hitherto entirely in the third person. Soane had, he admitted to himself at least, reached breaking point.

13

RECONCILIATION AND DEATH

Ever since the suspension of his lectures, Soane had inadvertently found himself a focus for discontent at the low status of architecture at the Royal Academy. James Elmes, who later became a prolific writer on architecture, proposed a breakaway body.[1] He offered Soane the presidency of the Academy of Architecture, as yet unborn. He detailed his disillusion with the Royal Academy. 'The circumscribed state of the Library, the want of models, instructions, lectures etc. but especially the illiberal deprivation of the benefits that would have arisen from your very instructive lectures and extreme liberality of illustrations to them, more than warrant such a proceeding.' Soane's lectures had been the first useful architectural contribution that he had received, he said, in the eight or nine years since he had been a student there.[2]

Elmes was a useful ally although Soane had no taste for a splinter institution; he was a loyal Royal Academy man whatever the storms and discomforts of the voyage. He also had every intention of returning to give his lectures and spent long periods preparing new material. He used the hiatus to record work in progress from the office, his pupils' illustrations providing material for future lectures and an invaluable record of the architectural process. They began with the new Infirmary at Chelsea Hospital, finally on site in June 1810 (fig. 153).

In January 1813 the council of the Royal Academy decided that Soane had, by his actions, resigned as Professor of Architecture. Flaxman did not agree.[3] It was pointed out that the Prince of Wales would have to concur in removing him and Martin Archer Shee, another Soane supporter, praised his 'unparalleled display of drawings made at a great expense to illustrate his observations'. The Academy was damaging its reputation by constant argument. Compromise was in the air and Soane was ready to concede, as his friends knew. A motion to reinstate him was passed unanimously. Soane thanked the academicians and agreed to resume his duties.

Farington recorded Soane's high spirits. 'He came up to me and taking me by *the hands* he said he would thus address me whatever impression might be on my mind. I returned his address with kindness . . . Smirke [sen.] expressed much pleasure at Soane's business being thus settled.'[4] It was an auspicious start to the year. He and Turner were back on good terms.[5] In his notebook he records a flurry of celebratory expenditure; £4

153. A drawing from 1810 showing work in progress on the Infirmary at Chelsea Hospital, by Soane's pupil Robert Chantrell.

2s 0d for a scarlet cloak for Eliza and a £50 loan to Gandy.[6]

Soane recommended his lectures on 12 February 1813. Henry Crabb Robinson was there to hear the third lecture on 26 February and found it uninteresting. He was, however, struck by Soane's suggestion that all lovers of fine art replace the vow to King, Country and God by one to Painting, Sculpture and Architecture.[7]

The complaint against Soane, as ever, was that of incomprehensible delivery.[8] Yet despite the high pitch of his voice, Soanes was a marginally better speaker than his colleagues. Turner mumbled and gave his lectures so fast that one was over in thirty-five minutes. His notoriously odd pronounciation baffled his listeners and the constant attendance of Thomas Stothard, the elderly, deaf, librarian of the Royal Academy was another puzzle. When asked for the explanation, he replied 'Sir, there is much to *see* at Mr Turner's lectures – much that I delight in seeing though I cannot hear him.'[9] Soane's illustrations were similarly splendid. By contrast, the Professor of Painting, Fuseli, showed no images and spoke in a much-mocked, near incomprehensible guttural accent. The students at the Royal Academy were well used to the short-comings of their professors.

Humphry Repton was intrigued by the rumours of the professor's 'brilliancy of remark and severity of criticism' and decided to join the audience. Repton had a mild grudge against Soane; years before 'he overturned my beautiful plan for Port Eliot . . . my design for bringing together the house and the Abbey did not suit the fancy of my fanciful friend (who knows but little about Gothic) so the plan was totally changed'.[10]

Perhaps hoping to settle the score, Repton hurried to Somerset House. 'The room was very full and had he seen me amongst the crowded audience, he might perhaps have softened or qualified a most severe attack on the "pretensions to architecture" of him who he was pleased to call 'the most celebrated of landscape gardeners' but I heard myself abused and held up to ridicule without mercy.'[11] There was, apparently, no rule against criticising a living landscape gardener.

'On descending from the rostrum he seemed surprised to see me – and still more so at my thanking him for having done me the honour to think me worth so much notice.' Repton then bantered with Soane, parrying 'I shall have a push at you and perhaps *pin you* to the bank!' The encounter ended amicably, the two men shook hands. 'I believe he has as much good nature as he has seeming asperity' wrote Repton. Like several of those well disposed towards Soane, he preferred to emphasise the pleasant aspect of Soane's character rather than the unpleasant.

One man who saw little of that good nature was Robert Smirke. Soane and he were again in competition. The position that both men craved was that of Surveyor-General at the Office of Works. Smirke hurried to London on hearing of James Wyatt's sudden death on 4 September 1813 in a carriage accident, to activate his patrons, Lords Bathurst and Lonsdale, on his behalf. Lord Liverpool responded coldly to Lonsdale's approach, 'stating that when arrangements were being made, he should consider who would be most proper'.[12] Benjamin West, Farington wrote, 'pitied those who had obligations upon them to leave London at this season so favourable for professional application'. Lobbying for these positions required the full personal attention of the hopeful candidate.

Soane, who was genuinely fond of Wyatt (the only architect Royal Academician to have supported him in 1810), was more concerned with according the debt-ridden architect an official ('*Academical*') burial and had visited West to request this mark of respect to be told that 'Wyatt did not [hold] a situation in the Academy such as to make particular attention to his funeral a proper measure for the Academy to interfere in.'[13]

Soane's affection for Wyatt was surprising since he had defeated his ambitions at Westminster. But Soane mourned 'my lamented friend . . . Peace to the ashes of James Wyatt . . . His life was gentle and the elements so mixed in him that he will long live in the memory of those who, like myself, participated in his social hours.'[14] Wyatt's charm left no one untouched. Later on, Soane was a prime mover in trying (unsuccessfully) to raise a subscription for Wyatt's needy widow Rachel.

Soane's restraint in pursuing the surveyorship could be ascribed to his confidence in Lord and Lady Liverpool's favour (he had drawn an attractive conservatory for Coombe in 1812, similar to that for Pitshanger) as well as his realisation that Nash, even though a royal favourite, was viewed as an unsafe pair of hands, given his elasticity in professional matters. Soane also had close contact with at least one of the committee members dealing with the reorganisation of the Office of Works, Henry Peters from the Bank of England, his client at Betchworth, in Surrey, and in London.[15] Charles Bosanquet was also a member. Soane may well have known about the planned changes.

Like Soane, the Prince Regent was deeply saddened by Wyatt's sudden death; he wept when Philip, his son, arrived with the news, adding that having 'just found a man suited to his mind' he had now lost him. Meanwhile other Wyatt relatives, in particular his nephew Jeffry (later Wyatville), lost no time jockeying for his post. Smirke, for all his efforts, was realistic and 'thought Soane was the most likely to succeed. He being employed by Lord Liverpool, and indefatigable in pursuing any object which he has in view.'[16]

In fact, the new organisational structure at the Office of Works, from now on to be directed by an administrator, provided positions as joint 'attached architects' to Soane, Nash *and* Smirke.[17] The regime was radically different, with strict controls on all aspects of the work and the possibilities for corruption greatly reduced. The establishment headed by the efficient Colonel Benjamin Stephenson took time to set up officially, coming into being in April 1815. Nash's careless approach was to exasperate Stephenson, while Soane and Smirke were always highly professional. The immediate task was to clear up the confusion that Wyatt, unbusinesslike and dilatory, had left behind him.

In the meantime, the deficiencies (and, oddly, the charms) of the British seat of parliament continued to intrigue visitors (fig. 154). A Swedish visitor to the House of Commons in 1810 described a mean chamber even though it had been enlarged at the time of the Union with Ireland. What was interesting to him was exasperating to Soane. There was no sense of ceremony; girls were dusting when he arrived and the members 'walk, stand, sit (read the papers and chat, too, when the debates are not interesting) . . . as best suits their convenience, in top-boots, with hats on and in great-coats, or go up into their gallery and lie at full length to listen to the speeches'.[18]

154. The House of Commons in 1808 as shown in Pugin and Rowlandson's *Microcosm of London*. The cramped conditions and lack of ceremony remarked upon by visitors can be glimpsed even in this polite rendering.

Despite the clarification of the architects' roles after Colonel Stephenson's reorganisation, the processes of official patronage still remained obscure and unpredictable. In Prussia, where in 1810 Karl Friedrich Schinkel had been appointed *Geheime Oberbaurat* (Privy Councillor for Public Works) the position was very different. Schinkel had been charged with remodelling the historic centre of Berlin and his powers were almost unlimited.[19] The Prussians and the French, especially under Napoleon, approached public works with an autocratic thrust that Schinkel's English counterparts could but envy. Geijer's observation upon the House of Commons – 'It is interesting to see this carelessness of every kind of display . . . which touches the public' – had wider implications.

In 1813 Soane went to look at the route for Nash's proposed New Street. It involved the demolition of almost 750 houses, more than half of which were, fortunately, Crown property and mostly south of Piccadilly. Nash was 'architect, surveyor, valuer, estate agent, engineer and financial advisor'[20] for the building of Regent Street; it was a massive undertaking, unusually bold for London. Soane followed the project closely but never illustrated Nash's work in the lectures and only referred to one early building, that in Bloomsbury Square.

Soane continued relentlessly to pursue his own dream commission – the House of Lords. Every year from 1800 onwards, Soane entered one or other of his designs at the Royal Academy.[21] In 1812 he submitted the old Senate House design (made in Rome in 1779) but in 1814 his sole exhibit was 'View of part of one of the designs for a New House of Lords'. He had no way of knowing when the opportunity to improve on Wyatt's deficient works at Westminster might fall to him.

Meanwhile, the transformations at Lincoln's Inn Fields continued. Eliza was keeping well away and wrote from Bath in May 1813 to inquire after progress: 'you are going on . . . I suppose with the house. Lady B [Bridport] longs to see it. I shall return with them next week.' Old Lord Bridport was looking very ill and John now needed an inhaler and regular drugs. Earlier that year Soane had at last conceded that his son was seriously ill.[22] By the beginning of June Eliza was back in Chertsey, looking daily in the papers for news of peace with France. 'However, when you want me, whether peace or war, let me know and I will return.'[23] William Soane, now over seventy, was in poor health, although his wife Mary was better than she had expected.[24] Solicitously Eliza told her husband not to stand about at the house and catch cold.[25] She then asked for a report on prgress: 'You forgot to tell me . . . Could not the second floor be painted and finished, for the weather is now very drying and I long to see some part quite done?' Soane's chronic inability to draw matters to a conclusion was exasperating. No. 13 Lincoln's Inn Fields was proving an interminable project and a frustrating prospect as a family home.

At the end of July, John's wife Maria delivered a stillborn son in Chelsea. Eliza, two months later still exiled in Chertsey, had become aware that the foolish flirt from Devon, Norah Brickenden, was in London and buzzing round her husband again. Even Richard Holland, who had introduced her to Soane was surprised at his behaviour in his wife's absence, 'I was surprised and a little hurt to hear that . . . you should be *noticed* gallanting about another lady with attentions that arouse great *suspicions*. I have not yet read it in the public papers, but I have private intimations, which, as a friend to both yourself and Mrs Soane, I have felt it a duty to notice, for fear of further exposure.' Soane had been seen at the early summer social round of public events and exhibitions with a female companion; no one in London fashionable circles knew who she was and Holland, disingenuously, hoped 'for the sake of your character, and particularly for your easy reconcilement with Mrs Soane, when she comes to know such extraordinary attentions, that it had been . . . Norah Brickenden'. Presumably Holland felt that Eliza would feel reassured since Norah was his friend and he considered her 'of strict virtue and honour'. He ends, 'I fear you gave [these women] too much encouragement at Coombe Royal, but this you need not tell Mrs Soane.'[26] On 5 July the unusual entry in Soane's notebook is three exclamation marks, without explanation, and on 22 July he notes cryptically a 'letter and handkerchief found in my closet at the Bank'.[27]

Norah, as her later letters reveal, had nursed a *tendresse* for Soane since the Coombe Royal gathering, and it was warmed up over discussions of Rousseau that summer. Soane was lonely and flattered by her attentions. Norah Brickenden, a suggestible unmarried woman who shared Soane's interests in romantic literature, could read volumes into a look. Eliza Soane, tipped off about the friendship, was suspicious and Holland's reassurances gave her no confidence.

Eliza wrote to her husband cuttingly: 'I really think that there is much more fuss made about Miss B than she deserves. For in my opinion any woman turned *thirty* that affects to be romantic and professes *platonic* love, tis only a cloak for *intrigue*'.[28] There are, Eliza reminds him sourly, gossips in London as well as in the country. The Daniells, back in Chertsey, had reported meeting her husband and 'congratulated me on your good looks'. Eliza was surprised that his friend Holland, 'who certainly *knows the*

the government of France too much for the improvement of the people. The one must keep pace with the other, or mischief must ensue – too much liberty will do more harm than good. With respect to this country I think we want a frugal, plodding minister, rather than a great man.' Lord Liverpool was a perfect candidate.

Fellowes did not share Soane's metropolitan hero-worship of Bonaparte. 'An old Roman would have fallen on his sword, instead of wetting his handkerchief.' He felt that Napoleon had acted so many parts at different stages in his life that it was difficult to consider him one person. Rowland Burdon, who after his bankruptcy had put his energies into farming, also kept a lively eye on politics. He wrote to Soane, commenting that Louis XVIII had taken on a difficult nation of subjects and wondered whether Dr Willis's services (George III's doctor in his madness) might also be of use in France. There were no illusions in England about the fitness of the Bourbon Restoration king for his role.

There were several direct results of the peace for Soane.[47] The visit of the Allied Sovereigns to London beginning on 7 June 1814 led to a flurry of festivities and entertainments, including a pioneering venture in gas lighting – a pagoda erected in their honour in St James's Park and lit by 10,000 burners which ignited in succession, like a rocket. Unfortunately it went up with the fireworks on the first night of the celebrations.[48] A more gentle outing for the Emperor of Russia, Alexander, and his sister the Grand Duchess (Duchess of Oldenburg) was an expedition to see the Bank of England and to partake of a 'cold collation'.[49] Escorted from the Lothbury Gate through the building by the governor and directors, Emperor Alexander was greatly impressed and asked to be introduced to the architect. According to Soane, he congratulated him and asked him to bring drawings of the Bank to the Pulteney Hotel on the following Sunday.[50] Typically, Soane took the opportunity of showing him a number of other drawings (no doubt including those for the House of Lords) and presented them to the imperial couple. He was following the example of Ledoux, who had dedicated his volume *L'Architecture considerée...* to the Emperor and sent him almost 250 drawings.[51] He believed, as did Soane, in the monarch as patron.

As the British streamed across to France once more, there was traffic in the opposite direction. The Parisian architect of St Vincent de Paul and the man who would embellish the Champs-Elysées and alter and elaborate the Place de la Concorde (the old Place Louis XV), Jacques Ignace Hittorff, later remembered his impressions of the Bank: 'l'œil et l'esprit sont frappés des combinaisons ingénieuses qui ont présidés à la distribution de la lumière. Les effets de celle ci et de la perspective, calculés pour les localités et les donnés de l'Architecture, sont souvent merveilleuses.' Canova had also been hugely impressed – Hittorff recorded his 'éclatant hommage'.[52]

Soane himself was eager to travel, profiting from Napoleon's abdication and exile to Elba that spring. He had not been across the English Channel since his return from Rome in 1780 but through those friends and Royal Academy colleagues (including Turner, Flaxman and Fuseli) who had been there in 1802, as well as through the French students in his office and his own French teachers (for Soane continued to polish his French much of his life) he had kept well abreast of developments. Finally he could again see Paris for himself.

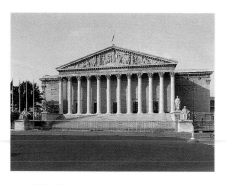

158. The Palais Bourbon became the Chambre des Députés under Napoleon and was transformed by Bernard Poyet's addition of a large Corinthian portico in 1808, one of many changes which Soane would have noticed between his visit to Paris in 1778 and that of 1814.

Soane set off for Paris on 15 August 1814 and returned on 5 September. Assuming a travelling time of two or three days each way, he spent less than a fortnight in the city. Unfortunately no record has survived of what he saw during these days but an itinerary given to him prior to his return visit in 1819 and those buildings which were illustrated or described in his lectures suggest the range of architecture he visited.

Fortunately another traveller, John Scott, the editor of the *Champion*,[53] left a lively, detailed account of his late summer visit to Paris that year. The English were popping across the Channel like corks released from a bottle, eager to visit a country that had been so long out of bounds and Scott's account catches the excitement and strangeness vividly. On arrival at the northern Paris customs barrier (that 'ring of stone' to which Ledoux had contributed many of the structures, mostly now destroyed), he found the *douaniers* and guards stabbing the sides of each waggon load with steel blades to check for contraband; the harsh authoritarian atmosphere which met the visitor was decidedly alarming.

The city itself was visibly battered by its recent past, Scott observed. Rich and poor jostled, decayed aristocrats and uniformed military men living on different floors of the same run-down mansions. The poverty in the streets contrasted with the architectural magnificence of the city, both from the *ancien régime* and recent official patronage.[54]

Scott was immediately impressed by the Place Louis XV standing at the core of the city and offering, in its immediate vicinity 'an extraordinary burst of sumptuous decoration, combining the beauties and magnificence of architecture, sculpture, and gardening'. Central avenues bisected the gardens of the Tuileries and the woods of the Champs-Elysées, while Gabriel's colonnaded pavilions were linked by Perronet's Pont Louis XVI across the Seine to the Palais Bourbon (now the Chambre des Députés), adorned by Bernard Poyet's massive Corinthian portico of 1808 inscribed 'A Napoleon le Grand' (fig. 158). Along the riverbank Scott glimpsed the Hôtel de Salm, 'lately the Palais de la Légion d'Honneur'. Pierre Rousseau's great hotel with its entrance colonnade and triumphal arch ornamented by winged victories had been built in the mid-1780s. One of several important pre-revolutionary Parisian buildings, like Victor Louis' impressive Palais Royale for the Duc d'Orléans which had offered both a setting and a pretext for revolutionary fervour and which demonstrated to Scott the Parisian 'air of bustling dissipation and lounging sensuality' even early in the day, these were buildings added since Soane's last visit, which he would be able finally to see for himself.

Behind the Hôtel de Salm loomed the huge, recently gilded dome of the Invalides. Everywhere were reminders of the man who now awaited events on Elba and of the circumstances that had led to his rise. Behind L'Arc du Carrousel, designed by Napoleon's architects Percier and Fontaine, the walls of the Tuileries, 'the scene of so many interesting events', as Scott remarked with a degree of understatement, were pitted by the imprint of cannon balls. In front of the immense length of the old sixteenth-century palace, 'a broken mass of small windows, unequal stories, frittered compartments, petty pilasters' Scott enjoyed the sight of the 'gay promenaders' as they strolled between the intent newspaper readers, 'seated on hired chairs . . . among the marble Atalantas, Apollos, Daphnes and Satyrs'.

A great avenue ran to the Barrière de l'Etoile, and between the two checkpoints rose the incomplete Arc de Triomphe; Napoleon's wooden facsimile, surmounted by himself in a horse-drawn chariot, was gone. Now the stone arch was revealed at impost level. Scott commented 'Perhaps it would be as well if all the commemorations of governments and dynasties were made of wood here. There is seldom time to finish them.'

The rue de Rivoli, planned from 1803 onwards to link the Tuileries with Perrault's Louvre (fig. 159), conducted visitors to the great gallery, now filled with the booty from Napoleon's overseas exertions. As Scott put it, 'the stranger finds a banquet spread out before him, and put within his reach'. Soane must have revelled in these riches, such a contrast to the limited offerings on public view in London.

159. Hubert Robert *La Grande Galerie du Louvre* (*c*.1795). The Louvre was greatly admired by visitors from London, still without a national gallery.

Other memories of the recently departed emperor and his imperial architecture included incomplete projects such as the Temple de la Gloire (later completed as the Madeleine) by Ledoux's pupil Pierre Vignon and Brongniart's Bourse. In the middle of the Place Vendôme stood Jacques Gondoin's spectacular triumphal column 'erected by Napoleon in honour of his own victories', modelled upon Trajan's Column in Rome but now denuded of Bonaparte, who had been replaced by a white Bourbon flag.

In an attempt quickly to eradicate the Napoleonic symbols, artists, wrote Scott, 'were racking their ingenuity to discover the neatest methods of turning the letter N into an L, for Louis, or an H, for Henry the Fourth'. Fleurs de lys were stitched over the bees on the carpets in the spectacular apartments which Percier and Fontaine, Napoleon's favourites, had designed within the Tuileries. It was all testimony to how 'governments, creeds, and other such serious matters, are here introduced, danced for a while before the eyes, and finally displaced, as if they were so many figures of a magic lanthorn'.

Soane, a tireless walker, would have found the city greatly enlarged since the new boundaries introduced by the *Fermiers Généraux* in 1784 and marked by Ledoux's ring of toll-gates – many now destroyed as exemplifying the repression of the monarchy. Soane could familiarise himself with buildings which he had only before seen on the printed page – those noted by Scott but also, of particular interest to him, Ledoux's Hôtel Théllusson and the rue de Colonnes.[55] Soane was critical of the 'tawdry' gilding of the dome of the Invalides but was impressed by Napoleon's splendid Vendôme column 'perpetuating his victories by a magnificent monument formed with the brass artillery taken from his enemies'. The identity of the enemy did not concern him.

As Soane returned, to the very day, Eliza Soane set off from Brighton to Dieppe with a party of friends, writing the same day to tell her husband of the apparently impulsive scheme. Although the plan was for a brief jaunt, lasting from Tuesday until Friday, the party was forced to remain in France for eight days, caught by contrary winds at Dieppe. Their destination was Rouen. Scott had arrived in France by the same route and perceptively described that undefinable feeling of foreignness. For the traveller, leaving his own country for the first time (as was the case for Eliza Soane) 'everything comes upon him with the force of a first impression; and nothing startles him more than the numerous resemblances to those objects and habits with which he is familiar'. Even from the packet-boat as it arrived in harbour, voices could be heard 'talking a language which we had been accustomed to consider as the proof of a liberal education'. A beautiful French girl and her companion, 'a fierce fellow, with a cocked hat and cockade', watched in amusement the disembarkment of the dishevelled and seasick passengers after a long night at sea. In the crowds men were wearing oddments of military uniform, the detritus of a just disbanded army.

Having enjoyed the picturesque huddle of Dieppe on a Sunday, women with rosaries leaving church but the shops as busy as on a weekday, Scott who had also preceded Eliza and her friends on this route, left the town through a military checkpoint. He was charmed by the villages of Normandy and impressed by excellent roads along which the odd-looking, but comfortable, French diligence ('a mixed species formed by the union of a waggon with a stage coach . . . [with] many of those advantages which are found to result from crossing breeds') moved along at a good pace. There were signs everywhere of the years of revolution and social upheaval; ruined and abandoned châteaux housing poor families, their children playing in the overgrown gardens and roofless, windowless summerhouses. By contrast the farms in this part of Normandy looked well tended and the breaking up of estates 'into the hands of persons of active habits' appeared to bode well for the countryside. The small towns along the road were lively and the people cheerful while in Rouen, Scott saw people pouring out of the theatres, crowded into cafés and, everywhere, music playing. Eliza Soane was equally delighted by it all and longed to return.

The following year Lady Bridport hoped that Eliza would accompany her husband to Somerset 'as I do not think from the present state of the Continent, she will be inclined to put her plan of travelling in execution or that you would consent that she should – you must both have experienced sufficient anxiety for your son. I rejoiced to hear that he was returned in safety.'[56] Her brief excursion had whetted Mrs Soane's appetite for travel and a meeting with John in France would have been a useful pretext for another journey.

The pleasures of France in 1814 were quickly dissipated for the Soanes by harsh reality. George's financial situation was grave and his behaviour had become atrocious. As usual at times of family stress, Mrs Soane had retreated to Chertsey but at least calm had been restored to her marital relations. Sometimes the easy domesticity of a thirty-year marriage comes into their correspondence; in October 1814, she advised Soane that it was too late in the season for fishing and reassured him that his brother (whose wife had died the previous December) was well and happy.

During 1814 George had systematically demanded money from, first his family, then long-suffering family friends. He had written to Soane in March asking for £350 per annum or, he threatened, he would be forced to seek his living on the stage. Later his mother heard that he had played the part of Shylock at the theatre in Richmond, to general derision. By the autumn he had involved young Henry Beechey, Sir William's son, as well as the kindly and unfailingly generous Mr Pennington, the equally patient Edward Foxhall of whom he asked £300 and who finally became convinced of George's 'perverse and intractable disposition', and James Spiller.[57] On 8 September George's house was repossessed. Eliza had finally been forced to adopt a hard line with 'that scape-grace'. She told him that she did not have £800 and if he could not arrange his affairs within the month, he would have to go to prison.[58] No longer adopting unconvincing tones borrowed from Soane, she writes in the angry misery of a mother faced by the unpalatable truth, that her son is an emotional blackmailer, a bully and a cheat.

John Taylor, the newspaper editor and close friend of both Soane and James Boaden, had been interceding on George's behalf but Mrs Soane wrote to tell him the harsh realities of the situation. Sixteen months earlier Soane had settled George's debts and given him money to go on with; since then he had received another £700. George and his wife owed £57 13s 0d to a pearl-stringer, £184 to two upholsterers and £121 to the wine merchant. There was little sign that they were practising economy and Eliza pointed the finger at Agnes – in the hope that Taylor might pass this back to her father. 'In the first three years of our marriage we had but one servant – Mr Boaden's daughter must have two, and a man to attend to clean knives, shoes etc. I felt it my duty to go to market. Mr Boaden's daughter found it less trouble to put her household on board wages and have the tradespeople come for orders.'[59]

Taylor replied, adding that the Boadens had their own troubles (probably financial ones) and he would spare them the contents of her letter. Eliza must have remonstrated with him in person and he relented. He reported back, having read her letter to Boaden who defended his daughter, saying that the luxuries were gifts from George. 'He observed that if you and Mr Soane had so little control over your son, deriving as he did, and does, everything from you, how could it be expected that he should have any influence.'[60] His logic was inescapable.

Soane had washed his hands of George, having finally again met him, face to face. He had money to lend to clients in short-term financial difficulties (such as Stephen Thornton of Mogerhanger, to whom he had given a draft for £500 in June[61]) but not funds to subsidise George's stubborn refusal to live within his means. Over two days a series of 'councils of war' took place between George, James Spiller and Robert Pennington, culminating in a confrontational meeting between George and his father on 20 October. They had failed to persuade him to list his debts which now amounted to over £1,400, including his mother's repayments of sums advanced by his brother and Edward Foxhall. Since George would not fall in with any of the plans proposed and Soane would not bail him out, George was now bound for prison. Soane's reaction was to summon Spiller to Lincoln's Inn Fields to witness his new draft will, since 'I expect to be murdered this evening!'

The contents offered some surprises, in particular a bequest of £1,000 to Eleanor (Norah) Brickenden. He left Eliza £1,500 and the house, John a bequest of £500 ('if he gives up claim to our house, No. 13 Lincolns Inn Fields') and George, one shilling. William Soane would receive an annuity of £100 per annum. Mrs Britton and Mrs Hofland ('kind to me during my illness') each received £500, as did Pennington and Spiller himself (they, with Eliza, were designated trustees). In the event of Eliza's death everything was to be sold and the funds passed to John's eldest daughter. Soane also left instructions for a bequest to the Royal Academy, for 'improving the study of architecture, by giving facilities to the pupils in that art or profession'.[62] The will was never revealed, certainly not to

160. The King's Bench Prison as shown by Pugin and Rowlandson. Described by one visitor as 'an entirely isolated world in miniature, not unlike a small town, except that it is surrounded by thirty-foot high walls.' For some debtors such as Lady Hamilton life in prison was not hard but George Soane, 'a scapegrace' of twenty-four, imprisoned for both debt and fraud, was not provided with any comforts. However, the law had been changed in 1813 to be less harsh for small debtors.

Eliza, but it vividly conveys the unstable and confused state of Soane's mind that day.

By early November George had surrendered to the Marshall of the King's Bench and entered prison for debt and fraud (fig. 160). The latter charge was for obtaining £46 under false pretences from the bookseller Priestley; the penalty was transportation. His parents provided £50 per quarter, a weekly allowance of £3 17s. His conditions in prison, in which a comfortable standard of living could easily be arranged and where recent incumbents included Lady Hamilton, were probably better than those his wretched family were enduring at their liberty.

Agnes, who had given birth to twins in September, had since lost one infant. Old family friends, despite their dwindling sympathy for her husband, tried to help her. George behaved characteristically, veering between threats and promises. He claimed to be considering suicide and poison was found in his possession. Two days before Christmas he wrote to Soane, a torrent of invective and misery. 'In my earliest years you treated me with cruelty and coldness; even at this moment I remember, perfectly, the horror and aversion which your presence inspired in me.' He laid the guilt for his child's death at his father's feet. George Soane, cornered, could be vicious. He wrote to his father referring to his knowledge of the 'history of the family', which he hinted he could be persuaded to keep to himself and he slandered his sister-in-law Maria (sensing a receptive ear, given his father's attitude to her) who was kind to her parents-in-law 'from expectation'.[63] Soane, in self-defence, began to construct a theory that George was not his son, but a foundling, substituted at birth.[64]

Meanwhile George wrote inveigling letters to his mother, hoping that she might intercede with his father and playing his parents off one another. In January she repaid Priestley £61 15s 8d which included his legal costs, thus saving George from the criminal charge of fraud. His demands continued; he now wanted £4,000 and an annuity and played mercilessly upon his mother's divided loyalties. But she had become toughened in her dealings with him and when he threatened to publish an account of his father's life she riposted with appropriate sarcasm: 'no doubt it will produce so much *profit* and *credit* that all further pecuniary assistance from either of us will be unnecessary'.[65]

Even after George had come out of prison ('this stye of abomination') early in 1815, Eliza continued to borrow money from friends to stave off further incarceration for George. 'I have nothing to give to others – or lay out upon my self', she wrote pathetically. All these transactions were kept secret from his father; her close confidants remained Foxhall, Spiller and Pennington.[66] Later in the year, Eliza heard that Foxhall had found an inexpensive house for George in Marchmont Street, near Russell Square, and had furnished it for them.[67]

Soane had changed his mind about letting John and his family live at Chelsea, invoking rules laid down by the board (which as John pointed out, had been equally in force when Soane gave him 'quiet possession' of the house at the time of their marriage in June 1811). The real explanation lay elsewhere. He had offered the house 'in the full belief that you had determined henceforward to the study of Architecture and to the discharge of as much of my professional duty at Chelsea Hospital (particularly) as you possibly could'.[68] This John had failed to do.

The family, John, Maria and little Bessie, left for Paris in February 1815, with no farewell from Soane. 'His unkindness and his cruelty have not sufficiently steeled my heart' John wrote to his mother but they hoped she might join them in Paris. Before many weeks had passed, Napoleon's phoenix-like re-emergence sent them hurrying home, where they stayed in Upper Cadogan Place – possibly through the good offices of John's godfather Richard Holland.

Now that the clerk of works' house at Chelsea was empty, Soane began to carry out improvements in the spring of 1815, transforming the small cottage at his own expense. The remodelling was Soane's reward to himself. He regularised a small brick cottage, with an odd tower attached, into a two-storey villa, its only external mark of eccentricity the prominent and elaborate paired chimney shafts with their jar-shaped smoke pots retaining the height of the now-demolished tower (fig. 161).[69] In the early summer Henry Parke was sent to draw the building, before and after Soane's improvements. After the flamboyance of Pitshanger Manor, Soane concentrated on making a comfortable and practical family residence, in which some of the recent difficulties and misunderstandings between himself and Eliza might be ironed out.

Hardly was the work complete, and John and his family unexpectedly back, when Soane changed tack again – bemusing them – and offered John the whole, newly improved house 'except two parlours, two chambers, two rooms in the basement and the two new rooms, the coachhouse and stables (if any should be allotted to me)'. The new clerk of works' house had five rooms on the first floor but with Soane's requirements, there was not a great deal of space for a couple and their small child and the servants of both establishments. Whatever space this arrangement did allow the young Soanes, 'the whole [is] free of any taxes and repairs of every kind'.

Soane's recent work for the board, as opposed to for himself, included a neat little bakehouse surmounted with immense chimneys and a new

161. The Clerk of Works' house at Chelsea, which Soane rebuilt as his reward for an often thankless appointment. Here it is seen from the rear with its vegetable gardens; the 'raisin jar' chimneys are prominent.

stable block (fig. 162), begun in 1814, its eastern elevation an onion-like succession of slender brick blind arches, peeling away to reveal a pair of lofty doors and lights and a huge central arched entrance to the yard behind. Screens had always intrigued Soane since his experiment with the lodges at Tyringham. The seventeenth-century French urban device, offering a dramatic introduction to the courtyard and *hôtel* beyond, appealed strongly to him. Ledoux had taken it further. Soane always took pleasure in reworking and playing around with his favourite motifs and here he used one to dignify a modest stableyard.

Soane did not yet feel compelled to echo the architectural style, or emulate the materials, of his 'most justly celebrated'[70] predecessor at Chelsea, Sir Christopher Wren.

The Soanes had recently met Barbara and Thomas Hofland, respectively a writer and a painter. Soon her son Frederick was reporting back to her, and she in turn to Soane, on one of Flaxman's 1812 Royal Academy lectures which he had been unable to attend.[71] In May 1813 she had sent him, at his request, some of her work, which although it was written for children she felt he might enjoy reading in his 'domestic solitude' while Eliza was in Bath. Soane thanked her, particularly enjoying *The Son of a Genius*. He hoped that she would continue to write 'for the advantage of the rising generation'. A fortnight later, he reciprocated her gift of 'mental food' with some freshly caught fish, as he put it, laboriously, 'the fruits of my labours in a dispossessed hour of yesterday'.[72]

Barbara Hofland was to become a central figure in Soane's life; one of the rare women friends who did not fawn, flirt and flatter but was a friend to both Eliza and John Soane. Mrs Soane, so she told her mother, had 'sought me unknown, unintroduced; invited me for the express purpose of being good to me, a stranger in London . . . struggling with great difficulties, and my past distresses as well as my past situation utterly unknown'.[73] The two women warmed to one another. Once, showing her a portrait of her husband, Eliza exclaimed 'with a glow of pleasure I never shall forget, "Oh, he was so handsome once" suddenly checking herself as if she had forgot any one was near.'

In September 1814 Soane found himself (by name) an incidental char-

162. Chelsea Hospital, the stables. Soane's handling of brickwork was never more skilful than here, transforming a simple element (the entrance to the stableyard) into a dramatic feature.

acter in a novel. In Barbara Hofland's *The Merchant's Widow and her Family* published in September 1814, a boy, modelled on her own son, asks his mother to 'make me a Mr Soane'. After his mother and the architect had discussed poetry and other adult subjects, 'Mr Soane took me by the hand, and led me into a very beautiful place like the inside of a house, open from top to bottom; and it was full of beautiful tops of columns and pieces of pillars, and statues . . . and he told me which of these things came from Greece, and which from Rome, and told me they were objects of study to him.'

The boy had also been shown the rotunda at the Bank and had discussed ways in which genius, implicitly architectural, manifests itself, in the eyes or the mind. In the story the boy goes on to be a diligent student of architecture, with 'every reason to hope that he will become the Soane or the Wyatt of a future day'.[74] Soane took exception to the extract, and the use of his name, perhaps made uncomfortable by the public revelation of his views about his own genius and equally because of the unfortunate conjunction with events in his own sons' lives. Tactfully Mrs Hofland withdrew the offending copies and altered the title, reissuing the revised text later.[75] Her generosity ensured that their friendship did not suffer from the incident.[76]

Mrs Hofland was herself a woman of considerable intellect and resilience. Born Barbara Wreaks in Sheffield, in 1796 she married a merchant who died of consumption leaving her with an infant son, Frederick Hoole. Already a published writer, she turned to her pen for their survival. In Harrogate, where she ran girls' school, she met the impecunious landscape painter Thomas Hofland and they married in 1810. He was a mediocre artist, much involved in the British Institution, and a philanderer who fathered an illegitimate son in 1816, whom Barbara uncomplainingly took in and brought up. In Hofland Soane found another enthusiastic fellow angler. Despite her troubles, Mrs Hofland produced a stream of novels, an estimated sixty in her lifetime. Miss Mitford, her friend and fellow novelist, described her as 'independent as a skylark'.

It may have been Hofland who invited Soane to be present at the inaugural meeting of the Artists' General Benevolent Institution (AGBI) on 20 June 1814. Soane became a member of the provisional committee of directors and took an active role in the organisation for the rest of his life, both as a trustee and steward for the annual dinners and as a generous contributor to their funds. Hofland was an active promoter of the new body and a year later J.M.W. Turner was elected Chairman, with Hofland his deputy. John Young, of the British Institution, was the Secretary. The Trustees for several years were Soane, Turner and Chantrey – three men who had risen to eminence by ambition and ability alone. Their support of the AGBI was a form of recognition of their own good fortune, much as Hogarth had applied himself to support Captain Coram's Foundation at the Foundling Hospital. In time the AGBI broadened its remit to assist architects who had fallen on hard times.[77]

The early summer of 1815 was a happy period for the Soanes. In June preparations were being made to get the Chertsey pond ready for a fishing weekend. As Sarah Smith added in a postscript to Eliza's letter, 'if a quarter of a hundred perch are not caught it shall not be for want of proper tackle'.[78] The Abbey stream was too overgrown for fishing with a

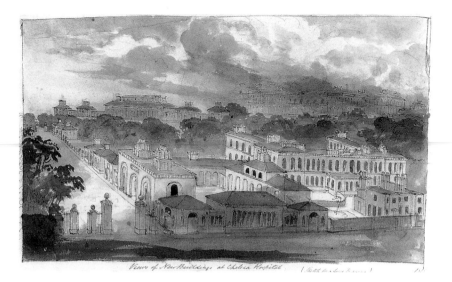

163. A composite drawing of Soane's work at the Chelsea Hospital in 1818; the stables are immediately to the right of the entrance (Wren's work is out of sight to the left). To the right is the infirmary with Soane's own house on Paradise Row, to the front. The secretary's office (in fact, to the left) has been, for these purposes, relocated in the distance.

reel, 'the trees, weeds, stinging nettles and giddy heads not very accommodating' and she suggested he bring his own tackle. They were dining with the Smiths and the Clarks on Saturday evening and Eliza was arranging to dress the venison at The Swan. She asked Soane to bring two or three bottles of port and some sherry 'as perhaps you may want it'. She was off to play a rubber with 'the old Chamberlain's lady'.[79]

By late August Eliza was in Cheltenham, with Sarah Smith as her paid companion, suffering from gall-stones. Dr Jenner was not available, since his own wife was seriously ill. Eliza was dependent on Pennington's instructions, conveyed by Soane. After a month of taking the waters she felt better. She wrote to Maria: 'They tell me I shall renew my lease of life for twenty one years – after that I can only expect to be a tenant at will, liable to be turned out every quarter day . . . Pray give my love to your idle husband, and tell him when I return I shall be so full of health and spirits, that if ever I see him contrary, pettish or ill-humoured he may expect what he never yet experienced.'[80]

Any momentary reassurance given Soane by Eliza's improved health or appreciation of his work, such as that in Richard Brown's *The Principles of Practical Perspective* (1815),[81] dedicated to Soane and offering tribute to his public works and his 'scientific and instructive lectures', was harshly shattered in September. Two long and particularly vicious articles on Soane's work were published in a respectable, recently founded, Sunday newspaper called *The Champion*. Initially edited by John Scott, that observant visitor to France, the publication aimed 'to satisfy the curiosity of the public on *literary* as well as *political* subjects'[82] and had a strong line in theatre criticism provided by its critic and second editor, J. H. Reynolds. Early contributors included Keats, Wordsworth and Hazlitt.

The tone of the articles, savaging Soane's work at Chelsea Hospital (fig. 163), 13 Lincoln's Inn Fields and the Bank, was choleric and frequently puerile. The clerk of works' house and the stables at Chelsea attracted the writer's particular attention. 'Not that . . . there is a manger in the architect's house or a drawing-room in the stables, but the style of architecture is the same . . . on the top at the back are two large raisin jars . . . fresh, to all appearance from the grocer's shop.' (Brown had singled out the Vanbrughian outline of the chimneys for praise.) 'Fronting them, ranged in military array, appears a little regiment of chimney-pots with white heads, like so many well grown cauliflowers; the house has two wings, one of which has windows and the other a door.' From this 'monster in the art of building', attention turns to the Infirmary, 'exquisitely ludicrous in this unison of contrarieties . . . Disproportion is the most striking feature in the works of this artist.'

Then followed a swingeing attack on the Bank, exhibiting 'extravagances, which are too dull for madness and too mad for the soberness of reason' and then on the artist's house in Lincoln's Inn Fields, where the exterior exhibited, 'exceeding heaviness and monumental gloom . . . it looks like a record of the departed and can only mean that considering himself as defunct in that better part of humanity – the mind and its affections – he has reared this mausoleum for the enshrinement of his body'. Passing on to the interior, the ground-floor library is a 'satire upon the possessor, who must stand in the midst of these hoarded volumes like a eunuch in a seraglio; the envious . . . guardian of that which he cannot enjoy'. Beyond is 'a narrow lofty cave, ycleped the museum; it is lighted at the top by a lantern of stained glass . . . here are urns that once contained the ashes of the great, the wise and the good; here are relics broken from the holy temples of Greece and Italy; here is the image of the Ephesian Diana, once the object of human adoration, but now only valued as a rarity that by its high price may feed the grovelling pride of its possessor'. After that, the author moves on to Somerset House, in a vain effort at even-handedness.

From the choice of buildings and personal tone of the diatribe, Soane knew immediately that the writer was George, but it took him some time to prove it. He was mortified and enraged. The pursuit of a suitable revenge took all of his energy and thought for several weeks.

He tried to keep the articles from Eliza while she was in Cheltenham but eventually she read them. Soane recorded her reaction.[83] 'Those are George's doing. He has given me my death blow. I shall never be able to hold up my head again.'

She wrote to S. Turner, one of her go-betweens with George, asking him to return her £200; presumably intended for George.[84] It was to be an autumn of sickness and death and another blow followed. Edward Foxhall, of all the close family friends the most steadfast, provider of early financial and professional support and Soane's colleague on numerous commissions, died in early November.

On the morning of Tuesday, 21 November, the Soanes had breakfasted together at Lincoln's Inn Fields, 'very cheerful and kind as had been the case more particularly at Cheltenham and since her return',[85] Soane remembered. Although Eliza had complained of severe pains, they passed and she went off to market to purchase a dessert for dinner. On her return she was taken ill again and retired to bed. It was too late by then to cancel that evening's dinner guests so Mrs Shee, wife of Martin Archer Shee RA, took her place at the head of the table. Pennington, a fellow guest and her doctor over a long period, prescribed medicine and returned the following morning at 8 a.m. He told Soane that Eliza's condition was grave. Soane asked Dr Pemberton for a second opinion but he could offer no hope. At twenty minutes past one she died, the cause of her death never determined. There is little doubt that George's behaviour, the tensions that he exacerbated between his parents and the misery he caused her personally were major contributors to her death, her physical symptoms brought about by intense stress.[86] A few hours after her death, a cheerful letter with family news arrived from her 'daughter' Maria in Brighton, addressed to 'Dear Mother'.

Sarah Smith did not arrive until after Eliza's death, despite a desperate dash to Chertsey by Joseph Beynon, the Soanes's manservant, to fetch her. John arrived from Brighton at 1.30 the following morning. Of George there was no sign. The distraught Soane was given a sleeping draught by Pennington.

Over the following days, a steady stream of Mrs Soane's friends came to visit her coffin, which remained in the house for the next week. Until the Tuesday it remained open. On the evening before the funeral, the coffin was placed in the library and, now covered in black velvet and black ostrich feathers, it awaited the journey to the burial ground at St Pancras the following morning.[87] Over that week, the pages of Soane's notebook remained blank.

The next entry was on Friday, 1 December. 'Melancholy day indeed! The burial of all that is dear to me in this world, and all I wished to live for.' The funeral procession was made up of the young John Soanes, James Spiller, Martin Archer Shee, John Taylor, James Perry and Robert Pennington. Three pupils attended, George Basevi, Henry Parke and Edward Foxhall jun., and the servants Joseph and Mary. There is no record of the funeral service. Soon afterwards, Soane framed up George's 'Death Blows' and hung them prominently in the house.

Over these terrible days, Thomas Keate, their surgeon friend from Chelsea, counselled father and son to support one another, despite John's 'cold, teasing and irritating' manner. He pleaded with Soane 'to call in the aid of religion' and to settle their differences in Eliza's memory, 'a person so excellent, so capable of judging accurately, administering consolation and healing differences'.[88] Perhaps as a result, there was a brief reconciliation, with Pennington and Spiller as intermediaries and allowing Soane to feel, briefly, optimistic and that 'the past will be forgotten and that we may live united and as happily as the late sudden and dreadful event will allow'.[89] But wrangles with Maria over Eliza's possessions and continued tensions at Chelsea were not conducive to the new harmony.

In those weeks Soane called upon George Dance, their first meeting for many years; perhaps in response to a message of sympathy. Other friends gathered to provide support and distraction. On Christmas Eve Soane's companion was J.M.W. Turner, a reflection of Eliza's friendship with Turner as much his own. He spent Christmas Day at Chelsea, dining with John and Maria. It had been, he observed, a gloomy day. New Year's Eve was spent drinking tea with the Brittons and on New Year's Day he summoned Tyrrell at seven o'clock, followed by three clerks. He was remaking his will.[90]

On 5 January, the *Gentleman's Magazine* published a lengthy obituary of Elizabeth Soane, which while giving her parents' names wrongly as 'John and Elizabeth' painted a perceptive and affectionate portrait of her vivacity, intelligence and literary talents (a letter writer 'scarcely excelled by a

Sevigné, a Woolstoncraft or a Montagu') as well as her ability to hold her own and offer decisive and informed opinions at the dinner table, surrounded by 'eminent artists, literati and men of science'. Moreover: 'what are usually termed the fashionable elegancies of ladies, she despised; for she justly remarked that they were merely calculated to make women the dolls or puppets of men – the playthings and not companion of husbands'.

14

THE YEAR OF MISERY AND BEYOND

Soane's 'first year of misery'[1] was one in which he took on almost no new work. Every effort to nerve himself to deliver his Royal Academy lectures had failed, he wrote to the secretary Henry Howard.[2] Meanwhile the news of Soane's tragedy spread amongst his friends, some of whom must have been alerted by reading Mrs Soane's obituary in the *Gentleman's Magazine*. In Norwich John Patteson's daughter had shown it to her father and he immediately wrote to Soane; he had known deep personal tragedy himself, having lost three sons to fever in as few days twenty years before. 'I have no one for whom I feel great friendship nor in whose prosperity I have more sincerely rejoiced'[3] he assured him and offered him the only comfort, the relief that time brings.

For the coming weeks, Soane's mourning process consisted of his immersion in designs for Eliza's tomb, the family vault.[4] Rowland Burdon did not hear of her death until February, when Soane wrote to ask his advice on inscriptions. He too drew on his own experience of bereavement – for his first wife and daughter had died in 1791 – and his insights into Soane's depressive disposition (he, like Patteson, had known him for almost forty years). 'I . . . am disposed to think, that literary quotations should be used sparingly, as they do not occur naturally to us under the immediate pressure of the calamity; and we rather wish to dwell on the character on the object we lament than upon the duty we are ourselves performing.' He suggested the Ode of Horace on the death of Virgil or the Bible, which, he said, had always provided many 'just and . . . affecting descriptions of a virtuous woman'.[5]

While Burdon had found his Christian religion a great comfort, for Soane there was no consolation from that quarter. Another old friend, John Coxe Hippisley suggested travel as a palliative and was, accidentally, nearer the mark.

The commemoration of Eliza in cold stone above the brick vault in which her body lay was a painfully difficult task. The burial ground for the parish of which Soane had long been a vestryman had been recently opened, one of several which relieved the pressure on city churchyards and crypts. Old St Giles's burial ground was next to St Pancras churchyard on the northern fringes of London. Later the dividing wall was removed to combine the two as a public garden. The physical reality in 1816 was very bleak. Here Soane built an unconventional, free-standing structure, dominating the still almost empty graveyard. Significantly this was to be his monument as well as Eliza's grave (fig. 164).[6] Perfecting the design took several weeks.

He conceived it with a core, a block of Carrara marble – the quarries having just reopened after the Napoleonic wars – on which the inscriptions would be carved. The block was sheltered by an inner aedicule (also in marble) with Ionic columns and an outer canopy of Portland stone, surmounted by a shallow, heavy dome. One further 'layer' was the outer balustrade (instead of the usual iron railings), a Portland stone parapet with Coade stone balusters and a flight of stairs leading down to the vault, sealed with a stone slab.

Soane avoided Christian ornament entirely. A pine cone, the Egyptian symbol of regeneration used widely throughout classical antiquity, surmounts the dome and below it a serpent is coiled, swallowing its own tail, symbolising eternity.[7] The lips of the curved, segmental pediments are scratched with a wavy continuous line and above the squared shafts of the supports are incised 'capitals'. Below, panels with Greek boys holding snuffed torches are interspersed with the balusters. The inscription, lines by Barbara Hofland rather than Horace, is to the west: Soane's own epitaph, above the steps down to the vault, would be the one to confront future visitors to the monument.

George Basevi and Henry Parke began to draw up the designs in mid-February and in April two views were on show at the Royal Academy, though Soane did not feel able to attend the private view.[8] But Old St Giles's burial ground was a place of no natural beauty whatsoever, close to the encroaching terraces of north London with the little church of St Pancras beyond, a far cry from the contemplative calm of Rousseau's much-visited grave in its island setting – or indeed from the dignified

164. A design of early 1816 showing the Soane family tomb in Old St Giles's burial ground in a pleasing and entirely imaginary leafy landscape (St Pancras church can be glimpsed to the right).

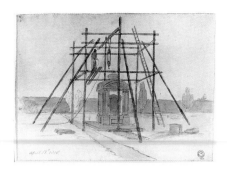

165. The tomb under construction in April 1816, before the addition of the surrounding balustrade and steps down to the vault. The burial ground is revealed as empty and treeless.

avenues of Pompeii or the Via Appia that Soane had so admired, the ranks of former citizens in their mausolea dignifying the approaches to Roman towns.

The tomb was erected over Easter by Soane's trusted mason, Thomas Grundy and Parke and the other pupils recorded the process (fig. 165). Soane could not bring himself to visit it for many months but Barbara Hofland went on his behalf in early June 1816. 'I saw the monument last evening. It is exceedingly beautiful and appropriate, there is an air of dignified simplicity, and solid character about it, which I never saw in anything else in my life.'

The monumental gravity and the lack of Christian motifs may have disconcerted her but she was discreet. 'I wish you would muster courage to look at it yourself' she continued, with her usual good sense, 'as I think you would feel some satisfaction from witnessing the fulfilment of your wishes in its appearance, and the consciousness that you had left nothing undone which could evince your esteem and affection for her you loved.'[9]

The obituaries and the accounts of the tomb soon flushed various long unseen members of Mrs. Soane's family out of the woodwork. Mr J. W. Palmer, a nephew of George Wyatt, began to pester Soane, having fallen on hard times since the death of his uncle. Asking first for work in 'some inferior department of surveying', he came to see Soane and then continued a lengthy, bitter correspondence, threatening to expose what he saw as the unequal treatment of his family by the Soanes, grown wealthy at the expense of their relatives. Gathering in strength, the attacks were opportunistic attempts to milk Soane, despite Wyatt's completely even-handed will in 1790. Foolishly Soane, rather than ignore the unpleasant tide of letters, reacted angrily.[10]

At Chelsea, where Soane and his wife might have settled happily in their later years, the young John Soanes had moved into the remodelled clerk of works' house in mid-December 1815.[11] Of George there was no word. One sketch for the family tomb includes a writhing skeleton, hurling a spear, below the fourth side – where George's epitaph would have been under other circumstances.[12]

Soane was avoiding Lincoln's Inn Fields where possible. There were rows about the dispersal of Mrs Soane's effects between Sarah Smith, Maria Soane and Soane, who seemed unwilling to accept that they too were mourning Eliza deeply and wished for items by which to remember her. At Chelsea the house-sharing arrangements soon fell apart. There had been a series of furious arguments with John and Maria, culminating with a visit from his small granddaughter Bessie. Bringing in a plate of biscuits she had looked around and accused him of taking her nursery carpet and her bed. She then asked her grandfather if she could play in the garden. Aware that she was simply repeating her mother's grievances, Soane furiously copied the innocent phrases into his notebook.[13] On 24 February he symbolically took his toothpowder, combs, corkscrew and decanters to Chelsea to emphasise his intention to spend more time there. John and his family went back to Paris in April. George had written to his father but there was no further contact.

Despite his desperate state of mind, not all jobs could be stalled. Soane was considering new work at the Freemasons' Hall although in February he felt unable to face a dinner at James Perry's to meet the Duke of Sussex.

His responsibilities at the Office of Works led to a series of meetings with the Lord Grenville and Lord Liverpool in March, and he was back at Coombe House working privately for the Prime Minister.[14] In early April, that untiring independent bloodhound on the track of public expenditure, Henry Bankes MP 'having noticed the repairs which were going on in the front of the Secretary of State's Office, Whitehall, moved for estimates of the probable expense'. The Chancellor of the Exchequer assured him that they were authorised by the Office of Works (in the person of Soane), due to the dangerous state of the building. On this occasion Bankes retreated but he was keeping his powder dry for future engagements.

166. The Dropping Well at Knaresborough, drawn by Francis Place, 1711.

The rapprochement with George Dance, who had retired from practice in 1815, was a great comfort. Dance suggested that Soane take some distracting excursions: 'the wisest thing you could do would be to court dissipation in every innocent shape'.[15] Barbara Hofland also realised that congenial distraction would lighten Soane's angry solitude and depression. She persuaded him to join her on a summer tour and pointed him towards Harrogate, which she knew well from her efforts to set up a school there, but which was a new watering place for Soane. The town offered scenes without any poignant associations with Eliza and lay within easy reach of many architectural destinations and natural wonders. Her choice was inspired; Harrogate, about which she had written a rather good poem,[16] ran the gamut of choice for anyone in search of the picturesque.

Neighbouring Knaresborough had a spectacular gorge, the rock-hewn chapel of Our Lady of the Crag, a cliff-side hermit's cave, hanging gardens and a 'dropping' well with remarkable properties of ossification (fig. 166), reached through an enchanted woodland walk. Excursions from Harrogate included the Plompton Rocks, Ripon, Newby Hall (with its classical sculpture gallery and sarcophagi), Hackfall, Fountains Abbey and Studley Park, with York and Castle Howard, Harewood House and Masham easily accessible in a day.

Soane arrived in Harrogate in the first week of July, after spending a miserable night at The Angel at Doncaster, dirty, expensive and 'd—-d bad'. The North Yorkshire town had only recently developed into a fashionable spa resort, with the disadvantage of a shorter season than its southern counterparts but the volume of visitors to Harrogate now supported several large inns, two of which vied for the society visitors. The Granby was known as the 'house of peers', The Green Dragon being the 'house of commons'. Soane stayed at the latter.

Kept indoors by almost continuous rain, he divided his time between bathing, drinking medicinal waters and reading. He was also translating the *Observations* of the Abbé Laugier.[17] Soane was in retrospective mood and the writings of the Jesuit theoretician, offering a neat historical progression from the primitive hut to the architecture of classical antiquity, offered a rational benchmark against which Soane could measure the conflicting architectural arguments with which he struggled. There were nine copies of Laugier's treatise in his library. Perhaps the mental exercise of the translation helped to distract him, while the reiteration of the familiar text was a comforting rosary, running through his brain and offering a link to the past. He was desperately missing Eliza's company; 'here we should have rambled together and held converse sweet' he wrote in his notebook.[18] Later in the stay he wrote to 'Miss Bee', Norah Brickenden.

241

On kinder days Mrs Hofland conducted him to scenes she judged would best provide emotional release and catharsis. Before leaving he had been immersed in her novels and she knew that he was thirsty for scenery that might mirror his melancholic mood. Grandeur, natural gloom, even a touch of vertiginous menace could all be provided in accessible and miniaturised form around the spa town. Mrs Hofland had quoted some lines from *King Lear* which might be suggested by one precipitous view: 'Here lies the place – stand still. How fearful, and dizzy 'tis, to cast one's eyes so low! The crows and choughs, that wing the mid-way air, show scarce as gross as beetles.' The heavy rain intensified a mood of Shakespearean tragedy. Mrs Hofland well knew Soane's needs.

Of the party for some of the time were Mr and Mrs Edward Conduitt. The Conduitts, tenants at 3 Albion Place, had been early callers on Soane after Eliza's death.[19] Mrs Hofland thought Sarah (Sally) Conduitt might make an ideal non-resident housekeeper. A period in each other's company in Harrogate was a good way of testing their compatibility. At the end of the holiday Soane noted that she had ordered a black dress 'how kind! But she is good indeed!'[20] The purchase of mourning dress signalled that she was considering taking the post. This and the visits that week to 'Howard's house' (Castle Howard) as well as to Studley Park, Fountains Abbey, Ripon Minster 'and market place' had cheered him up considerably – 'saw so much' he noted.[21]

Joseph Gandy was also playing his part in the effort to rally Soane's spirits. He suggested following a picturesque route home from York to Lancaster, through Wensleydale, which would pass a number of castles and churches of interest to the architect 'if he collects for the future' as he charmingly put it.[22] He also recommended Soane look at a number of recently built gaols, the largest programme of public works going on around the country, including those at York, Lancaster (Thomas Harrison's Gothic Revival scheme which he had completed) and, especially, Gloucester.[23] Conway Castle, with its cyclopean walls, was worth a detour as was the valley; 'if you rise with the sun and set with it, you will frequently enjoy the sublime'.

The ten days between leaving Harrogate and his return home remain a blank in Soane's notebook and journal, but his high expenditure for the month away of almost £200 suggests that he may have followed Gandy's route. John Britton, his pupil George Bailey and manservant Beynon had joined him in Harrogate, as well as 'Storace', his old friend Nancy. Perhaps some, or all, of this party accompanied him on the tour. Gandy did not, 'I wish I could travel with you; my ready hand, and your mind, would be perhaps useful; pardon my presumption, I am teaching what I want to be taught.'

The letter illuminates the relationship between the two 'scarred romantics' as Sir John Summerson memorably described them.[24] Gandy's perceptive eye supplied scenes of grandeur and beauty for Soane's highly suggestible spirits. Finally, though he could ill afford to, Gandy offered Soane his immense watercolour of Merlin's Tomb (fig. 167) exhibited at the Royal Academy the previous year, 'as a mark of my esteem and gratitude'. The painting, glowing from its very core, illustrates the line 'the tomb itself did brighten all the cave', from Harrington's translation of *Orlando Furioso*.[25] It is a haunting image in which architecture *is* imagination.

Gandy shared Soane's fascination with *lumière mystérieuse*. The architecture in *Merlin's Cave* is based upon features in the Rosslyn Chapel,[26] a mysterious and strangely ornamented fifteenth-century gothic structure in Scotland, a few miles south of Edinburgh. The twisted column, the so-called 'Apprentice's Pillar' and the elaborate squared one beside it, 'The Mason's Pillar' – telling the tale of the over-industrious apprentice, a timeless fable – had become important within masonic symbolism. Britton knew and had published engravings of the chapel, a famous romantic destination which Turner had also painted.[27] Britton's Volume III of the *Architectural Antiquities* – dedicated to Soane – described the setting; 'the sylvan and romantic beauties of hanging woods, beetling rocks, precipices, hills, dales and mountains . . . the castle and chapel, not only fine . . . in themselves, but rendered more so by their union with such natural charms, must afford a rich intellectual treat to the architect and antiquary'.

Twelve of the fourteen plates devoted to the Rosslyn Chapel were by Gandy, the other two by James Elmes. Few other subjects in Britton's extensive coverage were given as much space, either in plates or prose.[28] He quoted Walter Scott's invocation of the legend of the chapel being seen in flames but unharmed in his *Lay of the Last Minstrel* (canto VI): 'Seemed all on fire within, around/Deep sacristy and altar's pale/Shone every pillar, foliage bound/and glimmered all the dead men's mail'. One plate was dedicated to Scott. Britton's text ends by remarking that the Lords of Rosslyn were 'formerly *hereditary grand masters* of the free-masons of Scotland'. The masonic symbolism in *Merlin's Cave* would have been clear to Soane.[29]

Gandy's offer was an attempt to comfort Soane in his terrible state of bereavement but Soane never received the painting; Gandy's desperate financial situation meant that his intentions may have been forgotten in the confusion.[30]

However, it must have been in these months that Gandy began to plan his first great compilation piece for Soane. *A selection of buildings erected . . . between 1780 and 1815* was exhibited at the Royal Academy in 1818 (fig. 168). Under the pendentives of a 'handkerchief' dome, an array of Soane's major buildings is assembled, like architectural models in a tiered display. The family tomb, draped in a black cloth, stands to one side while the whole is dominated by the Bank of England (Tivoli Corner in the most prominent position). Every available surface is covered by plans, folios and framed perspectives. The eye is drawn into the vortex at the centre of the picture by the glow of a single powerful stage lamp.[31] By leaving whole areas of the picture surface shadowed almost to obscurity Gandy bathed the whole of Soane's career in a theatrical *lumière mystérieuse*.

The companion piece, shown at the Royal Academy two years later, *Architectural Visions of Early Fancy and Dreams in the Evening of Life* (fig. 169), drew together, this time in a landscape setting, Soane's architectural disappointments and a few of his remaining faint hopes. A wash of clean early morning sunlight alights on the British Senate House but the city is uninhabited. The only figures are the youthful dreamer, yet to pass under the arch leading to the city within and the contented fisherman upon the lake (possibly Soane in retirement) while far away along the winding route past Soane's unbuilt parliaments and palaces are mourners following a state funeral procession (in fact Nelson's).

167. Joseph Gandy's luminous watercolour of Merlin's Tomb exhibited at the Royal Academy in 1815 and which he offered to Soane after Eliza's death, thinking that its masonic symbolism and the *lumière mystérieuse* would appeal to Soane.

Back home in mid-August, Soane set about altering what he referred to as 'the monk's cell'.[32] Fresh in his mind from Knaresborough was the stained-glass of the tiny rock-built chapel and the lingering presence of the hermits who had lived in the honeycomb caves in the outcrops – history to flesh out flimsy gothick fiction. He continued with his morose improvements and entertained old friends who called to comfort him, among them Rowland Burdon and Norah Brickenden.

The depressing arrangements at Lincoln's Inn Fields almost became self-fulfilling when a marble crashed down, narrowly missing Soane who had just moved from his seat. As he noted later, 'all my miseries would have been completed had I remained only two minutes longer in the chair!'

Barbara Hofland, practical as ever, had a plan for Soane. As he had now arranged his 'beautiful Marbles beautifully', could he not consider 'the valuable antique . . . on the banks of Tame and Anker . . . and add it to your collection'? She thought that Soane should consider obtaining a seat in parliament, that of Tamworth Castle in Staffordshire. The closed borough was divided between the Manor interest and the Castle interest, the former in the hands of Robert Peel I since 1790 and the latter those of the Marquises of Townshend. The second Marquis of Townshend had died in 1811, disinheriting his heir, and by 1814 the estate was for sale. John Robins, Soane's friend and client, and who was a creditor, bought it for £94,700 and, not wanting to take on the parliamentary interest, sold off the property in lots. In 1816 the Tamworth Castle seat was available.[33]

Mrs Hofland's idea of 'the Castle' would act both as a palliative for his broken spirits and be 'a new charge . . . being alike honourable and useful'. She suggests that his 'tried integrity and a situation of known independence' mark him as an ideal candidate for the seat, even invoking his 'probable longevity' in his favour.[34] Soane was grateful: her compliments proved, he said, the blindness of friendship but there was a 'vacuum that can never be filled and to which time cannot administer any lenient remedies'.

Mrs Hofland, who as she reminded him, had had her own share of sorrows, was alert to signs of self-indulgence in his mourning. Well before his other friends dared to touch the subject, she rebuked him and suggested

168. Joseph Gandy *A Selection of Buildings Erected from the Design of J. Soane Esq. RA between 1780 and 1815.* The Bank of England takes centre stage; every commission of which Soane was particularly proud is illustrated including small works such as the stables at Betchworth Castle (left foreground), an armorial stove for Bentley Priory and various monuments, including that for Lord Bridport and, of course, Eliza Soane's, draped in black. In the upper shadows to the right can be seen Norwich Castle and the gothic library at Stowe, significantly not omitted from this catalogue of his finest work. A solitary figure sits at a plan-strewn table – perhaps the artist.

that he was unworthy of her for whom he grieved. 'To . . . be determined not to accept of contentedness in lieu of happiness, is surely rather a romantic grief, than a rational respect for her memory; it destroys you, but does not therefore honour her – far from it.'[35]

Soane thanked Barbara Hofland for her 'excellent' letter. He wanted her advice over certain 'hellish machinations', a mixture of domestic complications and gossip. Mrs Soane's friend and companion from Chertsey, Sarah Smith, had stepped in to act as his housekeeper but they had parted acrimoniously. Her sister Sophia succeeded her but soon departed too. Meanwhile life was complicated by the hovering Norah Brickenden. Mrs Hofland warned him, without naming names. 'When she comes to town, see her neither too often nor too seldom . . . bring yourself to endure the society of other women.' The Tamworth scheme had been her attempt to distract him, 'eradicating one passion by another'. She was sure that he would marry again, having no daughter or niece to take the head of his table, but in the meantime advised that he should 'struggle on for a time'. Barbara Hofland did not want to see Soane taking a foolish step, on the rebound.

169. Joseph Gandy *Architectural Visions of Early Fancy and Dreams in the Evening of Life.* At the centre is the 1779 British Senate House, bottom right is the House of Lords and left the Gold Medal Triumphal Bridge. Wending uphill into the left upper corner is Nelson's funeral cortège. The painting catalogues Soane's many dashed hopes: all the figures remain outside the gateway to the promised city, except those which follow the funerary procession.

Soane felt her letter had gone too far. He had asked her advice, whether he should 'give up housekeeping altogether and retire abroad, or. . .have a proper housekeeper, that my table might be suitably arranged, if health and spirits should again allow me to see my friends as formerly' but she had embarked on flights of fancy and he was angry. He did not want her views on the Smiths; '*I* am no stranger to their qualities' he added sarcastically. Mrs Hofland must have felt rebuffed but, tactful as usual, she dropped the subject and preserved the friendship.

Meanwhile Mrs Conduitt became Soane's housekeeper, receiving £50 per annum towards expenses and paying a merely nominal rent for the house in Albion Place. She was an ideal woman companion for Soane, becoming increasingly informed in architectural matters and all his professional concerns, travelling with him and accompanying him to functions. Sally Conduitt could escort Soane without giving rise to gossip of the kind Miss Brickenden provoked. An intelligent and attractive woman,[36] she became a great favourite with Soane's friends and clients, who were always delighted to find her at Lincoln's Inn Fields, where her presence lightened the atmosphere enormously. John Taylor, his journalist-poet friend, called her 'the fair Samaritan'. Her duties involved overseeing the running of the house and keeping the accounts, although she and her husband, who went fishing with Soane and sometimes travelled with them, continued to live in Southwark.[37] Soane was very generous to her and her family, as George later discovered.

For Christmas 1816 Soane sent John and his family a turkey, while claiming to be unaware whether they had yet returned to Chelsea from Paris. His own Christmas dinner was spent with the Brittons. Margaret Tyndale, an attentive and always kindly neighbour, had kept him company one evening but the early days of January were mournful and solitary; 1 January set the tone. 'At home and *alone* all the evening. Thus ends the first day of the New Year!'[38]

John's Christmas gift to his father was thoughtfully chosen – the complete writings of Winckelmann, the arch-priest of neoclassicism. On his return from France, John did his best to repair relations with his father. On 19 January 1817 they spent a companionable day together, returning to Chelsea in the evening. Ten days later they went to East India House, and in the coming weeks they breakfasted or dined together regularly.

On 20 February 1817, despite trouble with his eyesight, Soane opened his new Royal Academy lecture season. He presented the first of his two sets of lectures, considerably revised, completing it on 27 March.[39] John Moyes, his printer, wrote to congratulate him on the '*éclat*' which the lectures had received and the full houses which they had attracted.'[40]

At the dinner table in Lincoln's Inn Fields, Eliza's chair still remained inviolate. On the first anniversary of the installation of her monument he walked to St Pancras but 'had no resolution to go nearer!'; it took another year for him to approach 'the monument of my never to be forgotten friend'. March became the month for his annual visit to her burial place.

However, Soane's responsibilities and work, with its insistent pace, were helping to pull him back to life. The new Earl of St Germans (the former John Eliot) had ideas of his own for his stables at Port Eliot and Soane had to ensure that his client was not running away with the job. Each year he paid his annual visit to Mells, where Colonel Horner and his wife, Sir John

Coxe Hippisley's daughter,[41] offered him the pleasures of friendship diluted by the frustrations of their perpetually indecisive and contradictory behaviour as clients. Both Chelsea (where he was planning the guardroom and privies) and the Bank required his attention again.

At home Mr and Mrs Conduitt dined with him, usually weekly. In April 1817 Soane invited both John and Maria to Lincoln's Inn Fields, suggesting a conciliatory mood. There were constant sad reminders of Eliza; items which he found tucked away in her desk and the arrival of a dividend from her savings (sadly diminished by George's incursions).[42] Meanwhile Miss Brickenden remained in the wings. Soane saw her regularly but he did not invite her to the house. Dinner guests were the old friends; Pennington, John Taylor, the widowed Mrs Foxhall and her family, the Flaxmans and Miss Denman, Mrs Flaxman's sister.

Almost despite himself, Soane was healing. He began to go out into society, attending his first public dinner since Eliza's death, among old friends at the Artists' General Benevolent Institution where he was a Trustee and considerable benefactor. On 3 May he was at the private view and dinner of the Royal Academy. His pleasure in the theatre was reviving and in early June he saw J. P. Kemble and his sister perform a renowned *Macbeth* at Covent Garden.[43] Henry Crabb Robinson, an admirer of the pair for twenty years, joined the crush to see the production and was rewarded by 'the astonishing powers of . . . Mrs Siddons . . . [who] in the night scene raised herself to a level with all my recollections of her youthful powers'.[44]

Norah Brickenden was unable and unwilling to read any significance into the distance that Soane was keeping between her and the rest of his life. She had been to one of his Royal Institution lectures – more popular versions of the Royal Academy lectures designed for a wider public including women and given in the summer social season, May and June – and wrote a gushing letter of praise.[45] Mrs Hofland, too, had attended one and complained that it was too brief. She thanked him warmly and sincerely for the pleasure of hearing him. James Perry dared to proffer some advice about Soane's lecture delivery. He suggested that, given the splendour of the illustrations, they should be shown at a slower pace. 'The truth is that one of your Lectures contains matter for two and whenever you have a quotation to recite, you prove by the clearness of your delivery, how articulate you can be when you please to be deliberate. I know that you will receive this hint in the kindly spirit in which it is hazarded.'[46]

Perry was unusual among Soane's circle in that he was frank but tactful, thus avoiding the usual furious reaction to any hint of criticism. But flattery from women brought out Soane's 'more-sly-than-shy gallantry',[47] a suavity in female company that sat oddly with his usual manner. The tone of Norah Brickenden's letters was increasingly alarming. 'Six years ago – at Coombe Royal – was my fate decided!' The day before she had seen four of his closest friends, the Brittons, Mrs Conduitt and Mrs Hofland all in deep conversation 'I doubt not, in high admiration of you – but . . . there is no one *feels* like your own, Ellen' she signed her missive. She referred to their friendship as of 'so *peculiar* and *sacred* a nature' that his favourite Rousseau would have understood. (George, in contrast, considered Soane a 'pupil of Voltaire'.)[48] The following day she hoped to meet him. She was becoming obsessive.

170. An early design (May 1811) for
Dulwich Picture Gallery, which finally
opened to the public in 1817. Soane's top
lighting was only partially effective and the
glazing was later altered. The shape of the
top of the drawing echoes the curve of the
pendentive.

In late June Soane attended the first Annual Dinner at Dulwich. Farington recorded the seating plan for the thirty guests, amongst whom were George Dance, Henry Fuseli and Sir William Beechey as well as other Royal Academicians, who would be invited by rota each year. The bequest allowed for a lavish feast; at six o'clock they sat down to turtle soup and venison, washed down with madeira, claret, port, sherry and champagne. Carriages were called for ten.[49] Soane must have felt satisfaction as his old friends and sparring partners dined handsomely in the fine new gallery, thanks to Mrs Desenfans's bequest.

Dulwich Picture Gallery (fig. 170) was now open to the general public although Royal Academicians and invited visitors had been welcome since 1815, the year in which the three bodies were placed in the mausoleum. Those who were interested in visiting the gallery had to purchase tickets in advance from designated shops in central London and then make their way out to Dulwich village as best they could.

Soane's family responsibilities at Chertsey, long taken care of by Eliza, were now his alone. He shouldered the various tasks, settling accounts for his brother's household, visiting the family friends the Clarks and the elder Smiths (despite the recent disagreement with their daughters). Before long Sally Conduitt had assumed Eliza's role as supervisor of family affairs there, while he and Edward Conduitt sat companionably with their rods on the banks of the Abbey River.

In July 1817 Soane went back to Harrogate, taking 'Bee' (his manservant Joseph Beynon, not to be confused with 'Miss Bee', Norah Brickenden) and Mrs Conduitt. They revisited Fountains Abbey and his favourite, emotive scenes around Knaresborough followed by a wider circuit, this year, of the architectural attractions of West Yorkshire, Leeds, Wakefield, Rotherham and Wentworth Park. On his journey home Soane visited Clumber, Welbeck, Warwick Castle and Banbury and then stayed a couple of days at Stowe, to discuss a commission from the second Marquis of Buckingham, the son of his old patron and the man who as Joint Paymaster-General had been a key to the Chelsea Hospital appointment. Buckingham was considering altering family apartments at Stowe and soon Soane was working for the marquis on designs for Sudeley Castle (unexecuted) and later, after a devastating fire in 1820, at Wotton House in Buckinghamshire.

Shortly after his return to London from Harrogate, Nancy Storace died. She had been a tragic figure since her rupture with her younger lover and colleague, Braham, on which occasion Soane had proved a firm and fair friend and adviser to both parties, mediating in the prolonged and bitter division of their property, a wrangle which descended even to sharing out the cutlery. Her death was another break in the chain that stretched back to Italy. Soane now became entangled in another bitter dispute, honourably representing the interests of their son, Spencer, between the opposing parties of Braham (in general, behaving responsibly) and Nancy's mother. Again Soane behaved in an exemplary fashion in someone else's family disagreement, bringing measured advice and good sense to the situation as he so utterly failed to do in his own and earning the affection of Spencer, as he could not with his own sons.[50]

On a visit to Hampton Court in October he had lunched with his student

15

PARIS AND LONDON

In February 1819, George Dance sensed a change for the better in Soane's mood. They had been on a congenial visit to the Bank to see the recent work 'the new Room and the house in Old Jewry'.[1] Dance prevailed upon him to remove the sinister glazed and framed 'Death Blows' – George Soane's articles in the *Champion* – from the drawing-room at Lincoln's Inn Fields and hang it elsewhere.[2] Since Dance had in 1817 presented Soane with an album of drawings by Sir Christopher Wren in a moving gesture of reconciliation, he was probably the only man able to broach the subject with any hope of success.

Soane's commission to build a new National Debt Redemption Office had become subsumed – in his mind – with the idea of a Cenatoph to Pitt. It was appropriate that he should show the result to Dance, whom he had taken out to Holwood to meet Pitt many years before. The building as designed consisted of three storeys wrapped around a full height, top-lit, tribune at the core of which sat Richard Westmacott's statue of Pitt (fig. 175). Soane was in retrospective mood and his single exhibit at the Royal Academy in 1819 was Pitt's Cenotaph 'now building'. John Taylor neatly conflated their two reputations.

> honours here designed for Pitt,
> Are shrewdly blended with thy own.[3]

Soane was active on the Royal Academy Council that year; he, like Turner, was behaving badly. Callcott complained that it was difficult to get on with the business 'owing to the improper behaviour of Soane, jeering what was said by members and treating business with ridicule; added to which the incessant talking of Turner made it impossible to proceed with any dispatch'.[4] Despite that, he delivered his lectures again: eager to make a good impression on the audience, he felt that he had read them too fast. The six lectures, his 'first series', were delivered between 18 February and 25 March. The professors at the Royal Academy were mutually supportive; in January, Soane had taken his dinner guest William Hazlitt to the first of the aged Henry Fuseli's lectures, possibly in the hope of interesting the critic in his own forthcoming series. The expedition may have had the opposite effect; by the fourth of Fuseli's talks the audience had been reduced to just Soane and Henry Howard, the secretary. For whatever reason, Hazlitt did not review Soane's lectures:

175. The National Debt Redemption Office, a section through the full height tribune, as it appeared in 1819, combining its function with that of a Cenotaph to William Pitt. Westmacott's statue of Pitt is now at Pembroke College, Cambridge.

James Perry had taken on Hazlitt as his Parliamentary reporter at the *Morning Chronicle* in 1812, after which he had become a critic and essayist. Perry may have introduced Soane to Hazlitt[5] and they must have soon discovered a mutual fascination in Napoleon. Hazlitt's *The Life of Napoleon Buonaparte*, his four volume 'epic' final work, was not published until 1828 but he was already mesmerised by him, as demon, radical and man after his own heart, a peg upon which to hang his own political convictions. For his part Soane, like Goethe, took Napoleon to epitomise the romantic figure of genius, an 'imaginary' historic person, or even several people, whose heroic and contradictory myth was conducive to the notion of the artist as hero. A tyrant, he had 'sublime ideas yet [was] vulgar in soul' as Ugo Foscolo, the Italian poet put it.[6]

Napoleon, whether the youthful Consul or the brooding figure who had looked out from Elba, embodied the irresistible rise of a man of talent and vision – a potent icon to the ambitious. Whether judged as a brilliant, intuitive general or as an administrative and political opportunist he offered a model, from whose many-sided career and personality his admirers (as various as the facets of their hero) could pick at random.

At the popular level, in the years immediately after Waterloo Napoleon proved his commercial potential. The Waterloo Museum (97 Pall Mall) and the Waterloo Exhibition (1 St James's) vied with one another to attract the London public. The latter exhibited clothes and objects gleaned from the very battlefield but the Waterloo Rooms (94 Pall Mall) beat off the opposition by displaying Napoleon's stallion, Marengo, complete with war wounds. Despite the bullet lodged in his tail, he was, the public was assured, so gentle that even the most timid lady could approach him.

Inevitably, it took the flair of William Bullock of the Egyptian Gallery on Piccadilly to whole-heartedly exploit the market, recognising its short-term nature. He had begun with a display of Napoleon's carriage, complete with a coachman, two horses, his camp bed and travelling case (fig. 176).[7] Later

176. George Cruikshank's impression of the public passion for Napoleonic relics, *A Scene at the London Museum, Piccadilly or A Peep at the Spoils of Ambition, taken at the Battle of Waterloo* (1816).

on Bullock took it all on tour, a very profitable venture. He then added an exhibition of artefacts 'executed for and connected with the history of the ex-Emperor of the French'. By 1819 the interest was waning but there was still an insatiable market for Napoleonic relics which Soane played his part in sustaining. Bullock's exhibition was finally sold and the star exhibit, the statue of Napoleon that had been toppled from the Column of Peace in the Place Vendôme, was bought by William Beckford for £33 12s.[8]

In the summer of 1819 Soane finally decided to return to Paris, with plenty of time on this occasion, to absorb himself in the architecture, with a view to providing new material for the lectures. The regular routine of a stimulating summer journey had proved to be an effective anti-depressant and he had explored Harrogate and its environs to the limit over the previous three years. This visit to Paris, compared to 1814, would be in congenial company and be a well-organised stay of five weeks. His pupil, the former painter Henry Parke, was coming with him to prepare the lecture illustrations.

Thomas Keate had been in Paris for some weeks, visiting his goddaughter Adele Thompson, a great favourite with Soane, who had helped her learn Italian the previous year.[9] Having observed the positive effects of travel on Soane on previous occasions, Keate had written to encourage him although he could not in all honesty avoid conjuring up the inevitable hardship of the journey. He was beginning to recover from a three day, 150 mile ordeal, the coach rumbling over paved roads 'shaking every fibre of the frame, almost every second'. He assured his friend that the pleasures of Paris ('this sink of vice and corruption'[10]) would be a palliative.

Unfortunately, Keate ended his letter, he could not acompany him to 'more southern climes'. This is the first and only intimation of Soane's plan to extend his journey, perhaps at last to Roman Provence and surely from there to Rome.

J.M.W. Turner had set off in August for his first visit to Italy, having prepared himself thoroughly for the journey since 1817. The discussion of Turner's plans may have encouraged Soane to consider another visit to Rome. His former pupils' vivid letters from Italy and the knowledge that Francis Chantrey, Humphry Davy, Thomas Lawrence and many others were heading there, must have tempted him strongly to make the journey. He could show 'his' Rome to Turner or even meet John in Italy, introduce him to the city and let it work its magic, making an architect of him at last.

In fact the two would cross paths; John was characteristically sarcastic about Turner's manners and person, having seen him 'making rough pencil sketches to the astonishment of the fashionables, who wonder of what use these rough draughts can be'.[11] Turner's voracious delight in everything around him, in Naples and its surroundings as in Rome, to which he returned ten years later, was in marked contrast to John's reactions.[12]

Eventually, sadly, Soane settled for Paris alone. The prospect of the length and discomforts of the journey to Italy and the continuing responsibilities and opportunities at the Bank and the Office of Works deterred him. Paris would offer him a rich enough treat.

Soane set out on 21 August 1819, taking a letter of credit for £1,000 – enough to see him extend the journey to Italy in comfort, if he changed his mind. He spent a night at Dunkirk, where he encountered his client Lord Carrington, and continued via Abbeville and Beauvais, arriving in Paris

177. Lecture illustration by Henry Parke of the Père Lachaise cemetery in Paris, an arcadian scene compared to Old St Giles's burial ground in London (see fig. 165). Soane visited the cemetery at the very beginning of his stay in Paris in September 1819.

to join the Conduitts, his housekeeper-companion and her husband, at lodgings at 10, rue Vivienne, four days later. The journey had exhausted him and Keate hurried round to check up. Soane was not going to spend his valuable time in Paris in bed and by the next day he was out walking the boulevards with Mrs Conduitt.

In contrast to the journey of 1814, Soane left a full – if staccato – record of this stay in Paris. There is significance in the order in which he visited the buildings, both those which had formed his education forty years before and those sanctioned by the Napoleonic regime, deemed by Soane to be the very epitome of enlightened public patronage.

His first visit on the first day was to the Pont de Neuilly, with its memories of Perronet, followed by the Invalides and the Palais du Roi de Rome which had been at the top of his list of buildings to visit.[13] The latter, Percier and Fontaine's grandiose Versailles-scale structure at Chaillot only existed in the form of foundations.

After dinner Soane visited the Père Lachaise cemetery (fig. 177), first mooted under the *ancien régime* and sanctioned by Napoleon I in 1804, the largest of three burial grounds established on the outskirts of Paris. Once the country estate of Louis XIV's confessor, features from the eighteenth-century gardens were incorporated within A.-T. Brongiart's arcadian lay-out. It was a revolutionary approach to the design of burial grounds, a garden city for the dead and, Soane must have found, a contrast to the featureless suburban field in which Soane's own family monument now stood. Parke was detailed to draw general views and in particular Soane pointed him to the tomb of Abelard and Eloise.[14] That first day had been so ambitious that it laid Soane low again but one restful day ensured that he could follow his exhausting programme over the coming weeks without difficulty.

Soane was eager to show Mrs Conduitt the sites which held the greatest significance in his own work – rather as he had to Eliza in the weeks before their marriage. On 30 August they walked to Boullée's chapel at Sainte-Roche and then rode out to Vincennes to see the medieval château and chapel with pavilions added by Le Vau. In the evening he took her to the Arc de l'Etoile (Arc de Triomphe), by then looking more like a ruin

to Greece and Albania and returning via Sicily. Basevi, too, went on to Greece and Turkey. Even John's enthusiasm was growing; he was toying with a visit to Greece in early 1820 and, as he wrote to his father, 'the pleasure of surprizing you with a few marble fragments from our beloved Greeks'. John had been seduced by the beauties of the coast of southern Italy, 'the scenery so sweetly described by your favourite Horace' but by the time they had reached Naples he was unwell. Maria was pregnant again; the plan was foundering.[31] In the event, John's health prevented a journey to Greece.

Their second daughter Maria was born in Naples in mid-January 1820 and the family stayed on for mother and baby to regain full strength. Tactfully, he spared his father the morose observations that he shared with old Uncle William in Chertsey. 'Let the discontented visit the Continent: the distress and misery of France can only be exceeded by that of Italy! . . . the wretchedness that prevails under the imbecile government of the Pope; surrounded by bad and designing men and fools . . . I mean to reserve all I have seen and heard for your pipe and winter's evening.'[32]

Periodically self-pity rose to choke Soane. Forty-two years to the day since he had set out for Italy he marked the anniversary in his notebook on 18 March 1820. He had finally recognised that he would never return and that sending John, in his place, had been a failure. Two days later he went out to Ealing. As he walked around he grieved. 'O John! John! What has idleness cost you' he wrote that evening.[33]

From Italy, John thanked his father for buying him a winter season ticket for Drury Lane. He may have appreciated the irony of his father and brother now being employed, nominally at least, under the same roof. In January 1820 George had provided an Ode of Triumph to beef up an abridged *Coriolanus* with Kean, playing the title part as if he were Richard III. It lasted four performances. Fortunately for the wider health of the theatre, King George III died at the end of the month which allowed, once more, *King Lear* to be performed.

During the later deranged years of the king's life, the play was forbidden out of respect for his sufferings. Now the two patent theatres, Covent Garden and Drury Lane, competed, with all possible speed, to put a production of the great tragedy back on the boards. In the meantime George Soane's poetic adaptation of *Ivanhoe*, called *The Hebrew*, provided a useful stopgap, opening on 2 March 1820. It ran in competition with another version, called simply *Ivanhoe*, at Covent Garden. As Hazlitt put it 'Mr Walter Scott no sooner conjures up the Muse of old romance . . . than Messrs Harris and Elliston, with all their tribe, instantly set their tailors to work to take the pattern of the dresses, their artists to paint the wild-wood scenery or some proud dungeon-keep, their musicians to compose the fragments of bewildered ditties, and their penmen to connect the author's scattered narrative and broken dialogue into a sort of theatrical join-hand.'

Hazlitt did not wholly dismiss George Soane's efforts (an author, he added, 'of some pieces which have been well received') judging it ill-constructed as a play but better as a poem. Despite ludicrous incidents and a weak story-line, 'there are individual touches of nature and passion, which we can account for in no other way so satisfactorily as by imagining the author [i.e. Scott] to be a man of genius'. Kean played Isaac of York, his acting being 'such as to terrify us when we find from the play-bills that he is soon to act Lear'.[34]

Covent Garden won the race to produce *King Lear*, Macready opening in the leading role on 13 April. Drury Lane followed on 24 April, their production being a fantastic affair of flashing coloured lights and storm effects, so noisy that much of the dialogue was inaudible, while Kean's performance divided the critics (Crabb Robinson thought 'his representation of imbecile rage was admirable. His exhibition of madness . . . exquisite').[35] *King Lear* ran for twenty-six performances and then was taken off to be replaced by *Virginius*, prologue and epilogue by George Soane, with Kean again in the title role. The epilogue was lost in the cacophony of disapproval. This theatrical disaster managed two performances and was never heard of again.[36]

Outside the theatre, George's serious literary prospects appeared to be improving. His knowledge of German, acquired in preference to the Italian and French that his father so loved, had led to his translation of some excerpts from Goethe's *Faust*, the first in English. These he turned into verse. In 1822 Goethe read his translation and liked it. With this accolade, George embarked on a full version, for a German publisher called Bohme. Yet none of this would provide an income and meanwhile his financial and domestic affairs were in a far worse state than anybody knew. His bohemian personal life, the details of which his father would not discover until ten years later, appeared to be modelled on that of his circle in the theatre and literary worlds.[37]

In November 1821, George wrote to his father expressing his willingness to enter into any profession 'even study architecture in your office . . . having been informed that the want of a son to follow your profession is to you a source of real unhappiness'. Now he had his own family, he wrote piously, he could understand Soane's wish for a successor more sympathetically.[38] Ignorant of the extent of George's current troubles, Soane was, perhaps, nursing his position at Drury Lane in the faint hope that he could hand it to George at a future date – as he had hoped to pass Chelsea over to John.[39]

Perhaps the reappearance of *King Lear* on the stage, his favourite Shakespearean tragedy, had suggested to Soane's close friends that it was time to approach the matter of his prolonged and increasingly self-indulgent mourning. James Perry, with nerve perhaps gained during his years as the editor of the major Whig newspaper, the *Morning Chronicle*, was as usual the most courageous – breaking a taboo by sitting in Mrs Soane's vacant chair at the dinner table. He wrote with engaging candour that he had taken the long-empty place 'as a prelude to my arguing with you on the topic'. He felt that he had the right, given his own experience as a widower in tragic circumstances. (His own wife had been kidnapped at sea by Algerian pirates and was never heard of again.) Noting that the passage of time was having little effect upon Soane's grief, 'to the detriment of your energies and the affliction of your friends' he pointed out that 'keeping constantly before your eyes, symbols and testimonies to keep alive the source of your suffering . . . [is] a species of self-torment that increases in strength with its indulgence . . . I make no apology for this expostulation, because it proceeds from a true motive of friendship, and cannot be misconstrued by you upon serious reflection.'[40]

Due to the death of the president of the Royal Academy, Benjamin West, Soane's 1820 lecture series had been cut short. That year, to Soane's displeasure, Robert Smirke had become Treasurer on the death of John Yenn and Thomas Lawrence took West's place. By the following year, the state of Soane's eyes made reading impossible. As he wrote to Howard 'the pain I feel in writing this letter, must account to you for the delay in answering'.[41]

In 1821 Soane embarked on the design of the Surgeon's House for Thomas Keate at Chelsea, ingeniously combined with the hospital wash-house. The house bears many of Soane's light domestic touches: the shallow saucer-dome, ball beading and vestigial mouldings among them. The interior has been given that extra fillip that Soane reserved when he was working for a friend. But tragically Keate was not to live to enjoy the house.

Another tragedy in November the previous year had brought Soane an unexpected job. Lady Charlotte Williams-Wynn (Lord Grenville's sister) wrote to her daughter with news of a devastating fire at the Grenville family home in Buckinghamshire.

181. A drawing showing Wotton House, Buckinghamshire comparing the elevation before (left) the disastrous fire of November 1820 and after Soane's alterations (right), lowering the attic storey and adding a tiny row of windows at parapet level.

> Poor old Wotton . . . was burnt to the ground on Monday last, thank God without the loss of any lives . . . Its aimiable owner, however, with that reverential attachment which he has always so strongly felt, looked at nothing in the first moment that he heard of the destruction but restoring it and actually sent off Soane's foreman for that purpose the *same evening.*

The fire had found its way around the copper roof and forced its way down the wooden stairs at each end and into the centre of the house. Her next letter continued; 'the poor people at Wotton after having worked like horses as long as there was any thing to be done sat themselves down in front of the poor old walls and cried'.[42]

Soane reacted as the marquis knew he would, sending his clerk James Cook ahead and following the next day. He spent four days on site and ten days later had drawn up a scheme. He altered the attic storey (fig. 181) but concentrated on the gutted interior. He persuaded his client to insert a full-height central tribune (fig. 182), top-lit as usual, wrapped by the main stair, as well as an axial passage running east-west linking the principal rooms of the house and disguising the service quarters. He punched apertures above the arches along the passage, to light the house from end to end, and adjusted and softened the proportions of the boxy early eighteenth-century principal rooms.[43] Soane subtly curved corners and added his large-scale ball mouldings. The skirtings and all other mouldings on doors and shutters were identical, effaced as simple incisions into the woodwork.

Three years later, Wotton was whole again. His transformation of the house from a chunky Queen Ann mansion into an archetypical Soane house was carried out with an assurance that had grown through the continual refinement of a relatively limited vocabulary. His client could not have been more delighted, 'your plan and the execution of it are perfect and beautiful. You have restored to life my old mansion.'[44]

As Soane busied himself at Wotton, he decided that Henry Parke, who

182. At Wotton House Soane entirely remodelled the interior, piercing the centre with one of his top lit tribunes or halls (later blocked off) and carrying out numerous alterations to the entire satisfaction of his client who wrote 'you have restored to life my old mansion'.

had proved such a willing and observant companion in Paris, might be the man to benefit from a journey to Italy, in contrast to John, with his burdensome family and bad health. Soane offered Parke a stipend of £100 for a two year journey and in 1821, a politically uncomfortable moment, he set off to meet his fellow pupil Charles Tyrrell in Rome.[45] Before embarking for Sicily, Parke spent time in Naples, where he was maddened by the constant shuffling around of archaeological finds. Investigations had continued after the French had gone but it was all very unsystematic. Previous discoveries were published (in his experience inaccurately) and then removed to inaccessible warehouses, in order to make room for the new material.

Parke gratefully drew the second £100 and thanked Soane for his thoughtfulness in obtaining a ticket for his sister for the coronation of George IV of which she had written 'a most rapturous account'. He also wrote to thank Soane for his teaching; 'the lectures, it is true, are known and appreciated by all the world, but the principles which led to their existence are, I regret to say, only to be found under your roof'.[46] Parke's words are a rare glimpse of Soane the pedagogue, bringing his passions to life in front of the young men in whom he was now vesting his hopes for the architectural future.

At home, Soane was increasingly seen in company. Benjamin Robert Haydon saw him at a *conversazione* of 'celebrated men' in the spring of 1821, 'smiling and talking to several, a man of a good heart and caustic temper which renders life a burthen'.[47] The fiery Haydon recognised a man with a similar temperament to himself. In November 1821 Soane became a Fellow of the Royal Society, vouched for by Earl Spencer and John Rennie among others. Over dinner at East Cowes Castle on the Isle of Wight, John Nash told his guest Joseph Farington that he believed Soane to be worth at least £100,000 by now.[48]

Just as Soane showed real signs of emerging from his depression and self-pity, he found himself under attack again, in the pages of the *Guardian*, along with Gandy, who the writer unkindly said, could no longer be considered an architect. The review of the architectural entries in the Royal Academy exhibition of 1821, signed 'T.O.' and 'F.T.' described Soane's 'manner' as pernicious and vitiated. 'Nature, common sense, propriety, simplicity, are all immolated to his idol – novelty.' Soane's 'deterious mixtures' are compared unfavourably to the (absent) Greek revivalists – Smirke, Harrison and Atkinson. Soane's entries, 'a bird's eye view of a royal residence' and three sketches for a 'church proposed to be built in the Regent's Park',[49] were the sole architectural entries (Gandy excepted).

Soane, never one to bow his head and let criticism pass, was enraged but it was Gandy who made a fool of himself, unleashing a torrent of lengthy, incoherent letters on the newspaper.[50] James Spiller cautioned Soane against any reaction, 'I am inclined to think that silence will inflict the deepest wound' as did John Taylor ('your best course is to treat it with contempt'). The *Guardian* he points out, is an obscure paper and the matter 'wholly unworthy of your notice'. He ends, knowing Soane as well as he does; 'it is vexatious to be prevented from punishing unprovoked malevolence, but I do not see an adequate remedy in prospect'.[51]

John Britton found himself under fire too. Despite having ensured that Soane's name was regularly in his columns since the first issue of his *Magazine of Fine Arts*, he made the mistake of alluding in them to the

Guardian criticisms; 'if an able professor of architecture allows his name to be attached to slight or to tasteless drawings . . . he had better 'repent and sin no more' than endeavour to control or repress the temperate language of criticism'.[52] Soane was sure that Britton knew the name of the author of the original review but while assuring him that George Soane had no part in the matter he refused to reveal the writer's name. Over the summer months Britton and Soane remained on extremely rancorous terms.

Britton's inaccuracy, as Spiller put it 'the consequences of the loose and offhand way of writing usually indulged in by those who are bound to furnish a certain quantity of writing in a certain time' had already angered Soane.[53] Although William Beckford had heard that Britton was 'the most agreeable, lively, continentalish and knowing little personage in the world' and entrusted him with publishing one of the accounts of Fonthill Abbey,[54] Britton's prolific output made him careless. Yet he had already argued in his columns for an adjudicating architect among the Commission for the New Churches, quoting Soane on the subject, and so was justifiably pointing out that Soane's initial church designs were lacklustre, betraying his unhappiness at such a cut-price approach to commissioning new buildings. The criticism was perfectly valid.

The Act for Building New Churches of 1818 was a response to the exploding new urban population and they were to be funded out of a £1 million allocation. The limit for each was a paltry £20,000. The cheeseparing spirit of the funding was frustrating. The architects produced 'ideal' designs as models: Soane submitted just two designs to the commissioners; one gothic, one classical. Nash submitted ten (in both styles) and Smirke four – all variants on the Greek Revival. In the end each built churches for the commissioners; Smirke's both in and out of London, Nash's two (one of which was All Souls, Langham Place) and Soane's three in London. In order of construction his churches were St Peter's Walworth (1823–5) (fig. 183), Holy Trinity, Marylebone (1824–6) and St John's Bethnal Green (1826), although he had first considered the design of Holy Trinity as early as 1820.

By December 1821, Soane's paranoid tendencies were at their worst. Even Gandy was now considered an enemy, having been in friendly contact with Britton, whom Soane still believed to be harbouring the identity of his assailant.[55] Gandy had also miscalculated badly by supporting John Britton's suggestion that Soane might consider using the repentant George's services 'to . . . prevent or answer, anonymous letters and fastidious newsmongers'.[56] The author of 'Death Blows', the wicked articles that had contributed to Eliza Soane's death, was hardly a good choice to defend Soane from malicious criticism. Finally Soane accused Gandy of passing off his designs as his own, which was 'absurd', an accusation 'the same as treason by a minister against his king. Did I not respect you beyond myself?'[57]

183. St Peter's Walworth, 1823–5, the least compromised of Soane's cut-price Commissioners' churches.

16

POLISHING AND PURCHASING

In the spring of 1823 Soane was approaching seventy but showed no signs of preparation for retirement. As Rowland Burdon put it, 'you are much more like the man of 1778 in Sicily, than your friend'.[1] Nevertheless Burdon felt that Soane was more preoccupied by professional matters than he should be 'at our period of life'; he, a 'laughing philosopher', was content to accept the onset of age and slow down. But Burdon's actions belied his words; three years later he was trying to encourage Soane to join him in a visit to the latest engineering wonder, Thomas Telford's suspension bridge over the Menai Straits, 'the great lion of North Wales',[2] and in the 1830s became embroiled in a project to modernise the harbour at Hartlepool and link it by rail to the nearby coalfields.

At least Soane was winding down his country house work. His final commission in 1822 was Pell Wall in Shropshire, for Purney Sillitoe, a wealthy London iron merchant. The link seems to have come through Mrs Sillitoe, formerly Miss Davies.[3]

The new house, for which the plans were settled in May 1822 and which would take Soane on nine long journeys to Market Drayton between then and autumn 1828, exacted 'his best energies' but it was to be the end of 'his private professional labours'.[4] The discomforts and dangers of long distance travel – particularly by night, a foolhardy practice which 'all especially medical men' condemned, particularly after Soane had been involved in an accident[5] – were more than an elderly man could endure, even one as tough as Soane. On the other hand, at Pell Wall – a job which he published but never exhibited at the Royal Academy (in fact he showed none of the late country houses, nor illustrated or referred to them in the lectures) – he could continue his development of an exaggeratedly personal style.

Soane drew the critics' fire himself in his *Designs for Public and Private Buildings* (1828): 'if the several buildings considered together do not form a suitable and convenient residence for its liberal-minded, wealthy owner and his family, the faults are not to be charged on Mr and Mrs Sillitoe, further than having placed the most unbounded confidence in the professional character of their architect!'

The two lodges, the kitchen garden with garden house and fruit sheds, its walls surmounted by elaborated finials, the stables, offices and the house itself – which cost in all almost £21,000 on completion – were, like

Tyringham thirty years before, the result of his unified vision at the service of a fully supportive client. Even though, unusually, he invited tenders and used a general builder for the shell of the house, the fitting-out was carried out by the trusted team from London – the same men who had worked at Lincoln's Inn Fields, the Bank and many other of his important jobs.[6] Thomas Grundy, the stonemason who had worked on the family tomb, made the chimney-pieces in London. The first clerk of works on the job, Thomas Ward, ran into the usual difficulties with local workmen. Ward had found three joiners 'one of them is a handy man and the other two are but indifferent . . . I fear we shall not get country men to work the mouldings as not any of them have tools sufficient to do good work'.[7] The men, rather than the tools, seem to have been the problem.

Many of the polished Soane details re-emerge at Pell Wall; the generous bow-front overlooking the park, the increasingly abstracted remnants of pilasters and capitals on the external stonework (fig. 184) (as if the front elevation at Pitshanger had been flattened and then stripped off, leaving just its imprint), the dominant top-lit stair, the star-fish vaulting and canopy dome in respectively the ladies' morning room and the lady's dressing-room and the ubiquitous ball-bead mouldings. Yet the meeting of the gothic and the classical in the triangular lodge (fig. 185), with its pointed windows and hexagonal lantern (a miniaturised version of that in the big house), marked another stage on Soane's journey away from the easy reiteration of his domestic repertoire towards the enormous difficulties of an inclusive style. It says much for his vigour in old age that he was prepared to embark on such an untried path.

Soane considered his rightful position to be at the head of his profession working within the public sphere. He had no intention of 'ceasing his labours' in this area and was continually pulled back to his office by unfinished business, above all the prospect of finally building some part of the Palace of Westminster.

The month after Soane's seventieth birthday, his crabby, invalid son John died of consumption in Brighton, leaving his widow Maria with three daughters and a son, another John who had been born a few months earlier at Chelsea. Despite a quarrel prompted by Soane's discovery that John had, the year before, sold £100 of his East India Company stock and given it to George, his father mourned him deeply, although his death cannot have been unexpected, and he visited Brighton twice that autumn. Now Soane had out-lived his eldest son – a terrible fate for a parent. 'Poor John . . . Alas my Dear Boy' he noted on 21 October, the day of his death.[8]

He ordered a fine funeral, organised by John Robins.[9] The coffin, cased in black velvet with brass studs and handles was placed on a hearse pulled by six horses, their heads ornamented with black ostrich feathers. Four pages accompanied the cortège which left Brighton at 5 a.m. on 28 October. On arrival in London it formed a procession, with two further coaches also garbed in black velvet and black ostrich feather plumes. They reached Old St Giles's burial ground at 11 a.m., 'where the remains were deposited by the side of his Dear Mother!'.[10] John's inscription was added to the family *Domus Aeterna* 'eternal home', as Soane later referred to the tomb.

John's shadowy and unfulfilled life, spent unsuccessfully and unenthusiastically carrying out his father's intention that he become a great architect,

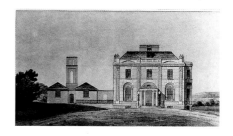

184. Pell Wall, Shropshire. The last of Soane's country houses, it was far more conventional than the estate buildings, see fig. 185.

185. Pell Wall. Here, in a tiny lodge, Soane introduced a novel synthesis of gothic and classical styles.

was over. His small son John rapidly became the object of his grandfather's dynastic plan. Soon old patterns began to re-emerge: John was to study suitable subjects and his grandfather took charge of his schooling. The pressures which had ground his own sons down began to build up over the heads of the next generation. Meanwhile Soane, master of self-deception, immediately began to ease his son's memory back into favour.

The fortnight following John's funeral, Soane returned to his new schemes at Lincoln's Inn Fields. He had only just finalised the purchase of No. 14 for £1,480.[11] The plan was to rebuild the front part of the site, the rent from which would be a secure source of income for his heirs, and to retain the rear in order that he could build a new ground-floor picture room with, below, a set of monkish spaces to elaborate the gothic theme begun at Pitshanger and in a small way at No. 13.

He spent Christmas Eve 1823 'arranging crypt' and a new spate of work ensued. His friends understood the efficacy of the activity; John Taylor had written to him a couple of years earlier, admiring the new arrangement of the Museum. 'I hope it will be long before you are satisfied with it, as the pursuit weans you from thoughts of a very different nature.'[12]

Soane's current programme of transformations at Lincoln's Inn Fields was more self-conscious than those which had preceded it. This house, with or without a member of his family in residence, was now to become a museum – his memorial and a symbol of his individual achievement. If it had begun as a conversation piece, the house now became a family portrait – without the family – as the modern Japanese architect Arata Isozaki has described it.[13] With only the estranged George and two grandsons, too young to become architects in his lifetime, his dynastic hopes were becoming very faint. Soane had no religious belief to support him, only the continuing vitality of his ambition. He would turn his house into an Academy of Architecture, with himself acting as the perpetual Professor of Architecture. Students had been welcome since at least 1812 but now he embarked upon a much more wholehearted attempt to make his house a museum, his collecting activities fuelled by a new sense of purpose.

George Booth Tyndale, Soane's neighbour, heard a hint of plans respecting an intended new house at No. 14 from their mutual friend Mr Pennington. 'As we have continued for so many years on the most neighbourly and friendly terms I am willing to indulge a confident hope that there would be no dimunition of the same at No. 14.' he wrote, circumspectly. He was interested in leasing the new, smaller, house from Soane and giving up possession of No. 12.[14] He offered £150 rent for fourteen years and agreed to a covenant, on a £500 penalty, not to let the house as barristers' chambers. Despite arriving at this agreement the Tyndales never occupied No. 14, their lease was not executed and the house remained empty until Soane entered into a new agreement with the lawyers, Williams and Bethell.[15]

Significantly, for his plans at No. 13, Soane had been back to Harrogate again in 1824 after a six year interval. He paid two visits, the first with Mrs Conduitt and Miss Rowsell, the second with Gandy with whom he was, once more, on the closest of terms.[16] He had, no doubt, taken Gandy to his favourite haunts, the little chapel in the rock and the hermits' caves in the Knaresborough Gorge. Soane was preparing for his most whole-hearted exercise in the gothic yet, helped by the clear eye-

through, as well as pouring down in great shafts from the dome beyond. Here Soane was finally reproducing the effects of Tyringham or the Bank, the use of passages or low-ceilinged vestibules to make dramatic introductions to a major space. Soane had aimed at an effect 'rather solemn than gloomy, and the pictorial breaks of light and shade will be duly appreciated by the students and lovers of art'.[33] Turner seems to have been aiming at similar effects; the 'comparative dungeon' of his dining-room opening into the wonderful lightness of the gallery above.[34] The culmination of these effects was at Dulwich, with a profound dimension added by Soane's thoughts on mortality:

> fancy the Gallery brilliantly lighted for the exhibition of this unrivalled assemblage of pictorial art, – whilst a dull, religious light shews the Mausoleum in the full pride of funeral grandeur, displaying its sarcophagi, enriched with the mortal remains of departed worth, and calling back so powerfully the recollections of past times, that we almost believe we are conversing with our departed friends who now sleep in their silent tombs.[35]

Refracted light and diffused colour, stolen views and reflected space, death, memory and association: Soane was absorbed in perfecting his house during these otherwise grim months, as he became increasingly fearful that he would lose his sight, like his brother.

In fact the condition of Soane's eyes meant that he was ready for surgery. Treatment for cataracts depended on allowing the crust upon the retina to build up to the point at which it could be knocked off, a process known as couching. His operation finally took place in December. Soane was immensely relieved and immediately optimistic about the prospects, although the long term prognosis remained uncertain.

Nothing pointed more clearly to Soane's singular status in the mid-1820s than the interior of his house-museum in Lincoln's Inn Fields. The contrast between the magnificent display of marbles and casts there and Smirke's temporary shed where the newest treasure acquired for the nation by the British Museum, the Elgin Marbles, had been exhibited since 1817, was eloquent.[36]

Meanwhile remarkable Egyptian material was returning to Britain following the 1816–17 mission of Henry Salt, British Consul-General in Egypt. Many of the most spectacular finds had been excavated by Giovanni Belzoni, an Italian hydraulic engineer who had a brief but celebrated career in England as a strong-man, but who had gone to Egypt in 1815 to work for Mohamed Ali, the Pasha of Egypt. One of his tasks was to put into working order a pumping machine presented to the Pasha by the Prince Regent. Belzoni's practical abilities were soon diverted to the excavation and retrieval of some of the greatest finds in the Valley of the Kings, including the Great Temple at Abu Simbel – missions which were funded by Salt. According to B. R. Haydon Belzoni's companion at the heart-stopping moment when he entered the burial chamber of the Pharoah Sethi I, was Henry Beechey, Sir William's son, and Salt's secretary, which suggests that Soane may have had prior notice of their astonishing finds. Sethos, the eponymous hero of the Abbé Terrasson's 1731 novel – upon which *The Magic Flute* was based and which was widely

189. Soane's purchase of the sarcophagus of Sethi I and its display, a short distance from the British Museum who had rejected it, was one of his master-strokes. In 1825 he gave a three-day party to celebrate the acquisition.

known and translated – had given rise to the Egyptian symbolism within freemasonry, another reason for Soane's interest.[37]

The jewel among the treasures shipped to England in 1821 was Sethi's alabaster sarcopaghus (fig. 189). The tomb had been robbed and the cover broken, but even so, the huge translucent casket with its indecipherable and intricate hieroglyphics was a magical object. Yet, despite their involvement in Salt's mission, the trustees of the British Museum, led by Sir Joseph Banks, lost nerve in the face of Salt's initial valuation of £8,000 for his trophies. Some argued for the purchase, including the Earl of Hardwicke's nephew, Charles Philip Yorke, who declared that it would be a national disgrace if the collection were to be lost to an overseas buyer. In the meantime, at the Egyptian Hall on Piccadilly the unstoppable William Bullock constructed a one-sixth scale plaster of Paris model of the tomb, coloured after Belzoni's drawings and lit as if at the moment of his entry, in an exhibition which ran, with great success, for a year.[38]

Finally in 1822 the museum trustees agreed to pay £2,000 for the entire collection – except for the sarcophagus to which Belzoni claimed part-ownership. He valued it alone at £3,000 and they declined it. Among the eleven trustees present at the meeting were Sir Charles Long, Sir Humphry Davy, Henry Bankes MP,[39] Richard Payne Knight and Soane's next-door neighbour, George Booth Tyndale (a legal Trustee for the Cotton family).

Belzoni died in west Africa in December 1823 and did not live to see the outcome. Soane asked for first refusal and Tyndale acted as his intermediary.[40] In April 1824, one month after Bankes had instigated a Select Committee investigation of Soane's new Law Courts at Westminster, his offer of £2,000 was accepted – the purchase price of the *entire* remainder of the Egyptian collection. On 12 May Soane noted 'sarcophagus bought this day'. It was Soane's most flamboyant acquisition yet; possibly, too, a gesture of defiance to the most persistent of his critics.

After his purchase of the Belzoni sarcophagus, as Soane always called his treasure, he bought a number of smaller items, also associated with Belzoni, from the Yarnold sale in 1825. He was also very aware of Napoleon's strong *égyptomanie*. Like many in England, Soane had admired Napoleon's use of the 1798 Egyptian campaign to further archaeological and antiquarian interests.

Soane's admiration for Napoleon was, as we have seen, long-standing and intense, greatly fuelled by his two visits to Paris. Soane's hero-worship was uncritical and apolitical and took in, without any sense of paradox, the mesmerising figure of Josephine, elevated and then wronged, a very romantic heroine. Soane's collection of Napoleonic items – prints and paintings, books and drawings, sculptural casts and bronzes, medals and even a pistol said to have been presented to Napoleon by the Tsar at Tilsit – represented aspects of the great man's career from start to ignominious finish. Soane pondered Napoleon's achievements and personality with increased attention after his death in 1821. Later, in the *Description* of his house, he devoted an entire section to his Napoleonic collection, complete with the provenance of the major items. Among Soane's three most precious possessions left in his will of 1834 to his grandson John and his descendents 'as heirlooms' was a ring with a strand of Napoleon's hair.

The question arises, when the massed ranks of his heroes are seen displayed in his Museum, whether they were there to humble Soane in the presence of greatness – as in Alexander Pope's Temple of Fame – or to provoke a flattering comparison. Despite his own enormous egotism, the towering figures in the arts and literature, Shakespeare (to whom he paid homage with his Shakespeare Recess on the stairs at Lincoln's Inn Fields in 1829) and Milton or the busts of Raphael and Michelangelo which he had wanted to flank his own (fig. 190) in the final arrangement at Lincoln's Inn Fields, held Soane in thrall.[41] They were figures who represented his aspirations but even he could not see them as peers.

There was also a personal dimension as Shakespeare's *King Lear* evoked for Soane the tragedy of his own life, a man almost destroyed by the acts of his own children. Soane's admiration for Jean-Jacques Rousseau, a genius self-consciously at odds with his society and the man who held that reason and sensibility were not inimical, was enduring. Similarly, Le Sage's fictional Gil Blas, a figure continually undermined by circumstance was to become an *alter ego* for Soane (and many others, William Beckford included).[42] Continually baffled by the gulf between his own expectations (in particular, of his genius) and reality, Soane sought empathy, rather than insight, from his literary or fictional heroes. Soane's own contradictions were mirrored in the puzzling conundrum offered by the personality and achievements of his fallen hero Napoleon.

As well as his faith in his heroes, Soane enjoyed the company of the famous and in March 1825, he held a massive three-day party.[43] Guests were invited to view the 'Belzoni Sarcophagus and other antiquities . . . by lamplight'. The centre-piece was by then triumphantly in place in the basement (having come in through the back wall).[44] The sarcophagus was Soane's coup as a collector and his most expensive single purchase, symbolising the 'human industry and perseverence' of its makers, celebrating antiquity and mystery (in particular freemasonic mystery). The event was, in every sense, a personal and professional celebration for Soane. It marked the fine state of his house-museum and his own optimism and activity, after the professional setbacks of 1824, enhanced by his restored eye sight.

890 invitations were sent out for the party. John Britton helped with the practical arrangements, the two pupils[45] and his assistant George Bailey with the preparations and writing invitations. The doors opened at eight o'clock, with tea, coffee and cakes for the guests, who would have dined beforehand. Soane organised the lighting himself. Only the ground floor and basement were illuminated, with over one hundred specially ordered lamps, chandeliers and candelabra. In the breakfast room Soane depended largely on the mirrors (fig. 191) (of which there were by then more than a hundred) to reflect the two five-light candelabra. The exterior of the house was hung with 'bucket' and 'barrel' lamps. Enormous quantities of wax lights and candles were ordered.[46]

Soane could now fully enjoy the shimmering light and dramatic effects, no longer blurred images on a foggy retina. Illuminated, both inside and out, the house and its central trophy glowing at the very core of the space[47] (its transparency, when lit from inside, was commented upon by Belzoni in his original account of the discovery) became a thrilling display of intense shadow and luminous contrasts.

190. Soane's bust by Chantrey. 'Will you come to me on Thursday morning and bring your head with you?', he wrote to his friend Soane on 15 May 1827.

James Christie the younger – the man who had sold Pitshanger Manor for Soane – accepted his invitation enthusiastically; commenting that to see the collection by lamplight would help his own speculations upon the lamplight exhibition at Eleusis. (Gandy had painted a scene of Eleusis for Soane.) Soane's friends and guests would never forget the evening. Newspapers recorded the 'distinguished fashionables', from the worlds of politics, royalty, literature and art as well as countless beautiful women. Turner jostled with Coleridge and the phrenologist Spurzheim. On the first night Mrs Belzoni[48] was a guest and on the last, Robert Peel. On the grandest evening of all, Saturday, 26 March, Lord and Lady Liverpool, Sir Thomas Lawrence and Sir Charles Long were among the throng of dignitaries, from home and abroad. As Soane well knew, 13 Lincoln's Inn Fields was an eloquent statement to the committees of taste, the jealous architects, his detractors and, above all, to his surviving but outcast son George (fig. 192).

B. R. Haydon, writing to the novelist Miss Mitford,[49] conjured up a

Cretan labyrinth; curious narrow staircases, landing places, balconies, spring doors, and little rooms filled with fragments to the very ceiling. It was the finest fun imaginable to see the people come in to the library after wandering about below, amidst tombs and capitals, and shafts, and noiseless heads, with a sort of expression of delighted relief at finding themselves again among the living and with coffee and cake . . . smirking up to Soane *lui faisant leurs compliments* with a twisting chuckle of features as if grateful for their escape.

Pushed up against the 'red face and white waistcoat' of Turner, Haydon turned to see the Duke of Sussex asthmatically 'squeezing and wheezing along the narrow passage, driving all the women before him like a Blue-Beard, and putting his royal head into the coffin'.

Later Mrs Hofland evoked the memorable scene. 'By degrees this space becomes peopled – figure after figure emerges from the crypt and corridors, where they had loitered in the gloom: they assemble round the sarcophagus, which sheds from within a pale, unearthly light upon the silent, awe-struck beings that surround it . . . the rank and talent of this country' but, she continues, 'Had any of one of that . . . company been placed *alone* in the sepulchral chamber, at the 'witching hour of night' . . . it is probable that even the healthiest pulse would have been affected with the darker train of emotions.'[50]

One person missing from the splendid celebration was George Dance – he had died in January 1825, after some years of failing health, aged eighty-five. His son Charles wrote to Soane immediately; 'my beloved father expired without the least apparent pain, and as quietly as if he was asleep . . . I think you will be glad to hear that I have determined upon his being buried in *St. Pauls*'.[51] The difficulties between the old master and pupil were long forgotten and Soane willingly bought Dance's architectural drawings for £500 when they were offered to him in 1836, including a special cabinet in which they were stored. He was fittingly recording the heaviest debt of his professional life. Soane also inherited Dance's position as a trustee of the Royal Academy.

So near to the British Museum, its trustees fiddling while fine objects slipped through their fingers, Soane's collection was now vying with theirs.

It was mentioned in London guidebooks and interested individuals beat a path to his door. Margaret Tyndale, his former neighbour and tenant, had been amused when passing to see several people sketching his house.[52] Meanwhile at the British Museum the rebuilding stumbled forward in fits and starts (fig. 193), in Smirke's increasingly frustrated hands, a job which proved little easier than Soane's own work at the Houses of Parliament. Soane must have felt a degree of *schadenfreude*. Hamstrung by the Treasury and earnestly protecting themselves from public outcry over any apparent extravagance, the Trustees were indecisive and nervous, and the new Museum did not materialise until after Soane's death.

As he adjusted to the loss of John, rose-tinting his memories, Soane's relations with his daughter-in-law deteriorated. Although he now turned his dynastic hopes to little John Soane, he also began a poisonous correspondance with Maria, accusing her of deception and lies and of taking the house at Chelsea from him.[53] None of her reasoned replies satisfied him. Before long, several of the officers at Chelsea began to intercede on her behalf. Colonel Le Blanc wrote in her defence in August 1824 and again in September, pointing out the strength and legitimacy of her claims upon the grandfather of her children. Over the coming months Maria Soane reported to her father-in-law on her reduction in household expenses and her economies in schooling her daughters. Soane's only concession was that when young John was five, or earlier if she wanted, he would 'charge myself with the care of his education and every expense attending him . . . as I do for my other Grandson'.[54] Soane continued to deluge Maria with implacably cruel letters. She had no option but to remain in contact and in November 1825 wrote to him from Chertsey to report on William's worsening health. Mrs Clark in Chertsey had earlier told Mrs Conduitt – who had offered to go immediately to help – that William was now 'quite blind' as well as helpless. Soane's brother died on 1 December.[55]

Soane's mercurial temperament was not always obvious. Charles Mathews, who had been a pupil of Augustus Pugin, was the son of the famous comedian and impersonator of the same name, a friend of Soane's. He warmed to him: 'I contrived to ingratiate myself into the old gentleman's good graces, for he was by no means easy of access, but he took quite a fancy to me, and gave me unceasing proofs of his goodwill.'[56] Soane took young Mathews along to the Bank and encouraged him to make sketches of the construction, while offering him valuable advice. 'He was a most singular old man.' Soane granted Mathews unrestricted admission at all times to his 'marvellous gallery . . . his portfolios and splendid library'.

One day, unnervingly, he crossed an invisible line. Seeing the 'Death Blows', the black bordered display of George's fatal words in the *Champion*, Mathews, sitting at Soane's bedside while he had breakfast, naïvely 'ventured to expostulate with him on the sad spectacle. . . and urged him to remove this constant reminder of his wrongs, and remonstrated with him upon the impropriety of keeping alive vindictive feelings, which, if left to time, might gradually become extinct'. Immediately 'he put me in my place . . . with a burst of ungovernable passion, and I took care never again to recur to a subject which was the height of presumption in me to have approached at all'. In the early 1830s, Mathews became a district sur-

191. Detail of the dressing-room, off Soane's study (fig. 212) at 13 Lincoln's Inn Fields; the skylight (rimmed with angled mirror glass) is a miniature of the lantern which Soane designed for the Freemasons' Hall.

192. A view of the museum, the heart of 13 Lincoln's Inn Fields, showing the Belzoni sarcophagus in the distance, see also fig. 189.

193. George Scharf's drawing of the building of Robert Smirke's British Museum in July 1828.

veyor, leaving an unusually entertaining record of the thankless job ('Shades of Vitruvius! was this architecture?'), before turning to the stage, where he prospered.

Soane's simmering fury with George and his hapless daughter-in-law Maria, his continual fear of blindness and further printed criticism combined to explosive effect in these years. An attack in 1824, published in *Knight's Quarterly Magazine*, was in Arthur Bolton's phrase, comparable to 'boys who tie kettles to the tails of cats'[57] and unworthy of his prolonged attention but drove Soane into paroxyms of rage and the determination to find of the perpetrator.

The writer begins with Soane's work in Regent Street, 'the Emporium of Messrs Robins and Co., Auctioneers and Land Agents', crediting him with a new, sixth Order, the Boeotian, 'his own *invention* and not a revival'. Specifically, the 'Bœotian Order' – the word derived from a distant corner of Greece thought to have been populated by rustics and bumpkins – involves suspension of the classical rules of propriety, as between the relative proportions of columns and pilasters and the apparent lack of support for the roof structure, 'leav[ing] the arch miraculously suspended by the back, like the stuffed crocodile on the ceiling of a museum'. The instances given are the picture room at Lincoln's Inn Fields and the new Law Courts. The writer notes the 'immense field which . . . opens to invention'. Citing a variety of Soane's particular touches, he wonders is the Professor a geologist, botanist, conchologist, astronomer, undertaker, *and* optician? The coloured glass in the courts will 'shed the yellow hue of guilt on the face of a criminal, and the rosy tint of modesty on the face of a barrister'.

Other targets include the front of 13 Lincoln's Inn Fields, ornamented with the *spolia opima* of Westminster (the gothic corbels), the Rotunda at the Bank, where the author mentions a problem with the acoustics, 'this sacrifice of the convenient to the beautiful . . . in defiance of the lungs of stock-brokers, and the Babel-stunned ears of the public'. Then follow aspersions on Soane as a wrecker and despoiler of ancient buildings and mockery of his publications.

Soane, he writes, has been courageous: 'unmoved by the *Brutum fulmen* of this parliamentman's oratory, or the perilous pop-gun of this pressgangman's ridicule'. A skit on Gray's *Ode to Eton College* becomes an *Ode on a distant prospect of Dulwich College,* with 'Chimney groups that fright the sweep, and *acroteria* fifty deep.' Alluding to the current Westminster dispute ('where saving *Bankes* doth rise, Catching the Speaker's eye, to make *The Courts* a sacrifice . . . [but] Shall hard *Sir Charles's*[Long] alter'd eye, Mock the great plans he lately prais'd?'), the writer appears to be offering a measure of support to Soane. He did not see it in that light. The suspected writer was Thomas Stedman Whitwell, a student whom Soane had turned down as an assistant for his lecture illustrations and whom he had earlier suspected as the author of of the *Guardian* attacks.[58] In 1825 the embittered Whitwell joined Robert Owen in America to design his Utopian settlement of New Harmony but left again in 1826 'excited by disappointed pride, ambition and revenge'.[59] On his return he built the Brunswick Theatre in London which collapsed spectacularly in 1828.[60]

Soane again unwisely took recourse in the law, mounting an action against the publisher, Knight, despite having been advised not to rise to 'a . . . dreary exhibition of a feeble and perverted mind'. His lawyer pointed out that 'the law has no sympathy with personal feeling unless . . . the aggravation tends to a breach of the peace'. Such a prosecution only drew attention to the author, usually to his advantage. Nevertheless Soane subpœnaed Colonel Stephenson of the Office of Works to give evidence on his behalf. In June 1827 he lost his case, a conclusion which took seven hours to reach, and was ordered to pay Knight's defence costs. The action cost him £211 7s 10d[61] and gained him no credit. James Elmes, always willing to see the best in Soane, suggested that it had been his 'painful disease of the eyes' which had driven him to this unwise action.

While Soane had been immersed at 13 Lincoln's Inn Fields, J.M.W. Turner had been painting a work for the house. *Forum Romanum for Mr Soane's Museum* (fig. 194) was shown at the Royal Academy in 1826. The critics did not welcome Turner's newly introduced 'intolerable yellow hue . . . whether boats or buildings, water or watermen, houses or horses, all is yellow, yellow, nothing but yellow, violently contrasted with blue.'[62] Turner, unabashed, was proud to have taken '*all* yellow to my keeping this year'.

Tentatively he asked Soane 500 guineas for the painting. Although he cheerfully and honourably paid the agreed price Soane wrote to Turner 'the picture did not suit the place or the place the picture'. Turner took its rejection in good part, 'I like candour and my having said that if you did not like it when done I would put it down in my book of Time!!'[63] Picture and cheque remained in Turner's possession, while in its place in the picture room before long hung a huge cool, north Italian lakescape by Callcott, Turner's friend.

Turner's move to a Mediterranean glowing light had not been unannounced. George Basevi wrote to Soane of his growing admiration for Turner, noting that 'without having even ever visited Italy, he has devised the effect of an Italian sun, and borders on the eastern'.[64] Now after his 1819 visit to Rome – when he had, perhaps, hoped to visit the Forum with Soane beside him – Turner offered him a recompense for his missed opportunity to revisit Rome and a demonstration of what that city now meant to him, in large part thanks to his friend's introduction. The framed view, a structural version of Gandy's sweeps of theatrical curtaining or possibly a nod to Soane's penchant for buildings seen through screens and arches, included the Arch of Titus (seen before its 1822 restoration, crusted with knobbly accretions) and a panoramic view of that most evocative scene of Roman antiquity, the Forum itself. Unlike Turner's other large scale Italian compositions, compilations of architecture, history and myth, such as the *Rome from the Vatican* or the *Bay of Baiae with Apollo and the Sibyl* he had restrained himself, representing the scene much as it stood.

There were, perhaps, clues for Soane in the composition, such as the priestly file of figures to amuse the anti-cleric and the perfect inscription and lettering on the arch (corrected just before he sent it to the Royal Academy) to please Soane's love of the marks of antiquity. (There was also a cryptic set of letters on a stone block in the foreground A[ ]GM[ ] SRMMPA). It was a composition not just for the museum but for Soane himself.

Knowing each other as they did, there was no bad feeling when Soane rejected *Forum Romanum*, perhaps on the grounds of the over-heated tones or its non-conformity to the plan for the room. Soane's hang was as care-

194. J.M.W. Turner *Forum Romanum for Mr Soane's Museum* which Soane rejected, perhaps because of its strong yellow tones, its large dimensions or its subject matter. The painting, a celebration of Turner's journey in 1819, brings together the major buildings of antique Rome while offering a reminder of modern Roman Catholicism.

fully considered as the architecture itself. Later George Jones's painting of the *Opening of London Bridge* hung near the large Turner which Soane purchased in 1831, the calm, Dutch scene of Admiral Van Tromp's barge at the entrance to the Texel. It was as if Turner had painted a tonal rejoinder to the Callcott. Jones noted, 'even Turner's picture is improved by your arrangement and where his can be mended mine must be made'.

When Sir Thomas Lawrence died in 1830 Soane sent his carriage and servants to the funeral on 20 January, to mark his respects. The next year Soane wrote to Turner at the Royal Academy, offering £1,000 towards the purchase of Lawrence's Old Master drawings. It was more self-revealing than many of his letters. 'Allow me to add a few words. Success, my dear Sir, has caused me many enemies, always anxious to ascribe improper motives to my conduct; I shall therefore, that I may not be misunderstood, take this opportunity to state briefly the principles on which I have acted.' He then recites his familiar litany, beginning with the years of study in Italy under the auspices of George III and Sir William Chambers, his desire to mark his 'debt of gratitude never to be forgotten' and ending 'In the same feeling – to a sincere regard for the Fine Arts, and the grateful recollection of what I owe the Royal Academy for favours conferred in early youth, and subsequent honours, I have been induced to make the offer contained in this letter.'[65]

The letter mirrors exactly the spirit of the thirty-one-year-old Turner's introductory words to his first Royal Academy lecture series: 'I cannot look back but with pride and pleasure to that time, the Halcyon perhaps of my days, when I received instruction within these walls; and listened, I hope I did, with a just sense and respect.'[66] The two great individualists in painting and architecture of their era, spoke with one voice on the remarkable start in life that the Royal Academy had offered them.

A perplexed, but intrigued, visitor to 13 Lincoln's Inn Fields in 1826 was the Prussian architect Karl Friedrich Schinkel.[67] He noted the extraordinary proliferation of objects, ingeniously exhibited, crammed into a tiny space and yet lit both from above and from the side. 'Medieval, antique and modern works are intermingled at every level; in courtyards resembling cemeteries, and in chapel-like rooms, in catacombs and drawing-rooms, ornamented in Herculanean and Gothic styles. Everywhere little deceptions.' Schinkel appreciated the theatrical element in all this, the quality of the collection (he commented on the Belzoni sarcophagus and the two Hogarth series in particular) and the complexity of the labyrinthine arrangements within little more than a 'Second Rate' London terraced house spilling out at the rear into a pair of adjacent yards.

Schinkel also visited the Bank of England where Soane's programme was almost complete. Between 1823 and 1826 he had rebuilt the remaining, southern stretches of outer wall, particularly those on Threadneedle Street (fig. 195). The first designs show their elaborated outlines following the new synthesised gothic-classical forms which he had applied at Pell Wall. The Bank, now employing 900 staff on the site, was the object of great attention. All visitors to the City of London included it on their itineraries, along with the Guildhall, the Mansion House and the other key monuments of the area. Schinkel joined them; on 1 June 1826 he noted 'Bank, many rounded corners, Corinthian, handsome courtyard, much that is useless, a simple set of pillars divides two courtyards, one of the triumphal arches is the best thing about the building.' There is no evidence that he went inside the Bank and so his comments (thoughts confined to a private journal and in German) – in marked contrast to his admiration for the stern production of Robert Smirke at the British Museum – do not reflect his thoughts upon the remarkable sequence of interiors (fig. 196), large and small, that was now complete within.

Elmes and Shepherd's *Metropolitan Improvements* (1828) heaped praise on the Bank. In a style 'at once masculine, appropriate and novel' Soane's complex redevelopment of a difficult site, an irregular rhomboidal figure, offered 'stability and strength, harmony and apt decoration and above all appropriateness or fitness of means to its ends'. There was high praise for the Tivoli corner and for the external walls where he 'carried on his bold design upon a lofty base, emulating the beauties of his predecessor Vanburgh, whose talent Mr Soane has often honoured in his lectures'.

With Joint Stock companies now free to set up business anywhere beyond a 65 mile radius of the City, the Bank needed to adopt a countrywide system itself. It was essential to increase the circulation of notes to the provinces and to protect itself against competitors.[68] Soane's work for the Bank was, from now on, largely outside London. George Bailey and Walter Payne crossed the country, first to Gloucester, then to Manchester, Swansea, Birmingham and many more towns. Soane himself went to Liverpool (no doubt after a visit to Pell Wall). First they had to survey existing buildings and then decide whether new premises were needed or if the old ones be adapted. In many ways this would have been the obvious moment for Soane to retire but with such able lieutenants he could still do the work, without the continuous travel.

In March 1827 Robert Fellowes offered Soane his advice.

I well know what you will feel on giving up your professional business, but yet I cannot but recommend you to do so . . . I wish you to retire to the society of your family and friends, the *Otium cum Dignitate*. Though you will certainly be deprived of many of your present enjoyments, yet you will get rid of much uneasiness . . . I hope when you have retired . . . I shall be alive to see you here.[69]

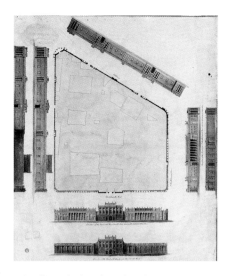

195. Soane's drawing, dated 1823, showing the outer, screen walls of the Bank of England completed – his last major programme of work on the site.

196. Soane's Four Per Cent Office of 1818–23, a refined version of the earlier banking halls of the 1790s. The corner piers now melt into the pendentives and the roof light has become a tiered cupola. See also figs 102 and 124.

Maria Cosway, by now esconced in a convent at Lodi, wondered in her New Year letter in 1825 whether he would ever visit Italy again and offered him 'a room as English as it can be made here'. By August 1826 she realised that her old friend was now unlikely to make the journey. 'But you are too heavy in wealth and work to move so quickly. Is it not true?' It was then almost fifty years since they had first met and she continued to write until 1835, still hoping that he might visit her, and commiserating about a sorrow that they shared, failing eyesight.

Whatever Soane's state of health, he battled on. His instincts for self-preservation, as often with the heavily self-absorbed, were strong. Friends came to the house regularly, sure of a welcome from Sally Conduitt even if Soane was feeling out of sorts. Haydon called one summer evening; he found him 'crabbedly good-natured and happy to see me . . . On Soane's chimney piece were bits of paper to light candles with, crumpled architecturally in his peculiar style.'[70] Soane's architectural idiosyncrasies infected everything about him.

In March 1827 little John Soane was christened in the chapel at Chelsea Hospital, with Maria's brother and the kindly Colonel Spicer, the deputy treasurer of Chelsea Hospital and an unfailingly sympathetic friend to Maria, standing as his godfathers. His grandfather replied to the invitation with bad grace, saying he was surprised that he had not been baptised already. He neither accepted nor refused, but did not attend. A few months later Maria wrote to tell him that she had received a proposal of marriage from Lieutenant-General Sir Frederick Robinson. Soane further distanced himself by responding in the third person; 'Not having been consulted on her first marriage he cannot interfere with any subsequent arrangement Mrs John Soane may be advised to make.'[71] She did not remarry – the General could not obtain a home posting – and the difficult dealings with her father-in-law over John's education continued. In 1829 John went to Mr Morice's small school at Parsons Green and moved to a school in Thames Ditton attended by Colonel Spicer's son in 1833.

As John grew up, Soane became more involved in his life and virtually ignored George's existence apart from his quarterly £50 payment. George's engagement at Drury Lane had been extended for three years 'on the same terms' – confirmed on 12 January 1825 – and his adaptation of Carl Maria von Weber's *Der Freischutz* was the fifth and most successful version to be seen in London, running for seventy-two nights. George described his work (a romantic opera in three parts) as 'partly original and partly altered from the German opera of Friedrich Kind'; and with its impressive special effects of thunder, lightning, meteors, eclipses, transformations of trees to men and skeletons to dust, it would have been churlish to bemoan the loss of the original story or the deficiencies of the music.[72] For the Christmas season a pantomime based on the Incantation scene was introduced to extend the appeal of the melodrama to another popular audience. For one visitor, Henry Crabb Robinson, the latter was greatly preferable to the main attraction ('a tiresome performance').[73]

Among the audience, the French painter Eugène Delacroix was struck by Clarkson Stanfield's and David Roberts's sets; of the many extraordinary effects, the torrent of water which became a column of fire had impressed him most. Schinkel also saw the production. He was very critical; 'dreadful depiction of the Wolfs' Glen, poor musical performance', but thought the theatre very fine. He might have been surprised to know the connection between the adapter of Schiller's work and the architect of the Bank, which he had revisited that morning.[74]

George Soane's verse tragedy, *Masaniello*, was his next offering: Elliston accepted it although he was blind drunk during the reading. Kean, back from a tour of America, took the lead part, on horseback (animals were popular props, then as now). On its opening on 17 February it was denigrated. 'Kean made no exertion whatever and assisted in the condemnation.' It ended early, without prologue or epilogue, and the following evening Kean requested that it not be repeated. Elliston's handling of the theatre was as out of control as his life. Winston's post-mortem of the 1825 season, well-attended but unprofitable, noted 'the successful pieces so huddled upon one another . . . as to ruin both, others brought out without any chance of success . . . and, to crown all . . . a piece [*Masaniello*] badly written by a once great author, against which there was a national prejudice'. He does not clarify if the prejudice was against the subject matter, a stirring seventeenth-century tale of a Neapolitan fisherman turned revolutionary, or the author.

Fortunately, George had greater success with another adaptation that season. His melodrama *Faust* was based (very loosely) upon his own partial translation of Goethe's work, which had been approved by the author. It opened on 16 May 1825. Again Delacroix saw, and wondered, at the staging – by Stansfield, Roberts and Marinari. Daniel Terry, who played Mephistopheles, had assisted in writing some of the dialogue and various characters had been added to flesh out the piece. Crabb Robinson, who was in the audience on 19 May, was unimpressed. 'This piece has borrowed the name of Wagner from Goethe but not a tittle remains besides . . . though the sarcastic tone of Mephistopheles partakes of the character of Goethe's hero.' George Soane had already given a devilish figure the characteristics of his father.[75]

George had added an apologetic prologue, adding 'For the greatest that learning or genius e'er knew,/Their minds from Romance the first nourishment drew.' The *Times* judged it 'trash' but other judges concurred in considering *Faust* too refined and subtle to be staged at all and found it, in the circumstances, a good 'serious pantomime' in the apt term used by the *New Monthly Magazine*. By December 1826 it had been performed fifty times. George Soane's *Faust* was the favoured version for a later production in New York, from which, presumably, he drew no financial benefit.[76]

The company George kept was, as his father well knew from his own dealings with Drury Lane, a collection of theatrical dissolutes. Elliston's drinking and extra-marital affairs (he fathered a child by a fifteen-year-old just before his wife's death) were only challenged by Kean's who, if minded, could wreck a play in a night. In such circumstances, Drury Lane's contractual agreement with George Soane was worth nothing as he soon found at the end of Elliston's last season.

As Soane's eyesight worsened again, the twenty-four-year-old George Wightwick, a friend of the Beechey family, became Soane's amanuensis in the autumn of 1826. After a punishing interview, which reduced

Wightwick to tears, Soane changed tone and told him he had liked his simple and well-expressed letter, thought he could be useful and asked him if he would accompany him to Bath. They agreed to meet there at nine in the morning the following Tuesday.

On arrival Wightwick found Soane at a table with his writing things, a screen dimming the direct light thrown from the window. He stood between the screen and the fire. 'He was certainly distinguished-looking; taller than common; and so thin as to appear taller . . . He was dressed entirely in black.' An impressive figure with a black velvet waistcoat, knee breeches and silk stockings and a frilled shirt, he had not followed fashion, by then short jackets over long trousers, but 'the Professor unquestionably *looked* the Professor and the gentleman.' A brown wig compounded the anachronistic dress.

Wightwick read to Soane in the evening as well as working in his office by day (mostly transferring Soane's anger over the House of Lords and other disappointments into coherent prose) and sensed the old man's desperate need to retain his professional identity. His account of his time with Soane in the winter of 1826–7 is an illuminating, intimate portrait. Soane went from Bath to Pell Wall and they remet in London, where the routine continued. Wightwick found him sympathetic and terrifying in almost equal measure. Having been treated miserably all day in the office, working without break and buffeted by a succession of furies and moods, which changed from one hour to the next, he was disconcerted to be offered a glass of wine and treated civilly as he settled down to read the familiar passages from *Gil Blas* in French. From behind the screen, which now shielded his strained eyes from fire and candle glare, there came 'in a tone of admiring and compassionate interest, "P-o-o-r Gil!"' as well as occasional corrections to his pronunciation. Sometimes *Gil Blas* was replaced by a recitation of Soane's miseries and his conviction that he was dying of a broken heart. Having guided him up to his bedroom with a candle, Wightwick, exhausted by the vicissitudes of the day, went back to his boarding-house to entertain his fellow occupants with his tales.

George Bailey and others around Soane did their best to ease Wightwick through the rough patches but he could stand it no longer. He left a letter of resignation and went without notice. Soane returned from the Bank, in excellent spirits, and addressed a young assistant, mistaking him for Wightwick. Informed that he had left, nothing more was said. Some weeks later, he inquired after him and sent a message that he would be very pleased to see him again. Later Wightwick called with a copy of his book *Select Views of the Roman Antiquities* and Soane gave him considerably more than the price of the book and asked him to be sure to call again and tell him how he was getting on.[77]

One of Soane's recent commissions at the Office of Works had been to rehouse the Insolvent Debtors' Court (fig. 197) from its premises on Essex Street to a house across the square from Soane's, 33 Lincoln's Inn Fields backing on to Portugal Street. The new building that eventually opened on the site in 1825 greatly pleased the First Commissioner in Bankruptcy who praised both the new facilities and its architecture.[78] Since changes in the law, from 1813, a small debtor could now spend a token period of two months in prison, during which time a schedule of his debts was prepared. He then appeared at the Insolvent Debtors' Court and surrendered his property. George must have become all too familiar with the court.

In *The Pickwick Papers* Charles Dickens described the depressing scene some years later; 'a lofty room, badly lighted and worse ventilated' with 'three or four gentlemen in wigs . . . a box of barristers on their right hand . . . an enclosure of insolvent debtors on their left'. The Commissioners of the court sat in front. The people, like the place, were seedy, a mixture of the indigent, the fraudulent and the genuinely impoverished, abandoned by changed circumstances.

George was still in touch with Pennington, despite periodic outbursts against him, and wrote to Sarah Smith in 1826 to ask if she had heard of an accident that the doctor had sustained. 'He is now, indeed, recovered but for many days I felt more pain and anxiety on his account than I should be willing to own to himself being quite sure that he would not believe a word of it. With all his oddities, I firmly trust in him as the best and sincerest of friends, and were I ever to be deceived in him, should have no faith in any human being.'[79] George's ability to change his views about people, from positive to negative and back again overnight, was one of the surest proofs of his paternity.

In February 1827 George sold a comedy and two melodramas to a Mr Price for £100, including copyright. Elliston was now at the Surrey Theatre (across Blackfriars Bridge) and George Soane followed him as did Henry Crabb Robinson, that tireless theatre-goer, who went to a play there 'on a mere resource against Ennuie . . . Bad acting – coarse scenery and trumpery pieces'.[80] George's luck was running out. That year saw the first of his many approaches to the Royal Literary Fund.[81]

As often, it was the genuine plight of George's family which moved old family friends to offer help. On 29 November 1827 George's sixteen-year-old daughter Caroline died, after a lengthy illness. In one of the blackest of all the tragic family episodes, Soane had steadfastly refused George's pleas for funds for medicine and a change of scene for his ailing daughter. He even remonstrated with the Reverend Dr George Chisholm, Frederick's schoolmaster, who had agreed to conduct her funeral, and receiving a stinging reply from him; 'I would officiate for a criminal's funeral, if asked'.[82] George could not ask Sarah Smith to come to town (she was tied to Chertsey for reasons only George knew) 'but write to me at all events . . . you are the friend of my mother. All my early recollections are connected with you and your family.'[83] His plea to Soane for Caroline to be buried in the family vault at Old St Giles's burial ground met with no response.

These years saw the end of several of Soane's oldest friendships – more often through dispute than death. He argued bitterly and irrevocably with James Spiller over money (he had advanced him a sizeable mortgage in 1800) – a man almost as irascible as himself but from and with whom he had formulated his strongly held ideas upon the evils of speculative building and other professional matters. He even briefly fell out with the faithful John Taylor. Robert Pennington's support of George made him Soane's enemy for a period; his friend and doctor of forty years wrote wistfully in 1832 that he would like to be 'reinstated in your favour' and soon after, he was readmitted.

John Britton, to whom Soane had entrusted the precious task of publishing an account of 13 Lincoln's Inn Fields to be entitled *The Union of*

197. The Insolvent Debtor's Court on Lincoln's Inn Fields of 1823–5. Soane had argued against Treasury short-sightedness and forced the construction of a purpose-built court rather than the conversion of unsuitable domestic premises.

198. Detail of title page of the first published description of Soane's house, John Britton's ill-fated *Union of Architecture, Sculpture and Painting* (1827). The setting is the Monk's Parlour (see fig. 186).

Architecture, Sculpture and Painting (fig. 198) was continuously treading on eggshells. Overstretched, financially and professionally, he had enlisted W. H. Leeds to assist, 'disposed as we both are to do full justice to your professional works, to the extent of our united judgement and talents'.[84] In fact Soane found both wanting and the folio volume, published in 1827, cost him a great deal – both in advances to Britton and in the disappointment he felt in the final, unsaleable, volume. There were further arguments about the rights to the plates. John Britton's publications on Fonthill and on Deepdene were company Soane had wanted to join but Britton's effort did not satisfy him. Soane decided to follow the example of Horace Walpole, who had published his own account of Strawberry Hill: he would write the description of 13 Lincoln's Inn Fields himself.

Soane also remained confident that he could give his Royal Academy lectures in 1827, writing to Henry Howard that his sight had improved considerably lately 'and is daily improving'. But Pennington, by now himself retired, had warned Soane that reading for even an hour by lamplight (practising to see whether he could deliver the lectures) would risk his total loss of sight and forbade him from doing so. The spectre of near-blindness was terrifying. Robert Fellowes, eleven years his senior sympathised.[85] 'I am very nearly in your situation, not being able to attend to any thing in dark weather, and in the clearest day but for a very short time. I cannot see to read a newspaper of any sort, and scarce any printed book.' Added to that, he was deaf 'so that I am shut out of all society, except of a single person'. He asked why Soane did not retire, 'you will get rid of much uneasiness'. Yet Soane, as Fellowes half suggested, needed his 'present enjoyments', however vexing they were.

The terror induced by failing eyesight was probably often at the root of Soane's illogical rages. Other health problems did not improve his temper. Soane was having difficulties adjusting to some dentures and was an entirely exasperating patient, quick to berate his dentist. A kindly man, the latter wrote that he did not want his fees but just wanted to relieve Soane's problems, which he could only do if he persevered.

In 1829, Soane was corresponding again with Henry Howard about delivering his lectures himself, but was mortified to find his new reading glasses, for which he been waiting impatiently 'after repeated trials' were little better than the old ones. 'This is', he said, 'one of the most serious disappointments of my life . . . I make this communication . . . under a depression of mind more easy to be felt than described – but such is the fate of, dear Sir, your always obliged and faithful, John Soane.'[86] In this mood he embarked upon work on the little Monk's Cell.

But Soane could still harbour hopes of an architectural dynasty as long as there remained a grandson carrying the illustrious name. His Christmas letter in 1828 had been addressed to 'my dear, dear grandchildren' and went on 'I love you all most dearly . . . my dear little boy I hope in a few years you will be a great architect and reap the fruit of your labours'.[87]

17

WESTMINSTER AT LAST

Soane's programme of official work throughout the 1820s and beyond meant that full retirement remained a distant prospect. Despite his failure to find favour with royalty, from 1820 he had been caught up in a succession of state occasions, both tragic and celebratory, in his role as Attached Architect to the Office of Works, responsible for Westminster. The death of George III and the show trial of his daughter-in-law, the spurned Queen Caroline (fig. 199), for which Soane designed a temporary conversion of the House of Lords, were followed by the long postponed Coronation of George IV.

The queen's divorce trial which began on 17 August 1820 required heavy security as well as the adaptation of the House of Lords to accommodate the enormous numbers. Popular sympathy for Queen Caroline was running high and trouble was expected. On the opening morning more than 250 peers entered the House, via Westminster Hall, and the crowd of lawyers, witnesses, pressmen, officials and curious spectators, including many MPs, filled Soane's specially inserted galleries, with their gilded supports, to capacity.[1]

Responsibility for another transformation of Westminster Hall and the adaptation of Westminster Abbey for George IV's coronation, which finally took place on 19 July 1821, also fell to Soane but he told Colonel Stephenson that he would find the burden too much. Once again enmeshed in a spate of criticisms, this time those in the *Guardian*, Soane either intentionally or simply because of his distractions, let the job slip him by. The coronation was a memorable piece of theatre[2] and the king revelled in the occasion, looking, according to B. R. Haydon, like a 'gorgeous bird of the East'. George IV flourished in a theatrical habitat, whether it was the oriental exoticism of Brighton Pavilion or the lavish, overweighted interiors that Nash would provide him at Buckingham Palace. Perhaps Soane had also sensed his own unsuitability as the designer of a suitably florid setting for this coronation.

But it was at the coronation, with Westminster Hall revealed in its full magnificence, cleared of the Court of Chancery and the King's Bench, that Lord Liverpool realised that the remarkable medieval building must be permanently emptied of its occupants and the courts rehoused. The job fell to Soane. An awkward adjacent site squeezed between (and behind) Vardy's irregular Palladian stone building on St Margaret's Street and the

199. The Trial of Queen Caroline by George Hayter, showing the House of Lords as adapted by Soane in 1820.

north-west tower of Westminster Hall and 'trammelled with the [six] buttresses of the Hall' as Soane put it, was allocated for the new court accommodation.[3] By December 1821 he had submitted his plans to the Treasury and two months later, showed his designs to the king.[4]

Soane also knew that the new king felt that the monarch's approach to the House of Lords was insufficiently grand and had remembered George III's liking for an ante-room decorated by a series of triumphant history paintings. The idea of commemorating 'great public actions and distinguished talents', the House of Lords becoming the national site for monuments in preference to Westminster Abbey, was a favourite with Soane.[5] In 1822, having shown his designs for the new law courts to the king, Soane also finally achieved his ambition to work at the House of Lords with a commission to provide a new Royal Entrance, with a grand stair (the Scala Regia as he always called it, in homage to Bernini's stair at the Vatican). 'The new entrance and *Scala Regia*', wrote Brayley and Britton in 1836, 'is said to have originated with his late Majesty, whose taste for shewy and expensive architectural works led him to consider the old entrance to the House of Lords as mean and insignificant, altogether unworthy of forming the passage for a British monarch to his official station at the head of a national legislature.'[6] The additions to the south-west corner of the Palace of Westminster, soon amplified with a gallery and ante-room, closed one of the longest episodes in Soane's career. The work involved demolition of substantial sections of the medieval Palace of Westminster and provoked an outcry in parliament.[7]

Unfortunately Soane's desperate desire to be favoured by the monarchy was widely known – and mocked – and in 1823 a disrespectful ditty was sent anonymously to him, dedicated to 'old Johnny Scragg':

> of that rubbishing nonsense in Old Palace Yard
> Common talk goes to prove the King shows no regard
> . . . More whim and caprice by a mind in disorder
> And which seems on insanity strongly to border.[8]

Meanwhile, in preparing his brief for the new courts Soane had taken great trouble to sound out the views of judges, lawyers and officials on the defects of the old buildings and 'determined to dovetail into my design as many parts of the old Buildings as were capable of alteration and useful repair' – for reasons of economy rather than sensitivity to the existing fabric. He absolved himself of responsibility for the demolition of the sixteenth-century Exchequer Court alongside the hall but his own careful approach was not guided by 'any apprehension of the plaints of a Gayfere, the ravings of a Carter, or the lamentations of a Capon' (three antiquarian watchdogs) but by the functional need to integrate the new and the existing buildings. Gradually a workable scheme evolved. Soane, in his role at the Office of Works, had already worked on and around Westminster Hall. In 1819 he had repaired the gable. His respect for its 'magnificence and unique character' was genuine. Nevertheless, every episode in Soane's troubled history of public commissions suggested that he would choose a classical treatment for the north front of the new Law Courts. He used Vardy's Palladian elevation as his justification but it was also a memorial to his own thirty-year long history of schemes for the

House of Lords. Neither Soane's pride nor his architectural tastes would have allowed him to design the new law courts in flimsy castellated gothic. Soane's recent visit to Paris was fresh in his memory and a classical solution was the only one to offer the appropriate associations.

On 18 March 1824, ironically the anniversary of Soane's journey to Italy, Henry Bankes MP moved for a Select Committee of the House of Commons to examine the new courts, already under construction. Although Bankes saw himself as a guardian of the public purse, at a time when the control of expenditure and bureaucratic expansion were on a collision course, he couched his complaints on stylistic grounds; classical buildings had been 'grafted on to the old Gothic', in 'abominable taste'. Work was suspended. Members of the committee included the Chancellor of the Exchequer (since the previous year) Frederick 'Prosperity' Robinson, Bankes and his antiquarian son, as well as Sir Charles Long. The voice of the self-appointed arbiter of taste has a modern ring to it; Soane was faced with a 'Committee of Taste', interference which would have maddened the most placid of architects, let alone the irascible, bereaved and now near-blind Soane. The committee, advised by the weaselly chancellor, Robinson, who turned on designs he had previously approved, lambasted the 'incongruous style of architecture which thus comes into immediate contact with that magnificent and enriched specimen of Gothic architecture'.

Soane had an intellectual and aesthetic distaste for *ersatz* gothic but also a practical one. As a former pupil, Robert Chantrell, later wrote to Soane from Leeds, 'Even with good proportions this Gothic Architecture requires many decorations to characterise it' and even where there was plentiful good building stone 'the buttresses, pinnacles, indented parapets and other appendages will cause the *expence* of Gothic buildings to exceed considerably that of Grecian or Roman'.[9]

Nothing would placate Soane's critics in the House of Commons.[10] On 23 June demolition of the offending corner began (although construction had not gone far) and the New Palace Yard façade was rebuilt in Soane's most unconvincing Tudor-gothic style, with a stair turret. The ignominy of the demolition rankled and the enforced rebuilding in a weak style which he despised, shamed him deeply: he brought the subject up continually. Yet Soane had to continue to deal personally with Robinson, in 1825 designing the state dining-room, an ante-room and other improvements for him at 10 Downing Street, since Lord Liverpool was still living at Fife House. Presented with a selection of ceiling designs, Robinson chose the characteristic 'star-fish' vault which still presides over the official dinner table. On 4 April 1826 Soane dined in the handsome panelled room at Robinson's invitation: 'I wish you to be of the party that you may see how well it looks when lighted up'.[11] Soane also worked at 11 Downing Street, where his first floor drawing-room and dining-room also survive.

In October 1826 George Wightwick, at that period as his secretary daily engaged in expressing Soane's grievances in written form, visited both the Law Courts and the Kings Entrance, and reported to Soane that he was even more impressed than he had expected to be, although he was nervous in saying so, fearing that Soane might imagine that he was attempting to 'further *my interests* by flattering *your talents*'.[12] When Henry Crabb Robinson met him, over dinner at the Flaxmans', (the night before

200. The Court of Exchequer in Soane's new Law Courts drawn in August 1826. The exterior had been rebuilt in a crude gothic style, forced upon Soane after his classical designs had been rejected and demolished. The alterations meant that the site was reduced and Soane had to struggle to maximise the light and space from a cramped, unsuitable site. As usual he concentrated on top lighting and ceiling details.

201. The Court of Chancery (from where, ironically, Soane's own estate was to be later administered) with Soane's distinctive hanging arches ornamenting an upper gallery, itself lit from an upper clerestory.

their host's death in December 1826) Soane 'talked about the New Law Courts, and with warmth abused them. He repudiates them as his work, being constrained by orders.'[13] Having mulled over the matter at obsessive length, he finally produced one of his splenetic printed pamphlets, *A Brief Statement of Proceedings respecting the New Law Courts at Westminster, etc.* (1827), the gist of which would reappear in all his subsequent publications.

While Soane's scheme for the exterior had run into major problems, the interior never particularly interested his critics. Nor were they aware that by setting back the building line they cramped the layout so that the courts were scarcely larger than before. In the final plan Soane envisaged Westminster Hall as the main foyer to all the courts. Soane's ingenuity on plan, a skill thoroughly honed at the Bank, came to the fore as he fitted seven new courts into the narrow canted site. Much of his attention went into lighting the boxy rooms and in breaking up the visual effect of their considerable height. As so often he had to take all illumination from overhead (fig. 200). Soane introduced hanging arches (recalling those in the Library at Lincoln's Inn Fields), tall tribunes, clerestory or lantern lit, panelled walls and heavy plasterwork put together in different combinations and to different effects. There was an elaborately contrived gallery at the Court of Chancery, below which the pendentives were pierced with *oculi* to allow light to the corners. The spine corridor between the court and Westminster Hall was top-lit.[14] Soane was so injured by the attacks that he made less of his considerable achievement with the interiors than he might have done. After his death, some of the protracted battles over his will would take place under the elaborate ceilings of his Court of Chancery (fig. 201). By the time his estate came out of Chancery, the New Law Courts were approaching the end of their life. By 1883 they were gone.[15]

For once, Soane's grievances were justified and clear. John Nash told him that he felt he had not been fairly treated, as did many others. The unpleasantness of the whole episode brought Soane sympathy on all sides.

Running concurrently with his work at the Law Courts, the House of Lords was a job which Soane supervised closely and personally. Nash had been surprised, calling to see how the Scala Regia was progressing, to find him there in person, overseeing the workmen. 'I have your figure before my eyes, a thin black shadow standing on the foundation walls . . . with arms folded contemplating the mode of laying bricks.'[16] Nash himself would have left well alone, but for Soane his professional reputation rested as much with the quality of the craftsmanship as with anything else. If he was working for the king, at last, then the job was too important to leave to a clerk of works. His craftsmen respected him as much for his standards as for the fact that he stood by them. Nash, who had just been appointed to design the new Buckingham Palace (a job which should have been Soane's by rights) wrote: 'It occurred to me that our appointments are perfectly Constitutional, I, the King, you, the Lords and *your* friend Smirke, the Commons . . . It then struck me that you wanted to be both King and Lords.'[17] By employing his wit and charm Nash could get away with saying the unsayable.

On the completion of the Royal Entrance (fig. 202), in late January 1824, Soane offered his workmen a celebration dinner.[18] At the last moment Colonel Stephenson of the Office of Works saw the printed invitation and, a stickler for propriety, thought it inappropriate since 'so extensive public an entertainment . . . may draw down some unpleasant animadversions from those under whose authority this Department is placed'. He was worried that the Treasury might object (or perhaps, was second-guessing Henry Bankes's response) even though it was at Soane's expense. Soane agreed to absent himself as a face-saving exercise and John Britton took his place as host to the 120 workmen at the Freemasons' Tavern.

Apologising to Stephenson afterwards, Soane wrote: 'My chief object in giving the dinner was to have an opportunity of complimenting the workmen and of expressing my grateful acknowledgements to all those persons who by the most extraordinary and unusual exertions had enabled me to finish such extensive works with almost incredible promptitude.'[19] Soane never underestimated the importance of his workforce as a contributory factor to his success. The *Essay on the Qualifications and Duties of an Architect* had offered sound advice, echoing down half a century, 'Be civil and complaisant to tradesmen and ready, whenever you find an honest and industrious tradesman to recommend him. By this carriage no small advantage will rebound to yourself; the workmen will work more cheerfully under you, do their work better, and complete it sooner, than otherwise they perhaps would do.'

The programme at the House of Lords must have been a terrible strain on Soane, whose eyesight was deteriorating fast. It was the willingness of tradesmen, who by now had worked on most of his major commissions, the carpenters, Richard and Thomas Martyr, the mason Thomas Grundy, the painter and glazier William Watson and the plasterer Thomas Palmer, to tender low prices and to work night and day that had made the job possible. Last minute additions required building works to be carried out in the recess. Soane hated the pressure: he knew that sound workmanship took time. Their Lordships, and behind them the Treasury, were turning out to be nightmare clients.

None of his other public commissions was quite such a battlefield as the Law Courts but compared to work for private clients, and Soane was deep in Pell Wall, his last private house job, the planning and execution of public works was chaotic.[20] Further difficulty came from the changing face of government. The nascent departments of state, the recognisable ancestors of modern ministries, could not be housed on an *ad hoc* basis. Soane was caught between the old ways and the new order.

John Nash's own disastrous collision with Bankes and the unofficial scrutineers lay ahead with the Select Committee of 1828 but it made Soane's struggles pale into insignificance.[21] Soane's relationship with Nash, which might have been poisoned with professional jealousy, was always informed (and sweetened) by his knowledge – gained long before on Rowland Burdon's Wearmouth Bridge scheme – that Nash was careless on fine points. If his estimates were accurate, then he failed to consider contingencies, while the constant supervision and close attention to detail upon which Soane prided himself were, as Nash admitted, not his *forte*. Added to that, Nash was involved in speculative ventures and was therefore liable to be acting in more than one capacity on any major scheme. Nor, despite his position as a royal favourite, was he active in the political arena or involved in the Royal Academy.

202 The Royal Entrance of the House of Lords, as designed in 1794, a dream of Soane's which finally came true thirty years later. In reality a quite narrow passage, he dignified it with groined vaulting and a sternly classical vocabulary of ornament. See also figs 205 and 206.

203. A photograph from 1910 showing, to the left of the picture, Soane's only contribution to John Nash's New (Regent) Street, a group of buildings for John Robins, an auctioneer and already a client and friend.

The one project, among their 'extra-mural' duties at the Office of Works, that brought Soane and Nash into constant contact was their involvement, with Robert Smirke, in the building of the Commissioners' churches, an unsatisfying episode in Soane's career. Indeed George Wightwick commented that 'he had such an aversion to Sabbath 'laziness' that I wondered he had compromised his principles of perpetual industry by building any churches'.[22]

Relations between Nash and Soane were amicable. They dined with one another, Nash thanking Soane for 'the sumptuous dinner you gave my trio at your elegant, doublefaced mansion' and hoping that Soane would allow him to return the hospitality, especially since 'Brother Soane, you was in a miff when I saw you at the head of your Masons'. Nash teased Soane about his freemasonry but 'one of the Masonic rules, I am told, is to acquire a meek and humble spirit. I fear therefore you are not qualified for Grand Master.'[23] Nash had three redeeming features; enormous personal charm, wit and a spark of theatrical brilliance as a designer of grand urban projects, which Soane could not fail to appreciate. Compared to Smirke or the elder Cockerell, Nash could fly and if any architect could bring French panache to London, it was he. The bombast and the unreliability that Soane had experienced and which Rowland Burdon never forgot after their dealings in the early gestation of his bridge, writing to Soane that he worried whenever he saw his name joined to that of Nash, could also be transformed into an astonishing breadth of imagination – a civic vision. Soane was envious but properly admiring.

In many ways, Soane and Nash, the two kings of the profession, could travel on separate, parallel tracks within their world. When Soane worked under Nash's overall control in 1820, designing Nos. 156–170 Regent Street for John Robins and others (fig. 203), the arrangement was harmonious. Although Nash was in charge of the elevations on the new street 'if a person presents a design for the elevation of a building, and I do not see a material defect, it would be invidious of me to find fault with it; I return it as approved by me. Mr Soane made a design, I could not object.'[24] He was content to let the stern, odd terrace stand sentinel in the midst of the more flamboyant, commercial classicism of the developing street. Between 1822 and 1824 Nash built a large double residence for himself and a relative at 14–16 [Lower] Regent Street, over shops. Inside was a 70-foot long gallery (fig. 204), housing casts, architectural models and a collection of many sixteenth century Italian paintings, an altogether very Parisian affair, a 'flutter, multiplicity of mouldings, filgrain, and gold leaf' in Elmes's words.[25] Nash had himself been to Paris in October 1814 and again in January 1818.[26] The contrast between Nash's gallery and Soane's picture room, as between Nash's new castle at East Cowes on the Isle of Wight and Pitshanger Manor, spoke volumes.

However the arrangements at Regent Street were confusing to clients and led to misunderstandings. In 1791 Soane had been the architect to Ransom and Morlands' Bank in Pall Mall, later he had worked for them at the New Bank Buildings and no doubt assumed he would be asked to design their new premises on Regent Street. Furious to find he was not to be their architect, he withdrew his valuable account. The Hon. Douglas Kinnaird, whose family had been the Soanes's neighbours in Ealing days,[27] was mortified. To lose Soane's business 'will unquestionably be the most painful event that has hitherto occurred to me as a banker.'[28]

Kinnaird, knowing Soane's views on speculative building, had been careful not to offend him by asking him to undertake a demeaning job. Citing his 'an over-scrupulous delicacy towards yourself . . . [which] has unfortunately been mistranslated into neglect' Kinnaird explained; 'Our elevation has been, as a condition . . . of the New Street Commissioners furnished by Mr Nash, and is still in its details to be controlled by him . . . our house is to be built by contract – and certainly if under these circumstances . . . you would have condescended to meddle with it, unquestionably we have all been in error.' Their mistake had been founded upon 'the sincerest delicacy and respect towards you as the Head of your Profession'. Soane did not relent and never banked with them again.

In his *Metropolitan Improvements* (1828) James Elmes devoted considerable space to Soane's one contribution to Regent Street, perhaps to put the record straight after the Bœotian attack in *Knight's Quarterly* to which he felt Soane had over-reacted. He has 'in one or two instances deviated from those sound rules of Grecian architecture which are not too lightly to be sacrificed or deviated from' and only a 'great master' could afford to take such liberties: 'Mr. Soane I consider to be such a master . . . as long as he keeps within the bounds of good taste, and runs not into a capricious riot of doubtful vagaries'. He sternly quoted the words of Chambers on the danger of tampering with 'the primary forms invented by the ancients'.

Soane was eager to take his place in the growing numbers of social and intellectual institutions in London. He was an original member of the Athenaeum Club, which met at 12 Waterloo Place from its foundation in 1824 until it moved to Decimus Burton's fine building on Pall Mall in May 1830.[29] Soane joined at the same time as J.M.W. Turner and there were Monday *conversazioni* through the winter and spring on topics of general interest. Later Soane also joined the Garrick Club. The clubs, like the institutions, were the core of a spreading cultural life in the capital.

James Christie, twenty years younger than he, was impressed by his health and strength in the spring of 1828. Soane's physical stamina was inherited from his mother and had been shared by his brother William. But his creative longevity was exceptional. Christie admired his ability to plan and execute 'works of intricacy and grandeur, and to superintend the engraving of designs from them when I, your junior . . . scarcely had strength to hold a pen'.[30]

Soane's vigour was sustained by a great scheme of his own. The pettifogging interference of Henry Bankes MP, the Chancellor of the Exchequer and many before him had, he felt, denied him the chance to give London the public buildings it deserved. He would put his ideas on paper and in the form of a processional route, which he envisaged George IV taking on state occasions. In *Designs for Public Improvements in London and Westminster* his own dreams and his public commissions were blended in a scheme which in scale and aspiration harked directly back to French academic neoclassicism and forward to the fully uniformed dress of the Victorian imperial capital that London would shortly become. Soane offered a plethora of symbolic public structures – richly decorated in conformity with the classical rules of hierarchy – that failed to match the national mood or the reality of the time. It was less a route imbued with 'architectural testaments to the legitimacy of [the king's]

204. John Nash's own gallery at his house on Regent Street, engraved by A. C. Pugin in 1836, so different in its plan and ornament from Soane's ingenious Picture Room at Lincoln's Inn Fields (see fig 204).

reign'[31] than a valedictory statement from an embittered man who, despite appearances to the contrary, felt that he had been cheated of his architectural deserts.

The king, never his whole-hearted admirer, was an intrinsic part of the fairy-tale. Imperial Rome was Soane's reference point; making London a 'fully-clothed' Rome brought together the city that had formed him with the city that had made him. If Paris could be remodelled around its key public buildings, why not London?[32] He adjusted the fabric of the city to suit his scheme.

From Windsor Castle (itself a commission that had recently slipped Soane's grasp and been awarded to Jeffry Wyatville) the king would enter his capital through two triumphal arches, one at Kensington Gore, the next at Hyde Park Corner, past a great palace on Constitution Hill (another dream, his retort to Nash's Buckingham Palace) and on, skirting a sepulchral church in the park (with strong resemblances to that designed for Praed at Tyringham many years before), commemorating the Battle of Waterloo. The king would pass a monument to the Duke of York (who had died in January 1827)[33] and then enter Downing Street, marked by triumphal arches to both west and east ends, turning out into Parliament Street where Soane's own works could finally be seen in reality – the Board of Trade and Privy Council offices and, beyond, at Westminster, the New Law Courts and the House of Lords. Soane's natural abilities, offering intensity and subtlety within confined dimensions, were strained to the limits by his efforts to give an inflated, public dimension to his architecture as well as to telescope virtually his entire *œuvre* of public works into this scheme.

One wonders what point was Soane trying to make. Both he and the king were in their seventies; if it was a manifesto, the timing was curious. Any argument for heavy public expenditure after the gross indulgence of the king's youth and the current political volatility (the Reform Act was only four years away) made no sense whatsoever. As a rejoinder to Nash's Regent Street, if that was also the intention, then the comparison was not in Soane's favour. Nash and Decimus Burton's sequence between the Wellington Arch, Marble Arch and Buckingham Palace, completed in the 1830s was the nearest that London would ever come to a triumphal route. Soane's scheme, so close in spirit to Gandy's earlier compilation of his work *Architectural visions of early fancy and dreams in the evening of life*, was both introspective and retrospective, both over-ambitious and under-considered.

Despite the pretext of the royal route and the pleas for national patronage and memorials to recent victories, *Designs for Public Improvements* was in reality Soane's combined autobiography and memoir, comparable to 13 Lincoln's Inn Fields in which every object, every juxtaposition, every moment referred to his life, achievements and failures. There, he was still hard at work perfecting the arrangements, purchasing further items for the rooms, and preparing a strategy whereby it could be passed on, intact.

There was, too, another reason for *Designs for Public Improvements*. Sir Charles Long's *Remarks on Improvements in London* had been privately printed in 1826.[34] Although he had little to say about Soane's existing work in the city, while lavishing praise on Nash's New (Regent) Street and giving Wyatville his dues, Long was arguing Soane's point[35] – if not for him personally, then in terms of public patronage and a grander stage for the monarch and his parliament. Long, from his perspective close to the workings of government, referred to the urgent need for a State Paper Office (although he suggested that the Banqueting House might suit the purpose) and sternly reprimanded the House of Commons as 'unfit to decide' on their accommodation, everyone wanting something different. As he put it, 'public buildings can never be directed by such a body as the House of Commons, they can only be carried on the Government of the country'. The slim document had gone to both king and Prime Minister.

Soane well knew that an idea planted by Lord Farnborough, as he became in 1826, ran a good chance of being taken seriously. After his long years of power, during all of which he had known Soane, Long had latterly pursued a course which reflected his own passion for the arts. His wife was a regular exhibitor at the Royal Academy and was the (anonymous) author of the observations on parks in the *Remarks*. Long was a trustee of the British Museum, where he had enthusiastically advocated the purchase of the Elgin Marbles, was a prime mover for the establishment of a national gallery and the government's purchase of the Angerstein collection in 1823 and headed the British Institution. Farington had earlier referred to his powerful position at court, calling him 'Mr Long who appears to be Minister to the Regent for the Department of Art'. That influence continued during the reign of George IV, although politically time was running out.

In November 1826 the king ceremonially opened parliament, which he had not done for some years. The fully blown ceremonial, using for the first time the approach up Soane's Scala Regia (fig. 205) and along his regal gallery (fig. 206), greatly impressed an overseas visitor, Prince Puckler-Muskau. 'At two o'clock, cannons announced the approach of the King in state . . . At half-past two the King appeared, the only man in full dress, in fact clad from head to foot in the old royal regalia, with the Crown on his head and the Sceptre in his hand. He looked pale and puffy, and had to sit for some time on his throne before he could get enough breath to read out his speech.' In the meantime he threw 'loving glances' at some favoured ladies.

Lord Liverpool and the Duke of Wellington stood to his either side. 'All three looked so miserable, so ashen-grey and exhausted that it seemed to me that human greatness had never looked so pitiable . . . The whole scene, with its entrances and exits and the King's costume, [was] striking in its way . . . One could see clearly that the monarch was delighted when his task was ended, so that the exits went rather more vigorously than the entrance.'[36] The theatre the visitor saw, set within Soane's staging, does not suggest a vital era of new patronage, rather the dragging footsteps of two tired regimes, those of monarch and Prime Minister, heading towards a finale.

Nevertheless as a kindly gesture, knowing of Soane's perpetual struggles with his political masters, in 1827 Farnborough took Soane's drawings for a new royal palace to the king since 'it will be gratifying to him to have a design of yours in his Portfolio'.[37] Soane offered the drawing then on exhibition at the Royal Academy.[38] The king accepted, which was 'one of the most consoling circumstances of my life', especially since it was 'the only

205. (above, left) Soane's Scala Regia (Royal Staircase) at the House of Lords, besides which gigantic statues of monarchs were to stand.

206. (above, right) The narrow, but elaborate gallery of the House of Lords, along which the king passed to reach the house.

opportunity I have ever had of . . . having any design of mine fairly before the Sovereign since His Majesty was Prince of Wales'. Touchingly, Soane later thanked Farnborough by asking him to become a trustee for his grandchildren in 1829.[39]

This renewed contact with royalty, Soane told Farnborough, had encouraged him to collect his designs for 'the improvement of London and Westminster' and dedicate them to the king. This was, in effect, the first edition of the *Designs for Public Improvements*, which reached George IV by late September, with autograph drawings instead of engravings.[40]

The timing of the second edition of the *Designs* was no accident. In 1828 Henry Bankes MP had unleashed another Select Committee into the conduct of the Office of Works and the public building programme, this time with Nash in his sights but also questioning Soane's designs for the Privy Council Office and the Board of Trade building on the corner of Downing Street and Parliament Street (fig. 207). Soane had earlier argued, to Colonel Stephenson's order that he choose his tradesmen by competitive tender, that: 'The execution of the exterior of the Board of Trade . . . is of such vital importance to the Office of Works that I most sincerely trust that a tried and faithful tradesman accustomed to such works, may not be passed by for the saving of a few pounds'.[41] He had won his argument and fielded the usual trusted team. The building was continually altered and the work dragged on from the autumn of 1824 until later 1826, when Soane was ordered to remove the balustrade.

The select committee considered the history of this unsatisfactory saga and although unwilling to point the finger and apportion blame, 'the system cannot be good which has produced such a result'.[42] Robinson, now Viscount Gooderich, had briefly been First Minister, in a rapid succession of changes after Lord Liverpool's paralytic stroke, followed by George Canning's death. He himself resigned after six months to be replaced by the Duke of Wellington. However he continued in government and at the select committee hearings revealed himself to be particularly interfering and only half-informed.

No wonder that Soane wanted to have the last word, on the page at least.[43] *Designs for Public and Private Buildings*, as Soane retitled the subsequent revised editions, included a 'Roman temple altered into a casina'. The caption to the plate read that this design had been worked up in Rome fifty years before, following 'the suggestion of Mr Pitt . . . and of Mr Bankes, afterwards Member of Parliament for Corfe Castle, Dorsetshire'. Soane, as always resorting to the personal, had got his own back.

Other public commissions in these busy years included Soane's adaptation of 16 Downing Street and the four adjoining houses, carried out during 1825–6, but proving almost immediately inadequate to the needs of a rapidly expanding Foreign and Colonial Office. There was further work on 10 and 11 Downing Street; houses he had worked on thirty years earlier. Finally came the State Paper Office (fig. 208). In 1828 the need for a new building had become urgent and the Treasury board accepted Soane's design on 29 December 1829. He was still at work on the Office in 1834, aged eighty. He had, somehow, taken a deep breath of fresh air and designed an Italianate *palazzo* as modern as anything that Charles Barry was offering. Barry's Travellers' Club and Soane's State Paper Office, built at the same moment, shared the honour of spear-heading the new preferred style for banks, clubs and libraries in the 1830s.[44] Young Barry himself was close on Soane's heels; before long he had largely replaced Soane's work at the Board of Trade and built the brand-new Houses of Parliament.

Thirty years after it was built, the State Paper Office was demolished for the new Foreign Office and by 1900 scarcely anything of Soane's work in Whitehall was still standing – apart from some interiors in Downing Street, the refronting of the Banqueting House in Portland stone and, scarcely recognisible after Barry's attentions, the Privy Council – to testify to Soane's desperate and miserable struggles with the self-appointed arbiters of taste and the unquestioning servants of the new bureaucracy.

Battered but not yet defeated, Soane still had hopes for another major commission. In 1828 he took a new design for additions to the Freemasons' Hall to the Duke of Sussex at Kensington Palace: it was a mongrel of equally idiosyncratic classical and gothic motifs, 'appropriate to historic or national institutions'.[45] The design eventually chosen was simpler, with fireplaces oddly sited under windows.[46] Clerestory windows and a lantern flooded the hall with golden light from richly patterned and painted glazing. Another of his miraculous domes floated overhead, supported by iron struts which were cunningly disguised. Construction began in the summer of 1828 but the room was not complete until the early

207. Soane's model for the Board of Trade building in Whitehall, on the corner of Downing Street, another of the public commissions where interfering MPs and changing requirements caused him great difficulty. The Privy Council chamber remains in very residual form after a substantial remodelling by Charles Barry.

208. The State Paper Office, Soane's final official commission, demolished thirty years later. For the first time he has adopted an Italian Renaissance style, showing his awareness of Barry's work.

months of 1831. In 1832, upon the occasion of the celebration of the Grand Master's birthday, Soane personally donated £500 to the new building.[47] Soane had been involved in every detail, from the layout of the furnishings to the decoration of the organ case. That year Gandy exhibited the results of Soane's labours – and funds – at the Royal Academy, 'an evening view made after the completion of the building', the interior glowing in the lamp-light.

In his portrait by Sir Thomas Lawrence PRA (a man who had had little patience with Soane in the days of the Royal Academy disputes), which was painted in 1828 for the British Institution, Soane looks out with a slightly quizzical expression, the eyes a little clouded and on his head a jaunty wig of rich copper-coloured hair. A snappy pair of knee breeches show that his sartorial roots, as George Wightwick had observed, were still firmly in the Georgian era. Soane's first few sittings for Lawrence alternated with others for a small portrait, by John Jackson RA, this time showing him dressed in Masonic garb, with the Freemasons' Hall behind him. Soane had also commissioned a posthumous companion portrait of Mrs Soane from Jackson, with Fanny on her lap.

He also sat for a bust by his friend Sir Francis Chantrey RA from March 1829. He is in classical profile, the aquiline nose a distraction from the thin lips, on which an ambiguous expression hovers towards a smile. His eyes may have been very clouded but Soane was a man in excellent command of his faculties as he approached eighty. He had a considerable amount of unfinished business and was far from ready to fade into history.

18

STRANGE WORK

In 'Crude Hints towards the history of my house' Soane described himself spectrally visiting the ruins of 13 Lincoln's Inn Fields in 1830. Written in his deep despair and near mania of 1812, it was gothic fiction, worthy of George Soane. In reality, 1830 found Soane in excellent form, the Grand Old Man of architecture, honoured and busy.

The *Athenaeum* accorded him a lengthy profile, the seventh in a series on living artists. His 'peevishness or perversity of temper' had apparently been soothed into 'mildness and moderation'. (The portrait was being retouched.) His works should be illustrated and 'some safe and sensible friend . . . give an account of them and their author'. His biography, the writer noted, would be 'strange work . . . for the man and his works are not well understood'.[1] The article marked his recent knighthood.

Soane's solicitor John Bicknell wrote to offer his congratulations. 'I like tardy justice better than no justice and I like half justice better than none at all and therefore I was pleased to see that the King had done you even half, and tardy, justice in adding a title, not a distinction, to your name.'[2] The royal favourite Jeffry Wyatville had been knighted in 1828 but Nash's carelessness debarred him from a knighthood (although George IV had urged one) as well as causing his dismissal from the Office of Works. It was left to King William IV, the Duke of Clarence for whom Soane had worked forty years before, to honour Soane in 1831.

His friends knew how much it meant to him. Peter Coxe, an auctioneer and sometime poet, penned thirty-seven verses to mark his friend's elevation, ranging wide across Soane's achievements at the Bank, his Professorship and beyond:

Soane! The important task was thine,/With all thy thirst for classic lore,/To take thy own distinctive line,/And forms create unknown before. . .

SOANE! All regret is haply past,/Thy generous Sovereign owns thy claim;/And gracious binds the laurel fast, That knighthood yields to deck thy name. . .

Bold and peculiar in thy style,/ Whose structures shew a novel grace. . .

Thus still to act, may time allow,/Propitiously, with lengthened care,/Unfading bays to bind thy brow,/And decorate thy silvery hair.[3]

Turner, too, hurried to congratulate Soane, leaving a scribbled note and a drawing. 'I called in Lincoln's Inn Fields to congratulate you. . .and to have the pleasure of saying so in person. Likewise to offer with my most sincere regards the accompanying portrait . . . of Mrs Soane which I fortunately obtained at poor Jackson's sale'. (fig. 209).[4] His thoughtfulness in buying back John Flaxman's drawing for Soane (which Jackson had used as a reference for his posthumous portrait of Eliza with Fanny) was telling of the long, tender friendship of the two truculent men of genius.

In August 1831 Soane and Mrs Conduitt had a fine day out, quaffing champagne at the opening of London Bridge. They were well placed to watch the event. Some way distant, up on the lantern of St Paul's Cathedral, B. R. Haydon, grudgingly taking time off from the completion of his latest painting, *Zenophon*, had found a bird's-eye view of the proceedings for his family. Having waited for hours, they heard and saw the crowd, a distant mass of tiny specks, roar and raise their hats for the king, while a hot air balloon ascended and 'Mrs Mary Haydon the Elder had a pain in her stomach, and Master Harry Haydon wanted to suck, and Master Alfred was hungry, and Master Frederick wanted to drink, and Miss Mary said she was faint, and Master Frank Haydon said "is this all?" – and then they went down an infinite number of dark stairs and got into a coach and drove home . . . and *this* was pleasure.'[5]

Soane had commissioned a painting of the occasion from George Jones (fig. 210); Soane and Mrs Conduitt appear centre-stage. The king had commissioned one from Clarkson Stanfield and Soane was eager that an Academician should also have the chance.[6] He asked for a 'moderate-sized' picture, since his walls left little space for new work. He offered Jones 500 guineas, 'and I shan't quarrel with you if you make it a thousand'.[7] Soane had embarked on an ambitious period of patronage of British art – even though his rooms were already hung to capacity.

Soane's official apotheosis may have been under way but his fire was not dampened. He was engaged in another fight with the Royal College of Surgeons, the portico of which he looked at daily across the Fields, through the trees. In 1824 he had been asked to become honorary architect[8] and in 1831 Robert Keate (son of his late friend from Chelsea) asked if 'as a friend' he would look at the museum and see if altering the roof and adding another gallery would improve it: 'if you think such a plan feasible and desirable – or any other having the same object . . . I will talk officially to you and recommend its adoption'.[9] The next he heard from the Surgeons was a request to make a structural survey in 1833 followed by a peremptory command to submit proposals for the substantial expansion and rebuilding of the College headquarters.[10] Soane ignored them.[11] Charles Barry was the successful candidate, eventually earning over £2,000 but enduring a lengthy builders' strike and the usual difficulties of working for an inexpert committee. Soane, justifiably furious at the Surgeons' unprofessional and insulting conduct, remained implacably silent. The silence extended both ways.

Soane was, that year, preoccupied in seeing through the private Act of Parliament by which his own house in Lincoln's Inn Fields and its contents (still growing) became vested in trustees for the benefit of the public. He had first begun to explore the idea in early 1824 as he embarked upon the last major remodelling of the house after John's death. He had asked

209. Pencil sketch of Mrs Soane by John Flaxman, 1810, bought for Soane by J.M.W. Turner and presented at the moment of his knighthood.

Timothy Tyrrell, his friend and adviser since the 1780s, about choosing trustees. Tyrrell thought he should probably consider 'public characters the Presidents of the Royal and Antiquarian Society and the President of the Royal Academy with the Professor of Architecture there for the time being – your executors must be men of a different description and who may be trustees for family purposes'.[12] Over the intervening years, Soane refined his plan: now it was before parliament.

The Bill had its second reading in the House of Commons on 15 March 1833, introduced by Joseph Hume, MP for Middlesex.[13] Hume set the scene. 'Having derived everything from science himself . . . [Soane] wished that the Museum he had formed should be useful to others.' It was, he continued, 'unnecessary to eulogise . . . Sir John Soane . . . the person who prevented Belzoni's celebrated Sarcophagus from going abroad . . . for one manuscript alone he had given £500'. Hume suggested that honourable Members might like to pay a visit for themselves. He moved the second reading, supported by Sir Robert Inglis (MP for Oxford University)[14] who stressed Soane's 'disinterested course' and who drew the

210. George Jones's painting of the opening of London Bridge commissioned by Soane who can be seen, centre left, with his companion-housekeeper Mrs Sally Conduitt.

attention of the house to another generous donation, of which the public knew little and which deserved notice, that of Mr Payne Knight to the British Museum, a collection worth £60,000. More publicity for these benefactions might induce others to follow suit and he suggested that the directors of the National Gallery annually report to the House. The Bill was read and sent on its way.[15]

On 1 April, the day on which it was due to have its third reading, William Cobbett, newly elected MP for Oldham, presented a petition against the bill on behalf of George Soane.[16] Soane was incandescent with fury about his intervention and an additional clause, proposed by Sir Robert Peel, which would place the house and collection ultimately under the control of the British Museum.

In Soane's opinion the British Museum would display nothing but the pick of his pictures, consigning the remainder to their cellars. If the house and the objects within it were not considered an entity, the treasures ('his hobby') would go abroad; the Belzoni Sarcophagus to the Emperor of Russia, his Hogarths to the King of Holland and his coins to the King of Bavaria.[17]

On the floor of the House of Commons the combination of Cobbett's rhetoric and George Soane's melodramatic tale ensured a ringing presentation of their case. The petitioner considered that the passing of the Bill 'would be . . . a violation of those laws by which the society was held together' and, disingenuously, 'that his father must have been improperly importuned and persuaded at the ninth hour . . . to alienate so large a portion of his property, since, if he had contemplated such an act . . . previously, he must have made up his mind . . . before he had arrived at a period of natural decay'. He asked to be heard in person, by counsel or agent, lest the House 'reverse the fundamental laws of hereditary succession, and of testamentary law'. Cobbett added that he had never met either Sir John or his son until four days before.[18] On hearing of the distress of Soane's grandchildren, and considering the words of St Paul 'if a man take not care of his own house, he has denied the faith, and is worse than a heathen', he hoped that the House 'would pause a little' before it sanctioned the third reading of the Bill. Biblical incantations from a noted radical were not calculated to please Sir John Soane.

Hume corrected Cobbett, pointing out the provisions made for John's children, and said that the Committee had now heard George Soane's case and remained unanimously of the view that no injustice had been committed. One member at least, Mr Briscoe, was persuaded of George's case. From the little he had heard 'he considered it a case of extreme hardship and great moral injustice'. He suggested sending the objects to the British Museum, where they would be of more use to the public, and release further funds for the grandchildren.

Sir Robert Peel pointed out that Soane had accumulated his collection 'by denying himself indulgence' and that the nation should be duly thankful and gracious for his generosity. He was, however, intending to move a clause on the third reading, placing the property under the aegis of the British Museum, a course which could save the money required for a separate establishment. Lord John Russell supported the idea but hoped that the clause would leave the matter at the discretion of Sir John Soane himself.

Cobbett had not finished, replying that he considered the argument one of morality. The bill withheld from the donor's grandchildren 'that sustenance to which they were entitled . . . and needed'. He also mentioned Mrs Soane's '£30,000' from her uncle, which had, perhaps, 'been the occasion of the whole of [Soane's] celebrity and property'. George's return to his false charge, that Soane had appropriated his late wife's property, was his cruellest weapon and he ensured that Cobbett used it, unwittingly, at length. Fortunately an unnamed member and Hume between them pointed out the fallacy of George's case, supported by Messrs Hodges and Baring. Sir Robert Peel then moved his amendment, by which Soane's collection could be left to the British Museum, under his own name, but left the final decision to him.

That prompted a lengthy discussion on the difficulties of visiting the British Museum. A trustee both of the National Gallery and the British Museum, Alexander Baring claimed that application to the librarian would always facilitate entry 'for any gentleman who came there for any purpose connected with science or art'. (As long as, it was pointed out later in the debate, that they were in 'decent dress'.) James Morrison, MP for Ipswich and a supporter of Robert Owen's ideas[19] felt that it was unduly inaccessible to the 'vast numbers of persons interested in manufactures of the country [who] came to the metropolis for the purpose of obtaining information'. The labourer and the tradesman could not benefit from public access to the British Museum, only open from ten until four and closed in the holiday months of September and October ('when all the lawyers and parsons, and lords and loungers, were out in the country enjoying shooting'), as well as on public holidays. Soane's Bill had occasioned a wide ranging and thoughtful debate on the accessibility of museums to the public. The clause was agreed and the Bill passed. On 16 April, the House of Lords concurred and the whole matter satisfactorily concluded on Saturday, 20 April 1833, when the Bill was given Royal Assent.[20]

The Act contained a sub-clause to allow for that distant, but still lingering, hope that his grandson John might practice architecture. He and his family might reside in the house, on John attaining the age of twenty-five, but he could only use the library if he was practising architecture. In 1847 he applied to live at Lincoln's Inn Fields but the following year he died in Madeira.

Soane's endowment was to provide some £900 per annum for the museum, with around £200, the rent from No. 12. The curator was to be 'an English Architect who may have distinguished himself or gained any Academical prize': In his will Soane had nominated George Bailey, who entered the office as a pupil in 1806 and remained there until his death. Mrs Conduitt was to be the inspectress. The will also designated C. J. Richardson as assistant curator and assistant librarian – neither post being specified in the Act. Richardson who was articled to Soane in 1824, aged fifteen, had become his amanuensis and remained in the office after his term in articles came to an end in 1830.[21] The latter's practice of borrowing drawings by Soane and others (including Adam) ostensibly to make copies, led to many entering the collection of the South Kensington Museum (now the Victoria and Albert Museum).[22] As a result the museum possesses the only major holding of Soane material outside his museum.[23]

Richardson was not offered either of the posts that Soane specified for him in the will: there was not enough income.

His two most trusted helpers and friends, George Bailey and Mrs Conduitt, upon whom he had become increasingly dependent respectively in the professional and domestic areas of his life were well provided for in his will[24] and the income from Soane's endowment was adequate for present purposes. The four life trustees were Samuel Thornton, Francis Chantrey, Samuel Higham from the National Debt Redemption Office and John Laurens Bicknell (John Constable's wife's uncle and Soane's solicitor since 1828) – old friends spanning Soane's worlds, that of the Royal Academy and the arts, the Bank of England and the world of commerce beyond it. Five more trustees were to be appointed by the learned societies (much as Tyrrell had suggested). His house, in John Britton's words 'an index, epitome and commentary on the architect's professional abilities', was safeguarded in perpetuity.[25]

1833 was also the year in which Soane finally recognised that his professional career was drawing to an end and tendered his resignation to the Bank of England, after forty-five years of service. He cited his impaired sight, rather than his age (he was now eighty), as the impediment and offered any help that he could to his successor. Soane proposed George Bailey for the position but the Bank's own candidates were George Basevi, his former pupil, and C. R. Cockerell, of whose work Soane claimed to know nothing.

Basevi's career was the most distinguished of the many pupils who had passed through Soane's office (with the exception of the fleeting Smirke). A relative of Isaac d'Israeli (father of the future Prime Minister) and of David Ricardo, the economist, he had not shirked speculation, despite his years at Soane's side, becoming the surveyor to a number of large Kensington and Belgravia estates, the new fashionable residential areas west of London. He was also among those invited to submit his designs for rebuilding the House of Commons, before the fire. Soane would have undoubtedly been happier to see Basevi gain his old job than the successful candidate, Cockerell, Smirke's pupil during the Covent Garden Theatre episode.

Perhaps because of this ancient resentment, Soane was remarkably rude when asked by Cockerell's assistant Goodchild for a view of his drawings of the Bank of England. 'You'll tell Mr Cockerell I'll not leave a scrap, not a bit of paper for him to go to the water closet with.'[26] Not surprisingly, Cockerell's tribute to his predecessor was cool and impersonal. He pointed out that the 'office . . . must be held in future at a disadvantage: since it can neither be dignified by works of similar splendour, nor perhaps adorned with personal qualifications of so high a character'. He would welcome Soane's 'remarks and views' and considered it his duty to preserve its elegance.[27]

Perhaps Soane had also received an inkling of Cockerell's views on the Bank, confided to his diary years before. 'The lantern rooms all subject to inconvenience or air descending on the head . . . corridors are narrow . . . but highly studied and some beautiful effect.' The general impression was both 'little and great, the taste sometimes flat, sometimes unreasonably bold'. Now, ten or more years later, his first job at the bank was to grapple with the heating problems in the top-lit halls and to sort out the sulphurous atmosphere in the Stock Office.[28] His programme of work at the Bank included further careful alterations, in particular raising the height of the parapets while retaining a Soane-like vocabulary of ornament, to provide protection for the guard during the threatening 1848 Chartist uprising.

Now that Soane's office had virtually closed and there were no more new jobs (although he remained in post at Chelsea until his death) Soane turned as usual to his papers. He made a new will – having accomplished the transfer of the house and museum to the nation – in May 1833. As well as John Bicknell, his witnesses were a neighbour, Dr Joseph Moore and two old friends, the secretary of the Royal Academy, Henry Howard and Robert Rainy Pennington. The latter when asked by Soane to take this role, joked that if he was to be a witness he obviously was not a beneficiary.[29] The document ran to thirty-three pages and later three codicils were added. A few specified heirlooms were to be kept in the family. Soane's (replacement)[30] Royal Academy gold medal, the diamond ring presented by the Emperor of Russia, a gold ring with a strand of Napoleon's hair and some silverplate.

Bequests aside, the estate was to pass into a twenty-one year trust fund. £20,000 three per cent consols were set aside to pay for John's education. On his death, the fund passed to his children ('lawfully begotten'). Should there be no heirs, Edward Foxhall, son of his old friend, would be the beneficiary. This may have been because of some historic obligation to his father which Soane, who forgot so little, wanted to repay.[31]

His debts and obligations acknowledged, Soane pressed on with further work on the house and an energetic programme of purchases and improvements. In 1829 he had glazed in the ground floor loggias to extend the library; now in 1834 he similarly altered those on the first and second floors.[32] In the same year Henry Howard RA painted panels in the compartments of the dining-room and library ceiling, those in the dining-room told the story of Pandora from whose vase, in Milton's phrase 'issued all the cares and miseries of life' whilst that in the library represented the more cheering scene of Phoebus, Aurora and the Morning Star, the Hours and the Zephyrs. Visitors might make what they wished of the symbolism overhead.

Soane encrusted the breakfast room with convex mirrors (fig. 211), some so tiny that they are little more than crystal orbs, and inserted glass at every occasion, experimenting with panes of glass set over canted mirror glass and angled panes.[33] In the library, too, from the late 1820s onwards, Soane added more mirror glass wherever he could; it was now in the recesses behind the ornamental canopies above the bookcases, in strips between the bookcases themselves, in the fireplace, in the mullions and jambs of the window onto the internal courtyard. There was glass on the inside of the sliding shutters and a pier glass between the windows.[34] By day the north–south light was intensified. By night, with candles and fires, the room glittered and sparkled, throwing every detail back, often from unexpected angles or heights. The rich red walls with their almost lacquered sheen, the use of ebony and patinated bronze, intensified the jewelled effect and took it forward, a foretaste of increasingly heavy early Victorian interiors.

The use of mirror glass at every opportunity underlined the dramatic, self-referential aspect of Lincoln's Inn Fields, the very opposite to those

211. The breakfast room, a tiny room made intricate by its floating paper-thin ceiling and the introduction of mirrors (mostly convex) at every possible point. It was here that he drew up his will in 1833.

glittering rococo rooms of southern Italy, with their painted decoration on glass dissolving space and turning walls into air, or even those of Adam or Wyatt, reflecting Georgian society in the finest music and drawing-rooms of London. Soane's theatrical manipulation introduced an unsettling, illusionistic element. Shadows and light, memory and reflection, were at the heart of his house: enclosed within the labyrinth, the obsessive aspect of Soane's personality was completely at home (fig. 212).

Earlier, in 1830, Soane had printed at his own expense the *Description of the House and Museum* which included three engravings borrowed from John Britton's unsuccessful *Union of Architecture, Sculpture and Painting*. Other illustrations were lithographs by Haghe and the text was Soane's own, a factual account of the house and its contents, ending with a discourse upon 'the advantages, importance and utility of Architecture'. He included a section devoted to his Napoleonic collection, reprinted Belzoni's account of his discovery of the sarcophagus and referred to the burial rites of the Guanches of Tenerife – a confusing range of information.

212. Soane's 'little study' at 13 Lincoln's Inn Fields, with the dining-room and library seen beyond the doorway. A window (right) looks into the Monument Yard and the passage continues as the dressing-room (fig. 191).

The next edition, in 1832, used all but one of the plates, with two additional lithographs, and was dedicated to the Duke of Sussex. The introduction referred to the evidence of 'the almost certain successful results of industry and perseverance, so forcibly illustrated in two well-known series of prints by that great moral British artist, William Hogarth'. Emphasising his wish to promote British artists, the descriptive text is hardly amended, save for a mention of future plans to open the House, Museum and Library and an early draft of the trust deed.

In 1833 Soane also printed *Plans, elevations and perspective views of Pitzhanger manor-house*. It included early designs 'to bring back the recollections of the old Manor-house, formerly the scene of English hospitality' and rehearsed the history of the 'Roman ruins intended to puzzle the geologist and antiquary' (which were illustrated, as was their 'restoration') and 'the legendary lore . . . [that] the place had been occupied by a pious monk'. Soane's memories were giving him energy.

Finally he put together the definitive edition of the *Description*. It was published in a limited edition of 150 copies in late 1835, with a largely new text, including the 1833 Act, interspersed with descriptions of the unbuilt royal palaces and the saga of the Houses of Parliament, two poems in Mrs Soane's memory and an account of the Gold Medal presentation earlier that year. To Soane's text, Mrs Hofland had been asked to add 'pictorial and poetical remarks' in order to 'render [it] more pleasing and attractive to young minds'. Her mellifluous words were interspersed throughout, set in smaller print.

Recent changes in the house were inserted, including the relocated second floor model room with its views out over Lincoln's Inn Fields, Lindsay House (ascribed to Inigo Jones) and the Royal College of Surgeons, in the middle distance the dome of St Paul's and St Bride's steeple, with the Surrey hills beyond. Mrs Hofland, reflecting Soane, emphasises the links between the general view, the immediate exterior – the statues from the Temple of Pandrosus which ornament the elevation – and the 'classical impressions' within the gallery with its models offering 'exquisite representations of those ancient, magnificent, and far-distant edifices'.[35]

Barbara Hofland accurately reflected Soane's own thoughts: it was, in Arthur Bolton's words, 'a first hand appreciation by a sympathetic and impressionable lady, unquestionably responsive to the vigorous and original mentality of the Architect-Collector'.[36] Mrs Hofland guided the visitor past the Hogarths in the picture room ('a severe but powerful teacher of morality') through to the Monk's Parlour below, where she retold the story of Padre Giovanni – a parable of Soane's family disappointments.

The monk, 'unquestionably a gentleman', lived in retirement, surrounded by memories of his wife and beautiful daughter, both dead. 'The son, who should have supplied the place of both [has] become an alien to his home and his country'. Surrounded by objects of devotion, the monk's apartment was lit with 'that mellow lustre which aids the all-pervading sentiment . . . light subdued, not exhausted'. So unlike the profligate Prior of Alcobaça in *Vathek* (a dig at Beckford himself, perhaps), 'our imagined padre is the last representative of an order to whom . . . we are much indebted', a guardian of learning and the arts. 'B.H.' continues: 'Now Padre Giovanni is no more, his monastic refuge is ivy-covered, its floor of pebbles and bottle glass, his presence marked by a skull encircled by a laurel wreath.' Mrs Hofland had provided a coded text for Soane's friends, even to the detail of his fondness for wine.

In front of Hunneman's early portrait of Soane in the attic (where Soane now slept), Barbara Hofland muses on the treasures below, offering evidence of 'what one man during his own life may acquire and accomplish, when he unites industry to genius, and integrity to perseverance'.[37]

The objects in Soane's collection, the ivory chairs evoking Tippoo Sahib's fall from greatness (and 'British valour') or the likenesses of Napoleon 'that wonderful man, who so lately 'kept the world in awe' were 'in perfect keeping with the sentiments they tend to awaken'. The irony of celebrating both a British triumph in India and the heroism of the national arch-enemy, did not apparently occur to either Barbara Hofland or Soane.

He was fascinated by the associations of his possessions. 'The most original thinker, and even the wildest wanderer in poetic conception, must have some foundation on which to raise the superstructure that may prove the temple of his fame. Where shall he find one so broad, so safe as that supplied by the aggregate wealth of the mighty minds that have preceded him?' as Mrs Hofland put it.

Shakespeare, his bust cast from the monument in Stratford-upon-Avon by George Bullock, and examined by the phrenologist Spurzheim, presided over the Shakespeare Recess (a pair with the Tivoli Recess, also on the stairs, which commemorated Soane's favourite building, the Temple of Vesta at Tivoli). The house, with its many reminders of national genius, had become Soane's own version of the Temple of Worthies at Stowe. He extended his admiration well beyond Shakespeare, Milton and Dryden, to Garrick and Hogarth. Visitors could draw their own conclusions as to who might rank as a modern native genius.

Soane's 1835 *Description*, in both English and French editions, was distributed to old friends and distant contacts, as had been the earlier *Designs for Public and Private Buildings*. Letters of thanks came back, sometimes from a son or widow with the news of a recent death, often with touching notes in aged hands, from his grandson John and from lofty figures such as the King of Bavaria and Prince Metternich the Austrian Emperor's righthand man. Gandy's long-winded, evocative letter[38] conjured up the image of a continuing Soane architectural practice, 'your Hall, Craig and Payne [clerks of works] reigning here as sub-curators' and young John setting out on his career. The responses were always effusive but nobody could match the generosity of the new Emperor of Russia, now Tsar Nicholas, on whose behalf the Count Lieven thanked Soane in the spring of 1829 for the copy of *Designs* and his offer to show him the Belzoni sarcophagus, with the gift of a diamond ring, which Soane treasured as a personal heirloom and bequeathed to his family. Sometimes over the intervening years personal circumstances had changed, though rarely as dramatically as for the emigré teacher in Ealing who had become Louis XVIII of France. In the *Memoirs* Soane printed the queen's letter of thanks for a copy of *Designs* and regretting that were no drawings of 'votre jolie villa d'Ealing, qu'elle se souvient d'avoir eu le plaisir de visiter, il y a environs trente ans'.

Soane was frail but apart from his eyes his physical health was generally good and Mrs Conduitt and George Bailey between them looked after him and conducted his far from moribund affairs efficiently and tactfully. His needs were tacitly acknowledged by old friends. William Daniell would accompany him in the carriage to the 1834 Royal Academy dinner and although he could not sit near him, not being on the Royal Academy Council, he offered to lead him up to the Great Room on his arm. Rowland Burdon continued to send him interest (a steady £40 per annum) on the Wearmouth bridge. Soane was his very oldest friend (of fifty-seven years' standing) but 'I wish we could be oftener in each other's company'.[39]

Soane at over eighty did not behave like a man in retirement and it must have been satisfying when old clients came back with their practical problems. In 1835 Stephen Thornton wrote anxiously to report that almost two thousand panes of glass on his cold frames and hothouses at Mogerhanger had been shattered after a severe summer hailstorm. He wanted to fix it all before the onset of winter. Within ten days William Watson, who had undertaken the job twenty-one years earlier, dealt with the problem.[40]

Athough Soane's library was now available to students on two days a week, it was – despite Joseph Hume's kind words in the House of Commons – of little use to the Royal Academy architectural students confined in their employers' offices during the hours of opening. Nor was the library equipped to assist students; there were no tables for large folios, while the 1831 catalogue was rudimentary.[41]

Soane was also engaged in a gruesome exorcism of his family ghosts. He was working on his *Memoirs* and on accounts of his sons' transgressions in two extraordinary documents[42] in which he unleashed his resentment over the failure of his dynastic plans. In that devoted to John's family he concentrated on his battles with Maria Soane, reverting to the distant skirmish over her inheritance and, more recently, their disagreements over young John's education, printing a tedious catalogue of letters on the subject. He also included his recent displeasure with Bessie. Where George was concerned, Soane spared no detail of his disdemeanours.

All this was activated by new revelations. In early 1831 he discovered that George had fathered a son by Maria Boaden, his sister-in-law, in 1824. The affair had been continuing for several years before that. In 1821 Maria suffered a severe late miscarriage at an address in Marchmont Street, Bloomsbury. The unborn child had been George's, as was her daughter, Maria, born in the summer of 1822 but who died aged twenty months. Her surviving son, George Manfred Soane had been born on 24 September 1824 at Pancras Vale. Soane embarked on a dogged investigation culminating with an interview with Agnes.[43]

Soane took several depositions of evidence. One was from their landlord and Maria's doctor, Mr Dore. George's behaviour to Mrs Dore, using 'some of the most opprobious epithets possible', drove Dore to double, then treble, the rent in the hopes of dislodging his tenant. They moved to a neighbouring house, where Maria Boaden was already living. Dore's memories of the unhappy household included seeing Agnes pulled out of the room by her hair, forbidden to come downstairs and driven to seeking refuge with her mother. Frederick, his legitimate son, was frequently beaten by his father.[44]

Typically Soane wasted little sympathy on the wretched Agnes, who had been forced to accept Maria as a member of her household, posing as teacher for her daughters, and he started obsessively to piece together this final history of ignominy in the Soane name. In April 1832 he deputed Pennington to make enquiries of the Foundling Hospital (of which he was a Governor) – to inquire whether the child had been admitted – and obtained a copy of the baptismal certificate for George's children.

He discovered that the children of George and Agnes Soane had been baptised at St Mary, Southampton on 17 July 1829, the sponsors being Mr and Mrs Perkins (a local waterman and his wife), George's servant, Miss Warne, and the sexton. George's grown-up daughters, Clara-Agnes and Rosa-Maria, were followed in the register by little George Manfred. Frederick (born in 1815), his legitimate son by Agnes, had already been baptised. Their father had not given his occupation, resorting to the gentleman's title, 'Esquire'.

Soane persuaded Sarah Smith to give an account of what had occurred in 1824. Her deposition, dated 14 April 1832 and sworn before a Surrey magistrate on 9 May, told how George called upon her in Chertsey in early September 1824 to enquire (in principle) about admitting a child to the Foundling Hospital, since she was an inspectress of the institution. She said there would be no difficulty 'provided it was a proper object'. When told the father was a married man who was not 'out of the country' she informed him it would not be possible. He then asked, since Miss Smith lived in such a remote spot 'could I make it convenient to receive a young person to lay-in? – Every expense would be paid; – my brother [Richard Smith] could attend her, and under my matronly care, she would be sure to do well. I felt rather indignant at such a proposal and informed him my character was my bread.' At this point she claimed she had had no idea whose the child might be.

Later in the month she received a letter from George asking her 'as a great favour' to go to his house with a wet nurse and take an infant back to Chertsey. On going to the house she found Agnes Soane, who pleaded with her, 'it is my husband's yet pray take the child'. Touched by her misery, she went to a cottage about a mile away 'where I received the infant, a very fine boy, apparently about three or four days old'.[45]

The agreement was that Sarah Smith would receive £75 to care for the boy for four years; during these years George Soane visited his child just once, with a parcel from Maria. He had planned to remove the child to school in 1827 but his daughter Caroline's fatal illness that winter meant that George Manfred remained a further year in Chertsey. On 2 December 1828 Sarah Smith took a post-chaise to Egham and handed over the little boy to his unknown father. They travelled back to Southampton on the outside of the coach. 'From that time to this I have never heard of or from Mr George Soane, although he was considerably in my debt for nursing and clothing him, nor did I know where to address a letter to him.' (Soane reimbursed her.)

Leonard Lester, an apothecary, swore another supporting deposition on 3 May. He remembered attending a woman in labour at a house at Pancras Vale, George Soane having informed him on the way 'of his name and connections'. Characteristically George tried to corner Lester, asking him to find a nurse 'and for me to take the charge of looking after it, which I immediately declined'. Lester remembered Agnes Soane's distress and how she asked him for advice. 'My reply was that she must insist on her sister leaving the house as soon as she was able . . . as I thought it impossible they could reside under the same roof after such conduct. Some months after this, upon my attending some of the children I was much shocked to see Miss Boaden still residing with them.' After that he too never saw or heard of the family again.[46]

On 6 June 1832 the baptismal register was officially altered, at Soane's instigation. The sealed depositions from Sarah Smith and Leonard Lester were presented in order that the curate, Mr Cary, could alter George Manfred's mother's name from Agnes Soane to Maria Boaden. The provision of false information under the Baptismal Act incurred up to fourteen years' transportation, Soane discovered, but even he baulked at bringing a prosecution.

By 1832 George Soane and his family were living in Worthing, where 'Master M. Soane', presumably Manfred, now aged eight, was a boarder at the Reverend Mr Balfour's school. By February 1834 the schoolmaster had not been paid and having taken the child in at 'little more than cost' applied to Soane for a settlement of his bill.[47] By then the family had returned to London and was living on the Borough Road, Southwark, leaving the usual trail of unpaid bills, angry landlords, shopkeepers and tradesmen, all telling of George's false promises and credible stories. When pressed, he divulged the identity of his famous father. Soane continually received letters from George's creditors – no doubt at his instigation and sometimes bearing the mark of his dictation in their venomous tone. George also included Mrs Conduitt in his sights; she had prejudiced Soane in his 'unhappy state of mind' against his grandchildren, for her own benefit. 'What, Sarah Conduitt, is it usual for a housekeeper to have her lady's maid and her footman, to sit at her master's table and to ride about the country with him?'[48] He threatened, in his usual fashion, to 'expose' her.

Soane still refused to help Agnes unless she separated from George. By February 1834 she was reduced to pawning her clothes. She promised her father-in-law that she would not live under the same roof as Maria but George, according to the evidence of Samuel England, Soane's go-between at this time, would not be separated from his lover. There is no mention of their son. Agnes was placed in an impossible position; George was violent and abusive but there was no assurance that Soane would assist her, even if she and the children left. Relations between the two remained hostile. However, by the summer of 1834 Soane had relented sufficiently to instruct Praed's Bank to pay £200 per annum to Agnes and her family.[49] Agnes and Clara received £10 each quarterly, Rosa £5 and Frederick £25. In 1835 he sent £2,722 to Ephraim How, his stockbroker, but Agnes received £129 8s 4d, considerably less than he allowed for John's education that year.[50]

It was now Frederick's turn to receive the onslaught of his grandfather's hostility. Despite everything, Soane had always paid for his grandson's education: on Pennington's suggestion he had first attended the Reverend Dr George Chisholm's school in Hammersmith and then Mr Watts's in Barnes. Soane forwarded the money via James Boaden.

Over the previous three years Frederick, in his mid-teens, had often been seen with an unsavoury character, a Captain Westwood. In December 1834 Soane set Charles Richardson, from his office and the putative assistant curator of the museum, on a distasteful mission to trail the unfortunate youth. Given Westwood's criminal record and notoriety, his neighbours' tales of unpleasant incidents at his house involving children[51] and the hardship of Frederick's own home life, he was surely in need of help and protection, rather than undercover surveillance. For Soane, no one in George's family was innocent.

A sadly distinctive figure, tall and thin with a very odd gait due to his splay feet, Frederick was now learning architectural drawing with John Tarring.[52] By January 1835 Tarring asked Soane to remove Frederick from his care; he was neglecting his work, behaving insultingly and staying out late at night. In three months he had copied just two elevations. Soane's grandchildren were proving no more satisfactory than his sons.

Young John and his sisters remained higher in his estimation. Maria Soane and her family had moved to Paris. Their financial affairs had been improved by the death of their grandmother's cousin, Miss Woodmeston of Albion Place in 1829. Bessie, her god-daughter, received a legacy of £10,000 3 per cent consols and young Maria £1,000. The other children received smaller sums.

In January 1832 Bessie met a Captain Chamier in Paris. Son of a member of the Council at Madras and grandson of an Admiral, Chamier was a Royal Naval captain who as a thirteen-year-old had seen service in the Scheldt expedition in 1809. Frederick Marryat, who was also to turn his experiences into fiction and became a close friend, was on another ship on the same unsuccessful engagement. In 1810, Chamier claimed to have accompanied Byron to the ruins of Troy and swum the Hellespont with him. Literature and colourful exploits had filled the intervening years, during which he remained an officer on half pay.

Unfortunately, when Bessie Soane met the dashing Captain, he had just lost a considerable sum after a failed publishing venture, the *Metropolitan Magazine*. Two months later, Maria presented the couple to Soane – Bessie's legal guardian since her father's death. She introduced Chamier, with perfect justification, as a highly literate man, with a reasonable sum left by his father (£10,000) and an annual income of around £300 from his writing. As she wrote, 'his pursuits and Bessy's will particularly accord . . . As far as I am capable of judging, I think he will take every tender care of Bessy, *and prove a most desirable friend for John.*' The age difference of some fifteen years did not seem to be a major objection.

213. Soane as an old man by Daniel Maclise. He took great exception to the picture which catches his stick-like physique, anachronistic clothing and uncertain expression.

Her grandfather was not persuaded (fig. 213); perhaps the literary bent of the intended son-in-law was too much for him to contemplate, after George's unrewarding years. Residence in Paris also suggested the possibility of a man escaping his creditors in England. He refused his consent, disapproving of the 'extraordinary haste' and asked them to wait until she came of age. Thereupon the couple fled to Gretna Green and a local newspaper glimpsed their muddied carriage as it dashed through Carlisle, including the detail that the bride was 'a near relative, it is said, of the celebrated architect of that name'. Soane's fame had an unfortunate habit of rearing up at him in unhappy circumstances.

In late April, the couple took part in a 'remarriage' at Esher. Soane's objections remained. From October 1832 until August 1834 Bessie[53] and Frederick Chamier continued to live in Paris. Their only daughter Elizabeth was born there in late January. Later, summarising their life together, he wrote, depressingly: 'I married in a hurry . . . I made love as a hungry man dresses for dinner . . . Time passed onwards – we went through the usual life, jumbling in the ruts of discomfort and then mooning along the uninteresting road of macadamized quietude.'[54]

In other areas of his life Soane was more generous, never more so than to Gandy, to whom he left an annuity of £100. Soane's debt to him, as he knew all too well, was immeasurable. Soane frequently advanced money when Gandy faced ruin and, on a number of occasions, was imprisoned for debt. In the 1830s, Soane offered him a room at Chelsea for his family. In this relationship, it was Soane who continually beat a path to Gandy's door, 'I have been nearly two years endeavouring to see you' he wrote in October 1833,[55] trying to break down the painter's fierce pride and help his family from destitution.

214. J.M.W. Turner vividly recorded the Houses of Parliament as they burned in October 1834. Soane's work on the south-western corner of the building was less damaged than most but it was not retained in Pugin and Barry's rebuilt complex.

The tide of taste was set firmly against die-hard classicists by now. It must have given Soane peculiar satisfaction to see Sir Robert Smirke, as he now was, drawing most of the criticism, with a stolid and generally uninspiring stream of public building. In marked contrast, the year before George Wightwick had written a perceptive criticism of Soane's work in the *Library of Fine Arts*. Much of his comment was reserved for the Bank of England. In words which must have delighted Soane he compared the Bank to a volume of Shakespeare for exhibiting 'faults that would damn professional mediocrity; beauties that ordinary talent may worship, hopeless of affecting their equal'.[56] He cannot be imitated with 'servile accuracy. In the activity of his fancy, and the boldness of his daring, he sometimes hazards more than he gains.'[57] Perhaps Soane saw himself here equated with another solitary, unpredictable and brilliant man who took dangerous chances, Napoleon Bonaparte.

In the evening of 16 October 1834 the Palace of Westminster exploded into flames (fig. 214). The source was in the House of Lords, a smouldering box of tallies. The event was witnessed from its early stages by A.W.N. Pugin.[58] Westminster Hall survived, so 'There is nothing much to regret and a great deal to rejoice in. A vast amount of Soane's mixtures and Wyatt's heresies have been effectively consigned to oblivion. Oh it was a glorious sight to see his composition mullions and cement pinnacles and battlements flying and cracking.' The speed with which the fire spread was terrifying and the effect of flames raging behind the tracery 'was truly curious and awfully grand'. He continues: 'I am afraid that the rebuilding will be made a complete job as that execrable designer Smirke has already been *giving* his opinions which may be reasonable supposed to be a preamble to his *selling* his diabolical plans and detestable details . . . His career has gone on too long.' In fact Pugin was mistaken, Soane's work at the southern end of the building was largely preserved by the south-westerly prevailing wind.

Soane had himself offered 'a kind of prophetic intimation'.[59] Referring to the conversion of the Court of Requests into the House of Lords in 1800 he had written that the construction, largely timber and plaster, was highly combustible: 'should a fire happen, what would become of the Painted Chamber, the House of Commons & Westminster Hall? Where would the progress of the fire be arrested? The want of security from fire, the narrow, gloomy and unhealthy passages, and the insufficiency of the accommodations in this building are important objections which call loudly for revision and speedy amendment.'

Smirke's involvement was simply as the attached architect to the Board of Works. In May 1835 Soane wrote to Joseph Hume hoping that the new buildings would be properly fireproofed and, in his reply Hume, a member of the committee, assured him that entrants to the competition would be required to attend to this matter.[60] Entries were to be submitted in the gothic or Elizabethan style, the call to arms for the Battle of the Styles. Confidently heralding the triumph of the true gothic revival was the man who had crowed as Wyatt's cement cracked and Smirke's reputation crumbled.

A.W.N. Pugin's *Contrasts* (1836) – published before the author had built anything except his own house[61] – opened with the hope that 'it will not be imagined I have acted from any private feelings towards those modern Professors of Architecture, whose works I have placed in comparison with similar Edifices of a more ancient period'. If any reader was in doubt who those men might be, the montage of buildings in the frontispiece clarified the matter; Soane's ornamented pendentives from the Bank joined William Wilkins's National Gallery, Nash's All Souls, Langham Place and Robert Smirke in Pugin's rogue's gallery.

It was a book in the tradition of Soane's own polemical productions – but with a mission to right the world. Pugin's fluency and imaginative graphic format (the nearest to which, perhaps, was Repton's 'before and after' flaps in the Red Books) contrasting each work in bad (neoclassical) taste to a gothic equivalent, was refreshing and novel.

Pugin's main thrust was an attack upon plain, cheap churches, the erection of which 'has dwindled down into a mere trade' with a side-swipe at the Protestant church, as mean in spirit as in its structure and observance. By contrast with the magnificence of the buildings of the true Catholic gothic, made with loving craftsmanship and dependent upon vernacular skills, were 'those nests of monstrosities, the Regent's Park and Regent Street, where all kind of styles are jumbled together to make up a mass . . . We have Swiss cottages in a flat country; Italian villas in the coldest situations; a Turkish kremlin for a royal residence; Greek temples in crowded lanes; Egyptian auction rooms.'[62] To the buildings on his prefatory plate he added Buckingham Palace, the British Museum, Windsor Castle and Soane's Board of Trade. What is to be expected given the education of the architect, thundered the angry young man. The student 'lolls over his desk, draws the five orders, then pricks off plans', then come a few years at the Royal Academy, possibly a medal, and then off to classic shores, where he goes over 'for the thousandth time, the same set of measurements on the same set of cornices and columns' allowing him to come back 'a conceited bustling pretender'. On return he is more than likely to become 'a common surveyor – a man who writes architect on his door and on his card, but who is, in reality, a measurer of land, a valuer of dilapidations and a cutter-down of tradesmen's accounts'.

215. The young A.W.N. Pugin larded *Contrasts* with Soanean detail and also compared his house with one of the great French Renaissance town houses, in the rue d'Horloge, Rouen. In the second edition the plate had been removed.

Among Pugin's illustrations, Soane was honoured with the opening pastiche plate, the scored ornament and mannered acroteria easily recognisable, while 13 Lincoln's Inn Fields was singled out for a full page plate (fig. 215).[63]

On 20 June 1835 Soane was awarded a Gold Medal by the 'Architects of England'. The medal showed Soane's likeness on one side, modelled by Chantrey, the north-west angle of the Bank on the reverse. Silver medals were sent to foreign academies and subscribers received bronze versions.

At the presentation Sir Jeffry Wyatville received Sir John Soane in his own library at 13 Lincoln's Inn Fields. Soane was too overcome by the occasion to read his reply to the tributes and his solicitor John Bicknell did so on his behalf. It was announced that Soane had contributed £150 per annum for the Distressed Architects Fund[64] and the evening continued with a ball in his honour, held in Sandby's Freemasons' Hall. Owing to his frailty, he could not attend to bless the general festivities and quadrille dancing. Chantrey's bust – certainly smiling that evening – appeared in his stead, garlanded, in the good company of busts of Vitruvius, Palladio, Michelangelo, Jones and Wren.[65]

Inevitably most events in which Soane took part were valedictory. Yet Soane did not lose his powers; he kept iron control of himself and his descent towards death as completely as he had the other aspects of his life. His death, at a great age, was part of an orderly transfer. The house and museum, its collections and endowment secure, and, finally, published as he wished, would speak for him after his departure. Family affairs apart, there were no loose ends.

He died on Friday 20 January, 1837 at half past three, having caught a chill. He was eighty-three years old. One obituary referred to the cause being the uneven heating arrangements in the house, the benefits of Perkins's warming apparatus apparently not percolating up to the upper floors of the house.[66] The notice of his death in the *Times* on the following Monday was brief. Readers could easily have missed it, distracted by a colourful story in the same column, a description of an escaped royal stag careering up Guildford Street in Chertsey, pursued by the hunt in full cry.

As requested in his will, Soane's funeral was 'plain without ostentation or parade' and he was buried in the family vault at St Pancras. He had left no instructions for the manner of service and the funeral was so private as to pass unrecorded.

The professional courtesies began immediately. 'I stand not here to exaggerate or extenuate his failures, not to be the mere panegyrist of his merits' said Thomas Leverton Donaldson, President of the Institute of British Architects – having been just that when presenting Soane's Gold Medal in front of the same professional audience.[67] Anyone talking, or writing, of Soane and his work must have felt a sense of relief that he was no longer there to react to every word or nuance. Once Soane had departed the stage, he could be examined in detail.

Oddly, this did not occur. The criticisms of the 1830s and 1840s were little different from those of the 1790s. Soane had lost touch with his peers and their successors – as George Wightwick would so graphically show by depicting the 'Soanean' as a *cul de sac* off the progression of architectural styles. In a damning account of Soane's late work, Donaldson talked of his dependency on 'novelty in the employment of embellishments, trivial and unmeaning, and by the introduction of meretricious effects lowered the character of the art'. This was, indeed, no panegyric.

More revealingly Donaldson spoke of Soane as a teacher. Initially the lectures had excited the students but the professor had not moved on; his lectures had become repetitive and his audiences dwindled when the first and second series of his lectures had been read on his behalf by the Royal Academy secretary, Henry Howard, in 1832 and 1833.[68] Further, Donaldson hinted that Soane had missed a golden opportunity; a more diplomatic man might have used the Covent Garden dispute to open the door to constructive criticism of modern work (as several of his peers had wished). Soane, instead, had 'neutralised the advantages'.

Soane's unchallenged position remained as the leader of the profession, a model of rectitude and probity to those who would follow, as Donaldson acknowledged.

Within architecture the emphasis was elsewhere; the gothic revival was in the ascendant, the Renaissance revival the only acceptable classical language. Pugin's *Contrasts* was the talking point. Samuel Palmer, at the end of a picturesque tour of 'Ossianic sublimities' in north Wales, arrived at Tintern Abbey and found himself 'once more a pure quaint crinkle-crankle goth'. He wrote to fellow painter George Richmond:

> if you are a goth come hither, if you're a pure Greek take a cab and make a sketch of St Paul's Covent Garden before breakfast. [Joseph] Addison speaks of the cathedral of Siena (one of the richest in the world) as the work of barbarians – clever savages almost . . . he could not bear too *lofty* and *pointed* a style – pity he died before the area of Doric warehouses Ionic turnpike gates and Corinthian ginshops! – his taste outran his age – ours hobbles after.[69]

Soane, fitting into neither camp, with his awkwardnesses and his wilfulness (inevitably seen to be heavily bound up with his personality) was no better understood in the years after his death than he had been in the year of *The Modern Goth* attack. As Gandy had said twenty years before: 'you are the only one . . . [to] show that architecture is not an imitative art, whose models must be formed in the mind'. Early Soane, as Cockerell wrote in the 1840s offered a simplicity which 'has its admirers even to this day'. Late Soane, atonal and discordant as his work could be, found no champions.

George Wightwick's handsome volume, *The Palace of Architecture* ('a romance of art and history') was published in 1840. He found the work of his former master hard to categorise, as contradictory perhaps as his personality, but he made an intelligent attempt to consider it. He appended a map of ten 'leading varieties that constitute the empire of Architectural Design'; the eleventh was 'the Soanean' (fig. 216). Was the Soanean exterior, he wondered

> *more* than an episode? . . . Sir John Soane . . . struck out a style of his own . . . not . . . to be taken as model-worthy but certainly to be studied as containing much that is extremely beautiful and evincing a more playful fancy – if not a more vigorous genius – than had been exhibited for centuries. His reputation as a practiser of Roman and Graeco-Roman Architecture (for he was never *pure* Greek) is rather supported

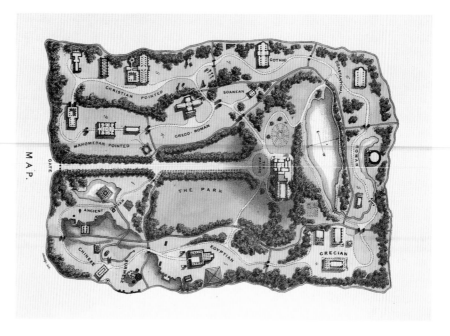

216. George Wightwick came to know Soane extremely well for a few months in 1826, acting as his amanuensis. Although the arrangement was not a success, Wightwick became a thoughtful critic and admirer of Soane's very individual style which he envisaged in this plate from his book as ending in a cul de sac off the Graeco-Roman, securely walled off from the gothic.

by his magnificent designs for Royal Palaces, Senate-Houses etc. than by his buildings; but there is enough in his own peculiar style (as exemplified in the Bank of England) to warrant a defence and high admiration.'[70]

Wightwick, characteristically perceptive, noted the particular level of hostility that his work attracted, and certain wonderful touches: the linear decoration, the way in which Soane could take the verticality of a pier directly into the curve of an arch, much as his rectangular ground plan effortlessly transformed into the characteristic flat-domed ceiling above. 'Whatever may be the faults and frivolities of the architecture of the late eccentric Professor', he continued, 'they are not more offensive than the mere plagiarisms which form the staple of certain other, less abused, and less imaginative architects.'

Elsewhere, Wightwick criticised Soane for repetition: 'he repeated himself till he became, as it were, the passive slave of his own mannerism' but praised his fight against 'the tyranny of precedent'. There was, for all his faults (and Wightwick did not let Soane off easily) 'virtue in his very faults, for they were corrective of those commonplace proprieties which only retard the advance of invention and originality'.[71]

An American visitor, Ralph Waldo Emerson, visiting London in 1848, made another anology, seeing Soane's house as a microcosm of England. 'Yes, to see England well needs a hundred years; for, what they told me was the merit of Sir John Soane's Museum, in London, – that it was well packed and well saved, – is the merit of England; – it is stuffed full, in all corners and crevices.'[72]

As might be expected, there was little sign of a Soane architectural legacy, beyond the warnings that he offered to those tempted to take a divergent path from their peers. George Wightwick pursued his own eclectic path in the west country, in partnership with John Foulston of Devonport, while Joseph Gandy's exhibits at the Royal Academy veered ever closer to the megalomaniac. Decimus Burton, an admirer of Soane's work,[73] had soared into prominence with a succession of public works but then faded from view. C. R. Cockerell had stepped into Soane's place both at the Bank and at the Royal Academy, and even assumed his colouring, exhibiting, in 1849, a drawing of the cumulative ancient and modern architectural styles entitled *The Professor's Dream*. Cockerell's lectures, which he began in January 1841, showed him far more intellectually able than Soane, a man of ideas, 'who knew far more than could ever be contained within such a course of lectures'.[74]

The new generation of promising practitioners was, of course, some fifty or sixty years younger than Soane. James Elmes, a stalwart supporter of Soane in print, was soon overshadowed by his son, Harvey Lonsdale Elmes, who won the first prize in a competition to design St George's Hall, Liverpool, in 1839 at the age of twenty-five. Perhaps only Alexander 'Greek' Thompson shared Soane's idiosyncratic approach to classical antiquity but – like Harrison before him – limited his influence by working far from London.

Only in north America, where influences came later and lingered longer, did Soane's legacy flourish, largely through the major public works of Benjamin Henry Latrobe, above all Baltimore Cathedral (fig. 217), a memory of Soane frozen at the Bank Stock Office and Rotunda, when Latrobe left the country. Half a century later, the Eastlake style (itself derived from an English text on ornament[75]) which became so dominant in American decorative arts in the 1870s, offered a synthesis of the gothic and the Arts and Crafts recalling Soane's late work, for example the lodge at Pell Wall.

Soane's pupils did not follow him – he had offered no clear direction, merely an unimpeachable view of the professional role. George Basevi, who quickly forgot his masters' strictures against speculation, built up a healthy practice developing South Kensington. In 1835 he won the prestigious competition to design the new Fitzwilliam Museum in Cambridge which he built in full-throated Graeco-Roman style. Ten years later he was killed, falling from the western tower of Ely Cathedral.

As if to emphasise the undeniable advantages of being well-born in architecture, the sons and younger brothers of Soane's contemporaries rose relentlessly up the professional ladder. Younger Playfairs, Hardwicks, Pugins and Wyatts were flourishing, a poignant reminder of Soane's failed family enterprise.

George Soane had wasted no time mourning his father. Five days after his death he re-applied to the Royal Literary Fund. He moved swiftly 'having just lost a father who rolled in affluence' as he put it. On 8 March, 1837 a delicately worded note told him that he had been awarded £50, 'in consequence of his acknowledged authorship, distress and the great liberality of his father, the late Sir John Soane to this Society'.[76]

George quickly challenged his father's will, with the support of John's children. His own annuity was £52 per annum and nothing more which, Soane had stated, was in response to 'his general misconduct and undignified behaviour and his determined and constant opposition to my wishes evinced in the general tenor of his life'. Agnes Soane received a £40 annuity 'not to be subject to the debts or control of her said husband'.

217. Soane's influence in his time was surprisingly limited, despite the interest in his work in recent years. One exception was Benjamin Henry Latrobe, S. P. Cockerell's pupil's before he left for the United States of America in 1795. By then he knew the Bank of England well and his work, especially at Baltimore Cathedral, echoes that of Soane.

The condition was that neither she, nor her daughters, live under the same roof as Maria Boaden.

On 6 March the *Times* reprinted a notice from the *Observer*. It bore the marks of George's pen. The executors and trustees of the will of the late Sir John Soane 'who carried his malevolent feelings against his only child down to the grave with him, have very properly refused to make themselves participants in the testator's bad feelings by taking upon themselves the trusts conferred on them by that document which consequently remains unproved'. George was appealing on the grounds of his father's insanity. 'During Sir John's life he gave small weekly allowances to his grand-children, which he ordered to be called for at a certain minute on a day named, and if they were a few minutes before or after the time or were ill and unable to come, they were to forfeit that allowance for that week.' Foxhall, 'a respectable trademan . . . in no degree related to or connected with Sir John', had been declared residuary legatee, after the death of all other legatees. The piece concluded by noting that the majority of these had honourably agreed to help restore the property, amounting to almost £200,000, to the Soane family.

The witnesses to the will, and to subsequent codicils, were required to provide depositions over the coming months. Three of Bicknell's clerks did so, as well as Dr Joseph Moore, Henry Howard and the seventy-two-year-old Pennington. They attested to Soane's excellent business sense, his clear rationality and, as asked, to the degree of his eccentricity. Pennington, who had known Soane for forty years and in the last three years of his life had seen him almost daily, judged him of extremely sound mind. He ended, 'I will . . . swear that it is my firm belief that Sir John Soane did not in any instance within my knowledge overstep the line which seperates or distinguishes extreme eccentricity from mental derangement; his perception was always correct and his mind was free from delusion.'[77]

On 1 August the judge at the Court of Prerogative delivered his sentence.[78] He told the court that the will was being disputed on the grounds that 'it was founded on an insane delusion that he (Mr George Soane) was not the son of Sir John but a changeling and really the child of a brick-layer's labourer'. He had examined the book (Soane's printed account of George's behaviour) and noted that 'not one of the facts in the book had been denied. The allegation must therefore be rejected.'

George appealed but on 26 November 1837 the suit was dropped.[79] Now George and the family turned their attention to the Museum. In February they petitioned the House of Commons to break up the museum, redistribute the contents between the national collections and divide the trust funds between them. The trustees counter-petitioned. By July, John Bicknell resigned as a trustee, exhausted by the continual family attacks, but his fellow trustees persuaded him to remain.[80] By the end of 1838 the estate entered Chancery and George was back in prison, now the Queen's Bench. His petitions and legal actions had cost him dear. He must have become a familiar figure at the Insolvent Debtors' Court.

Ironically, the first Soane to appear in architectural circles following Sir John Soane's death was Frederick Soane, his grandson, who applied to the Architects' Benevolent Fund in August 1843. His grandfather had brought him up an architect and then 'from motives which it does not become me to explain, refused to article me'. He was utterly destitute, living wretchedly in one room in Vauxhall, a pauper with a wife who was about to enter hospital.

Frederick Chamier, his cousin-in-law, was making strenuous efforts to help him, even writing to Sir Robert Peel. Frederick Soane had recently stood surety for his father in the sum of £300 and, George having defaulted, Frederick himself had been imprisoned. His £60 annuity from his grandfather's will had been sold to free them from prison. Chamier invoked the great value of Sir John Soane's bequest to the nation 'by which his wealth was turned from its natural current' in support of his grandson's case.[81] This appeal to the Prime Minister resulted in a swift and satisfactory outcome; Frederick was appointed to the Stamp and Tax Office at £2 a week. Chamier wrote to Peel a fortnight later offering heartfelt thanks on Frederick's behalf. Shortly after, the Chamiers moved to Paris.

John Soane, Soane's grandson stepped out of the shadows in 1847 and asked if he might live at 13 Lincoln's Inn Fields. He had married Mary Borrer in Brighton in 1844. Nothing came of the request and the following year he died in Madeira. The Emperor's diamond was still in his widow's possession at her death in 1886.

In December 1841 George went back to the Royal Literary Fund, his publisher Churton vouching for him as author of *The Life of the Duke of Wellington*, *Frolics of Puck* and *The Handbook of the Rhine*. Soane, now over fifty, was proving as dexterous as ever. This time he was awarded £30. In early July 1842 he turned up at Lincoln's Inn Fields, with one of his daughters. He asked George Bailey about the museum's surplus funds and was, no doubt, surprised to be told that the £900 per annum return on £30,000 3 per cent Consols was insufficient for the trustees to make the collection 'as useful they could wish'. Soane then asked his daughter to corroborate his claim that they had no beds and were reduced to eating dry bread: she did not speak.[82]

George Soane also wrote to the Prime Minister, Sir Robert Peel and to Queen Victoria, recounting his circumstances. He and his wife had a modest annuity of £80 between them and his daughters were helping to support the family 'in music and dancing taught as an accomplishment'. His father's 'prejudice' against him was 'considered by many private friends proof of insanity'. He appealed for pensions for his daughters, as for himself, or – failing that – a theatrical licence to reward his 'five and twenty years experience as a dramatist and manager'.[83] He had a position at the Princess Theatre, Oxford Street.

The bankruptcy of his employer may have precipitated the next crisis, George's own bankruptcy, which was posted in the London Gazette on 1 September 1843 for a declared sum of £10,000, largely contracted on 'post obit bonds previously to his father's death'. One of his landlords, Mr Hatton, 'conducted his own case with great pertinacity and something more, and afforded a greater degree of laughter than is usually met with in cases of insolvency'. Hatton had resorted to whitewashing the house, including the windows, and stopping up the chimneys in order to dislodge his unwanted tenant.[84] It was then that the unfortunate Frederick was imprisoned on his father's behalf.

In 1846 George Soane tried yet another (unsuccessful) application to the Royal Literary Fund: 'Many of my dramatic pieces have kept possession of

218. In 1864 the *Illustrated London News* included a feature showing various rooms from Sir John Soane's Museum, by then in existence for some thirty years and opened sporadically in daylight hours. Here visitors explore the basement.

the stage for thirty years, while my songs are upon every pianoforte in the kingdom', but his paternal and maternal inheritance had been 'alienated from me by an act of parliament'. Again in February 1852, from Greenwich and now a widower, he told the appeals committee that his daughters were still living with him but his son was overseas. The cause of his distress was 'in great measure attributable to illness, disinheritance, unforeseen losses and more than the usual vicissitudes of an author's life'. Added to this his youngest daughter was 'wasting away with consumption'. His application was vouched for by none other than John Britton who had, he said, known him personally for forty-five years. Another of his references was Mr Bernard Burke of *Burke's Peerage*.

In the summer of 1855, George applied again, now from Chorlton on Medlock, near Manchester, where he was living with his two daughters, 'one musical, the other upon the stage but both out of employ for some months'. There is no mention of Rosa's consumption, nor of sons, legitimate or illegitimate.

On 25 May 1858 the Vice-Chancellor's Court settled that Edward Foxhall junior's twenty-one-year reversionary interest in the Soane estate[85] be settled into eight equal parts, there being, as yet, no great-grandchildren to claim their inheritance. John had died childless ; his sisters Maria Sibbern and Harriet Niven had no children from their marriages.[86] The arrangement divided the £140,000 estate between Foxhall (who received four parts) and the four others – Elizabeth Chamier, Harriet, Maria and George. The financial affairs of Soane's legatees now went back into Chancery. By 1871 the estate was valued at over £180,000.[87] In October 1873, the unlikelihood of further heirs now accepted, three properties were offered for sale, a pasture at Dockmoor near Aylesbury (one of Soane's purchases for voting purposes), 80 Cowcross Street and 14 Lincoln's Inn Fields.

In July 1860 George died.[88] His catalogue entry in the British Library is far longer than his father's, but his reputation had faded long before his death. His career showed him industrious but a slave to literary fashion. His personal life might be reminiscent of Shelley's but he lacked his qualities.

The illustrious name of Soane was not destined to flourish, although the family spread widely. In 1878, following the death of Joseph Bonomi the younger, the curator, Frederick had written to the trustees regretting that he had not been appointed in his stead and asking for financial assistance. He was sixty-three years old. He died in 1880 and was buried in Hampstead. Nothing is known about the fate of the other surviving male Soane, the illegitimate grandson with the Byronic name, Manfred.

The Soane Museum, dark, difficult of access and little visited, took on its own mystique in the latter years of the nineteenth century (fig. 218). Henry James's proper young American, Laura Wing, promises to take her new friend and compatriot, Mr Wendover, to 'a charming place . . . to which she was afraid to go alone and where she should be grateful for a protector'. It was, she told him, 'one of the most curious things in London and one of the least known'. After exploring the house for half an hour, their emotions heightened by a furious thunderstorm, they descend to the basement, wandering between 'strange vague things' in a labyrinthine cave and seeming to be in the presence of shadowy figures revealed, by a flash of lightning and a shriek, to be Laura's errant sister and her lover. Henry James's novella *A London Life*, published in 1888 launched 13 Lincoln's Inn Fields as a suitably atmospheric setting for awkward fictional encounters.

Soane's own dramatic control over events was hard to improve upon. Down the years came a theatrical succession of openings of locked and sealed containers, as he had directed. The first had been on 22 November 1866 when the assembled trustees were invited to open drawers and cupboards containing mainly correspondence and accounts. Twenty years later, eight trustees and the solicitor gathered before his dressing-room cupboard, which revealed his privately printed accounts of the troubles with his sons as well as other letters and bills. Finally, in 1896, the same scene was enacted in front of a sealed bath, where further even more sensitive papers, had been entombed.

POSTSCRIPT

In the latter decades of the nineteenth century avant-garde designers in the decorative arts attempted to dispense with the catalogue of historic styles. Christopher Dresser – born three years before Soane's death – was a designer whose synthesis of styles was arrived at from the study of organic forms. In his view, historic styles provided the tool from which designers should produce 'new forms and new combinations in the spirit of the ornament of the past'. The search for novelty, so excoriated in Soane's lifetime, was now a legitimate pursuit, sanctioned by the profligate historicism of the high Victorians.

Soane's work did not appeal to the architects of the Arts and Crafts movement; the ambiguities and complexities of Soane's later interiors were the antithesis of the notions of truth to materials and fitness for purpose. For them, Soane's inverted mouldings and reticent detail were slightly unnerving, while his Roman public works were over-inflated. Soane, the architect who understood the business of building, revelled in the qualities of materials and construction detail – the man they might have appreciated – was subsumed entirely by his reputation as the architect of the wilful solution. Soane, wrote Bolton, 'appeals to those who desire to breach or expand the long line of classic tradition' and even in the inter-war years only classical revivalists bothered to look again at Soane.

Meanwhile, Sir Giles Gilbert Scott's K2 telephone box (fig. 219), its reassuring form so reminiscent of the Soane family monument – symbol of all Soane's miseries – was soon familiar in its successive variants in every town, village and rural cross-road. Scott became a trustee of Sir John Soane's Museum in 1925, the year in which his design was selected, suggesting that the link was more than mere coincidence.

Arthur Bolton, curator of Sir John Soane's Museum between 1917 and 1945, struggled to link Soane with art nouveau and then, more interestingly, identified the constant uncertainty of outcome in Soane's work as its enduring quality.[1] Bolton saw his independence as a position with 'a particular interest' in the 1920s but 'before he can be claimed as a modernist the attitude of that school to the classic art to which Soane was devoted must first be determined'.[2] Bolton, himself a classical revivalist, drew upon the vast archive of Adam drawings in the museum, which Soane had

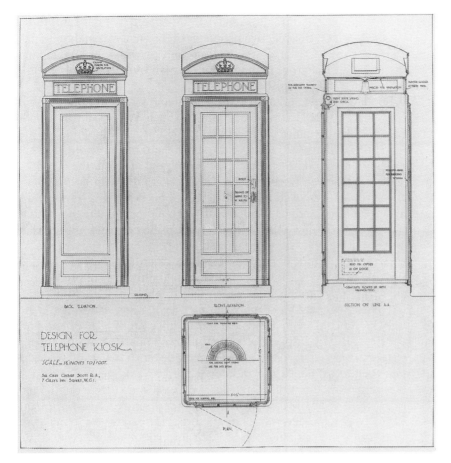

DESIGN FOR
TELEPHONE KIOSK.

SCALE 1½ INCHES TO 1 FOOT.

BACK ELEVATION.   FRONT ELEVATION.   SECTION ON LINE A-A.

PLAN.

219. Sir Giles Gilbert Scott's 1924 prototype for the K2 telephone box which was soon to be a familiar feature of the British landscape. Soane's shallow dome, used on the family tomb and elsewhere, characterises it. Scott became a Trustee of the museum the following year.

bought in 1818, for his Adam room designed for the British Empire Exhibition at Wembley in 1924 and 1925.

The centenary of Soane's death in January 1937 was marked by an eloquent tribute in the *Times* entitled *Architecture of the Mind* 'from a correspondent'.[3] The anonymous author, in fact John Summerson, saw the imaginative power of Soane as something more readily ascribed to English poets than architects. He described 'the amazing beauty' of the old Bank, effectively hidden since so few had been privileged to enter it and now gone. 'It had not architectural unity in the obvious sense . . . but Soane contrived to give the interiors an organic coherence and bonded the whole with his romantic and exquisite outer wall . . . As Soane left it, the Bank was a fantastic palace, in many ways more akin to Byzantine work than to the idiomatic Greco-Roman of its period.' He referred to the luminous, subtly coloured halls and then moved on to Dulwich where the 'toy-like but sinister mausoleum of Noel Desenfans strikes the true Soanic note, while the plain, curiously subtle brickwork of the gallery itself displays no less his intense preoccupation with the elusive fundamentals of architectural form'. He continued: 'The tragedy of John Soane was the tragedy of a mind in which spiritual adventure was crushed but never killed by the tyranny of an intellectual tradition.'

Summerson, who would become Bolton's successor as the curator of Lincoln's Inn Fields in 1945, wrote as a young architect and critic, intrigued by the insights into the creative mind offered by Freud and Jung. He was also at that time an active promoter of the International Style. He saw the destructive tensions, architectural and personal, around Soane and, against that background, judged him beaten by 'incompatible realities', rather than made by them.

Attrition and war dealt doubly hard with Soane's work in London – his city. The rapid loss of almost all his public work as Whitehall was rebuilt to reflect the new realities of govenment, the virtual demolition of the Bank of England (demolished ten years before the centenary) and Herbert Baker's portentious replacement,[4] the bombing of both the Chelsea Infirmary and Dulwich Picture Gallery in the Second World War (the latter quickly rebuilt) removed many instances of his best work. The bombing and demolition reduced several of his buildings to the ruins that Gandy had so fancifully depicted, in a spirit of literary and antiquarian romanticism, while they stood intact and robust.

The change of attitude towards Soane was sudden. Precisely his derided qualities, the 'wilfulness', his lively reaction to 'the tyranny of precedent', his adherence to an architecture which defied labels and would become referred to as 'Soanean' for want of another term, suggested some magic of which 13 Lincoln's Inn Fields existed to offer proof – as Soane had always intended. His stripped ornament allowed classicism to be reconsidered by modernists, his early use of iron made him a structural pioneer. On the other wing, his richly traditional public work pleased those for whom minimalism and reduction from the classical text were anathema. The reappraisal of Soane came with post-modernism, yet he was praised and valued by old and new school modernists.[5] He had begun to make an audacious call upon the attention of international architects, even at the polarities of academic classicism and neo-modernism.

Despite the swings of fashion, a cycle of mood and *Zeitgeist* into which Soane, like other towering figures such as Hawksmoor or Lutyens, have been swept, re-evaluated and then restored to equilibrium, there are other important aspects of Sir John Soane to remember – those revealed by the uniquely close-focused record of his life and practice that he left in such quantity in his house.

There is evidence in the long and often melancholy story of Soane's life that he was a man frequently beyond self-control. Despite that fearful temperament, so damaging to him, personally and professionally, many – friends, clients, employees – were prepared to exercise understanding and forbearance to see the best in Soane or to forgive him. He set standards of probity and care that remain models of professional conduct for the contemporary architect. He took as much care to detail a hinge or a wainscot moulding as some great set-piece at the Bank; he was as attentive to a good workman as to his Prime Ministerial clients (whose modern successors live under his Downing Street ceilings). He was rewarded by the loyalty of both.

And what of Soane, the 'accidental' romantic? The man, as angry as Benjamin Robert Haydon, as visionary as William Blake or J.M.W. Turner, as expressive as William Hazlitt, remains unimpeachably a mid-Georgian in his attitudes, his references and his Pittite view of the world. From a strenuously conducted programme of self-improvement and further education, professional diligence and probity, emerged John Soane, the architect. He poured his own money into buildings that he knew would provoke argument and criticism; for himself at Lincoln's Inn Fields and Pitshanger, and for others at Tyringham, Bentley Priory, Mogerhanger, Chelsea, Dulwich and the Freemasons' Hall. From a sense of profound spiritual unease, of unfulfilled ambitions for himself and his sons, of inexpressible frustrations, came the tension – the grit in his oyster shell. His fiercely held faith in the place of imagination and poetry in architecture make Soane, despite himself at times, if not quite the genius he believed himself to be, certainly among the great European romantic artists.

BIBLIOGRAPHICAL ABBREVIATIONS

The spelling and punctuation in the extracts from correspondence, diaries, notebooks and other manuscript material has been gently modernised.

ABRAMSON Daniel Abramson 'Money's Architecture, the building of the Bank of England 1731–1833' (unpublished Ph.D. thesis, Harvard 1993).

ACRES Wilfrid Marston Acres *The Bank of England from Within 1694–1900* (2 vols) (London 1931).

BOLTON PORTRAIT Arthur Bolton *The Portrait of Sir John Soane RA* (London 1927).

BOLTON WORKS Arthur T Bolton (ed.) *The Works of Sir John Soane RA Architect 1753–1837* (London 1924).

COLVIN Howard Colvin *A Biographical Dictionary of British Architects 1600–1840* (second edn, London 1978).

DU PREY EDUCATION Pierre de la Ruffinière du Prey *John Soane's Architectural Education 1753–80* (New York and London 1977).

DU PREY MAKING Pierre de la Ruffinière du Prey *John Soane, the Making of an Architect* (Chicago and London 1982).

EHRMAN PITT John Ehrman *The Younger Pitt* (3 vols): *The Years of Acclaim* (London 1969); *The Reluctant Transition* (London 1983); *The Consuming Struggle* (London 1996).

FD Kenneth Garlick and Alistair Macintyre (eds) *The Diary of Joseph Farington* vols 1–14; Kathryn Cave (ed.) vols 7–14; Evelyn Newby (ed.) Index (New Haven and London 1978–98).

HISTORY OF PARLIAMENT *The Commons 1754–1790* Namier & Brooke (3 vols) ; *The Commons 1790–1820* (5 vols.) K.G. Thorne (London 1986).

INGAMELLS John Ingamells *A Biographical Dictionary of British and Irish Travellers in Italy 1701–1800* compiled from the Brinsley Ford Archive (New Haven and London 1997).

KINGS WORKS Howard Colvin (ed.) *The History of the Kings Works*;Volume 6: 1782–1851 J. M. Crook and M. H. Port (London 1973).

REPTON MEMOIR Humphry Repton 'Memoir' BL Add MS 62, 112.

SOANE MEMOIRS John Soane *Memoirs of the Professional Life of an Architect* (privately printed1835).

STROUD DANCE Dorothy Stroud *George Dance, Architect 1741–1825* (London)

STROUD SOANE Dorothy Stroud *Sir John Soane Architect* (second edn London1996).

THORNTON & DOREY Peter Thornton and Helen Dorey *A Miscellany of Objects from Sir John Soane's Museum* (London 1991).

WORLD CITY Celina Fox (ed.) *London, World City 1800–1840* (New Haven and London 1992).

WATKIN LECTURES David Watkin *Sir John Soane: Enlightenment Thought and the Royal AcademyLectures* (Cambridge 1996).

NOTES

ABBREVIATIONS

BL British Library
BoE Bank of England
HLRO House of Lords Record Office
IGI International Genealogical Index
JSAH Journal of the Society of Architectural Historians
LMA London Metropolitan Archive
NRO Norfolk Record Office
PRO Public Record Office
RA Royal Academy
RCS Royal College of Surgeons
SAHGB Society of Architectural Historians of Great Britain
SM Soane Museum; SC: Soane Case; SNB: Soane Notebooks; ESNB: Elizabeth Soane Notebooks

1 BEGINNINGS

1 Thorvaldsen, the Danish classical sculptor, also a student of humble origins travelling on a scholarship, referred to his day of departure as his 'Roman birthday' and marked the day annually.

2 See p. 60 below; John Stuart his friend and client had been dealing with an unscrupulous money-lender and Soane found himself in the middle. Stuart wrote to him 'your letter is so confused from your agitation I can scarce make sense of it . . . you can never be imprisoned for bills you don't accept.'

3 Du Prey *Making* p.4.

4 Goring expanded greatly in the Edwardian era, becoming a riverside resort.

5 Soan and its variant spellings was not a very common eighteenth-century name in Berkshire or Oxfordshire but many hundreds were recorded in Hampshire, see IGI.

6 Walter Money *Stray Notes on the Parish of Basildon* (n.d.) p.12, cited du Prey *Education* ch. 1., n. 8. The Basildon parish records (in the front of the register of baptisms D/P 14/1/6) record the building of the tower by subscription in 1734. Churchwardens' records (D/A2 c.103) record in 1733 'our Tower and Bell out of Repair but now Repairing' and in 1734, 'Wee present the tower & bells Ought to Repare.' No builders' names are given in either case. Information kindly supplied by Berkshire Record Office.

7 SM: Vol. 40

8 Late in life Soane went to Basildon to 'examine' the parish register, possibly for some detail in his mother's life or even his father's involvement in the building of the church. SNB 208, 4 September 1830.

9 Stroud *Soane* p.17 mentions a probable Marcy nephew or cousin as vicar of Broughton, Oxfordshire in the late eighteenth century.

10 Du Prey *Education* Appendix A.

11 John Betjeman (ed.) *Murray's Berkshire* (London 1949).

12 First cited by T. L. Donaldson 'A Review of the Professional Life of Sir John Soane (with some remarks on his genius & productions, read at the first subsequent ordinary meeting of the IBA, Monday 6 February 1837)' (1837).

13 E. J. O'Dwyer *Thomas Frognall Dibdin* (Pinner 1967). Dibdin's research, such as the three volume *Bibliographical Decameron*, was only redeemed by its very beautiful typography and binding.

14 SM: SNB 1, 15 October 1784 'madre 1.1.0, sorella 10s 6d.'

15 *History of Surrey* (Vol. 2) by E. W. Brayley with John Britton and E. W. Brayley jun. (1841).

16 In his *Memoirs* Soane credits a 'close relative' with the introduction, however, another interpretation offered by Donaldson was that one of Soane's sisters was employed as a servant in the Dance household.

17 Later, Soane always referred to the Peacocks as 'Mr and Mrs Peacock of Chertsey' although there is no reference to them in records of the town (see Chertsey Museum names index). The Peacocks lived at 17 Finsbury Circus on the edge of the City of London.

18 Thomas Love Peacock's father Samuel, a Holborn glass-blower, died when he was a small child. The widow Peacock (*née* Love) came with her three-year-old son to live at her father's house in Chertsey in 1788. In adult life Peacock returned to the area.

19 Du Prey *Making* pp. 26–9 emphasises the importance of James Peacock's influence upon Soane who belatedly acknowledged the debt in his RA lectures.

20 FD Vol. I, p. 254, 10 October 1794. See du Prey *Education* pp. 20–21.

21 See John Summerson *Georgian London* pp. 97–8 (revised edition, London 1991).

22 Later Sir Nathaniel Dance-Holland.

23 See Stroud *Dance* p. 67.

24 James Peacock was confirmed as Dance's Assistant Clerk in 1771.

25 *World City*, see Andrew Saint 'The Building Art of the First Industrial Metropolis', pp. 51–76.

26 The others were Williams Chambers, John Gwynn (author of *London and Westminster Improved* 1766), Thomas Sandby and William Tyler, a sculptor and architect.

27 Album now at Royal Academy.

28 Eileen Harris 'Sir John Soane's Library' *Apollo*, April 1990.

29 Stroud *Dance* ch. 5.

30 Summerson *Georgian London* p. 128.

31 Robin Evans *The Fabrication of Virtue: English Prison Architecture 1750–1840* (Cambridge 1982).

32 Wyatt was employed again by Dance and the City Corporation ten years later, after the Gordon Riots had reduced the just-completed building to a fire-gutted ruin.

33 Peacock took the Joiners' livery in 1774. For this and other information about Peacock, see Colvin.

34 The firm traded with Lisbon, later becoming bankers to the Russian court. All three families in the partnership were linked by marriage. See J. J. Green *Biographical and Historical Notices of Jonathan Gurnell* (typescript 1914, Ealing Public Library).

35 Neither the RA schools register nor the Council minutes give any clues.

36 Bolton *Portrait* p.8. Letter of 13 December 1768: Tyler, Thomas and Paul Sandby to John Sawry Gilpin.

37 For the French system see Neil Bingham 'Architecture at the Royal Academy Schools 1768 to 1836' in *The Education of the Architect* 22nd SAHGB proceedings 1993.

38 Chambers excluded pattern or copy books and builders' manuals and, disliking the Greek Revival, was reluctant to accept the Society of Dilettante's volume *Ionian Antiquities* presented upon the foundation of the schools. See Bingham *ibid.* and Nicholas Savage 'The Academician's Library' *Apollo*, October 1988.

39 Du Prey *Making* pp. 61–2. See SM *Extracts from various authors on architecture abt. 1776* SC 140.

40 Sandby's colleague as the Professor of Perspective was Samuel Wales.

41 Colvin.

42 Henry Frederick, Duke of Cumberland replaced Lord Petre as Grand Master in 1782; he had been a freemason since 1767 and may have been in a position to argue for Sandby's appointment. The Grand Chaplain of the Order, the Reverend William Dodd, elected at the same time as Sandby, turned out to be a forger and was hung in 1777. Soane owned a bronze bust of Dodd.

43 For the diverging paths of British and Continental freemasonry see James Steven Curl *The Art and Architecture of Freemasonry* (London 1991) ch. 5.

44 Chambers at one point prepared his own lecture series, thinking that Sandby might be unable to continue as professor. See Watkin *Lectures* p. 30.

45 See du Prey *Making* p. 64, Watkin *Lectures* p. 55.

46 In 1775 Dance moved to Salisbury Street off the Strand, where he remained until 1791.

47 Soane *Memoirs*.

48 SM Letterbook 1802–16, Soane recalled 'this business was in some measure before me'; 3 November 1807.

49 Soane claimed the entrance hall had been completed from his own drawings, see du Prey *Education* pp. 33–4.

50 Soane's papers from his time in Henry Holland's office include a note of a painting job on Timothy Tyrrell's houses in Minster Street, Reading in 1777. SM: priv. corr XV.H.1 (2).

51 In 1773 Richard Holland gave his address as Mount Street, Soane's remained as before.

52 Half Moon Street was named after a public house on the corner of Piccadilly and was developed from 1730 onwards, the terraced houses mostly subdivided into apartments. See Ben Weinreb and Christopher Hibbert (eds) *The London Encyclopaedia* (London 1983).

53 Stroud *Holland* p. 28.

54 In 1775 Soane submitted his RA exhibits from Orange Court, Leicester Fields, before reverting to 'at Mr Holland's Mayfair' and in 1777 'No 7 Hamilton Street, Piccadilly'.

55 *Survey of London* Vol. XXXIX Grosvenor Estate pt 1 (London 1977), p. 120, pl. 14a. Also Vol. XL pt 2 (London 1980) pp. 286–9, pls 69 a and b.

56 The house was referred to as Pitt's 'West house in Hereford Street'. The houses attracted no interest and ten years later Pitt decided on another course, turning to Soane for assistance (see p. 65). Soane also supervised minor works on Camelford House in 1783–5, possibly in order that it could be let.

57 Holland entered the schools in October 1770 and is then listed again in January 1772.

58 SM: SC 139.

59 Du Prey *Education* Appendix B.

60 See John Brewer *The Pleasures of the Imagination* (London 1997) ch. 4.

61 Sidney C. Hutchinson *The Royal Academy Schools 1768–1830* Walpole Society, vol. 38, 1962, gives a list of students admitted from 1769 to 1830.

62 Described in Lecture XII (Watkin *Lectures* p. 659) as 'this masterly composition'. The Pantheon was used for masquerades, concerts and operas, and occasionally for trade exhibitions of wares such as stained glass or lightning conductors. Smaller rooms were set aside for tea, coffee and card playing.

63 Fanny Burney *Evelina* (1778), letter XXIII.

64 See *The London Encyclopaedia*.

65 See Colvin p. 48.

66 Robert R. Wark (ed.) Sir Joshua Reynolds *Discourses on Art* (New Haven and London 1975).

67 Sandby in turn had drawn on Piranesi's monumental bridge design from his first collection of designs *Prima parte di architecttura e prospettive* (1743). See Watkin *Lectures* pp. 55–6. Soane's scheme appeared as a model in the *Living Bridges* exhibition (Royal Academy 1996) pp. 76–81.

68 Du Prey *Making* pp. 78–9.

69 FD Vol. I p. 267.

70 See Eileen Harris (with Nicholas Savage) *British Architectural Books and Writers* (Cambridge 1990). *Designs* was reprinted in 1789, 1790 and 1797. See also Repton's comments below.

71 Stroud *Soane* pp. 284 et seq.

72 After Soane's death T. L. Donaldson discussed his abilities as a draughtsman. A close friend of Turner's he may have learned of Soane's difficulties from him. Referring back to the neat 'but timidly' drawn Italian works and praising the vitality of his pen sketches, he summarised 'at no period was Sir John Soane distinguished for mastery of his pencil; and his reputation has rested on the design, not on the drawing of his conceptions'.

73 Du Prey *Making* pp. 28–9; it deals with Newgate and to D[ance].

74 Bolton *Portrait* p. 401, George Wightwick's phrase.

2 TO ROME AND NAPLES

1 Matthew Brettingham the younger was responsible for buying statues and paintings for Lord Leicester, to form one of the greatest classical collections in the country, housed at Holkham Hall in Norfolk, which his father, with William Kent, had built. Some of his architectural drawings, including a few from Rome, later came into Soane's possession.

2 Bolton *Portrait* pp. 10–12.

3 *Sir William Chambers* (Victoria and Albert Museum 1996) see John Harris, introduction, p.4.

4 Bolton *Portrait* p. 12.

5 Du Prey *Education* ch. 3, p. 105; also *Chambers* pp. 28–32.

6 Robin Middleton and David Watkin *Neoclassical and 19th Century Architecture* Vol. I (London 1990) see ch. 4.

7 Antoine Picon *French Architects and Engineers in the Age of Enlightenment* (English edition, Cambridge 1992) pp. 346–9.

8 Perronet was elected to the Royal Society in 1788. In 1791 his bust was displayed at the Society of Arts alongside that of Benjamin Franklin.

9 Lecture XII see Watkin *Lectures* p. 662.

10 Since replaced, the modern Pont de Neuilly shares its name with a Parisian Metro stop and is the link between l'Arc de Triomphe and La Grande Arche (1989) at La Defense.

11 SM *Precedents in Architecture* (1784), Vol. 41, f. 3.

12 For those *hôtels* already built by the time of Soane's visit see Michel Gallet *Paris; Domestic Architecture of the 18th century* (London 1972) pp. 169–70.

13 See Watkin *Lectures* pp. 219–26. Soane, who also found common ground with Ledoux's perception of himself as a misunderstood genius, bought *L'architecture considerée . . .* (1804) in the year of publication.

14 SM *Precedents*, op. cit. f. 41. He described the columns as 'fulled'.

15 Some of the Duc de Chartres' garden survives as the Parc Monceau, Paris. For the modern state of the Désert de Retz see Diana Ketcham *Le Desert de Retz* (Cambridge and London 1994).

16 *Soane and Death*, p.72, I. 4 (Soane Museum 1996).

17 Stroud *Soane* p. 29.

18 Walpole Society, Vol. 32 (1946–8) *Memoirs of Thomas Jones* ed. Paul Oppé.

19 SM vol. 100, Tatham's letters and sketches from Rome, p.61, 7 June 1795.

20 Soane soon fell out with two of his fellow architects. John Henderson claimed that Soane's designs for the Bishop of Derry's new summer dining-room at the Downhill were plagiarised from his own proposals. Soane, always terrier-like in argument, put it to the vote. Brettingham adjudicated for Soane, Hardwick for Henderson. The verdict was inconclusive but Soane had little to do with Hardwick or Henderson thereafter in Rome. He included Henderson's designs alongside his own in his *Memoirs* of 1835 – he never forgot an insult. Henderson died in Edinburgh in 1786.

21 See Ingamells.
22 See du Prey *Making* pp. 148–51.
23 See James Mosley *The Nymph and the Grot* (reissued London 1999).
24 Soane *Memoirs*.
25 Du Prey *Education* p. 140.
26 BL Egerton MS Strange papers 1970, f. 27.
27 *The Yale Edition of Horace Walpole's Correspondence* general editor W. S. Lewis, to Horace Mann 13 April 1762 Vol. 22 (1960) p. 25. See also (when discussing the merits of various books on architecture) 'I have been consulting my neighbour young Mr Thomas Pitt, my present architect.' HW to Henry Seymour Conway Vol. 38 (1974) p. 198.
28 Tresham Lever *The House of Pitt* (London 1947) (Horace Walpole to Horace Mann 13 April 1762). For Pitt's own architectural work see his entry in Colvin and Michael McCarthy 'Thomas Pitt, Piranesi and John Soane' *Apollo*, December 1991.
29 Lever *ibid.*
30 Designs upon which Soane consulted Pitt included those for a *castello d'acqua*, an antique bath house and a succession of drawings for a Royal Palace – with elements of Vignola's Palazzo Farnese at Caprarola, Hadrian's Villa at Tivoli, Diocletian's Palace at Split, various Imperial Roman palaces and baths as well as the interior and portico of the Pantheon. It also boasted a double-skinned dome to admit *lumière mystérieuse* (borrowed from the Invalides, Saint Roche and other French examples) as well as 'a complete representation of the solar system' brought about by 'appropriate machinery'. The palace was an amalgam of Soane's sources and inspirations.
31 See Colvin.
32 Bolton *Portrait* p. 19, letter from Rome, 22 December 1787. Brettingham promised to send Soane's possessions on with Mrs Hervey's servants in a small box, as a trunk would be troublesome – the Bishop liked travelling light.
33 *Thomas Jones* Oppé op. cit.
34 *La Collezione Borgia* (catalogue Naples 1996).
35 Goethe *Italian Journey* (translated by W. H. Auden and Elizabeth Mayer, London 1962).
36 SM: Italian Sketches and Memoranda 1779.
37 SM: *ibid.* (29 December 1778).
38 Goethe *Italian Journey*, note 41.
39 Soane commented upon the monument to the poet Iacopo Sannazaro in S. Maria del Parto at Mergellina, the fishing port to the north of Naples, which showed him lying in an arcadian scene between the figures of Apollo and Minerva – a determinedly non-Christian iconography.
40 NRO Patteson correspondence Box 3; 11 and 12. Letters from Mrs Patteson to her son and from Henry Patteson to his brother (11), from John Patteson to his mother (12).
41 Du Prey *Education* Appendix G, pp. 374–6.
42 SM: Vol. 39 (mid-February 1779).
43 Soane *Memoirs* p. 15.
44 Du Prey *Education* pp. 168–9.
45 No. 45, *Vases and Volcanoes* (British Museum 1996).
46 SM: Vol. 39.
47 See *Vases and Volcanoes* pp. 42–3.
48 BL Add MS 36, 259.
49 Byres offered Yorke a Correggio at £1,400, followed by a Claude at the more modest £400. He bought neither. For Byres, see Colvin; Ingamells.
50 BL Add MS, 36, 260.
51 BL Add MS 35, 378 from Rome; 24 March 1779.
52 In 1787 Soane repaid Richard Holland £100 – a loan from when he was abroad. Holland was not in Rome with Soane and so he must have arranged for a note of credit from London at a moment when Soane's finances had reached a very low ebb.
53 Du Prey *Education* p. 182.
54 BL Add MS 35,378: 31 October 1778.
55 *Ibid.* 22 December 1778.
56 Du Prey *Education* pp. 184–5.
57 It had been built in the 1760s by Gaetano Barba.
58 SM: Vol. 39, ff. 34 onwards.
59 Du Prey *Education* Appendix G, p. 376.
60 Watkin *Lectures* Lecture VI, p. 566.

61 SM: Italian Sketches and Memoranda 1779.
62 *Richard and Maria Cosway* (catalogue, Scottish National Portrait Gallery, Edinburgh, 1995) pp. 41–2.
63 George Hadfield went to America in 1795 and became a prominent architect in Washington DC. Charlotte Hadfield married the satirist William Combe, the author of *Dr Syntax*; they later separated. William Hadfield, a painter, did not travel with the family.
64 Soane owned a bust of Paoli (Napoleon's hero and, possibly his godfather, in his early years in Corsica), by Flaxman.
65 Cosway catalogue pp. 45–68. Maria's affair with Jefferson apparently led to the opportunities offered to George Hadfield in America.

3 SICILY, ROME AND HOME AGAIN

1 Sometimes alternatively spelled Stewart, see Ingamells.
2 Richard Payne Knight *Expedition into Sicily* ed. Claudia Stumpf (London 1986).
3 John Britton claimed that Greece had been the original destination in his *Brief Memoirs* and Soane suggested so in his own *Memoirs*. Du Prey, in the absence of any mention of a visit to Athens by Patteson, Bowdler or Burdon, suggests that the whole idea was an embellishment, to give Soane some retrospective Greek credentials.
4 NRO Patteson Box 3.
5 Bolton *Portrait* p. 26.
6 Brydone's journey was in 1770; the book was in the form of letters to William Beckford, SM: AL 33D (2 volumes); Soane also owned a French edition of 1776.
7 There were also a number of illustrated guides in preparation. See introduction to Stumpf (ed.) *Expedition into Sicily*. All titles appeared from the early 1780s.
8 Burdon remembered them (in 1819) as 'hobgoblins'. The Villa Palagonia still stands and can be visited, see Paul Duncan *Sicily* (London 1992).
9 SM: Priv. Corr. III. B. 2 (14) for Burdon's reply. He remembered that the prince had been shut up by his relatives, there being a 'cloud' of witnesses to his insanity.
10 NRO Patteson Box 3/12, letter from Alicata, 23 May 1779.
11 *NACF Review* 1992, Andrew Moore 'The Patteson Bequest'.
12 NRO Patteson Box 3/11; letter from Norwich, 19 July 1779.
13 *Ibid.* 3 December 1778.
14 *Ibid.* 6 May 1779.
15 Stumpf (ed.) *Expedition into Sicily* p. 54.
16 See *Italian Journey*. Goethe translated and published Payne Knight's diary in 1810 although it did not appear in English until the British Museum publication of 1986, see Stumpf *ibid.*
17 NRO Patteson Box 3/12, 11 June 1779.
18 Bolton *Portrait* p. 532.
19 See Ingamells for Hippisley's time in Italy.
20 Farington (FD Vol. III, 8 July 1797, p. 865) recorded that 'Sir John Hippisley lived with Lady Percy 5 years – She quitted him – He was in ruined circumstances – followed her to Germany in vain. From then Lord Maynard carried him to Rome.'
21 Vignola and Peruzzi had drawn variants in early sixteenth-century Gothic which Soane also copied.
22 As Frank Salmon points out. The Academy of S. Luca in Rome required a personal reference; Dance's had been Piranesi, Robert Adam's Cardinal Albani. See Salmon 'Charles Heathcote Tatham and the Accademia di S. Luca' *Burlington Magazine* February 1998 Vol. CXL, No. 1139, pp. 85–92.
23 See also note 52, chapter 2.
24 See Bolton *Portrait*, pp. 41–2.
25 See David Watkin 'Soane's concept of the Villa' in Dana Arnold (ed.) *The Georgian Villa* Georgian Group 1996.
26 See guidebook to Kingston Lacy (National Trust 1987), also Anthony Clemenson 'Christmas at Kingston Lacy' *Apollo* December 1991.
27 *Henry, Elizabeth and George: letters and diaries of Henry, Tenth Earl of Pembroke and his Circle* edited by Lord Herbert (London 1939) p. 425, from Rome 7 March 1780.
28 Bolton *Portrait* pp. 27–8; 4 April 1780.

29 *Ibid.* p. 26.

30 Soane's copy of Dutens' *Itinéraire des routes les plus fréquentées*, which he bought in Florence, included a note of the distances between Lyon, Orange, Avignon, Montpelier, Marseilles, Nimes and Genoa, the clearest indication that he was planning a homeward journey to include this southward loop through Roman Provence. See du Prey *Education* p. 295.

31 This and following references from SM: Notes on Italy.

32 See du Prey *Making* pp. 186–8: Salmon op. cit. throws new light on the subject.

33 Stroud *Dance* pp. 70–1.

34 See Salmon op. cit. The earlier generation of student architects attached themselves to masters. Soane and his peers, usually mature Royal Academy medallists, remained independent.

35 SM: Notes on Italy.

36 See du Prey *Education* p. 324–5; Soane was 'among the French writer's least recognized but earliest spiritual children'.

37 Shanahan and the Bishop visited many other European bridges, producing almost thirty drawings which were then engraved, at the Bishop's expense, by dell' Acqua in Vicenza. Soane later owned a set.

38 Pierre du Prey 'Eighteenth-Century English sources for a history of Swiss Wooden Bridges' *Zeitschrift fur Schweizerische Archaeologie unde Kunstgeschichte* Bd 36 1979, pp. 51–63.

39 See Ted Ruddock *Arch Builders and their architects* (Cambridge 1979) p. 36.

40 Bolton *Portrait* pp. 31–2.

41 See du Prey *Education* p. 330.

4 RETURN

1 The first earl (created 1714) had consulted both Talman and Vanbrugh over plans to rebuild his manor house but nothing had come of the schemes. See Guide to Ickworth (National Trust, 1998).

2 See Soane *Memoirs*. For the dining-room see du Prey *Making* p. 116 for a detailed account.

3 SM: Vol. 80.

4 Alastair Rowan (ed.) *Buildings of Ireland: North West Ulster* (London 1979), introduction to Derry p. 367.

5 *Ibid.* p. 368, 'a very curious and handsome wooden bridge'.

6 Bolton *Portrait* pp. 36–7, 12 July 1780.

7 SM Vol. 100 copy of Tatham/Holland letters. Tatham claimed to be the winner, finding another patron who wanted a circular house and adapting his designs accordingly. Presumably he was paid properly on the second occasion.

8 SM: Vol. 80 – all other quotations from the same notebook.

9 Many of the Earl Bishop's acquisitions were confiscated in Rome when the French invaded Italy in 1798.

10 SM: Journal 1781–97 f. 15.

11 FD Vol. I, p. 279, 21 December 1794.

12 Bolton *Portrait* p. 40.

13 See Stroud *Soane* p. 49; Soane apparently arrived at Allanbank not having received the letter.

14 SM: Priv. Corr. IV.S.3 (5).

15 SM: *ibid.* (4).

16 SM: *ibid.* (7) 11 December 1780.

17 Gillian Darley *Villages of Vision* (London 1975) p. 109.

18 E. H. Coleridge *The Life of Thomas Coutts* (London 1920) vol I, various references. Allanbank, still heavily mortgaged, was sold in the next generation.

19 SM: Priv. Corr. IV. 5. 3. (12 & 13) 8 and 12 January 1781.

20 Bolton *Portrait* pp. 38–9, John Stuart to JS, 5 September [1780].

21 Lewis *Walpole's Correspondence* op. cit. vol. 25 (1971) p. 35.

22 Soane's friend Edward Foxhall's business, Foxhall and Fryer, was located in nearby Old Cavendish Street. The firm is first listed in the *London Directory* in 1797, as upholsterers.

23 See *Bath History* Vol. V 1994, Philippa Bishop 'The Sentence of Momus'.

24 See du Prey *Making*, letter from Bowdler to Wedderburn, p. 199. For the whole episode see ch. 10.

25 Robin Evans *The Fabrication of Virtue* op. cit.

26 It was there that Pitt first employed Soane to carry out a large programme of repair and redecoration in 1781.

27 BL Add MS 69, 328; 8 November 1786.

28 W. S. Childe-Pemberton *The Earl Bishop* (London 1924) vol. 1, p. 226.

29 See du Prey *Making* ch. 12, p. 245 et seq.

30 Stroud *Soane* p. 54.

31 For a list of drawings exhibited at the Royal Academy from 1772 until 1836, excepting the year 1778 and 1788–91, see *ibid.* pp. 284–91.

32 The design of the gallery harked back to Dance's Diploma design for the Parma Academy, see du Prey *Making* p. 25, fig. 2.3.

33 Soane's design did not provide for adequate ventilation for the hay, risking fire. See du Prey *ibid.* p. 10.

34 As Margaret Richardson points out, Smith obviously had a penchant for duplicates.

35 Pratt's commission was Ryston Hall (1785) and Collyer's was Gunthorpe Hall (1789).

36 SM: SNB 8.

37 Copies of the accounts and Forster's letter from photocopies of selected Gurdon papers at Letton Hall.

38 See Stroud *Soane* pp. 118–19, Soane's Hellesdon Bridge, designed in 1785, remained unbuilt.

39 Soane's 1788 alterations to Norwich Hospital were minor but the 1789 commission for the city gaol was a large job with significant repercussions; *ibid.* p. 139, pl. 85 also below, p. 127.

40 Dated to 1724 by the rainwater heads.

41 The temple has recently been discovered to be by Adam. There was, perhaps, an element of competition between Chillington and Weston Park, where Paine also had worked.

42 William Dunster was Governor of the Bank and Deputy Governor of the Levant Company before his death in 1754.

43 An unmarried brother William had set up the merchant house of Bosanquet and Willermin and lived at Forest House with Samuel and his family while old Mrs Bosanquet lived in the Dower House, Forest Lodge, nearby.

44 Stroud *Soane* p. 254.

45 Tyrrell received his title to be a Chancery solicitor and to take affidavits in the Queen's Bench in 1783 at which time he was living at Queen Street, Cheapside. In 1781 he was at Salisbury Court, Fleet Street.

46 SM: Journal 1781–97, including reference to work at Borough (ff. 13–14) and for Tollemache (f. 19).

47 SM: SNB 10.

48 George Wyatt, the son of William Wyatt, was admitted to the Draper's Company in August 1748, described as a joiner. From 1773 until 1785 he occupied No. 74 Bankside, known as Honduras Wharf, suggesting he was the owner of the adjacent wharf. His addresses in the *London Directory* of 1781 were, however, 65 Fleet Street and Albion Place, a speculative housing development close to the southern side of Blackfriars Bridge.

49 John Mosse 'The Albion Mills 1784–1791' *The Newcomen Society: Transactions* Vol XL 1967–8 (London 1971), pp. 47–60.

50 See *ibid.* John Robinson *The Wyatts* (Oxford 1979) includes a family tree; neither of the William Wyatts mentioned fits the known facts about George's father.

51 Guildhall Library St. Sepulchre, Holborn register of burials; 7223/2. Jonathan Smith of Cow Cross was buried on 17 June 1763, aged forty-two. A Jonathan Smith married Ann Wyatt (the name of George Wyatt's eldest sister) on 11 July 1750 at St Benet Paul's Wharf (IGI). An Elizabeth Smith appears in the baptismal records of St Sepulchre, Holborn (Guildhall 7220/2) as born on 22 April 1762, daughter of Jonathan Smith. Unfortunately the mother's name is recorded as Catherine.

52 LMA: Licensed Victuallers' Registers, Finsbury Division MR/LV/7/8. Jonathan Smith of the Castle, Cow Cross was licensed on Wednesday, 2 October 1751. On the erection of Mrs Soane's monument an anonymous member of her family (probably J. W. Palmer) with a grudge about the Wyatt inheritance sent the following to her widower. 'In Cow Cross Castle* I were born, Bet Smith my maiden name, Fame blew her trumpet at my birth, And at my Death the same.' SM: Priv. Corr. XIV C 3.

53 Probably by William Dance, George's brother.

54 Stroud *Soane* gives her age as twenty-three at the time of her marriage but without any documentary evidence.

55 Bolton *Portrait* p. 5 records their marriage by William Walker in the presence of George Wyatt and Elizabeth Levick. Only the index to the marriage register for Christ Church Southwark now survives [LMA X15/148] and Soane/Smith are No. 41. Their common licence (a standard procedure if both parties had reached the age of majority and did not wish or had insufficient time to publish Banns) was issued by the Vicar-General on 20 August 1784 (Lambeth Palace Library).

56 George Wightwick *Hints to Young Architects* (1846) dedicated to C. R. Cockerell.

5 ESTABLISHED

1 SM Account Book 1781–6.

2 SM: Priv. Corr. VI.K (4) letter of 1826 from Eliza Walker asking for his assistance, her husband Henry having outlived his patrons and become a common labourer.

3 See introduction to Colvin *The Architectural Profession*.

4 Bolton *Works* Appendix C.

5 Sanders's premium on taking up articles for five years was £50 but John MacDonnell, the carpenter's son who followed him eighteen months later paid £105. See Colvin.

6 Margaret Richardson 'Learning in the Soane Office' in *The Education of the Architect*; proceedings of the 22nd Annual Symposium of the SAHGB 1993.

7 BL Add MS. 69, 328, 9 February 1787.

8 *Ibid.* 18 August 1786 to Thomas Pitt in Lausanne. For the problem with unknown tradesmen cf. Soane's difficulties at Piercefield and Pell Wall (jobs thirty years apart), see pp. 82 and 269.

9 *Ibid.* 10 June 1787 (JS writing from Exeter).

10 SM: Priv. Corr. IV.P.2 (3) 19 February 1786.

11 Wyatt's wide-ranging construction business included all the main building trades and he was, in addition the City paviour.

12 SM: Precedents 1784 Vol 41 f. 25.

13 SM: Priv. Corr. II.R. 10 (1) 19 February 1795.

14 Red Book for Tendring quoted in Dedham Vale Society newsletter, summer 1995, 'Tendring Hall and Park' John Wallace p. 18.

15 Soane too often appeared in such arbitrations, see Laurence Kinney 'John Soane and property disputes: the Argyle Rooms & All Souls College, Oxford', *Architectural History* Vol. 41, 1998.

16 Du Prey *Making* p. 313. See ch. 14 for detailed account of the Tendring job and disputes.

17 BL Add.MS 69,328, 23 April 1787.

18 See *History of Parliament*, entry for Alexander Hood.

19 Cricket Lodge estate, and the house, survived to become a Mr Blobby television theme park and is, at the time of writing, about to become a holiday village.

20 Christopher Woodward 'William Beckford & Fonthill Splendens' *Apollo* February 1998.

21 FD Vol. III May 1797 pp. 840, 842.

22 In 1808 Beckford was constantly complaining of Foxhall's furniture; including 'infamous' chairs and 'the most horrible mess of colours' but on 11 November 1815, hearing of his death, he wrote 'I haven't failed to perceive and feel the horror of the loss of Foxhall' Boyd Alexander (ed.) *Life at Fonthill 1807–1822* (London 1957).

23 SM: Priv. Corr. IV.P.2 (8) (26 September 1786).

24 I am grateful to Christopher Woodward for emphasising the hidden nature of the house and Soane's rare privilege in gaining access to it.

25 SM: *Precedents* 1784 Vol 41 f. 66.

26 Letter dated 14 January 1793 from Piercefield, loose in *ibid.*

27 BL: Add. MS 69, 328 (19 June 1787 from Boconnoc).

28 SM: Priv. Corr. IV.P.2 (11) (8 February 1787 from Montpelier).

29 SM: Ledger A and B. The visits tailed off after 1786; he made four in 1787 and one more in 1791.

30 Repton *Memoir* BL Add MS. 62,112, f. 58. The document ('part 2') begins in 1788. The period in question was from December 1792 to summer 1793.

31 Pitt arranged a clerkship in the Auditor's Office for Repton's son.

32 Ehrman *Pitt* Vol. III pp. 75–9.

33 See Lever *House of Pitt* op. cit. p. 282.

34 *Ibid.* pp. 282–3 letters 16 January 1789, 9 March 1789 both from Carnoles, Monaco.

35 Soane used the opportunity to work at nearby Skelton where he altered an existing house and built an elegant stone stableyard.

36 By his last visit to the estate, the expenditure on the job had reached £8,398 2s 6d (accounts at Mulgrave Castle).

37 Mulgrave's wife died in childbirth in 1788 and his own bad health caused his resignation from politics in 1791. He died the following year.

38 Taxes levied in 1777 (and again in 1812).

39 One, at least, is still in good repair. Accounts for the materials at Mulgrave Castle, XI.1/24, 25, 33.

40 A few years later, Mulgrave's heir became involved in the building trade, shipping the raw materials for Atkinson's cement down to London. He also employed the eponymous William Atkinson to completely remodel Mulgrave Castle in castellated splendour, from 1804 on.

41 BL: Add MS 69, 328 19 February 1788.

42 John C. Van Horne (ed.) *The Correspondence of Benjamin Henry Latrobe* (New Haven and London 1986) Vol. II, p. 248 (July 19 1806).

43 SM: Ledger B, f. 97 (27 May 1790).

44 *Details Respecting the Conduct and Connections of George Soane* (n.d. but *c.* 1835).

45 Repton *Memoir* op. cit. f. 197.

46 *Ibid.* f. 205.

47 Member of the Corporation, trustee of the Suffolk Amicable Insurance Company, Justice of the Peace, governor of the Grammar School, a proprietor of the Assembly Rooms and *ex-officio* guardian were among his many public roles. Jane Fiske (ed.) *The Oakes Diaries* Vol. I, introduction (Ipswich 1990).

48 Salmon op. cit.

49 Bolton *Portrait* p. 319, 1 September 1821.

50 SM: Priv. Corr. IV. P.2 (15) 3 December 1787.

51 BL: Add MS 69, 328; 31 March 1788 from Boconnoc.

52 *Ibid.* 3 July 1788.

53 SM: Priv. Corr. IV.P.2 (13), 7 July 1787.

54 Repton mentions the continued popularity and high repute of *Designs* 'for its *fanciful* taste, among those who build pretty things from such books'. (*Memoir* op. cit. f. 204).

55 See Watkin *Lectures* pp. 301, 661. Soane used an attributed quotation of some length (and an illustration) from *Nutshells* in his twelfth Royal Academy lecture. Peacock died in 1814 after some years of illness.

56 Bolton *Works* p. 32.

57 BoE X81.

58 BoE M5/471.

59 At Forest House Soane built a portico and stables and added a balustrade. The family tomb, built after Samuel's death, in July 1806 commemorated three generations of Bosanquets as well as William Dunster, Samuel's first cousin.

60 Bolton *Portrait* p. 25, letter from near Monaco 6 February 1789. Reveley did not, in fact, return from a long tour through Italy, Greece and Egypt until 1789 which suggests that the candidate list for the Bank was a random selection of names, rather than one fine-tuned to the moment or the task.

61 See Daniel Abramson 'The Architectural Progress of the Bank of England' in *Architectural History* 37, 1994 pp. 112–29.

62 BoE M5/748.

63 Linda Colley *Britons* (London 1992) pp. 228–36.

64 BoE M5/748.

65 The modern spelling is Moggerhanger. The Thorntons, leading figures in the Clapham sect, became another staunch family of clients, employing Soane for over thirty years. Samuel Thornton engaged him at Albury Park, Surrey, and at 22 St James's Square, while Godfrey Thornton's son, William who changed his name to Astell, was his client at Everton, Bedfordshire. C. G. Thornton was the client for Marden Hill in 1818.

66 BoE ORG/B443.

67 See Abramson.

68 Colvin, Taylor entry.

69 David Kynaston *The City of London* Vol. I (London 1994) p. 13.

70 BoE X81, 29 April 1790.

71 Wyatt's will provided generously for the various members of his family.

Despite their complaints many years later, the Palmer family was left money but the bulk of the estate was divided between George Russell, his nephew and the Soanes. Each inherited freehold properties; Ann Levick, another niece, and George Russell each received £2,000 and Elizabeth Soane £1,000 and the contents of his house. Russell and Soane were the executors.

72 I can find no substantiation for the claim that George was a proprietor (included in Colvin, 1995) and nothing further has emerged during work on the Soho Archives currently being undertaken at Birmingham City Archive. A. D. Insull's 1955 BA dissertation, held at Birmingham Central Library, gives the names of the proprietors of the five original £12,000 shares in the Albion Mill Company as S. Wyatt, J. Frere. N. Bates, a joint share in the names of Matthew Boulton and Watt, and, early in 1786, Mr Wolff.

73 Repton *Memoir* f. 200.

74 George Dance's portrait of Joah Bates in *Sketches from the Life* (1808) remarked that he was a proprietor of Albion Mills and 'a great sufferer by the fire which destroyed them'.

6   LINCOLN'S INN FIELDS

1 The architect was William Tyler RA, a leading freemason, close friend of Thomas Sandby and also founder member of the Royal Academy.

2 SM: SNB 24. Thursday, 22 August 1793.

3 SM: many transactions are noted in Journal 2 and Ledger B between 1788 and 1793.

4 Margaret Richardson *Learning in the Soane Office* op. cit.

5 See Ian Bristow *Architectural Colour in British Interiors 1615–1840* (London 1996) pp. 206–8.

6 Megan Aldrich (ed.) *The Craces: royal decorators* (catalogue, Brighton 1990).

7 Soane owned a landscape by George Barret sen. of Norbury Park. SM: P246.

8 Dan Cruickshank 'Soane and the Meaning of Colour' *Architectural Review* January 1989.

9 SM: Drawer 32/2A/5: 28 August 1792.

10 FD vol. II p. 403.

11 However, Eliza Soane was not always eager for social life; on 13 July 1796 she told her Chertsey friend Sarah Smith that she had been 'dragged to Ranelagh . . . much against my will and was so illy disposed for the amusement that I would not be at the trouble of dressing, so after sauntering round the room an hour or two, I returned home half dead with the headache and have had a bad cold ever since'. SM: Priv. Corr. XIV. C. 1 (1).

12 Information kindly provided by Susan Palmer, also see Peter Jackson *George Scharf's London* (London 1987) pp. 104–5.

13 SM: Priv. Corr. I. F 2 (3) 30 July 1792.

14 FD vol. I p. 146.

15 Bolton *Portrait* p. 53 14 January 1794.

16 SM: SNB 15.

17 Harrison had designed a triumphal bridge over the Thames in 1776–8 and built the first flat British bridge on the lines of Perronet's Pont de Neuilly, at Lancaster, completed in 1788.

18 Soane had begun Baronscourt in 1788; Mordaunt Crook describes Bentley Priory as the 'Holland House' of the Tories. In 1790 the earl became the first Marquis of Abercorn.

19 John H. Gebbie *Introduction to the Abercorn Letters* (Omagh 1972) pp. 166.

20 SM: Journal 1, f. 164.

21 See Christopher Hussey 'Wimpole Hall' part III, *Country Life* 14 December 1967. The visitor was the daughter of Charles Yorke and married into the Eliot family.

22 Christopher Woodward 'Dancing Soane' *Apollo* April 1999.

23 See guidebook *Wimpole Hall* (National Trust, 1991).

24 The *castello d'acqua* was levelled long ago; Soane's preparations included careful investigation of water courses and levels. He included it in *Sketches*.

25 The bookroom is not to be confused with Gibbs's earlier library which housed the Harley collection.

26 See p. 204.

27 Guidebook, *Wimpole Home Farm* (National Trust 1999).

28 The earl was President of the Board of Agriculture in 1814.

29 See his entry *Dictionary of National Biography*.

30 See *Survey of London* (London 1960) Vol. XXIX pp. 360–2. Soane returned in 1813, this time to work for the second Marquis.

31 The house was on part of the site of the present RAC Club.

32 *Not* William Mackworth Praed.

33 George Grenville died in 1770; he had been MP for Buckingham for thirty years. In 1791 Soane had worked for Buckingham's brother-in-law Lord Fortescue again, at his London house at 43 Hill Street, and in 1792 he was also employed by his widowed sister Charlotte Williams-Wynn at Taplow. Her husband was Sir Watkin Williams-Wynn, Bt, MP for Denbigh. He died in 1788.

34 William Grenville had been introduced to Anne Pitt when she was seventeen but she had refused his earlier proposal of marriage. See Peter Jupp *Lord Grenville 1759–1834* (Oxford 1985) pp. 109–16. Grenville and Hardwicke were close political and personal friends.

35 In 1779 Praed became a partner in the New Cornish Bank, Truro, which his father and Sir John Molesworth had founded in 1774. The bank was heavily involved in financing the copper industry. The Hon. John Eliot with his elder brother Edward, also a Cornish banker, joined Praed as co-founder of the London bank of Praed & Co.

36 *History of Parliament* Praed's entry.

37 BL Add MS 41,135.

38 SM: Account Journal, 8 June 1793.

39 SM: Letterbook 1793–5 to Dr Scott, 28 August 1793.

40 See Thomas Whately *Observations on Modern Gardening* (1770) on bridges 'though they cross, they do not close the view'. Soane bought a copy of the volume as early as 1778.

41 SM: Letterbook 1793–5, 8 July 1793.

42 SM: SNB 33d,18 August 1796.

43 John Summerson *Sir John Soane* (London 1952) referred to the years 1791–1806 as the Middle Period (between the Early Practice Period 1780–1791 and the Picturesque Period 1806–21, ending with the Last Period until 1833). On the evidence of Tyringham in particular, Soane was designing with a picturesque sensibility from the early 1790s onwards.

44 Bolton *Works* p. 20. Dance was struggling with a house in the country, probably Coleorton for Sir George Beaumont, which would plague him 'to death' (letter dated 2 August 1802).

45 SM: drawer 8/3/15.

46 SM: Letterbook 1793–6, 23 February 1795. For Woodgate see Bolton *Portrait* pp. 50–2.

47 Margaret Richardson 'Soane's Use of Drawings' *Apollo* April 1990.

48 SM: Priv. Corr. XIV.C.1 (2) 22 July 1796.

49 SM: *ibid.* (4) 3 August 1796.

50 Other references to old Mrs Soane include SM: *ibid.* (7) 20 June 1797 (JS to Richard Smith). The 'old lady' was moving house but Eliza was too unwell to come to Chertsey to help. A few months before Eliza had bought the 'old lady' a gown, *ibid.* (5) 14 October 1796.

51 SM: Journal 3 f. 84, 1–19 February.

52 Bank of England conversion tables (November 1998) value £1 in 1800 at £28.84p – a considerable change from 1790 when the value was almost twice that (£51.37p).

53 L. S. Pressnell *Country Banking in the Industrial Revolution* (Oxford, 1956).

54 SM: Journal 6 f. 253, 11 April.

55 See *Soane and Death* op. cit. XVIIc, p. 115.

56 William Praed is buried under a more conventional sarcophagus in the churchyard at St Uny, Lelant, near St Ives, Cornwall.

57 Cartwright held the country seat from 1797 until 1846, shifting to the rearranged constituency of Northamptonshire South in 1832. He proposed the parliamentary motion that Pitt's debts be met by the public, at a time when Soane, who was owed considerable sums for his work at Holwood, had just completed Aynhoe. See Ehrman *Pitt* vol. III p. 833.

58 The village is spelt without the 'e'.

59 I am grateful to Ptolemy Dean for drawing my attention to this reference from Northampton CRO C (A) 5147, quoted in his forthcoming *Sir John Soane and the Country Estate* (London 1999).

60 Bolton *Portrait* p.409.

61 SM Letterbook 1797–1801, 12 July 1798; 14 November 1799.

62 SM Letterbook 1793–6, 10 August 1793; for Stuart see SM: Priv. Corr. IV.S.3(19).

63 SM Letterbook 13 June 1795.

64 SM Letterbook 1797–1801, 16 July 1800.

65 SM Letterbook 1793–6, 19 July 1793.

66 *Ibid.* n.d. f.41.

67 Drawings copied at Lincoln's Inn Fields 9 November 1791, show a bridge, close to Paine's model; see E. L. Kemp 'Thomas Paine and his 'Pontifical matters'' *Newcomen Society Transactions* Vol. 49 (London 1979).

68 See John Keane *Tom Paine: a Political Life* (London 1995) p. 276. The metal was to be enamelled with melted glass against rust and the system was prefabricated, allowing its transport anywhere in the world.

69 J. G. James 'Some Steps in the Evolution of Early Iron Arched Bridge Designs' (the 18th Dickinson Memorial Lecture) published in the *Newcomen Society Transactions* Vol. 59 (London 1990).

70 J. G. James 'Thomas Paine's Iron Bridge Work 1785–1803' in *ibid* pp. 156–7 and 205 ff.

71 Keane op. cit., chapter 9.

72 In fact, it was Nash's preposterous Welsh stone bridge, a single span of 295 foot, that proved to be beyond him. He pressed on, building a more modest bridge, 95 foot long, but this time in iron. This bridge, at Stanford Court in Worcestershire, collapsed almost immediately but in 1797 he rebuilt it from parts manufactured at Coalbrookdale, registering his patent that year.

73 SM Estimates Book 1789–99; also Letterbook 1793–6, Soane's bill of £23 16 0 and Foulds' of £5 5 0.

74 James op. cit. p. 159.

75 Ruddock op. cit. *Arch Bridges*.

76 SM Letterbook 1793–6, 19 February 1795.

77 See Thornton & Dorey *Miscellany* figure 85, p. 85.

78 Two other bridges built on these principles failed but the Ticknell Bridge at Newport Pagnell of 1810 survives to demonstrate the system.

79 *History of Parliament* Burdon's entry.

80 J. G. James 'The Cast Iron Bridge at Sunderland (1796)' in *Newcastle upon Tyne Polytechnic Occasional Papers in the History of Science and Technology* No. 5 (1989).

81 Soane frequently put his own money towards his own favourite architectural projects but in late 1793 as the affairs of George Smith, his client at Piercefield and earlier at Marlesford and Burn Hall, worsened Soane was advised by Timothy Tyrrell not to advance a large (unspecified) sum to Mrs Smith to help her with a property purchase. SM Letterbook 1793–6, 4 & 6 November 1793.

82 SM: Priv. Corr. III.B.2 (12) 8 May 1818.

83 Bolton *Portrait* p. 532, letter from Castle Eden, 13 August 1836. Soane was contradictory about his views on iron bridges, even that at Sunderland, see Watkin *Lectures* p. 347.

84 Todd Willmert 'Heating Methods and their Impact on Soane's Work: Lincoln's Inn Fields and Dulwich Picture Gallery' *JSAH* LII March 1993.

85 Braham patented no less than eighteen inventions, beginning with his water-closet of 1778.

86 Picon op. cit.

87 Watkins *Lectures* analysis of lecture XII pp. 388 et seq.

88 Years later at the Freemasons' Hall he suspended the heavy bronze chandeliers upon iron rods, carefully disguised.

7 THE ASSAULT ON WESTMINSTER

1 *Annual Register* 1790 pp. 247–50.

2 Bolton *Portrait* p. 48.

3 PRO WORKS 4/17; 4/18.

4 PRO WORKS 1/5 f. 100, William Chambers to Henry Holland, 8 April 1791.

5 PRO *ibid..*, also WORKS 4/17, 13 January 1792.

6 Ian Toplis *The Foreign Office: an Architectural History* (London 1987) p. 9.

7 Soane would also have dealings with James Burges and George Aust, the Under-Secretaries. When Burges bought Beauport in Sussex in 1794, it was to Soane he turned for the improvements; Aust was a useful contact at the Royal Hospital, Chelsea.

8 See Peter Jupp *Lord Grenville 1759–1834* (Oxford 1985) pp. 98–100.

9 On Camelford's death, which was followed by those of his widow in 1803 and his heir, in a duel in 1804, Lord and Lady Grenville inherited Boconnoc with some 19,500 acres as well as Camelford House. They sold the Norfolk and Wiltshire estates. See Jupp p. 301.

10 Repton *Memoir*.

11 HLRO Lords Journals Vol. 43, 137b, 29 April 1801. SM Letterbook 1793–6, f.31 is an undated letter from Soane to James Wyatt laying down the conditions for entry; including total anonymity and confidentiality, a submission on a single sheet of 'antiquarian paper', the use of Roman characters to disguise the applicants' identity and any inscriptions to be made in another hand. These rules had been agreed to by James Adam, Robert Brettingham, Samuel Pepys Cockerell, Richard Jupp, James Lewis, Robert Mylne, Henry Holland and John Groves.

12 *Kings Works* p. 44.

13 John Harris *Sir William Chambers* (London 1970) p. 124.

14 Harris *ibid*.

15 PRO WORKS 14/8, 8 February 1794.

16 SM Letterbook 1793–6, letter from JS to Messrs Burgess & Aust, 28 November 1793.

17 Cuffnells was to become a frequent stopping place for the king on his way to Weymouth.

18 SM SNB 24.

19 See Ehrman *Pitt* Vol II p. 211.

20 *History of Parliament*, entry for Long.

21 Charles Long's own house, Bromley Hill House in Kent was 'partially adapted' from published designs by the designer of the Egyptian Hall, P. F. Robinson.

22 HLRO Lords Journals Vol. 43, 1 April 1801.

23 HLRO MSS E/77.

24 HLRO Committee Book 1794, committee constituted 17 June.

25 Leeds succeeded to the dukedom in 1789. Soane sent him drawings for a peachery and other garden buildings as early as August 1792 (and again in 1795). SM: drawer 8/3/27 and 45.

26 His proposal was in January 1794, see A. Aspinall (ed.) *The Later Correspondence of George III* (Cambridge 1967) Vol. II pp. 517–18, note 3.

27 *Survey of London* Vol. XXIX op. cit. pp. 175–9.

28 SM: SNB 23, 24 etc. for Soane's continual contacts with Rose and Smith, no doubt combining his business on their private commissions with his own lobbying.

29 SM: Letterbook 1793–6, 16 January 1795, to William Chambers.

30 SM: SNB 28, meetings recorded on 23 June, 30 June and 7 July. Always at 3 o'clock.

31 Soane claimed that he showed the plans to the king in person – perhaps in late May when he went to Chertsey and Hampton for several days and spent an unusually large sum of money on the hire of chaises. On 30 October 1795 two volumes of unspecified drawings and a portfolio were taken to Carlton House. SM: Journal 3.

32 SM Letterbook *ibid.* 17 June 1795.

33 SM: Journal 3, f. 181; 24 August 1795 onwards.

34 See Ehrman *Pitt* Vol. III pp. 86–8.

35 SM: Journal 3 f. 182; 6 August 1796 'with own horses'.

36 FD Vol II, p. 634.

37 Smith's partner in the leading banking house of Smith, Payne and Smith had been René Payne, for whom Soane designed various buildings at Sulby in Northamptonshire, from 1792 until Payne's death in 1799.

38 In Cornwall, that nest of rotten boroughs, the Eliots had the patronage of six parliamentary seats; one borough had just seven voters. Edward Eliot, widowed in 1786, lived at 10 Downing Street with Pitt until his death in 1797. His brother John lived at 11 Downing Street. In 1804 he became the second Lord Eliot and in 1815 the Earl of St Germans. See Richard Hewlings '11 Downing Street: John Soane's work for John Eliot' *Transactions of the Ancient Monuments Society* Vol. 39 (1995).

39 SM: SNB 36.

40 See Claire Tomalin *Mrs Jordan's Profession* (London 1994), p. 166.

41 *Ibid.* note 8, pp. 350–1.

42 FD Vol. II p. 287.

43 See Colvin pp. 33–4 (Introduction).

44 RIBA Box 1 HoH/2/7/2. 3 April 1795.

45 FD Vol. II p. 398.

46 *Ibid.* p. 417.

47 *Ibid.* p. 462; the other guests were Wheatley, Dance, Lawrence, Smirke, Hamilton and Tyler.

48 Of the five founder architect members of the Royal Academy, only Chambers, George Dance and Thomas Sandby had actually built anything – the latter very little.

49 FD Vol II p. 504.

50 SM: SNB 33a.

51 Aspinall op. cit., Vol. II, p. 465, item 1379 Downing Street, 9 March 1796, 11.30 p.m.

52 Minutes of the Society, Vol. XXV p. 430. The Society of Antiquaries was notably classridden; Soane only became 'Esquire' after his election to the Royal Academy, remaining 'Mister' until then. Carter, regarded as humbler still, was given no title at all. (Information from Dr J. Mordaunt Crook.)

53 *Archaeologia* XII (1796). As Margaret Richardson points out, this is a very early example of a public conservation battle.

54 See Evans *Fabrication* op. cit., figure 140 shows plans for the later extension of the prison far beyond the confines of the Keep.

55 Soane's anger in 1826 was stoked by Wilkins's commission to replace his work at Norwich Castle with a new gaol. Wilkins pointed out that the magistrates had been critical of the former one. SM Priv. Corr. II.W.8 (I) 13 February 1826.

56 FD Vol. II, p. 416.

57 To his earliest clients among the Bank Directors Soane had now added the Thellusson brothers, Peter Isaac and Charles (whose aunt had been Ledoux's client in Paris) and Samuel Beachcroft. On 20 October 1790 (see SM Ledger B) he took into the Bank three working drawings for Wiston Hall, Beachcroft's Suffolk farmhouse.

58 Donaldson op. cit., pp. 17–18.

59 P. E. Jones 'The Office of the City Remembrancer' *Transactions of the Guildhall Historical Association* vol. IV pp. 176–84 (1967).

60 BoE M1/32.

61 Abramson *Bank* p. 338.

62 Sir John Summerson *The Evolution of Soane's Bank Stock Office in the Bank of England* reprinted in *The Unromantic Castle* (London 1990). See also Daniel Abramson's 1997 MS catalogue of drawings for the Bank Stock Office (SM).

63 Daniel Abramson, lecture at Sir John Soane's Museum 19 June 1997.

64 Abramson *Bank* fig. 144.

65 See James Ayres *Building the Georgian City* (New Haven and London 1998) p. 107 (pl. 159 shows cone-shaped 'bricks' from the Bank).

66 Abramson *Bank* p. 346 'Commercial activity to a classically trained architect was not a public activity like that of religion or government.' Soane always emphasised the importance of appropriate ornament.

67 See Bolton *Works* pp. 62 et. seq.

68 Abramson *Bank* p. 351

69 *Ibid.* pp. 355–7. Soane's own walls proved insufficiently impregnable in the 1840s, leading Cockerell, his successor, to heighten them.

70 Daniel Abramson 'C. R. Cockerell's Architectural progress of the Bank of England' *Architectural History* Vol. 37, 1994.

71 Bolton *Portrait* p. 62.

72 FD Vol I p. 287, 2 January 1795.

73 B. H. Latrobe remarked on the acoustic problem in a letter but it was not until the attack of 1824 that it was criticised in print. See p. 280.

74 Bolton *Portrait* pp. 63–5.

75 *Constable* (catalogue Tate Gallery 1976) notes to items 88, 89 and 108. Also see 'John Constable's Correspondence IV' edited R. B. Beckett (*Suffolk Records Society*, vol. X, 1966) letter of 18 April 1819. The 'e' on Greswold was an addition of 1818.

76 John Keay *The Honourable Company* (London 1991).

77 Bolton *Portrait* pp. 71–2, Jupp to Henry Holland (copy 3 May 1797).

78 *Ibid.* p. 65, 17 June 1796.

79 Dance's sixteen-year-old son George, had travelled to Bengal in 1794

aboard the *Lord Camden*, the East Indiaman in which the family had a financial interest.

80 SM: Estimates Book 1789–99. The estimate for Dunninald, complete with suitably hibernian ornament, came to £16,530 7s 6d. Soane delivered the details to Scott at his house in Harley Street on 21 December 1795. The house was never built since Scott's career came under attack in the late 1790s and he lost his fortune.

81 SM: PC 10/2 *A Letter to the Earl Spencer KG from John Soane Architect* (1799).

82 See C. H. Philips *The East India Company* (Manchester 1961) Appendix II. Jacob Bosanquet b. 1756/7, a cousin of Samuel, remained a director of the East India Company for forty-six years (until his death in 1828), see Grace E. Lee *The Story of the Bosanquets* (Canterbury 1966).

83 SM: Priv. Corr. XIV E, 4 July 1796.

84 Nicholas Brawer 'The Anonymous Architect of the India House' *Georgian Group Journal* Vol. VII 1997, unravels the background story. Quote from India Office Records E/1/95, letter dated 5 August 1796.

85 Bolton *Portrait* pp. 68–9.

86 *Ibid.* p. 70.

87 The following summer a small French force sailed from Ireland and landed at Fishguard on the south-western extremity of Wales but were quickly repelled.

88 Ehrman *Pitt* II pp. 639–41.

89 See Acres Vol. I p. 279.

90 *Ibid.* Vol. II p. 351.

91 *Ibid.* Vol. II p. 592.

92 See David Bindman and Gottfried Riemann (ed.) Karl Friedrich Schinkel *The English Journey* (New Haven and London 1993).

93 See Acres Vol. I pp. 291–8.

94 SM: Priv. Corr. II.S.14 (6) 8 September 1796.

95 FD Vol. II, p. 623.

96 See J. Mordaunt Crook, Ph.D. thesis 'The Career of Sir Robert Smirke RA' pp. 21–2.

97 FD Vol. III, p. 703 Soane much admired his drawing. Farington also mentions that Daniell had washed in the sky for him; his father's friends were already proving useful.

98 FD Vol. III, p. 740.

99 FD Vol. III, p. 875.

8 DISAPPOINTMENTS AND ACHIEVEMENTS

1 See letter SM from J. P. Brooke-Little, Norroy and Ulster King of Arms, 24 May 1989. Joan Corder *A Dictionary of Suffolk Crests* Suffolk Records Society vol, XL (Ipswich 1998) p. 74, cites a near identical crest in the names of Soane, Sone, Soone of Wantisden, Halesworth, Ubbeston.

2 SM: Journal 4, 23 April he applied to be a magistrate and later, on 5 July 1798, dined at the Clerkenwell Sessions House. In 1802 he became a vestryman of St Giles in the Fields.

3 FD Vol. III, p. 1141, 20 January 1799.

4 The Duchess of Leeds remained both client and family friend, see Bolton *Portrait* p. 90.

5 Aspinall op. cit. Vol. IV. Item 2799, Windsor, 26 September 1803.

6 Bolton *Portrait* pp. 164–5; 1 February 1815.

7 *Ibid.* p. 89, 27 July 1800.

8 HLRO Lords Journals Vol. 43, 84a, 1 April 1801.

9 *Annual Register* 1803 Vol. 46, p. 630.

10 FD. Vol. IV, p. 1529, 29 March 1801.

11 *Statement of Facts respecting the designs of a new House of Lords* 1799.

12 He had altered Spencer House, the family town house overlooking Green Park from 1785 onwards and soon after began work on Althorp, their country mansion. As Soane knew, Holland was also currently working on Wimbledon Park House.

13 See 'Letter to Earl Spencer', op. cit. ch. 7. Other directors and MPs in the company interest from whom Soane would have expected support included George Thellusson MP, (the third brother for whom he had worked) a Director in 1796 and 1799, and two Thorntons.

14 Bolton *Portrait* p. 78.

15 Aspinall, Vol. III. Item 1969, Pitt to the king, Wimbledon, 9 June 1799.

16 FD vol. IV p. 1230, 20 May 1799.

17 Bolton *Portrait*.

18 John Carter, the antiquarian, had accidentally found out the identity and had to give evidence, see Bolton *Portrait* p.77.

19 *The True Briton* (Law Report 18 May 1799).

20 SM: Letterbook 1797–1801, 6 August 1799.

21 Lever *House of Pitt* p. 284, Bishop of Lincoln to George Rose, 18 August 1801.

22 For Pitt's financial problems see Ehrman, *Pitt* Vol. III, ch. XVI.

23 Norman Gash *Lord Liverpool* (London 1984).

24 For the lecture theatre at Albermale Street the managers brought in James Spiller whose proposal was estimated at £10,000. Thomas Webster, their clerk of works eventually won the day but Soane may have suggested Spiller, whom he knew from the City and with whom he would forge a close working partnership and friendship.

25 The bankrupt John Martindale was the proprietor of White's Club and Gandy's father's employer.

26 SM: 'Diary of Joseph M. Gandy, ARA' (largely correspondence), p. 63 letter to his brother, 1 April 1795.

27 *Ibid.* p. 84, 4 July, 1795.

28 *Ibid.* p. 147.

29 *Ibid.* p. 226.

30 *Ibid.* p. 234, 2 June 1797.

31 *Ibid.* introductory notes p. 2.

32 SM: Priv. Corr. III G.1 (16) 8 March 1816.

33 John Summerson in 'The Vision of J. M. Gandy' *Heavenly Mansions* (1948).

34 Especially pronounced in his two publications, both of 1805: *The Rural Architect* and *Designs for Cottages, Cottage Farms and other Rural Buildings*.

35 See *Panoramania!* (catalogue 1989).

36 FD Vol. V p. 1741.

37 *Ibid.* p. 1746, 10 February 1802.

38 In 1802 Beckford's lawyer had contacted him about meeting mounting legal expenses and mentioned that he had asked Edward Foxhall 'to assist me from your funds on the occasion, which he declined, but very liberally accommodated me from his own'. Foxhall was more than just Beckford's upholsterer; he had some control over his finances and was also, it appears, a very rich man in his own right. In 1806 when Beckford sold the house and contents he tried to persuade Foxhall to sign an agreement to buy it all for £16,000. See Boyd Alexander *England's Wealthiest Son* (London 1969).

39 FD Vol. V p. 1754, 2 March 1802.

40 Presumably they attended as they both accepted the invitation (RA records).

41 SM: SNB 18, 12 March 1792. Although Soane mentions Turner in his notebook that day the reference is actually to the topic under discussion by the Architects' Club that evening, see p. 125.

42 FD Vol. V p. 1788, 15 June 1802, other guests listed by Farington were Nollekens, Garvey, Smirke, Daniell, Shee, Zoffany, Heath and Woodforde.

9 THE PITSHANGER DREAM

1 SM: ESNB 1.

2 The work at Pitshanger distracted Soane from a project that he was toying with at the office in May 1800, the redevelopment of the east side of Lincoln's Inn Fields, an entirely speculative notion on his part. For the transaction with Winter, see Stroud *Soane* p. 74.

3 SM: Account Book 1797–1803 ff. 15–17.

4 SM: 7/G/6 (3) gives the chronology of Soane's dealings with Captain Peyton (Mrs Gurnell's second husband) from 21 July onwards. Peyton wanted £5,000; Soane was offering £4,500. On discovering that the property was not freehold but copyhold under the Bishop of London (to whom 14s 7d was due annually) Soane lowered his offer, arguing that he would be unable to demolish the house or clear any trees. Finally he and Peyton agreed on £4,500.

5 Palmer *Soanes at Home* op. cit. p. 65.

6 Cosway catalogue op. cit., pp. 78–9.

7 Peter Hounsell, *Ealing and Hanwell Past* (London 1991).

8 SM: drawer 32/1/5 and others; all November 1801. In the end Soane's estate did not run to lodges.

9 SM: 4/B/7 (4).

10 SM: drawer 31/3/65. 9 March 1801. Other drawings show much more heavily planted gardens.

11 SM: Journal 4, 5 February f. 277.

12 Soane knew Thomas Sandby's 'classical' landscape at Virginia Water, between London and Chertsey, which was included by Whately, as was the nearby landscape at Claremont, where he had worked with Holland. In 1826, a genuine classical ruin from Leptis Magna was incorporated into the landscape at Virginia Water.

13 Watkin *Lectures*, p. 213.

14 SM: Priv. Corr. II. T.14 (13) 27 February 1808.

15 SM: AL Soane Case 31. The 'history' bound with *Crude Hints* was written in 1802.

16 'The sons of the sons'.

17 See Bristow *Architectural Colour* op. cit. p. 180.

18 SM 4/B/8/4: 4 September 1803 from Margate. Richard Bosanquet had been back in London since 1797 and in 1806 Soane provided designs, apparently without taking payment, for a small house in Falmouth. His fortunes had obviously been restored since the 1770s.

19 FD Vol. VI, p. 2370. Mrs Wheatley remarried in 1807, to Alexander Pope, the actor. As Clara Maria Pope she became a well known flower painter. Her portrait of Norah Brickenden, which Soane owned, ensured the end of her friendship with Mrs Soane around 1813. Eliza was not impressed by Norah's pursuit of her husband and thought her friend disloyal.

20 Soane *Memoirs*.

21 The Patteson family had been devastated in August 1796 by the deaths of three of their six sons from scarlet fever, within the space of three days.

22 Surprisingly, I have been unable to find a single memoir of Pitshanger and its delights from any of the regular guests. Mrs Soane's diaries show that they continuously entertained, but not on the scale that Soane claimed in the *Memoirs*.

23 For this and several following references to original colour schemes and details see Emmeline Leary *Pitshanger Manor; an Introduction* (1990).

24 See Thornton and Dorey p. vii.

25 Hughson *Circuit of London* (1808).

26 Soane owned two copies of *The Monk*, one inscribed with his name in the year of publication. He also owned Lewis's *Tales of Wonder* (1801), an anthology of poems, his own and others translated from German.

27 Lewis had been MP between 1796 and 1802 of the 'pocket borough' of Hindon in Wiltshire, formerly young William Beckford's. His major speech in the House of Commons concerned a bill to 'relieve the suffering of prisoners committed for debt'. See *History of Parliament*.

28 Boaden had also adapted two novels by Ann Radcliffe, *Romance of the Forest* became *Fontainville Forest* for the stage in 1794, while *The Italian* emerged as *The Italian Monk* in 1797.

29 Without evidence of the original paint schemes or coloured glass and with its marginally medieval ornament, consisting of heraldic bosses and Tudor roses, Soane's gothic is hard to judge from this distance but his collection of architectural fragments may have helped to produce a suitably gloomy and evocative atmosphere.

30 Bolton *Portrait* p. 97, 13 July 1806.

31 As a long-term admirer of Rousseau, being in George's phrase a 'son of Voltaire', and an admirer of D'Alembert's *Encyclopédie* and owner of Volney's insurgent text *Les Ruines*, Smith was virtually listing Soane's reading matter. *Twelve Miles from a Lemon* compiled by Norman Taylor and Alan Hankinson (Cambridge 1996). See SM: SC13.

32 Arthur Young *The Autobiography of Arthur Young* ed. by M. Betham-Edwards (London 1898). In 1793 Young became Secretary to the Board of Agriculture but ended his life as rector of a country parish.

33 Now a public open space, Walpole Park, Ealing, London.

34 Dorothy Hood *The Admirals Hood* (London 1941) p. 207.

35 SM: ESNB 3.

36 Eileen Harris op. cit.

37 Watkin *Lectures* chapters 3, 4 and 5.

38 David Watkin makes the point that there was an element of posturing in Soane's self-criticism.

39 John Carter, a fanatic in his pursuit of the true gothic and of the iniquities of 'Wyatt the Destroyer' was an admirer of Soane's firm grasp on the classical style, describing his designs for the Palace of Westminster as 'open and manly'.

40 See Howard Colvin *Unbuilt Oxford* (New Haven and London 1983), pp. 151–4.

41 C. R. Cockerell's memories of talks with Turner many years later suggest that architecture was an enduring subject of fascination to him.

42 *Autobiography of John Britton FSA* (1850) Vol. I, chs 3 and 4.

43 The second (1809) volume of *Architectural Antiquities* was dedicated to Thomas Hope. The third (1812) was dedicated to Soane, with numerous plates by Joseph Gandy.

44 Referring to his inability to help Joseph Bonomi, whom Soane had referred to his office, he says that 'not having pursued my studies as a draughtsman in architecture beyond a geometrical drawing in Indian ink and landscape . . . much more is required to oppose the effect which the fascinating drawings of otherwise unformed and inexperienced young men produce . . . in my general desultory business as a Surveyor he [Bonomi] is quite unable to afford me assistance' Bolton *Portrait* p. 103.

45 David Hill *Turner on the Thames* (New Haven and London 1992). Hill has painstakingly worked out the chronology of these journeys from Isleworth, entirely altering Finberg's dating of the sketchbooks. Soane and Tyrrell repeated the journey the following year, dining with the Austwicks in Reading before heading off to Pangbourne for two clear days fishing.

46 SM: Journal 5. Sykes's name appears among Soane's rough notes, some illegible, which also include 'the old house at Goring' and 'the Grotto'.

47 The Rev. William Chapman, who had been the curate at St John's church, was the dedicatee of the 1809 Guide to the area, the year he became the vicar. See *NUT conference souvenir* (1938) Margate Library. He died the following year aged fifty-three. His obituary in the *Kentish Gazette* of 21 September 1810 was long and, by the standards of the times, noticeably sincere. Among his other accomplishments, his obituarist noted 'In his instruction of youth there are few men who have been more successful in the art of teaching.'

48 SM 4/B/8/3/6: 19 September 1809.

49 BL Add MSS 39,780 (Flaxman Papers).

50 Dance was a son of the actor James Love (Dance) and first took command of an East Indiaman in the late 1780s. He commanded the *Earl Camden* on five voyages.

51 SM: Priv. Corr. XIV.B.2 (1) 9 November 1802. By 1806 Soane's East India Company holdings had increased sufficiently to give him three votes. In February 1805 he received £200 and in August 1805 £50 in settlement of the first voyage and £200, the first payment on the second expedition. See SM: Journal 5. The last note on file mentions salvage value in 1813; the *Earl Camden* had come to the end of her useful life.

52 *Register of Ships* (London 1813).

53 BL (Oriental and India Office Collections): L/MAR/B/303 A–C.

10 THE ROYAL ACADEMY AND OTHER BUSINESSES

1 See Christopher Hibbert *George III* (London 1998) p. 343.

2 FD, Vol. II, p. 404. 16 November 1795; J. Mordaunt Crook thesis op. cit., p. 51.

3 In their youth Smirke and Thomas Daniell had trained together as crest-painters to the coach-maker Catton.

4 FD Vol. VI pp. 2196, 2203.

5 See William Whitley *Art in England 1800–1820* (Cambridge 1928) p. 55. He moved a resolution 'to prosecute the newspapers who have vilified the Royal Academy'.

6 See Watkin *Lectures* p. 69 and notes 20 and 21, also FD Vol. VI p. 2199, 22 December 1803.

7 SM 4/B/8/7 (4).

8 Wyatt's supporters were Sandby, Copley, Turner, Cosway, Tresham, Opie, Bourgeois, Beechey, Rigaud, Hoppner and Soane.

9 FD Vol. VI p. 2460.

10 The candidate reportedly favoured by Wyatt and his supporters was Joseph Bonomi (although he had yet to be elected an RA), who in 1790 had been Sir Joshua Reynold's candidate as Professor of Perspective (see Colvin).

11 Bolton *Portrait* p. 135, 10 April 1806.

12 Watkin *Lectures* p. 397 note 7.

13 John Brewer *The Pleasures of the Imagination* (London 1997).

14 The London Institution (1806) was originally sited in Old Jewry and moved to Finsbury Circus, the Russell Institution on Coram Street, Bloomsbury, and the Surrey Institution on the south side of Blackfriars Bridge.

15 For discussion of the new lecture techniques and their popularity see Trevor Fawcett 'Visual facts and the 19th century art lecture' in *Art History* Vol. 6 no. 4, December 1983. By the end of Sandby's time as professor he was showing over a hundred and twenty drawings to illustrate his lectures.

16 Abramson *Bank* pp. 361–70.

17 *Ibid.* p. 369.

18 An anonymous correspondent quoted by Bolton *Works* p. 53 hoped that Soane would make a 'bold open street from Lothbury to the Mansion House so as to show as much of it as possible to people passing'.

19 For example, there were considerable difficulties with the Grocers' Company, see Abramson *ibid.* pp. 375–7.

20 When Herbert Baker rebuilt the Bank, he turned it into a passage.

21 Acres, Vol. II pp. 592–3.

22 SM: SNB 70. See *Description* (1835) p. 18.

23 See Gash *Liverpool* op. cit. p. 65.

24 Information from Ann Hardy, Wellcome Foundation.

25 Repton *Memoir* ff. 204–5.

26 Repton's *Red Book* 1792 Bedfordshire CRO Acc 6014 Z 493.

27 Hippisley himself, who sat for Sudbury, Suffolk from 1790 to 1796 and 1802 to 1818, was a past-master at securing votes, lubricated by heavy payments to local publicans to keep the freemen in beer, as well as in the dispensing of favours and patronage. See Allan W. Berry *A Suffolk Country Town* (Sudbury 1997) pp. 229–31. The election in 1812 cost him £825 3s 1d in payments to innkeepers and others.

28 FD Vol. VII p. 2661, 16 December 1805.

29 FD Vol. VII p. 2735, 26 April 1806.

30 In 1810–11 Smirke designed a theatre at Bentley Priory for the Marquis's amateur productions. His work for Peel was in the early 1820s.

11 'THE ROUGH STORM OF LIFE'

1 SM: Letterbook 1802–15, 20 November 1806.

2 Abramson *Bank* pp. 398–9. The directors objected to the removal of Taylor's Court Room. Soane lost the argument.

3 FD: Vol. VIII, p. 3439, 21 April 1809.

4 The competition was judged by Rowland Burdon, among others, and won by Thomas Wilson with a variant upon the Sunderland Bridge. A late entry from Thomas Telford overturned the result.

5 In 1809 Soane also began work on Lord Liverpool's town house, Fife House, Whitehall, which he continued to use even after becoming Prime Minister in 1812.

6 C.G.T. Dean *Royal Hospital, Chelsea* (London 1950). Appendix.

7 Lysons *Middlesex* Vol. II (1810/11).

8 Plates 57–9. The house is shown much as built, although the conservatory is flanked at either end by fountains and a 'cloister', little more than a back passage, links the main stair to the outside.

9 *Soane and Death* (catalogue Soane Museum 1996) section X pp. 93–5.

10 SM: 4/B/8/6/1, 20 May 1813.

11 Surrey Record Office QS7/5/6.

12 Chertsey Museum. Later a Francis Soane was in minor trouble with the law. William's son is not on the family tree but we know he had a grandchild.

13 James Boaden was at Pitshanger on 29 June 1808 and he and his family came to dine on 14 August. SM: SNB 86 and 87.

14 RA LAW/1/198.

15 Bolton *Portrait* p. 125.

16 *Joseph Michael Gandy* (catalogue Architectural Association London 1982).

17 RA LAW/1/201, 1 November 1808.

18 *Ibid.* 28 October 1808. Farington recorded that Soane had already had

a fit of jealousy against Smirke, seeing his drawings hung more prominently than his at the RA exhibition. FD Vol. VIII p. 3269 30 April 1808.

19 The stone was still there (before the recent redevelopment), in a corner of the gentlemen chorus's washroom and read 'LONG LIVE GEORGE PRINCE OF WALES'.

20 *Covent Garden Journal.*

21 SM: SNB 88.

22 SM: Priv. Corr. I. F. 2(20) 10 November 1808.

23 SM: 4/B/6 f 5, 29 January 1809; later the boys claimed that they had very inadequate allowances from their father.

24 See Richard Holmes *Shelley: the Pursuit* (London 1974) ch. 4.

25 Bolton *Portrait* p. 107, 18 October 1809.

26 Watkin *Lectures* p. 288 note 6.

27 See John Gage *Colour in Turner* (London 1969) pp. 22 etc for discussion of Turner's probable early architectural training.

28 Maurice Davies *Turner as Professor* (catalogue Tate Gallery 1992).

29 SM: SC 152, rough drafts of lectures 3 and 4 (22 and 29 January 1810) include a list of RA members attending.

30 The builder was Alexander Copland, who had learned his trade with Richard Holland and had worked with Soane on John Stuart's house in Wimpole Street in 1781 (SM: Journal 1781–97). His son was a pupil in Soane's office, 1817–20 (See Colvin).

31 FD Vol X p. 3515, 21 July 1809.

32 Erik Gustaf Geijer *Impressions of England 1809–1810* (London 1932) translated by Elizabeth Sprigge and Claude Napier.

33 In 1811 Robert Smirke the younger was elected an RA although he never exhibited on its wall thereafter.

34 Bolton *Portrait* p. 107.

35 Appearance in front of the Grand (i.e. large) Jury was equivalent to being summoned to a modern magistrates court.

36 SM Chelsea Reports 1807–12. Report to the Board April 13 1809. One drawing dated May 1809 is inscribed despairingly 'mihi turpe relinqui est', which Andrew Saint translates as 'it is a disgrace to me to be abandoned'.

37 Dan Cruickshank 'Complex Classicism' *Architects' Journal*, 26 November 1998.

38 *Ibid.*

39 FD Vol. VII p. 3439, 21 April 1809.

40 SM: 4/B/8/3/7, 24 September 1809.

41 SM: 4/B/7/4, (MS in JS's hand).

42 SM: 16/14/97 bill for £27 15s for advertising the house May–June 1809, 150 printed particulars.

43 SM: 4/B/8/3/5, 8 September 1809.

44 SM: 4/B/8/3/4, 8 September 1809.

45 SM: 4/B/8/3/7, 24 September 1809.

46 David Watkin *Thomas Hope and the Neo-Classical Idea* (London 1968).

47 See Gandy catalogue *op. cit.* and the information from John Harris. Thomas Hope, like Walpole and Beckford, had also written an exotic novel (although his *Anastasius* was not published until 1819).

48 SM: 4/B/6, 4 January 1810.

49 *Ibid.* 5 January 1810, f. 20.

50 SM: Copies of George Soane's correspondence etc 16/20.

51 Watkin *Lectures* publishes it, pp. 533–55, see pp. 317–23 for the analysis of the lecture.

52 Margaret Richardson points out that this dubious convention lives on between RIBA members.

53 *Ibid.* p. 544 and plates 104–5; the drawings are dated 20 December 1809. See also pp. 74–5. See pp. 88–96 for Soane's prolonged consideration of the arguments and the building, in the face of the outcry he had provoked. See pp. 343–4 for his discarded notes on the Greek Revival which had included criticism of Dance's Royal College of Surgeons.

54 *Ibid.* p. 542, note 11.

55 *Ibid.* p. 536, Soane's note 'L'. No illustration is included in the fair copy of the lecture, SM SC 38.

56 *Ibid.* Soane's note 'M' (illustrated).

57 *Ibid.* p. 541, Soane's note 'X'.

58 FD Vol. X p. 3599, 8 February 1810.

59 Bolton *Portrait* p. 152, Sir Francis Bourgeois to JS 5 or 6 February.

60 RA LAW/1/235 received 1 February 1810. In Soane's *Memoirs* written

in 1835 he wrote 'I must take this opportunity of observing that I never entertained other than the kindest personal feelings towards the Architect of Covent Garden Theatre, who had received his first principles in my office.'

61 FD Vol. VIII, p. 3593, 6 February 1810.

62 Bolton *Portrait* p. 152, 11 February.

63 FD *ibid.* pp. 3596–7, 10 February 1810.

64 FD *ibid.*, 14 February 1810, p. 3599 and 19 February p. 3602. The full list of Soane's home audience of fourteen is given in SM: Journal 5, f. 136: as well as friendly academicians (Bourgeois, Beechey, Cosway, Landseer and Tresham), it included old friends and patrons Coxe Hippisley, Patteson, Morland, the surveyors Pilkington and Spiller and the engineer Alexander.

65 FD *ibid.* p. 3603, 22 February.

66 SM: SNB 100, 14 September 1810.

67 Bolton *Portrait* pp. 166–7, 13 September 1810.

68 SM: Priv. Corr. III.H.10 (4), 21 September 1810.

69 SM: Letterbook 1802–15 to J. Faulkner, regarding a Bond of Arbitration between Bullock and Gandy, 7 July 1811.

70 Bolton *Portrait*, p. 126, 1 September 1810.

12 PLEASURES AND TROUBLES

1 SM: MS in archive, all quotations that follow from the document.

2 Soane had been working on alterations to the Elizabethan house belonging to the former Admiral Hood (Lord Bridport's brother Samuel) since 1807.

3 Soane may have chosen their lodgings for sentimental reasons. Henry Holland had adapted the seventeenth-century hostelry into a smart Georgian inn in the mid-1770s, possibly while Soane was in his office.

4 Remodelled in 1803 by either Thomas Harrison or John Foster the elder.

5 *George Bullock: Cabinet-maker* (London 1988) introduction by Clive Wainwright, chronology by Lucy Woods. Refers to 1809 Billiard Room (Rotunda) Bold Street by J. M. Gandy.

6 The area is now dominated by the University of Liverpool and the two cathedrals.

7 Probably the Welsh Bridge 1791–5 by Carline and Tilley.

8 Built between 1787 and 1793 by Telford after Haycock's designs it was cross-shaped with an octagonal chapel; Howard's bust was by Bacon.

9 Mrs Soane refers to it as Colnbrookdale throughout.

10 George Wightwick was born in 1802; his father drowned in 1811. See Colvin.

11 SM: 4/B/6 f. 21, letter dated 17 February 1811.

12 See *London: World City* op. cit. J. Mordaunt Crook 'Metropolitan Improvements: John Nash and the Picturesque' pp. 77–96.

13 SM 4/B/8/4/2 (letter from Eliza Soane with postscript from John, 22 April 1811).

14 SM 4/B/8/4/6, 20 May 1811.

15 SM: 4/B/8/4/5, 11 May 1811.

16 SM: 4/B/8/4/6, 20 May 1811.

17 Robert Mylne had held the post since 1766.

18 Colvin.

19 Soane *Memoirs.* Perhaps in sympathy John Britton dedicated the finest plate of St Paul's to Soane in the *Fine Arts of the English School* (1812). The other dedicatees for the plates of the great Wren building (the only architectural subject) were Porden and Tatham.

20 SM: 4/A/1/1/2 (copy) JS to Mrs John Soane (i.e. Maria).

21 SM: 4/A/1/1/3 JS jun. to JS 7 June 1811; also from Maria, 11 June 1811 with thanks, asking him for advice on disposing of the money 'advantageously' *ibid.*/4.

22 SM: 4/A/1/1/5 (copy), 12 June 1811.

23 Bolton *Portrait* p. 169.

24 SM; various letters including 4/A/1/1/9, 7 October 1811.

25 SM: 4/A/1/5/6, 7 January 1824.

26 SM: 4/B/8/4/9, 19 September 1811.

27 He wrote to his mother from Margate to give her the news; SM: 4/C/6/1, 15 July 1811.

28 SM 4/B/8/1/2, 4 June 1813.

29 SM: 4/B/8/1/1, 11 February 1812.

30 SM: 4/B/8/4/10, 22 September 1811.

31 SM: 4/B/6 f. 42, 30 September 1811.

32 SM: 4/B/8/4/13 20 October 1811.

33 SM: Journal 5, f. 213, 21 November 1811.

34 'Dulwich College and the Bourgeois Bequest' in *Soane and After* ed. Giles Waterfield (Dulwich Picture Gallery 1987).

35 Appendix 'The last testament of Sir Francis Bourgeois', *Soane and Death* (Dulwich Picture Gallery 1996).

36 For a general history see Giles Waterfield (ed.) *Collection for a King* (Dulwich Picture Gallery 1985). Also *Soane and After* op. cit., and *Soane and Death* op. cit. For drawings see *Buildings in Progress* (Soane Museum 1995).

37 Probably the first volume of the *Eve of S. Marco* since he refers, in a letter to Pennington, to having two volumes 'ready for the press' and 'am about the third', asking him to intercede with his father, 23 November 1811 (SM: 16/20).

38 Schiller was also a source of several of 'Monk' Lewis's adaptations.

39 SM: 4/C/6/2 17 April 1812, GS from Upper Baker Street.

40 SM: 4/C/6/3, 2 May 1812.

41 Humphrey Repton in his MS Memoir ff. 195–6 remarked of Sheffield Park, 'that Wyatt's natural good taste as been forced to yield to the reigning fashion of the day . . . *Modern Gothic* . . . that heterogeneous mixture of Abbey, Castle and Manor House for which a taste had been introduced by the experiments of Horace Walpole . . . and the same mongrel breed of architecture has been propagated ever since by buildings of all dimensions from the Palace to the Pigsty.'

42 SM: 4/C/6/4, 4 May 1812.

43 See *History of Parliament*. Lewis's later years were spent visiting Jamaica, where he had inherited large sugar estates and attempted to free his slaves. He died in 1818.

44 Louis Peck *A Life of M. G. Lewis* (Cambridge, Mass. 1961).

45 SM: 4/C/6/8, 11 May 1812. He protests that he is not idle but wishes to be 'industrious in his own way'.

46 The only connection that George Soane ostensibly had with the *Quarterly Review* was an advertisement for the *Eve of S. Marco* under new novels, p. 471 Vol. 7, June 1812.

47 JS jun. to JS quoting his father's remarks back to him, SM: 4/B/6 f. 51, 26 June 1812. It was an odd remark in view of Soane's delight in French novels such as *Gil Blas*.

48 See Holmes *Shelley* op. cit. p. 24.

49 SM: 4/C/6/13, 18 May 1812.

50 SM: SNB 8, 27 October 1811.

51 Soane observed that the word perspective was hardly mentioned. See Gage *Colour in Turner* op. cit. ch. 6. Also see Whitley op. cit. p. 184.

52 SM: Priv. Corr. III.B.1 (6), 5 June 1812.

53 See Whitley op. cit. pp. 202–2 refers to the gift of the chandelier in 1812 and pp. 240–1 to its dramatic collapse in 1815.

54 Draft of the sixth lecture. Susan G. Feinberg 'The Genesis of Sir John Soane's Museum idea 1801–1810' *JSAH* XLIII pp. 225–37, October 1984.

55 Watkin *Lectures*, p. 414.

56 SM: 4/B/8/5/1, 26 June 1812.

57 SM: 4/B/8/5/3, 4 July 1812.

58 The Tyndales' rent was £202 10s; they also shared the cost of constructing a passage between their house and the back entrance. The adjoining doors off Whetstone Park at the rear were lettered respectively, Mr Tyndale and Mr Soane (see fig. 147).

59 SM: 4/B/8/5/5, 30 August 1812 from Chertsey.

60 SM: 4/B/6 f. 53, 18 July 1812.

61 SM: 4/B/6 f. 54, 2 August 1812.

62 SM: 4/B/6 ff. 55–6, 28 September 1812. Mr Pennington, family friend and doctor, had spent some days with them in Brighton and, concerned about John's health, had confined him to the house for two days. He was still in Brighton in November.

63 *Ibid.* 18 July.

64 The closest similarities were with Praed's Bank on Fleet Street, which he was extending that year, using Portland stone, strongly articulated arcading and similar ornament.

65 Hunter had been Professor of Anatomy at the Royal Academy in Soane's student days.

66 Bolton *Portrait* p. 95, 2 August 1802.

67 RCS, various references within Minutes of Quarterly Court of Assistants Vol. I, also Minutes of Building Committee, 1799–1814.

68 *Ibid.* Minutes of Building Committee ff. 201–5. The Master of the College from 1802 was Thomas Keate, Soane's friend from Chelsea.

69 'Crude Hints towards the History of my House' ff. 30–1. Published in full in *Visions of Ruins* (catalogue, Soane Museum 1999).

70 Bristow *Architectural Colour* pp. 208–10.

71 Willmert op. cit.

72 Palmer *Soanes at Home* op. cit. pp. 10–12.

73 See Patrick Youngblood 'The Painter as Architect: Turner and Sandycombe Lodge' *Turner Studies* Vol. 2, No. 1.

74 Youngblood connects this motif with Soane's earlier Bentley Park and Hamels Dairy.

75 Ann Livermore 'Sandycombe Lodge: Turner's little house at Twickenham' *Country Life* 6 July 1951, pp. 40–2.

76 Turner sold Sandycombe Lodge in June 1826.

77 Albury Park was sold for £72,000 in 1811.

78 BoE M1/32.

79 FD Vol. VI, p. 2316, 7 May 1804.

80 See Watkin *Hope* op. cit. p. 218.

81 Watkin *Lectures* pp. 86–9 emphasises the importance of the *Appeal* (also 1812), another attempt to deal with the injustices meted out to him by the Royal Academy. As an instance of criticism of modern buildings he included a reprint of *The Exhibition* of 1779 by 'Roger Shanhagan' (in fact written by three Royal Academicians including the elder Smirke).

82 'Crude Hints' op. cit. f. 64.

13 RECONCILIATION AND DEATH

1 Elmes had already been involved in the London Architectural Society, founded in 1806. James Peacock was also one of the active members. See Colvin Introduction op. cit.

2 Bolton *Portrait* p. 139 and p. 154, letter dated 22 February 1810.

3 FD Vol. XII pp. 4284 (20 January), 4288 (26 January).

4 FD vol. XII p. 4290 (29 January).

5 SM: SNB 113, 5 November 1812 Turner and Britton called. He recorded at least three more meetings with Turner during the month

6 SM: SNB 113 Loans to Gandy were 'in all to this day' £200.

7 *Diary Reminiscences and Correspondence of Henry Crabb Robinson* selected and edited by Thomas Sadler (1869) Vol. I p. 411. John Soane even offered to prepare some lecture drawings; SM Priv. Corr. XIV.D.2 (23).

8 Hayes told Farington (FD Vol. XII p. 4315) 'Soane was the worst reader he ever heard, his words being often so expressed as scarcely to be understood.'

9 Whitley *Art in England* op. cit., pp. 179–81.

10 See Dean *Country Houses* op. cit. for Repton and Soane's exchanges over Port Eliot. The client may have found Repton's idea of linking his house with the abbey too radical but Repton preferred to lay the fault at Soane's feet.

11 Lecture 10 began with an account of 'ornamental buildings' and 'decorative landscape gardening'. See Repton *Memoir* op. cit. See Watkin *Lectures* p. 624 etc. The references to which Repton refers are not included in the completed text – they were perhaps *ad lib* additions.

12 FD Vol. XII p. 4423 (18 September), Bathurst felt that Nash was the likely candidate.

13 Wyatt's short-lived time as President could not have endeared him to West, from whom he had taken the post.

14 See Watkins *Lectures* p. 369 note 328.

15 See Stroud *Soane* pp. 177–9.

16 FD Vol. XII p. 4424.

17 See Kings Works pp. 109–13.

18 Geijer *Impressions of England* op. cit.

19 Gottfried Reimann, introduction to Bindman *Schinkel* op. cit.

20 See John Summerson *Nash* p. 88.

12 SM: Priv. Corr. XV. B. 25, 8 October 1826 to Soane at Gloucester. In Bolton *Portrait* p. 403 he described his task: 'Day after day, a somewhat differently worded preamble was our chief occupation . . . I . . . endeavoured to extract, and secure upon paper, the meaning of the disjointed utterances . . . the matter of his dictation.'

13 Crabb Robinson op. cit. Vol. II p. 370.

14 Full account in Alexandra Wedgwood *Soane's Law Courts at Westminster* AA Files 24.

15 The demolition of the Law Courts promoted another public row; this time between the promoters of Pearson, architect of the new work, and the youthful SPAB, recently founded by William Morris. See Chris Miele 'The Battle for Westminster Hall' *Architectural History* Vol. 41: 1998.

16 Bolton *Portrait* 18 September 1822 p. 253. SM: SC 145, Soane's own note for Saturday, 14 September 1822.

17 *Ibid.* p. 352.

18 Even Smirke had offered his workmen on Covent Garden a dinner at the Bedford Coffee House to mark it being 'covered in' see John Gore (ed.) *Creevey* (London 1949).

19 Bolton *Portrait* pp. 370–1.

20 The Stationery Office at Buckingham Gate was to be housed in converted domestic premises; the building was inadequate by the 1830s.

21 See Summerson *Nash* op. cit. p. 164. See also Colvin p. 580. 'Although its findings were scarcely to his credit, there was no actual reflection on his professional ability or his integrity'.'

22 Bolton *Portrait* p. 406.

23 Bolton *Portrait* pp. 351–2.

24 See *London World City* op. cit. p. 91.

25 See Summerson *Nash* op. cit. pp. 132–3.

26 Colvin and FD Vol. XVI p. 5745, 6 November 1821.

27 SM: ESNB 3, 10 May 1805, 'a mighty stupid party' at Lady Kinnaird's.

28 SM Ledger E. Soane's account with Morland & Co (one of three, for he also banked with Praed and Prescott & Grote) closed after 1818, when it was worth £14,640 (£3,000 less than in 1814). See SM Priv. Corr. I. K. 6 (2) (28 September 1820). However when he travelled to France in 1819 Kinnaird arranged circular bills of credit (a kind of contemporary travellers' cheque) for Soane through the bank.

29 Information from Sarah Dodgson, Librarian, The Athenaeum.

30 Bolton *Portrait* p. 445.

31 See Sawyer op. cit.

32 A view continually advanced until now; see Richard Rogers and Mark Fisher *New London* (London 1994).

33 Soane contributed £1,000 towards a monument to the Duke of York and in August 1829 designed a 'monopteral temple' to house a statue of the duke. Benjamin Wyatt's column was chosen instead in March 1831. See Bolton *Portrait* pp. 428–9.

34 SM AL 41A.

35 Long also concurred with Soane's arched entrance to Downing Street and argued for a Triumphal Arch leading to Buckingham House (later Palace), to be a London variant upon the Arc du Carrousel and the Arc de Triomphe. Nash's Marble Arch was under discussion from 1825 although it did not take shape, the work of several hands, until 1833. See Andrew Saint 'The Marble Arch' in *The Georgian Group Journal* vol. VII 1997.

36 *Puckler's Progress* translated by Flora Brennan (London 1987) pp. 51–2.

37 Bolton *Portrait* p. 424, 17 July 1827.

38 Presumably No. 977 'General View of a Design for a Royal Residence'. SM Catalogue of RA exhibitions 1811 to 1829.

39 Bolton *Portrait* p. 428, 7 August 1929.

40 See Sawyer op. cit. note 2.

41 See *King's Works* p. 133. Soane visited Nash's work at Buckingham Palace several times in April and May 1831, as a fellow Attached Architect at the Office of Works

42 *Ibid.* p. 559.

43 Elmes in *Metropolitan Improvements* praised the magnificent Privy Council Chamber, and the general accommodation 'simple and substantial suitable to the character of public offices' while mentioning the 'officious amateurs at the Treasury'.

44 Barry had married a Miss Rowsell in 1822, a connection of the Conduitts': Soane probably had contact with Barry through this link.

45 See Watkin *JSAH* op. cit. p. 411.

46 An arrangement which Soane also used earlier at Wotton, diverting the flues into nearest wall.

47 See *Ars Quatuor Coronatorum* Vol. 95 (1983) p. 201, quotes from Minutes.

18 STRANGE WORK

1 *Athenaeum* 8 October 1831, p. 206.

2 SM: Priv. Corr. I B 7 (7) 3 October 1831.

3 Peter Coxe *To Sir John Soane, Royal Academician* (privately printed 1832) it was a thirty-seven verse panegyric.

4 Drawing *c*. 1795 (see fig. 209). Jackson died in June 1831.

5 *Neglected Genius* op. cit.

6 Stanfield became an ARA in 1832 and exhibited his painting at the RA exhibition that year.

7 Bolton *Portrait* p. 475, notice from *Sunday Times* 27 November 1831.

8 RCS Minutes Vol. IV pp. 149, 199 (appointment, letter of acceptance). Perhaps to mark it, Soane gave a lecture there in 1824. See also Zachary Cope *The Royal College of Surgeons of England* (London 1959). Elmes' *Metropolitan Improvements* had offered a neatly phrased obituary to the portico; it was 'like a pension to a faithless patriot . . . a good thing ill-applied'.

9 SM: Priv. Corr. II.K. 1(20) 30 June 1831.

10 Others approached were Smirke, Charles Barry and a Mr Walker. Smirke refused, disliking the terms. The College was prepared to pay 50 guineas for the unsuccessful plans. More names were added by committee members, Deering, Kendall, Burton and Cockerell (the latter refused to submit plans).

11 RCS Minutes Vol. VI p. 153.

12 SM: 16/15/22 16 April 1824, TT to JS from the Guildhall.

13 The connection may have been through the Artists' General Benevolent Institution see FD Vol. XV p. 5170. Hume had also chaired the Select Committee on the House of Commons buildings in March 1833 to which Soane, among many architects, gave evidence.

14 Inglis (1786–1855) was an FSA and FRS. See DNB.

15 Hansard XVI 667.

16 Hansard op. cit. 1333–43.

17 PRO PROB 37/1062 testament of Dr Joseph Moore, attesting to Sir John Soane's state of mind in these years.

18 Soane, from an address in Worthing, had placed his petition on 25 March.

19 James Morrison (1790–1857) was a philanthropic businessman and radical politician, whose motto was 'small profits and quick returns' (DNB).

20 Journals of the House of Commons Vol. 88, 1833 part I; 154, 156.

21 Perhaps Richardson disappointed Soane; in a late, unproven codicil his bequest of £300 was reduced to £50 PRO op. cit.

22 The drawings were not offered to the museum until after George Bailey's death – the only man who would have known the irregular way in which Richardson had obtained them.

23 Pierre de la Ruffinière du Prey *Sir John Soane* (London 1985) in a series of catalogues of architectural drawings in the Victoria and Albert Museum. See introduction. Recent work suggests that there are fewer Soane originals than was thought.

24 SM: MS copy of will.

25 John Britton *Autobiography* p. 10.

26 See Watkin *Cockerell* op. cit. p. 216.

27 SM Priv. Corr. XIV J.1.(8) 2 November 1833.

28 Watkin *Cockerell* op. cit. pp. 66–7, p. 219.

29 PRO PROB 37/1062.

30 SM Priv. Corr. XV B.16 (1) Edward Foxhall had written in 1795 to say that he had found a Gold Medal for sale for 15 guineas and that the owner was prepared to take his name off before parting with it.

31 In November 1799 Foxhall had advanced Soane £200 and later Soane presented him with a bond for £1,200, the interest on which was demanded from Mrs Foxhall and which Soane bore on her behalf. SM *ibid.*, letters 2 and 3. The obligation is likely to have been incurred much earlier in Soane's career, for which no record has been found.

32 As he had done, years before, to great effect on the south front at Mogerhanger for Stephen Thornton.

33 Helene Furjan *Assemblage* 34 1997 argues that the mirrors incorporate the collection into the house, and vice versa. She also refers to the Burkean notion of extreme light obliterating objects just as much as darkness.

34 By good fortune, Soane's tenants at No. 1 Albion Place had been for many years the Plate Glass Company who paid, in the early 1830s, a half-yearly rent of £74 for the premises.

35 See *Description* (1835) p. 93.

36 See his edited version of Barbara Hofland's tour of the house, printed 1919.

37 See *Description* (1835) p. 96.

38 SM: SC 78 f. 59–60. Gandy described the 'dioptric light from unseen source . . . the number of revolving pictures and curved walls, folding doorlike, valve within valve, grading from shade to light, the many semblances of departed worth recalling us to human life'.

39 Bolton *Portrait* p. 531.

40 SM Priv. Corr. Division II.T. 7(8) 10 August 1835; Soane's response was written on the back, dated 20 August 1835. Watson's original bill SM: Journal 6, f. 36, 17 May 1814, paid William Watson for painters and glaziers work £430.

41 See Eileen Harris *Sir John Soane's Library* op. cit. pp. 246–7.

42 *Details respecting the Conduct and Connexions of George Soane also of Frederick Soane* and *Memoirs of Mr and Mrs John Soane, Miss Soane and Captain Chamier.*

43 *Details* op. cit. The copy appended to papers in the PRO (op. cit.) includes angry annotations in George's hand.

44 SM 4/C/11 (1-11), 4/C/12/5 etc.

45 Southampton Record Office PR 5/21/4.

46 *Ibid.* PR 5/21/5.

47 SM: 4/C/27 (6, 7).

48 SM: 16/20 GS to Sarah Smith. In October, responding to George's threat (22 January, f. 345) to set aside his father's will and throw the property into Chancery, Soane suspended George's allowance but Sally Conduitt pleaded with him to restore it for the sake of the children (f. 361).

49 SM Ledger D shows various payments, usually made by James Boaden.

50 *Ibid.*, all entries on his account at Praed's Bank.

51 See *Memoir of Mr and Mrs John Soane* op. cit. and for much of the following account.

52 See Colvin; Tarring was a pupil of Richard Brown, who had dedicated his 1815 volume to Soane.

53 Chamier described his wife as a pretty woman, with large dark eyes, a snub nose, a pretty mouth and exceptionally small hands and feet.

54 See P. J. Van der Voort *The Pen and the Quarter-deck* (Leiden 1972) p. 57 etc.

55 Bolton *Portrait* p. 521.

56 As Andrew Saint points out it is the Englishness of the comparison that weighs here; Racine could never be discussed in terms of broken rules.

57 See *Library of the Fine Arts* (1832) quoted in J. Mordaunt Crook *The Greek Revival* (London 1972) p. 116.

58 *Pugin* (catalogue Victoria and Albert Museum 1994) pp. 219/20.

59 *The History of the Ancient Palace and late Houses of Parliament at Westminster* p. 409 quoting Soane's *Designs for Public Buildings* (1828).

60 SM: Priv. Corr. XVI.D.3 (6) 7 May 1835.

61 Margaret Belcher 'Pugin Writing' in *Pugin* op. cit.; see also Rosemary Hill *Reformation to Millennium* op. cit.

62 *Contrasts* pp. 30–1.

63 The plate showing No. 13 Lincoln's Inn Fields had been removed by the time of the 1841 edition.

64 Founded in 1835, see Bolton *Portrait* p. 517.

65 Soane was invited to become the first President of the Institute of British Architects but his membership of the Royal Academy precluded it.

66 *Sunday Times* 29 January 1837.

67 Thomas Leverton Donaldon 'A Review of the Professional Life of Sir John Soane (with some remarks on his genius & productions, read at the first subsequent ordinary meeting of the IBA, Monday 6 Feb 1837') 1837. Dedicated to Wyatville, JS's successor as Senior of the Profession. Donaldson delivered his obituary reading on 6 February 1837.

68 Watkin *Lectures* see Appendix 5. Rowland Burdon wrote in May 1834 to tell Soane he had recently read his lectures in the *Herald*.

69 *The Parting Light* selected writings of Samuel Palmer edited by Mark Abley (Manchester 1985) pp. 50–1, 19 August 1835.

70 The Grand Master of the United Grand Lodge, the Duke of Sussex had died in 1843. His mausoleum, designed by Joseph Hansom, was a compilation of the styles, which Wightwick described as: 'a masonic riddle, teeming with multiplied significancy . . . wearing an aspect which . . . challenges admiration and defies criticism'.

71 Bolton *Portrait* p. 409 (Wightwick's account written in 1852).

72 R. W. Emerson *English Traits* (1856).

73 SM Priv. Corr. II.O.1 (17). (14 October 1824 from Harrogate) Oakley had dined with the Burtons, father and son, in Harrogate – enjoying a haunch of venison provided by Soane – and wrote to report their praise for 'the first architect in the land'.

74 See Watkin *Cockerell* op. cit. pp. 105–6.

75 Charles Locke Eastlake's *Hints of Household Taste in Furniture, Upholstery and other Details.*

76 Royal Literary Fund records op. cit. in BL.

77 PRO PROB 37/1062.

78 The *Times* 2 August 1837.

79 *Ibid.* 29 November 1837.

80 SM: minutes of the trustees, various entries.

81 *The Pen and the Quarter-deck* op. cot., Appendix IV, p. 166. From 14 Halkin Street West, Belgrave Square, 14 October 1843.

82 SM 4/B/2.

83 BM Add. MS 40, 492 (October 1842 onwards).

84 Unidentified cutting in RLF papers, op cit.

85 For legal purposes the estate was referred to in the name of Conduitt.

86 Maria's second husband was George Christian Sibbern (her first was the Swedish Baron Rehansen); Harriet's was the Reverend William Niven.

87 The *Times* 6 May 1871.

88 For George's will (of 16 April 1858) see SM: copy in family papers box. It was proved on 9 August 1860. Rosa-Maria later had four children.

POSTSCRIPT

1 *The Works of Sir John Soane* (London 1924).

2 Bolton *Portrait* p. 381.

3 20 January 1937. I am grateful to Alan Powers for this reference.

4 Described, surprisingly, in a remarkably inaccurate *Times* leader (also 20 January) as 'frozen music of much greater range and power' than Soane's lost Bank of England.

5 For example *Soane and After* (catalogue Dulwich Picture Gallery 1987). has comments by more than a dozen modern architects, see pp. 86–96 .

INDEX

PHOTOGRAPHIC ACKNOWLEDGEMENTS

James Austin 158; By courtesy of the Governor and Company of the Bank of England 58; The Bridgeman Art Library, London & New York/Leeds Museums and Art Galleries (Temple Newsam House) 11; The Bridgeman Art Library, London & New York/Guildhall Library, Corporation of London 76, 78, 160; The Bridgeman Art Library, London & New York/British Library, London 154; © The British Museum 75, 138, 160, 166, 193; Geremy Butler/House of Lords Record Office 96, 97; The Fitzwilliam Museum, Cambridge 7, 135; Martin Charles 156; Martin Charles/Sir John Soane's Museum 186, 187, 190, 191, 211, 212; Grosvenor Museum, Chester 171; The Conway Library, Courtauld Institute of Art, London 17, 36, 207; The Witt Library, Courtauld Institute of Art, London 25, 38, 108; By Permission of the Trustees of Dulwich Picture Gallery 132; Edifice 2, 27, 33, 34, 35, 37, 48, 49, 50, 53, 54, 60, 68, 69, 70, 88, 89, 94, 117, 162, 172, 183, 185; © English Heritage/NMR 46, 51, 52, 56, 57, 61, 62, 71, 72, 81, 93, 95, 197, 203; Glasgow Art Gallery 65; Abbot Hall Art Gallery, Kendal 42; Paul Larsen 173; Liverpool Records Office 142; The Museum of London 123; National Galleries of Scotland 20; By Courtesy of the National Portrait Gallery, London 5, 12, 63, 136, 199; National Trust Photograph Library 24, 30, 31, 84; Ashmolean Museum, Oxford 188; Photothèque des Musées de la Ville de Paris 19; R.I.B.A. 19, 39, 110, 143, 167, 219; © Photo RMN 159; The Royal Collection © Her Majesty Queen Elizabeth II 9; By courtesy of the Trustees of Sir John Soane's Museum 4 (P296), 8 (D4/4/16), 10 (12/5/8), 13, 14 (P400), 15 (P317), 16 (45/1/9), 22 (vol.42 p.148), 23 (P254), 26 (14/4/2), 29 (45/3/4), 32 (vol.27/3), 40 (vol.39 18v&19), 41 (45/4/3), 43 (79/1/13 recto), 44 (45/3/7),45 (vol42/128), 47 (64/3/100), 59 (SDR 21.31), 64 (13/5/8), 66 (2/9/31), 67 (2/9/5), 73, 74 (vol.60/20-22), 77 (76/4/1), 79, 80 (14/6/1), 82, 83 (6/1/5), 85 (8/3/25), 86 (Vol.60/72), 87 (vol.68/26), 90(3/5/37), 91 (vol.60/119), 92 (P370), 98 (vol.69/58), 99 (vol.69/31), 100, 101, 102 (11/6/8), 103 (vol.69/133), 104, 105 (vol.60/56), 106 (vol.6/133), 107 (P267), 109, 111 (1/8/12), 113 (vol.69/10), 114 (vol.90/1), 115, 116 (31/2/60), 118 (31/1/31), 119 (P229), 120 (P312), 124, 125 (P118), 129 (40/2/43), 130 (P350), 133 (15/2/1), 139 (67/5/25), 140 (14/6/5), 141 (18/9/1), 145 (P15), 146 (15/2/8), 147 (vol.32/3/42), 148 (14/6/3), 149 (vol.32/3/6), 150 (D5/7/1), 151 (74/4/1), 153 (vol.76/20), 155 (15/2/7), 157 (P142), 161 (vol.79/5), 163 (vol.60/102), 164 (63/7/33), 165 (63/7/10), 168 (P81), 169 (P87), 170 (65/4/17), 175, 177, 179, 180 (XP9), 181 (34/1/1/), 182 (34/1/34), 184, 189, 192, 195 (9/2/2), 198, 200, 201, 202 (71/1/3), 205 (71/2/72), 206 (Vol.61/28), 208 (P90), 209, 210 (P247), 213 (69/3/7), 216; Sotheby's Picture Library 112; © Tate Gallery, London 3, 121, 134, 137, 174, 194, 214; © Sterling and Francine Clark Art Institute, Williamstown, Massachussetts, USA 55; Yale Center for British Art, New Haven 21, 28, 144.